ASIAWEEK

An Investor's Guide to Asia's Top 1000 Blue-Chip Companies

ASIAWEEK

An Investor's Guide to Asia's Top 1000
Blue-Chip Companies

edited by

Alejandro Reyes
of
Asiaweek

JOHN WILEY & SONS (ASIA) PTE LTD
Singapore • New York • Chichester • Brisbane • Toronto • Weinheim

Copyright © 1998 by Asiaweek
Published by John Wiley & Sons (Asia) Pte Ltd
2 Clementi Loop, #02-01, Singapore 129809, Singapore.

All rights reserved.

Asiaweek is a registered trademark of Times Warner Inc. Its use is pursuant to licensing agreement with Times Warner Inc.

No part of this book may be reproduced by any means, or transmitted, or translated into a machine language, without the written permission of the publisher.

Other Wiley Editorial Offices

John Wiley & Sons, Inc.
605 Third Avenue, New York, NY 10158-0012, USA

John Wiley & Sons Ltd
Baffins Lane, Chichester, West Sussex PO19 IUD, England

John Wiley & Sons (Canada) Ltd
22 Worchester Road, Rexdale, Ontario M9W ILI, Canada

Jacaranda Wiley Ltd
33 Park Road, (PO Box 1226) Milton, Queensland 4064, Australia

Library of Congress Cataloguing-in-Publication Data

An investor's guide to Asia's top 1000 blue-chip companies / edited by
   Alejandro Reyes.
      p   cm
   ISBN 0-471-82905-6 (pbk.)
   1. Corporations -- Asia -- Finance -- Directories. 2 Investments-
-Asia. I. Reyes, Alejandro A.
HG4234.85.Z65I58 1998
338.7'4' 0255 -- DC21   98-36849
                                                                 CIP

Printed in Singapore
10 9 8 7 6 5 4 3 2 1

CONTENTS

Foreword	vii
Introduction:	
A Good Place to Start	3
Crisis and Opportunity	7
Mitsui Makes Magic: A Look at Asia's Top Blue Chip	11

Chapter 1:
Asia's Largest Companies by Sales — 13

Chapter 2:
The Best and the Biggest

The Largest Profits	89
The Biggest Losses	90
The Largest Assets	91
The Most Employees	92
The Biggest Equity	93
The Highest Market Value	94
The Highest Growth in Sales	95
The Highest Growth in Profits	96
The Biggest Profit Margins	97
The Highest Return on Assets	98
The Highest Return on Equity	99
The Most Profit Per Employee	100

Chapter 3:
The Largest Companies outside Japan — 101

Chapter 4:
Top Enterprises by Country

Australia and New Zealand: Crisis Victims	109
China: Steady and Stable	113

Hong Kong: Tiger's Misfortune 118
India: New Leadership, Old Problems 123
Indonesia: Crisis Ground Zero 129
Japan: On the Brink, But of What? 134
Malaysia: Do-it-Yourself Recovery 145
Philippines: Not Bad, But Could Do Better 150
Singapore: The Best of a Bad Lot 155
South Korea: On the Bumpy Road To Recovery 159
Taiwan: Calm Island, Tense Island 164
Thailand: First in, First Out? 169

Chapter 5:
Top Enterprises by Industry

Appliances and Consumer Electronics 175
Beverages, Food and Tobacco 177
Chemicals 178
Clothing, Textiles and Accessories 180
Construction 181
Electric Power 182
Heavy Industry and Engineering 183
Industrial and Farm Equipment 184
Information Technology 185
Media and Communications 186
Materials 187
Metals 188
Motor Vehicles 189
Oil and Gas 191
Resources 192
Retailing 193
Trading 194
Transportation 195
State Enterprises 197

Chapter 6:
Top Enterprises in ASEAN 201

Directory 207

FOREWORD

Investors often tend to forget that there are economic cycles. For the better part of a decade Asia could do no wrong and Asian economies and its companies were seen by many as being capable of defying gravity and perhaps even conventional economic theory. Since the last economic downturn in the mid-1980s, the region's economic expansion has been exceptionally strong and in some ways, unparalleled. The economic boom over the last decade has been one of the longest, even by the region's own standards. Previous to the mid-1980s, the region experienced a mild downturn around 1974-75 (following the first oil price crisis) and another one in the late 1970s (the second oil price crisis).

But just as Asia recovered from each of these previous downturns, it is likely to do the same again this time around – perhaps not immediately and not without the inevitable pain that accompanies each downturn, but the turnaround will come. Certainly, it is possible that things may get worse before they get better. However, just as it is impossible to pick either the exact 'top' of a financial market, it is equally impossible to pick the 'bottom'. At best, it can be safely said that we will most likely see a turnaround in the regional economies taking shape – probably, towards the end of 1999 and into the new millennium, assuming that like the previous downturns the present one too is roughly of a 24-36 months duration.

There is one important difference in the present economic downturn, however, compared with the previous dips. This relates to the precise cause of the downturn. In the mid-1980s, the economic dip, especially in Southeast Asia and South Korea, came on the back of strong public sector-led expansion in the early 1980s, large fiscal deficits and bloated external (mostly government) debt. While macro-economic policy failings have undoubtedly played a role in the present downturn, the crucial difference now compared with the past is the size of the asset-based economies across the region. The ownership (and in turn, prices) of financial assets (like stocks and shares) and physical assets (like real estate) had grown by leaps and bounds during the last decade. This asset bubble has now been pricked and the region is likely to see severe asset price deflation in the coming 2-3 years. It is this deflation that is now largely responsible for dragging down the so-called real economies of Asia.

For investors, this asset deflation implies that they will have to pay much closer attention to corporate balance sheets in the future rather than focus solely on a company's P&L statement. This is all the more so as many Asian companies, during the so-called boom years, tended to venture away from their core businesses and into unrelated fields like, for example, real estate development. It was not uncommon to find say manufacturing firms developing parcels of real estate in the hope of cashing in on the property boom. Often, these unrelated ventures would be undertaken with large borrowings.

Now, debt-equity ratios are likely to come under much sharper focus – and these figures may be more relevant than merely analyzing a company's earnings-per-share over the last 12 months. Earnings will undoubtedly be important, but without a strong balance sheet, it may all come to nought. Although earnings from core businesses may appear strong, large amounts of corporate debt are liable to ultimately lead to failures, especially in an environment where interest rates stay high. It is likely to be corporate balance sheets rather than P&L statements that will decide Asia's 'winners and losers' in the aftermath of the economic downturn of the 1990s.

Equally important will be a need for investors to assess the viability of earnings. As an ex-manager of mine would say, "there are only two ways to make money - either you increase revenues or you cut costs." During a time when revenues are likely to grow slowly, if at all, companies that pay equal attention to their costs are likely to do better. Trimming costs is never easy, and for many Asian companies, it could even be a first. However, this is not an exercise that can be put off indefinitely as sustained losses would eventually lead to a deterioration of the corporate balance sheet itself. It is in this respect that investors will have to assess if Asian companies have strong managements with core businesses on which they can ride out the current storm.

The name of the game in the coming months will be "cherry-picking" the Asian corporates. *An Investor's Guide to Asia's Top 1000 Companies* should be a most useful starting point in this respect. Beyond the financials, however, there is probably no escaping the well-worn exercise of "kicking and tires and slamming the doors" to determine if a business or company is indeed worth an investment. Often, the answer may be negative, but a publication such as this should help to better differentiate between the likely winners and losers.

SANJOY CHOWDHURY
Regional Economic Analyst
June 1998

Introduction

A Good Place To Start

Asiaweek's list of 1000 Asian Megacompanies is the best place for any investor in search of quality bargains to start the hunt. The list published here is based on the *Asiaweek 1000* list of the 1000 largest companies in Asia ranked by sales, which was released in November 1997. Compiled annually since 1992, the 1000 is put together by a special team at the Hong Kong-based magazine, with the aid of correspondents, staff, and representatives around the region. The data is gathered through a variety of sources, most coming directly from the corporations. Particularly in the case of privately held or unlisted firms, information is also obtained from accounts filed in company registries or published elsewhere. *Asiaweek* researchers check the figures before publication.

Though this list is based on corporate results for fiscal year 1996, the figures already foreshadow the Asian regional economic downturn. But when considering the information published in this book, bear in mind that the crisis is not yet reflected in the numbers. East Asia's financial markets are likely to remain volatile for some time. High interest rates in a number of economies are biting into corporate earnings. Banking systems are looking shaky, and even some of the most famous corporate names in Asia have gone bankrupt or are on the verge of doing so. Accounts for fiscal 1997 and 1998 will reveal just how badly Asia's corporations have been decimated by the financial turmoil.

What, then, is the point of compiling a listing of Asia's top 1000 corporations based on fiscal 1996 results? The answer, of course, is that Asia is hardly finished. If anything, its best days still lie ahead. The region has survived far more serious disasters. As for historical performance, it is a foolhardy investor — and even more foolish CEO — who does not bother to study the past, his own company's and that of his rivals. The likelihood is that companies that performed well in this list will be the ones that will withstand the full force of the economic crisis. Investor beware. Survival is by no means guaranteed, but if a company is well armed for the slump, chances are it will persevere and emerge in relatively good shape.

The 1000 — and the Crisis Effect

Total sales (in fiscal 1996) for Asia's 1000 Megacompanies were down 7.7% from the previous year to US$5.8 trillion. The main cause: Japan's stagnant economy and the weak yen. Though still by far the dominant group, only 709 Japanese corporations made it into the ranking — the lowest tally since the *Asiaweek 1000* was launched. Combined turnover for the Japan-based companies was US$4.6 billion, 11% lower than in fiscal 1995. While Australian, South Korean, Singaporean, and Chinese companies saw higher sales, the gains were not sufficient to offset the Japanese declines.

For the coming two years, sales results will be mixed. Much will depend on the business of the company. Many export-oriented firms could see sales rise on the back of a dramatic increase in purchases from overseas customers due to cheaper local currencies. Companies supplying mainly domestic customers will not enjoy such benefits unless they are able to re-engineer their operations to cater for export markets. Depending on their cost structures and whether they rely on imported raw materials in production, some companies might have to raise prices significantly, choking off domestic demand and overseas sales as well.

Breakdown of Asia's 1000 Megacompanies

As sales fall, so do profits. The combined earnings of Asia's 1000 biggest companies slipped 10.4% from fiscal 1995 to US$112.4 billion. Trouble in China was a key factor, as the combined returns of the mainland's 23 entries (two fewer than in the 1996 list) amounted to US$4.3 billion, down a massive 53%. Also in free fall: South Korea, where profits plunged 70%. Earnings in Hong Kong were up, however, along with figures from Southeast Asia and India. Japanese companies managed to make as much money as in fiscal 1995, despite slower sales.

COUNTRY	NO. OF COMPANIES	SALES IN $ BILLION	% OF TOTAL SALES
JAPAN	709	4,621.70	80.19
AUSTRALIA	67	240.10	4.17
SOUTH KOREA	63	354.60	6.15
SINGAPORE	34	97.40	1.69
CHINA	23	127.70	2.22
HONG KONG	19	67.80	1.18
INDIA	18	58.10	1.01
TAIWAN	18	63.10	1.10
THAILAND	15	38.10	0.66
MALAYSIA	14	43.90	0.76
NEW ZEALAND	8	21.10	0.37
PHILIPPINES	6	13.10	0.23
INDONESIA	5	15.50	0.27
PAKISTAN	1	1.50	0.03
TOTAL	**1000**	**5.8 TRILLION**	**100**

Initial results released at the beginning of 1998 already indicate that the crisis will cut into corporate profits in the coming two years. Again, much depends on a company's costs and where its customers are. After the first shocks wear off, a major exporter could run up significantly higher sales, taking advantage of local currency devaluation. A company reliant on imports or saddled with dollar-denominated debts will see profits shrivel up. Expect some of the more highly leveraged firms to collapse.

Profit Breakdown

Not surprisingly, total assets for the 1997 *Asiaweek 1000* companies fell 5.6% from the year before to $6 trillion, largely because the weak yen trimmed Japanese holdings in dollar terms. Collectively, Japan's top companies saw their assets dive 11% in value. India and Indonesia also slipped, but everybody else gained. Australia, China, Hong Kong, and South Korea had the biggest increases over fiscal 1995. Still, the Japanese companies accounted for the lion's share — 77.23% — of the assets of the *Asiaweek 1000*, though that figure is down nearly 5% from the 1996 compilation. South Korea now has 5.74% of the total assets, up from 4.48%.

COUNTRY	$ BILLION	% OF TOTAL PROFIT
JAPAN	57.0	50.70
AUSTRALIA	9.0	8.02
SOUTH KOREA	3.3	2.97
SINGAPORE	6.3	5.64
CHINA	4.3	3.78
HONG KONG	11.3	10.04
INDIA	3.4	3.02
TAIWAN	5.5	4.92
THAILAND	2.8	2.51
MALAYSIA	5.6	4.98
NEW ZEALAND	1.0	0.90
PHILIPPINES	0.9	0.82
INDONESIA	1.9	1.65
PAKISTAN	0.4	0.04

If there is one thing certain about the aftermath of the economic crisis, it is that asset values in Asia have plummeted significantly. Across the board, in the bombed-out economies, asset figures are expected to plunge over the next two years. The drop in currencies in East Asia means that, in dollar terms, hundreds of companies are now worth only a fraction of what they were before the turmoil hit, with many rendered technically insolvent.

Asia's top 1000 companies employed 13.1 million workers in fiscal 1996 — down 7% from the fiscal 1995 figure. The Japanese group, which accounted for half of all staff, had 67,000 fewer employees, while the staff rosters of the Chinese enterprises on the list were down 661,000 workers. The companies from India and the Philippines also had smaller workforces. But Australia's corporate giants had 80,000 more employees, while companies in Singapore showed an increase of 74,000 and Thailand's largest firms had 30,000 more staff.

Unemployment is expected to become a wider problem in East Asia as a result of the economic crisis. Even fairly well insulated economies such as Hong Kong have begun to see jobless rates rise. In the next two years, expect the staff numbers of Asia's top companies to be pared down significantly. The result: a worrying rise in social unrest, particularly in the hardest hit economies including Indonesia, Thailand, and South Korea. With reform efforts under way in China to rationalize loss-making state enterprises, the mainland's joblessness is also forecast to jump. East Asian countries typically have only rudimentary welfare systems to deal with unemployment, most relying on family networks to help. Some governments are using aid money to bolster safety-net programs, but funds are likely to be allocated to schemes for the poorest victims, mainly those in danger of falling below the poverty line.

CRISIS AND OPPORTUNITY

Though the financial turmoil in East Asia is altering the region's corporate landscape, the economic crisis spells opportunity for investors looking for bargain assets.

The investor's golden rule is to buy low and sell high. Rarely does the average punter manage to hit it just right. But once in a while, the chance to do so comes along. In Asia, that time is now. Take the example of Saudi Prince al-Waleed bin Talal Abdel Aziz. In Seoul one March afternoon this year, the jet-setting multibillionaire signed deals worth $150 million with two of South Korea's biggest companies, Daewoo Corp. and Hyundai Motor Co. His investments in the ailing giants were just the latest purchases in a buying spree across East Asia that has seen the royal tycoon pick up chunks of blue-chip companies including Singapore's HPL group, Telekom Malaysia, and Malaysian car manufacturer Proton.

Prince al-Waleed is not the only one sniffing out bargains. All over Asia, multinationals from the U.S. and Europe, private investors, and direct-investment funds — 'vulture funds,' as some of them have been branded — are scouring the region's bombed-out corporate landscape in search of quality assets going on the cheap. It is the classic investor's tale: in crisis, there is opportunity. In East Asia, there has certainly been enough bad news. The regional economic crisis sparked in July 1997 by the Thai government's decision to allow the baht to float freely saw currencies from the Korean won to the Indonesian rupiah plunge dramatically by as much as 70%. Stock markets, shocked by the meltdown, plummeted, wiping out billions in equity in a matter of weeks. Blame for the troubles rested on a range of factors. Among them: weak banking systems, inadequate monitoring of the financial sector, cronyism, a lack of transparency, the untenability of pegged exchange rates, and pressure from speculative currency trading. The carnage of the second half of 1997 and early 1998 left most of East Asia's economies battered, exposing the essential fragility of the once-lauded miracle that had prompted forecasters to predict that the 21st century belonged to Asia.

It still may. But for now, Asia is deeply engrossed in the serious business of restructuring, regrouping, and reforming. The recovery will take at least two years, probably longer in some economies. Crucial to the process will be a revamp of each country's banking sector. On the corporate side, the challenges are no less daunting. Only the fittest will survive. The better companies will rationalize their operations and rebuild. Those mired in debt will be taken over — or left to perish. Over time, new regulatory regimes will emerge to prevent the sorts of situations that led to the turmoil, including the rapid and unfettered accumulation of short-term debt by companies able to gain access to easy money from willing bankers. In short, East

Asia will rise again — leaner, meaner, and keener to pursue the dynamic destiny that the region's worst economic crisis since the Second World War temporarily put on hold. And ultimately, the region's megacompanies, including many of its large conglomerates, will flourish once more.

What that means for investors like Prince al-Waleed is that now is no time to sit back, but to act. Not only are prime assets being put on the block, but governments are rolling back limitations on foreign investment in once-restricted sectors such as banking and real estate and opening up their economies even more to overseas money. Call it the Great Asian Sale. Banks, buildings, blue-chip and bankrupt companies are crowding bargain basements in the region. Prices are down 20%, 40%, 60%, or more from pre-devaluation days, back to levels last seen in the early 1980s. And make no mistake — players with cash at hand and expansion strategies on the mind are already moving in, particularly in Korea and Thailand, the two crisis-hit economies that have been praised for taking the tough decisions necessary to getting their houses in order. But even in politically charged Indonesia, where economic reforms have not been implemented as quickly, overseas investors are quietly buying up small stakes in ravaged firms, some of them listed operations that, if not for the rupiah's nose-dive, would be regarded as the cream of the country's corporations. And throughout East Asia, there are more goodies going on sale every day, as shaky banks and companies seek new capital — or collapse. (Over 1200 firms went bust in January in Seoul alone.)

'The gainers [from the crisis] will be those who take the big-time risk buying up assets,' says Rudi Dornbusch, Professor of Economics at the Massachusetts Institute of Technology and an expert on economic transition and restructuring. 'If it works, they will be winners. This is a wonderful opportunity to get a piece of a *chaebol* very cheaply.' His advice to bargain-hunters still on the sidelines: 'Don't wait! If you missed the last one, get in now.' Kenneth Courtis, Tokyo-based strategist and chief economist for the Deutsche Bank Group Asia Pacific, has described the Sale as a 'once-in-a-lifetime' opportunity. 'I don't see anywhere else in the world where your risk can bring you four-to-five times the investment.' Alex Liu of management consultants A.T. Kearney in Hong Kong agrees: 'Many of my multinational clients thought they had missed the boat a few years ago. Now they're finding they can get in and at a better price.' Coca-Cola CEO Douglas Ivester is bubbling. 'This is a great long-term opportunity,' he says. The Atlanta-based soft-drink behemoth has gone crisis shopping, picking up 5% more of its Thai bottling operation, raising its stake to 49%, and taking 100% of its bottler in Korea.

Investment bankers are reporting that their mergers-and-acquisitions business is booming. Investors are lining up in the region's capitals to kick corporate wheels and check under the hoods of banks, property, and factories. Multinationals are taking advantage of the crisis to buy out joint-venture partners, or at least purchase larger stakes from other shareholders. Some investors are also thinking strategy, purchasing cash-strapped customers to ensure that they can continue buying the new parent's products. A.T. Kearney's Liu reckons that an Asian merger wave had been building anyway as part of a global trend. Many family-owned conglomerates that dominate Asian business have begun to realize they had over-diversified and needed to get more focused. Groups wanted to trade peripheral operations for assets that fit their core businesses. While Asia's family empires are more used to expansion than rationalization, they are no strangers to megabuck make-or-break deals. 'Big deals play to the strength of these tycoons; that's how they built businesses,' Liu says. '1998 will be the year of the big deals.'

The question for investors is whether to buy now or wait, in the hope that asset values may drop further if economic conditions deteriorate even more and currencies continue to fall. The tougher task is sifting through the corporate ruins and picking the right assets to buy. Even in the better-off economies, tangled ownership structures, opaque accounting practices, and fears of hidden debts will make the most-determined investors hesitate. 'It takes at least two years before you will really see what company balance sheets look like,' says Ernst-Moritz Lipp, a member of the board of managing directors of Germany's Dresdner Bank. He doubts East Asia will see a serious buying frenzy any time soon. 'I'm skeptical. In 2000 to 2001, you will see some takeovers. Now, you may see a few, but not a massive inflow of capital.'

But initial indications are that Lipp's skepticism may be unwarranted. If anything, the worry is that the Asian firesale could lead to resentment if foreign interests buy up so much of Asia's best assets. With governments and local businesses low on capital, a high degree of foreign participation in Asia's recovery is inevitable. 'Companies investing in the region need a great deal of sensitivity,' says Jaime Augusto Zobel de Ayala, CEO of the Philippines' Ayala Group. 'Maybe the investment will not be so welcome in two or three years.' For his part, Coke's Ivester maintains that his company is 'not trying to take advantage of people while they're down. We're good partners.' But pledges of good corporate citizenship may not be enough for laid-off workers, activists, and politicians pushing a nationalist line. Already, harsh restructuring terms imposed by the International Monetary Fund have spurred resentment and a patriotic backlash in some countries. If this attitude spreads, bargain-hunters may find themselves buying into industrial or political strife. Some may just stay away.

Buyer Beware

For those who do take the plunge, one warning: no deal is a sure thing. These bargain assets are cheap because they were in trouble. So don't buy the trouble along with the assets. Some tips:

Look before you leap

'Turn over the rock,' says economist Dornbusch. 'See if there is moss on the bottom and scrape it off first — I mean get rid of the debts.' A default on one small debt can touch off ruinous cross-defaults. Check the books, the accounting standards, and the corporate history, then check it all again. A warning — most recent accounts may not yet show the full extent of the financial meltdown's effects.

 ## Look for quality

Don't cut corners to snag a tasty-looking asset just because others are after it. There are a lot of good buys around, Dornbusch reckons, 'if you can tell the fake companies from the good ones.' Stay away, in other words, from shrimp farms that have been playing the derivatives markets. Parentage counts — scrutinize shareholders of the target and triple check any potential joint-venture partner. Buyers may want to go for management control, now that many governments allow majority or 100% foreign ownership. And even if the target looks attractive and the purchase makes strategic sense, consider the political risks. Why buy a factory now if, months later, irate workers angry about petrol-price increases burn the place down?

 ## Don't look too long

No sale lasts forever, and deals are already being signed. Thai Deputy Prime Minister Supachai Panitchpakdi warns investors considering a move against waiting for unmistakable signs that the target economy has bottomed out. 'If you wait so long, that can be a problem,' Supachai says. 'The situation can change. Prices will change.' While caution is good, remember: a faint heart never won a fair lady.

MITSUI MAKES MAGIC: A LOOK AT ASIA'S TOP BLUE-CHIP

Reaching the Number One position among Asia's 1000 Blue-Chip companies did not happen overnight. In fact, it took Japanese trading behemoth Mitsui & Co. more than 400 years. It began in the late 16th century when out-of-work samurai Mitsui Sokubei followed his wife Shuho's advice and opened a brewery. The enterprise prospered and expanded into a dry goods store, and later, into banking, paper, textiles, and machinery.

Mitsui has since grown into a diverse organization with regional interests in telecommunications, steel, chemicals, and mega-construction projects. It now boasts $833 million in investments in over 400 firms and projects. Among them is the power plant on Pakistan's Hub River, which it conceived, constructed, and runs. The facility, and projects like it, best represent Mitsui's current buzz words: BOO — build, own, and operate — and BOT — build, operate, and transfer. The formulas helped push Mitsui's turnover up 9% over fiscal year 1996, enough to edge past previous leading mega-company Mitsubishi Corp.

Mitsui's Tokyo headquarters puts the stellar performance down to a 'blossoming' of corporate efforts. No doubt, the appointment of Ueshima Shigeji, 66, as president in June 1996, and Japan's low interest rates helped. Pleased with what he views as Mitsui's new balance between trading and investment operations, Ueshima reckons that 'this is an era to approach business with a global point of view, not just a domestic one.'

Asia's financial meltdown has not discouraged Mitsui from pursuing its international approach. Executive managing director Shimada Seiichi, calling this an 'adjustment period,' is taking a 'calm and objective' stance. This includes urging 160 joint ventures in Thailand to 'shift more weight to exporting' to ride out the weak domestic market.

Part of the long-term strategy is expansion, most of it in crisis-torn Asia. Mitsui could be a leading example of a company that spots opportunity amid the turmoil. In October 1997, it beat German giant Siemens Nixdorf to secure a $50 million hydraulic power plant construction project in Nepal. It has also picked up a 10% stake in tire manufacturer Bridgestone in India, and has landed, with partner NEC, an order to install the world's first subway-train monitoring system in Singapore. By the year 2002, Mitsui says it will double its present $755 million investment in the telecommunications sector.

While thriving in Asia, Mitsui is determined to extend its global links. This region, Shimada asserts, 'has the greatest potential in terms of business opportunities and tie-up ventures with European and North American corporations.' Judging by the Japanese conglomerate's centuries-old history, a partner could expect a long and prosperous relationship.

Chapter One

ASIA'S LARGEST COMPANIES BY SALES

HOW TO GET THE MOST OUT OF THE ASIAWEEK 1000

Having the data at your fingertips is one thing; making the best use of them is another. The list of Asia's 1000 Megacompanies is designed to make it easy for you to learn as much as possible about a company on the list. All you need is a calculator.

• **Rank**
Based on their sales in fiscal year 1996, companies are compared with each other and their own past performance.

• **Company**
Commercial and industrial companies only are included in the 1000. Banks are ranked in the *Asiaweek Financial 500* list of Asia's top financial institutions.

• **Country**
This is where you will find a company's operational headquarters as opposed to its legal domicile, which may be outside Asia.

• **Main business**
The sector from where most of a company's revenues come.

• **Sales**
The most fundamental measure of a company's size. In the list, we compare fiscal 1996 figures to the year before by percentage change.

• **Net profit**
After paying the bills and taxes, this is how much remains. Divide by sales figures to calculate the profit margin — how much a company clears from $1 of sales. Warning: although profit margin is meant to place all companies on the same scale, it is not very useful to compare companies from different industries or countries.

• **Assets**
The value of everything a company owns, including cash, securities, land, equipment, and even intangibles such as goodwill and brand recognition. Subtracting equity from this figure gives a rough idea of long-term debt.

• **Equity**
The amount owners and investors have sunk into a company, as well as profits retained by the company rather than distributed to shareholders as dividends.

• **Employees**
Obviously, some industries are more labor-intensive than others. But along with the figure for profit per employee, readers can use this number to get an idea of how efficient a company is compared with others in the same business.

• **Market capitalization**
A company's worth — according to the corresponding stock market on Nov. 5. Divide by the figure for net profit to get the price-earnings ratio. P/E is a common measure to identify cheap or expensive stocks.

• **Profit ratios**
Another way to compare the performance of companies. These tell how much profit a company earns from its sales, assets, and capital.

• **Notes**
Important details about accounting periods, windfalls, and unexpected losses, mergers, exchange rates, and other corporate information.

Asia's Largest Companies By Sales

RANK 1997	RANK 1996	COMPANY NAME	COUNTRY	MAIN BUSINESS	SALES $ MILLION	%CHANGE	NET PROFIT $ MILLION	%CHANGE	RANK
1	2	MITSUI & CO.	JAPAN	GENERAL TRADING	150,081.5	9.1	333.4	19.4	84
2	1	MITSUBISHI CORP.	JAPAN	GENERAL TRADING	145,174.5	1.9	408.0	32.8	67
3	3	ITOCHU CORP.	JAPAN	GENERAL TRADING	140,347.6	12.2	114.8	6.8	248
4	5	MARUBENI CORP.	JAPAN	GENERAL TRADING	128,424.1	3.2	184.9	33.1	165
5	4	SUMITOMO CORP.	JAPAN	GENERAL TRADING	123,510.3	(16.9)	(1,338.6)	—	976
6	6	TOYOTA MOTOR CORP.	JAPAN	CARS, TRUCKS	112,555.9	14.2	3,547.7	50.2	1
7	7	NISSHO IWAI CORP.	JAPAN	GENERAL TRADING	81,719.2	(5.9)	141.8	—	205
8	9	NIPPON TELEGRAPH & TEL.	JAPAN	TELECOMMUNICATIONS	81,097.5	11.5	2,311.6	(8.1)	4
9	8	HITACHI LTD.	JAPAN	ELECTRONICS, MACHINERY	78,351.7	4.9	812.0	(37.7)	25
10	10	MATSUSHITA ELECTRIC INDL.	JAPAN	APPLIANCES, ELECTRONICS	70,563.6	12.0	1,267.3	—	11
11	12	NISSAN MOTOR	JAPAN	CARS, CAR PARTS	61,214.1	10.3	714.7	—	35
12	17	SONY CORP.	JAPAN	ELECTRONICS, MEDIA	52,060.4	23.3	1,282.0	157.1	10
13	13	TOSHIBA CORP.	JAPAN	ELECTRONICS, MACHINERY	50,132.3	6.5	616.6	(25.8)	44
14	19	HONDA MOTOR	JAPAN	CARS, MOTORCYCLES	48,660.6	24.5	2,033.2	212.4	5
15	11	TOMEN CORP.	JAPAN	GENERAL TRADING	48,155.1	(19.9)	43.7	6.5	457
16	14	TOKYO ELECTRIC POWER	JAPAN	POWER GENERATION	46,320.0	(0.3)	750.2	57.5	30
17	18	NEC CORP.	JAPAN	ELECTRONICS, COMPUTERS	45,490.3	12.5	841.9	18.7	23
18	20	FUJITSU LTD.	JAPAN	COMPUTERS	41,399.8	19.7	424.2	(26.9)	64
19	15	NICHIMEN CORP.	JAPAN	GENERAL TRADING	35,769.8	(20.7)	45.2	15.0	443
20	21	JAPAN TOBACCO	JAPAN	CIGARETTES	34,622.4	4.2	794.7	21.5	28
21	23	MITSUBISHI ELECTRIC CORP.	JAPAN	ELECTRONICS	34,245.2	6.1	78.4	(85.6)	322
22	22	MITSUBISHI MOTORS	JAPAN	CARS, TRUCKS	33,756.0	3.8	106.6	(8.9)	264
23	16	KANEMATSU CORP.	JAPAN	GENERAL TRADING	31,963.2	(27.7)	(253.1)	—	965
24	32	SAMSUNG CO.	SOUTH KOREA	TRADING, INVESTMENT	29,997.8	25.3	54.1	111.2	396
25	24	DAIEI	JAPAN	SUPERMARKETS	28,922.1	(0.3)	(109.5)	—	954
26	25	MITSUBISHI HEAVY INDS.	JAPAN	MACHINERY, AIRCRAFT, SHIPS	28,888.3	4.2	1,136.3	19.1	16
27	26	NIPPON STEEL CORP.	JAPAN	STEEL	28,142.0	3.6	31.7	(93.7)	533
28	27	ITO-YOKADO	JAPAN	RETAILING	27,752.0	4.4	683.3	(3.1)	36
29	31	CHINA PETROCHEMICAL CORP.	CHINA	CHEMICALS	26,874.5	5.6	662.6	(30.4)	37
30	36	HYUNDAI CORP.	SOUTH KOREA	TRADING, INVESTMENT	25,548.9	22.8	15.3	3.2	681

Company ranking by sales. Key to notes: All data are for fiscal years that ended between July 1997 and June 1998, except for companies with an asterisk (*) in the Notes column, which denotes data from the previous accounting period. The numbers refer to the month the fiscal year ended: 1 for January; 2 February; 3 March; 4 April; 5 May; 6 June; 7 July; 8 August; 9 September; 10 October; 11 November; 12 December. The letters denote publicly listed (L), unlisted (U), and state-controlled (S) companies. Financial results incorporate those of subsidiaries. Sales also refers to turnover, gross income, or revenue. Net profit is computed after deducting tax and minority interests while excluding extraordinary items. % Change is from the previous year's result in local currency. Sales per $1 Assets is equivalent to sales-to-assets ratio. Equity is the sum of paid-up capital, reserves, and retained

Asia's Largest Companies by Sales

1 to 30

ASSETS $ MILLION	RANK	SALES PER $1 ASSETS	EQUITY $ MILLION	RANK	EMPLOYEES NUMBER	RANK	PROFIT PER EMPLOYEE	MARKET CAP. ($M)	PROFIT AS % OF SALES	ASSETS	EQUITY	NOTES (Key Below)
69,727.7	7	2.15	6,148.3	56	7,783	332	42,832	11,924.8	0.2	0.5	5.4	3 L
88,802.7	5	1.63	10,108.3	25	35,000	69	11,658	12,683.2	0.3	0.5	4.0	3 L
67,486.0	11	2.08	4,517.4	80	6,999	351	16,405	4,721.1	0.1	0.2	2.5	3 L
69,409.3	8	1.85	4,715.3	74	65,000	30	2,845	4,400.1	0.1	0.3	3.9	3 L
49,613.5	18	2.49	5,132.1	68	5,931	400	—	7,329.4	—	—	—	3 L
116,793.8	3	0.96	52,186.3	1	70,561	25	50,278	102,534.3	3.2	3.0	6.8	3 L
49,774.7	17	1.64	2,490.7	163	6,398	377	22,157	3,010.5	0.2	0.3	5.7	3 L
151,453.3	1	0.54	49,093.7	2	230,000	5	10,050	135,008.4	2.9	1.5	4.7	3 L S
91,604.2	4	0.86	30,188.4	4	330,152	3	2,460	25,951.8	1.0	0.9	2.7	3 L
79,940.3	6	0.88	33,974.2	3	270,651	4	4,682	35,327.1	1.8	1.6	3.7	3 L
68,705.4	9	0.89	12,466.4	16	135,331	15	5,281	13,244.3	1.2	1.0	5.7	3 L
52,218.6	16	0.00	13,416.3	11	21,897	134	58,549	35,036.5	2.5	2.5	9.6	3 L
53,403.0	15	0.94	11,626.9	21	186,000	12	3,315	14,233.8	1.2	1.2	5.3	3 L
38,530.0	24	1.26	12,763.7	13	28,402	94	71,585	32,749.6	4.2	5.3	15.9	3 L
22,081.4	49	2.18	1,024.0	391	11,500	250	3,802	1,070.9	0.1	0.2	4.3	3 L
130,844.0	2	0.35	13,741.2	10	43,166	57	17,378	25,164.6	1.6	0.6	5.5	3 L
44,118.1	20	1.03	9,223.9	27	190,000	10	4,431	17,589.2	1.9	1.9	9.1	3 L
43,460.0	21	0.95	10,861.3	23	46,795	50	9,066	20,188.6	1.0	0.0	3.9	3 L
18,893.4	59	1.89	1,390.1	304	18,715	157	2,416	905.5	0.1	0.2	3.3	3 L
19,823.9	53	1.75	12,436.1	17	22,200	131	35,799	15,794.6	2.3	4.0	6.4	3 L
37,742.1	27	0.91	7,196.9	44	47,372	48	1,654	7,024.2	0.2	0.2	1.1	3 L
29,722.7	32	1.14	4,471.9	82	27,827	101	3,832	3,639.8	0.3	0.4	2.4	3 L
14,624.0	90	2.19	432.9	649	2,347	698	—	462.4	—	—	—	3 L
7,448.4	190	4.03	1,650.4	253	9,049	303	5,982	609.5	0.2	0.7	3.3	12 L
20,190.5	52	1.43	1,118.7	367	16,686	169	—	3,318.8	—	—	—	2 L
40,096.5	23	0.72	12,386.4	18	67,117	28	16,930	15,822.0	3.9	2.8	9.2	3 L
41,455.6	22	0.68	8,192.1	4	24,527	118	1,293	14,333.6	0.1	0.1	0.4	3 L
16,838.4	72	1.65	8,101.3	36	104,190	17	6,558	20,336.8	2.5	4.1	8.4	2 L
37,788.4	26	0.71	15,418.3	9	650,000	1	1,019	—	2.5	1.8	4.3	12 U S
572.6	877	44.62	195.0	791	614	922	24,896	199.4	0.1	2.7	7.8	12 L

earnings. Liabilities can be estimated by deducting equity from assets. Market Capitalization is the total value of all shares of listed firms as of **Nov. 5**. Profit as % of Sales is usually called net profit margin. Profit as % of Assets, return on assets; Profit as % of Equity, return on equity. All money values are in US$. Currency conversion uses average **1996** rates (except for Market Cap.); for Australia, A$1.2773 per $1; China, RMB8.3142; Hong Kong, HK$7.80; India, Rs35.433; Indonesia, Rp2.342.3; Japan, ¥108.78; Malaysia, RM2.5159; New Zealand, NZ$1.453; Pakistan, Rs36.079; Philippines, Pesos 26.216; Singapore, S$1.41; South Korea, Won 804.45; Taiwan, NT$27.50; Thailand, Baht 25.343. NA not available. Values less than $50,000 appear as $0.0; those less than 0.05% as 0.0%. Market Capitalization from Datastream. More notes on pages 84 and 85.

Asia's Largest Companies By Sales

RANK 1997	RANK 1996	COMPANY NAME	COUNTRY	MAIN BUSINESS	SALES $ MILLION	%CHANGE	NET PROFIT $ MILLION	%CHANGE	RANK
31	29	NIPPON OIL	JAPAN	OIL REFINING, DISTRIBUTION	24,456.5	3.2	115.6	(24.2)	246
32	28	KANSAI ELECTRIC POWER	JAPAN	POWER GENERATION	24,000.3	1.2	507.2	(11.3)	56
33	41	DAEWOO CORP.	SOUTH KOREA	TRADING, INVESTMENT	23,633.9	26.5	90.7	20.0	296
34	33	CANON	JAPAN	OFFICE EQUIP., CAMERAS	23,517.4	18.1	865.8	71.1	22
35	30	EAST JAPAN RAILWAY	JAPAN	RAIL TRANSPORT	23,108.9	1.6	649.6	3.3	40
36	35	JUSCO	JAPAN	SUPERMARKETS	20,576.2	11.9	279.0	12.1	107
37	34	CHUBU ELECTRIC POWER	JAPAN	POWER GENERATION	19,956.2	2.9	352.9	(19.6)	80
38	37	SAMSUNG ELECTRONICS	SOUTH KOREA	ELECTRONICS, APPLIANCES	19,733.4	(1.9)	204.1	(93.4)	148
39	45	KAJIMA CORP.	JAPAN	CONSTRUCTION	19,311.5	19.1	67.5	45.0	345
40	121	PERTAMINA	INDONESIA	OIL EXPLORATION, REFINING	19,276.5	26.0	578.1	58.9	46
41	43	IDEMITSU KOSAN	JAPAN	OIL REFINING, DISTRIBUTION	18,903.4	13.3	31.0	(47.5)	531
42	39	JAPAN ENERGY CORP.	JAPAN	OIL EXPLORATION & DEVT.	18,520.3	7.0	(425.5)	—	971
43	38	TAISEI CORP.	JAPAN	CONSTRUCTION	18,221.8	3.9	53.2	—	401
44	50	BRIDGESTONE CORP.	JAPAN	TIRES	17,999.9	16.1	646.6	29.9	41
45	48	SINOCHEM	CHINA	CHEMICALS TRADING	17,953.0	(1.5)	71.3	1.0	338
46	51	ISUZU MOTORS	JAPAN	CARS, BUSES, TRUCKS, PARTS	17,680.3	14.4	88.1	(74.5)	307
47	76	INDIAN OIL	INDIA	OIL REFINING	17,615.6	32.2	393.1	11.5	69
48	66	BROKEN HILL PROPRIETARY	AUSTRALIA	STEEL, MINING, OIL	17,474.4	12.6	320.0	(60.8)	89
49	74	LG INTERNATIONAL CORP.	SOUTH KOREA	TRADING, INVESTMENT	17,454.3	34.4	26.9	55.8	579
50	40	MAZDA MOTOR CORP.	JAPAN	CARS, CAR PARTS	17,413.1	2.8	(161.3)	—	960
51	44	NKK CORP.	JAPAN	STEEL	17,261.0	3.0	153.4	(68.2)	193
52	46	SANYO ELECTRIC CO.	JAPAN	ELECTRONICS, APPLIANCES	16,972.1	5.0	162.5	13.7	185
53	49	MYCAL CORP.	JAPAN	SUPERMARKETS, RETAIL	16,552.5	6.6	139.7	1,398.6	209
54	55	TOYOTA TSUSHO	JAPAN	AUTO-RELATED TRADING	16,497.4	10.4	56.0	169.9	387
55	52	SHARP	JAPAN	ELECTRONICS	16,460.6	8.5	446.3	7.2	63
56	47	NIPPON EXPRESS	JAPAN	TRUCKING, AIR CARGO	16,413.7	4.1	252.8	(1.1)	118
57	56	JIANGSU SUP. & MKTG. CO-OP.	CHINA	COOPERATIVE	16,303.3	(3.2)	185.9	(18.5)	164
58	53	MITSUBISHI CHEMICAL CORP.	JAPAN	CHEMICALS, PLASTICS	15,924.7	5.1	(110.1)	—	955
59	57	COSMO OIL	JAPAN	OIL-PRODUCTS TRADING	15,899.0	11.1	81.2	35.1	316
60	42	SHIMIZU CORP.	JAPAN	CONSTRUCTION	15,793.7	(5.9)	48.8	(27.9)	419

Company ranking by sales. Key to notes: All data are for fiscal years that ended between July 1997 and June 1998, except for companies with an asterisk (*) in the Notes column, which denotes data from the previous accounting period. The numbers refer to the month the fiscal year ended: 1 for January; 2 February; 3 March; 4 April; 5 May; 6 June; 7 July; 8 August; 9 September; 10 October; 11 November; 12 December. The letters denote publicly listed (L), unlisted (U), and state-controlled (S) companies. Financial results incorporate those of subsidiaries. Sales also refers to turnover, gross income, or revenue. Net profit is computed after deducting tax and minority interests while excluding extraordinary items. % Change is from the previous year's result in local currency. Sales per $1 Assets is equivalent to sales-to-assets ratio. Equity is the sum of paid-up capital, reserves, and retained

Asia's Largest Companies by Sales

31 to 60

ASSETS $ MILLION	RANK	SALES PER $1 ASSETS	EQUITY $ MILLION	RANK	EMPLOYEES NUMBER	RANK	PROFIT PER EMPLOYEE	MARKET CAP. ($M)	PROFIT AS % OF SALES	ASSETS	EQUITY	NOTES (Key Below)
27,194.3	35	0.90	6,007.4	57	11,533	247	10,023	4,786.3	0.5	0.4	1.9	3 L
63,356.7	12	0.38	11,234.7	22	26,265	109	19,310	16,926.1	2.1	0.8	4.5	3 L
11,500.1	131	2.06	2,309.7	172	12,274	228	7,389	795.5	0.4	0.8	3.9	12 L
24,069.7	41	0.98	9,026.2	28	75,628	21	11,448	21,343.1	3.7	3.6	9.6	12 L
67,884.4	10	0.34	6,614.4	49	78,624	20	8,262	18,764.2	2.8	0.0	9.8	3 L
13,741.8	100	1.50	3,128.8	131	39,006	60	7,153	6,755.6	1.4	2.0	8.9	2 L
56,959.2	13	0.35	8,679.8	32	21,024	140	16,784	12,368.8	1.8	0.6	4.1	3 L
19,688.6	55	1.00	6,327.0	54	59,086	36	3,454	4,977.2	1.0	1.0	3.2	12 L
26,368.6	38	0.73	3,521.8	110	13,877	201	4,866	4,148.8	0.3	0.3	1.9	3 L
14,205.5	94	1.36	6,372.2	53	33,333	76	17,343	—	2.0	4.1	9.1	3 U S
17,449.6	67	1.08	719.5	506	4,936	455	6,474	—	0.2	0.2	4.4	3 U A
15,028.2	87	1.23	829.0	458	4,888	459	—	1,597.5	—	—	—	3 L
27,672.2	34	0.66	3,598.2	107	21,757	135	2,443	3,338.8	0.3	0.2	1.5	3 L
16,198.7	77	1.11	5,686.2	62	92,458	19	6,993	16,884.3	3.6	3.0	11.4	12 L
6,600.0	219	2.72	1,000.0	402	1,322	837	53,933	—	0.4	1.1	7.1	12 U S
14,983.0	88	1.18	1,070.6	382	13,877	200	6,348	2,203.2	0.5	0.6	8.2	3 L
NA	—	—	NA	—	33,915	72	11,589	7,694.9	2.2	—	—	3 U S
28,759.9	33	0.61	12,693.2	14	61,000	32	5,262	20,565.1	1.8	1.1	2.5	5 L
1,726.0	641	10.11	349.1	704	1,352	830	19,925	173.6	0.2	1.6	7.7	12 L
13,030.0	107	1.34	3,166.7	129	24,891	117	—	3,779.3	—	—	—	3 L
24,226.2	40	0.71	4,263.1	89	16,161	176	9,495	4,570.7	0.9	0.6	3.6	3 L
23,148.2	43	0.73	7,131.9	45	67,827	27	2,395	6,208.0	0.0	0.7	2.3	3 L B
15,528.7	81	1.07	2,257.4	180	19,565	149	7,140	2,927.3	0.8	0.9	6.2	2 L
7,270.7	195	2.27	1,261.0	336	3,926	527	14,508	944.1	0.3	0.8	4.5	3 L
18,834.3	61	0.87	8,674.1	33	45,117	54	9,892	8,657.3	2.7	2.4	5.1	3 L
10,195.4	142	1.61	2,781.6	143	45,966	52	5,499	5,504.1	1.5	2.5	9.1	3 L
6,635.9	217	2.46	1,688.7	245	500,000	2	372	—	1.1	2.8	11.0	12 U S
18,223.9	63	0.87	4,428.6	84	12,512	223	—	4,554.5	—	—	—	3 L
11,832.8	126	1.34	1,744.7	240	3,395	575	23,931	1,427.6	0.5	0.7	4.7	3 L
22,327.9	48	0.71	3,236.7	126	14,658	189	3,330	3,383.7	0.3	0.2	1.5	3 L

earnings. Liabilities can be estimated by deducting equity from assets. Market Capitalization is the total value of all shares of listed firms as of **Nov. 5**. Profit as % of Sales is usually called net profit margin. Profit as % of Assets, return on assets; Profit as % of Equity, return on equity. All money values are in US$. Currency conversion uses average **1996** rates (except for Market Cap.); for Australia, A$1.2773 per $1; China, RMB8.3142; Hong Kong, HK$7.80; India, Rs35.433; Indonesia, Rp2.342.3; Japan, ¥108.78; Malaysia, RM2.5159; New Zealand, NZ$1.453; Pakistan, Rs36.079; Philippines, Pesos 26.216; Singapore, S$1.41; South Korea, Won 804.45; Taiwan, NT$27.50; Thailand, Baht 25.343. NA not available. Values less than $50,000 appear as $0.0; those less than 0.05% as 0.0%. Market Capitalization from Datastream. More notes on pages 84 and 85.

Asia's Largest Companies By Sales

RANK 1997	RANK 1996	COMPANY NAME	COUNTRY	MAIN BUSINESS	SALES $ MILLION	%CHANGE	NET PROFIT $ MILLION	%CHANGE	RANK
61	65	DENSO CORP.	JAPAN	CAR PARTS	14,937.5	14.2	656.2	43.2	39
62	62	SHOWA SHELL SEKIYU	JAPAN	OIL REFINING, DISTRIBUTION	14,709.2	11.0	55.7	(56.1)	392
63	54	KIRIN BREWERY	JAPAN	BEER	14,675.1	(2.3)	316.1	(14.2)	91
64	60	JAPAN AIRLINES	JAPAN	AIR TRANSPORT	14,406.4	8.1	(133.1)	—	958
65	81	KOREA ELECTRIC POWER	SOUTH KOREA	POWER GENERATION	14,393.4	15.6	742.8	(34.3)	32
66	75	HYUNDAI MOTOR	SOUTH KOREA	CARS	14,282.8	11.1	107.9	(44.6)	262
67	80	COLES MYER	AUSTRALIA	RETAIL	14,229.2	8.2	219.5	(33.8)	138
68	61	TAKENAKA CORP.	JAPAN	CONSTRUCTION	14,215.1	6.9	176.4	59.8	172
69	78	OBAYASHI CORP.	JAPAN	CONSTRUCTION	14,170.7	23.9	125.2	13.4	222
70	59	KOBE STEEL	JAPAN	STEEL, MACHINERY	14,096.9	3.8	160.9	(80.6)	187
71	58	TOHOKU ELECTRIC POWER	JAPAN	POWER GENERATION	13,899.8	(1.2)	251.1	(29.9)	120
72	67	SUZUKI MOTOR	JAPAN	CARS, MOTORCYCLES	13,811.6	8.8	308.8	26.1	93
73	69	DENTSU	JAPAN	ADVERTISING	13,612.8	10.0	124.8	(2.2)	225
74	63	SUMITOMO METAL INDS.	JAPAN	STEEL	13,400.9	1.8	243.8	23.1	126
75	70	SEKISUI HOUSE	JAPAN	HOME CONSTRUCTION	13,147.7	9.2	391.7	4.1	70
76	71	IBM JAPAN	JAPAN	COMPUTERS	13,100.5	8.9	511.2	40.0	55
77	64	KYUSHU ELECTRIC POWER	JAPAN	POWER GENERATION	12,998.6	(1.2)	364.2	(12.6)	78
78	68	KAWASHO CORP.	JAPAN	STEEL TRADING	12,985.7	4.1	11.4	12.0	716
79	115	WOOLWORTHS	AUSTRALIA	RETAILING	12,446.6	11.2	201.0	10.4	150
80	73	ASAHI GLASS	JAPAN	GLASS, CHEMICALS	12,293.6	4.6	222.2	(2.7)	135
81	96	RICOH	JAPAN	OFFICE EQUIPMENT	12,098.5	18.2	265.9	32.3	113
82	108	TELSTRA	AUSTRALIA	TELECOMMUNICATIONS	12,084.9	4.9	1,265.0	(29.8)	12
83	77	DAI NIPPON PRINTING	JAPAN	PRINTING	12,043.6	5.2	516.3	6.0	54
84	90	COFCO	CHINA	FOOD TRADING	12,021.9	(2.7)	92.9	(22.2)	290
85	87	CHINESE PETROLEUM CORP.	TAIWAN	OIL EXPLORATION, REFINING	12,019.4	2.2	276.4	(53.2)	108
86	109	POHANG IRON & STEEL	SOUTH KOREA	STEEL	11,989.7	11.6	735.1	(37.6)	33
87	72	SEIYU	JAPAN	SUPERMARKETS	11,938.0	0.5	(27.5)	—	922
88	82	ASAHI CHEMICAL INDUSTRY	JAPAN	MATERIALS, CHEMICALS	11,873.5	6.7	233.1	174.5	129
89	79	CENTRAL JAPAN RAILWAY	JAPAN	RAIL TRANSPORT	11,764.6	3.2	334.6	44.6	83
90	112	NEWS CORP.	AUSTRALIA	PUBLISHING, BROADCASTING	11,716.9	4.8	563.7	(29.4)	48

Company ranking by sales. Key to notes: All data are for fiscal years that ended between July 1997 and June 1998, except for companies with an asterisk (*) in the Notes column, which denotes data from the previous accounting period. The numbers refer to the month the fiscal year ended: 1 for January; 2 February; 3 March; 4 April; 5 May; 6 June; 7 July; 8 August; 9 September; 10 October; 11 November; 12 December. The letters denote publicly listed (L), unlisted (U), and state-controlled (S) companies. Financial results incorporate those of subsidiaries. Sales also refers to turnover, gross income, or revenue. Net profit is computed after deducting tax and minority interests while excluding extraordinary items. % Change is from the previous year's result in local currency. Sales per $1 Assets is equivalent to sales-to-assets ratio. Equity is the sum of paid-up capital, reserves, and retained

Asia's Largest Companies by Sales

61 to 90

ASSETS $ MILLION	RANK	SALES PER $1 ASSETS	EQUITY $ MILLION	RANK	EMPLOYEES NUMBER	RANK	PROFIT PER EMPLOYEE	MARKET CAP. ($M)	PROFIT AS % OF SALES	ASSETS	EQUITY	NOTES (Key Below)
15,644.6	79	0.95	8,994.1	29	56,961	37	11,519	17,419.3	4.4	4.2	7.3	3 L C
9,849.8	147	1.49	1,825.1	226	2,211	722	25,171	2,478.0	0.4	0.6	3.1	12 L
14,020.2	97	1.05	6,840.5	48	8,380	312	37,721	8,552.2	2.2	2.3	4.6	12 L
18,851.1	60	0.76	2,266.9	179	19,046	153	—	6,414.8	—	—	—	3 L
44,334.1	19	0.32	21,010.7	5	31,895	80	23,289	10,494.3	5.2	1.7	3.5	12 L S
9,943.0	145	1.44	2,074.8	194	47,174	49	2,287	864.9	0.8	1.1	5.2	12 L
5,534.9	253	2.57	1,916.2	211	152,744	13	1,437	5,828.8	1.5	3.0	11.5	7 L
14,870.4	89	0.96	2,835.5	141	14,013	198	12,586	—	1.2	1.2	6.2	12 U
22,338.9	47	0.63	2,772.2	144	11,856	244	10,562	3,915.1	0.9	0.6	4.5	3 L
21,494.0	50	0.66	3,403.7	118	13,437	206	11,976	3,261.7	1.1	0.7	4.7	3 L
35,539.2	28	0.39	5,742.9	61	14,730	186	17,048	8,082.3	1.8	0.7	4.4	3 L
9,281.4	154	1.49	3,201.0	128	28,813	90	10,716	4,798.1	2.2	3.3	9.6	3 L
7,185.5	199	1.89	1,667.4	246	5,629	416	22,179	—	0.9	1.7	7.5	3 U
22,396.3	46	0.60	4,978.3	71	49,791	45	4,896	6,723.6	1.8	1.1	4.9	3 L
16,450.6	74	0.80	7,251.2	43	14,006	199	27,968	5,999.5	2.0	2.4	5.4	1 L
8,657.2	162	1.51	3,270.9	122	20,689	141	24,711	—	3.9	5.9	15.6	12 U A
38,265.2	25	0.34	5,978.2	58	14,572	190	24,995	7,621.0	2.8	0.0	6.1	3 L
6,976.1	205	1.86	419.6	658	1,916	763	5,945	213.2	0.1	0.2	2.7	3 L
2,789.9	445	4.46	959.6	412	100,000	18	2,020	3,745.8	1.6	7.2	21.1	6 U
16,492.5	73	0.75	5,685.2	63	8,618	308	25,779	7,804.6	1.8	1.3	3.9	3 L
15,121.3	84	0.80	3,887.9	101	12,865	215	20,667	8,749.7	2.2	1.8	6.8	3 L
20,244.3	51	0.60	7,780.5	38	64,609	31	19,594	—	10.5	6.3	16.3	6 U S
12,963.2	108	0.93	7,641.7	40	32,061	79	16,104	14,684.6	4.3	3.0	6.8	3 L
4,142.0	338	2.90	1,369.9	308	26,000	112	3,573	—	0.8	2.2	6.8	12 U S
19,079.1	57	0.63	9,473.3	26	20,322	142	13,599	—	2.3	1.4	2.9	12 U S
19,524.1	56	0.61	8,115.8	35	28,093	98	26,166	4,889.8	6.1	3.8	9.1	12 L
14,156.3	95	0.84	749.8	494	18,790	156	—	1,052.3	—	—	—	2 L
11,499.5	132	1.03	4,069.0	95	26,721	108	8,722	6,190.7	1.0	2.0	5.7	3 L
56,748.5	14	0.21	4,161.7	93	22,920	128	14,599	—	2.8	0.6	8.0	3 U
32,379.2	30	0.36	17,407.0	6	28,200	96	19,989	9,570.5	4.8	1.7	3.2	6 L

earnings. Liabilities can be estimated by deducting equity from assets. Market Capitalization is the total value of all shares of listed firms as of **Nov. 5**. Profit as % of Sales is usually called net profit margin. Profit as % of Assets, return on assets; Profit as % of Equity, return on equity. All money values are in US$. Currency conversion uses average **1996** rates (except for Market Cap.); for Australia, A$1.2773 per $1; China, RMB8.3142; Hong Kong, HK$7.80; India, Rs35.433; Indonesia, Rp2.342.3; Japan, ¥108.78; Malaysia, RM2.5159; New Zealand, NZ$1.453; Pakistan, Rs36.079; Philippines, Pesos 26.216; Singapore, S$1.41; South Korea, Won 804.45; Taiwan, NT$27.50; Thailand, Baht 25.343. NA not available. Values less than $50,000 appear as $0.0; those less than 0.05% as 0.0%. Market Capitalization from Datastream. More notes on pages 84 and 85.

Asia's Largest Companies By Sales

RANK 1997	RANK 1996	COMPANY NAME	COUNTRY	MAIN BUSINESS	SALES $ MILLION	%CHANGE	NET PROFIT $ MILLION	%CHANGE	RANK
91	85	TOPPAN PRINTING	JAPAN	PRINTING	11,714.8	7.4	198.8	(45.5)	153
92	83	MITSUI FUDOSAN	JAPAN	PROPERTY	11,682.4	5.0	(404.4)	—	970
93	89	SUMITOMO ELECTRIC INDS.	JAPAN	CABLES, WIRES	11,610.5	8.8	296.1	14.7	99
94	113	JARDINE MATHESON	HONG KONG	GENERAL TRADING	11,605.0	9.1	536.1	(22.7)	52
95	101	FUJI PHOTO FILM	JAPAN	FILM, RECORDING MATERIALS	11,510.5	15.4	784.6	17.1	29
96	127	PETROLIAM NASIONAL	MALAYSIA	OIL, GAS, REFINING	11,480.0	29.8	2,892.0	28.2	2
97	84	TAKASHIMAYA	JAPAN	DEPARTMENT STORES	11,429.8	3.8	85.6	(53.1)	310
98	88	KAWASAKI STEEL	JAPAN	STEEL	11,329.0	5.8	73.3	(66.4)	332
99	99	KAWASAKI HEAVY INDS.	JAPAN	AIRCRAFT, MACHINERY, SHIPS	11,254.4	12.7	207.5	37.1	144
100	102	FUJI HEAVY INDUSTRIES	JAPAN	CARS, AIRCRAFT	11,243.0	13.5	364.0	103.0	79
101	91	SNOW BRAND MILK PRODS.	JAPAN	DAIRY PRODUCTS	11,165.4	4.0	48.7	(6.3)	421
102	98	ASAHI BREWERIES	JAPAN	BEER	11,142.2	11.4	75.7	24.6	326
103	86	WEST JAPAN RAILWAY	JAPAN	RAIL TRANSPORT	11,116.6	2.5	327.6	30.1	87
104	95	MITSUBISHI OIL	JAPAN	OIL REFINING, DISTRIBUTION	11,008.5	6.8	(95.7)	—	952
105	94	MATSUSHITA ELEC. WORKS	JAPAN	ELECTRICAL EQUIPMENT	10,960.6	6.3	286.5	23.9	101
106	106	DAIWA HOUSE INDUSTRY	JAPAN	HOME CONSTRUCTION	10,923.8	11.4	390.3	8.9	71
107	93	MITSUBISHI MATERIALS	JAPAN	MATERIALS, METALS	10,909.3	5.2	135.5	29.8	211
108	103	SEKISUI CHEMICAL	JAPAN	CONSTRUCTION, MATERIALS	10,869.4	9.0	285.3	18.6	102
109	92	SUMIKIN BUSSAN	JAPAN	GENERAL TRADING	10,612.1	0.6	6.9	2.2	778
110	104	KUBOTA	JAPAN	INDUSTRIAL MACHINERY	10,493.7	6.5	266.1	12.6	112
111	—	OJI PAPER CO.	JAPAN	PAPER	10,417.4	37.4	118.8	(19.8)	235
112	135	YUKONG LTD.	SOUTH KOREA	OIL REFINING, EXPLORATION	10,345.1	26.2	84.8	(33.9)	311
113	152	SUNTORY	JAPAN	WHISKEY, BEER	10,344.0	5.6	204.2	51.5	146
114	114	KOMATSU LTD.	JAPAN	CONSTRUCTION MACHINERY	10,102.2	9.0	166.9	27.1	181
115	107	NIPPON PAPER INDUSTRIES	JAPAN	PAPER, NEWSPRINT	10,050.0	2.6	263.2	18.8	115
116	155	CALTEX TRADING	SINGAPORE	OIL TRADING	9,872.6	30.1	10.5	(30.1)	729
117	100	ISHIKAWAJIMA-HARIMA	JAPAN	HEAVY MACHINERY	9,853.4	(1.2)	126.1	(29.7)	220
118	105	NITTETSU SHOJI	JAPAN	STEEL TRADING	9,798.1	(0.4)	(18.2)	—	914
119	97	KUMAGAI GUMI	JAPAN	CONSTRUCTION	9,732.9	(2.9)	(67.6)	—	945
120	120	TORAY INDUSTRIES	JAPAN	TEXTILES	9,623.4	11.2	213.0	27.8	141

Company ranking by sales. Key to notes: All data are for fiscal years that ended between July 1997 and June 1998, except for companies with an asterisk (*) in the Notes column, which denotes data from the previous accounting period. The numbers refer to the month the fiscal year ended: 1 for January; 2 February; 3 March; 4 April; 5 May; 6 June; 7 July; 8 August; 9 September; 10 October; 11 November; 12 December. The letters denote publicly listed (L), unlisted (U), and state-controlled (S) companies. Financial results incorporate those of subsidiaries. Sales also refers to turnover, gross income, or revenue. Net profit is computed after deducting tax and minority interests while excluding extraordinary items. % Change is from the previous year's result in local currency. Sales per $1 Assets is equivalent to sales-to-assets ratio. Equity is the sum of paid-up capital, reserves, and retained

Asia's Largest Companies by Sales

91 to 120

ASSETS $ MILLION	RANK	SALES PER $1 ASSETS	EQUITY $ MILLION	RANK	EMPLOYEES NUMBER	RANK	PROFIT PER EMPLOYEE	MARKET CAP. ($M)	PROFIT AS % OF SALES	ASSETS	EQUITY	NOTES (Key Below)
10,588.0	139	1.11	5,628.4	64	33,719	74	5,895	8,729.5	1.7	1.9	3.5	3 L
29,864.5	31	0.39	5,134.3	67	11,355	253	—	9,148.0	—	—	—	3 L
12,585.2	113	0.92	4,682.9	76	55,854	40	5,301	9,564.3	2.6	2.4	6.3	3 L
14,285.4	93	0.81	4,095.5	94	200,000	9	2,681	5,169.5	4.6	3.8	13.1	12 L
18,252.4	62	0.63	12,363.8	19	33,154	77	23,665	18,305.2	6.8	4.3	6.3	3 L
27,090.1	36	0.42	10,857.3	24	14,094	197	205,194	—	25.2	10.7	26.6	3 US
8,177.5	172	1.40	1,912.8	212	12,029	234	7,114	2,837.0	0.7	1.1	4.5	2 L
19,749.7	54	0.57	4,444.9	83	11,983	239	6,113	5,703.4	0.6	0.4	1.6	3 L
11,979.8	123	0.94	1,812.5	229	16,343	175	12,697	3,324.1	1.8	1.7	11.4	3 L
6,977.7	204	1.61	1,376.6	306	18,475	159	19,702	2,241.2	3.2	5.2	26.4	3 L
4,925.4	283	2.27	1,263.1	335	7,322	342	6,648	1,110.7	0.4	0.0	3.9	3 L
15,602.9	80	0.71	2,938.6	138	11,207	257	6,752	6,814.9	0.7	0.5	2.6	12 L
24,545.6	39	0.45	2,980.9	135	45,888	53	7,139	6,836.7	2.9	1.3	10.0	3 L
9,060.9	159	1.21	2,064.0	196	2,335	700	—	1,208.8	—	—	—	3 L
12,162.6	119	0.90	5,011.7	69	19,153	151	14,960	6,889.6	2.6	2.4	5.7	11 L
10,534.5	140	1.04	5,370.1	65	12,404	226	31,462	4,872.4	3.6	3.7	7.3	3 L
15,106.9	85	0.72	2,827.3	142	8,118	319	16,695	3,016.4	1.2	0.9	4.8	3 L
8,794.0	161	1.24	3,944.8	100	5,885	403	48,481	4,219.4	2.6	3.2	7.2	3 L
5,276.8	263	2.01	106.4	844	1,630	789	4,241	209.5	0.1	0.1	6.5	3 L
12,288.5	116	0.85	3,261.1	123	26,000	113	10,234	4,956.7	2.5	2.2	8.2	3 L
16,435.1	75	0.63	4,175.7	92	28,432	93	4,179	5,021.5	1.1	0.7	2.8	3 L D
12,104.5	121	0.85	2,671.6	149	6,022	394	14,079	1,096.3	0.8	0.7	3.2	12 L
12,143.5	120	—	2,030.3	198	20,000	146	10,208	—	1.0	1.7	10.1	12 U
13,906.3	98	0.73	4,981.9	70	27,007	107	6,181	4,976.8	1.7	1.2	3.4	3 L
11,751.4	128	0.86	3,050.9	134	14,520	191	18,125	5,154.0	2.6	2.2	8.6	3 L
1,037.4	797	9.52	82.6	861	84	980	124,738	—	0.1	1.0	12.7	12 U
12,258.3	118	0.80	1,888.6	218	25,431	115	4,960	2,881.4	1.3	1.0	6.7	3 L
6,922.7	206	1.42	27.7	894	736	909	—	133.4	—	—	—	3 L
17,097.2	69	0.57	2,093.1	191	10,000	278	—	644.2	—	—	—	3 L
12,801.0	111	0.75	4,399.7	86	33,790	73	6,332	7,077.5	2.2	1.7	4.9	3 L

earnings. Liabilities can be estimated by deducting equity from assets. Market Capitalization is the total value of all shares of listed firms as of **Nov. 5.** Profit as % of Sales is usually called net profit margin. Profit as % of Assets, return on assets; Profit as % of Equity, return on equity. All money values are in US$. Currency conversion uses average **1996** rates (except for Market Cap.); for Australia, A$1.2773 per $1; China, RMB8.3142; Hong Kong, HK$7.80; India, Rs35.433; Indonesia, Rp2.342.3; Japan, ¥108.78; Malaysia, RM2.5159; New Zealand, NZ$1.453; Pakistan, Rs36.079; Philippines, Pesos 26.216; Singapore, S$1.41; South Korea, Won 804.45; Taiwan, NT$27.50; Thailand, Baht 25.343. NA not available. Values less than $50,000 appear as $0.0; those less than 0.05% as 0.0%. Market Capitalization from Datastream. More notes on pages 84 and 85.

Asia's Largest Companies By Sales

RANK 1997	RANK 1996	COMPANY NAME	COUNTRY	MAIN BUSINESS	SALES $ MILLION	%CHANGE	NET PROFIT $ MILLION	%CHANGE	RANK
121	110	CHUGOKU ELECTRIC POWER	JAPAN	POWER GENERATION	9,569.4	(0.5)	250.3	(4.4)	122
122	111	MITSUKOSHI	JAPAN	DEPARTMENT STORES	9,507.2	1.6	(7.2)	—	898
123	124	NIPPON YUSEN	JAPAN	SHIPPING	9,416.5	14.9	125.0	307.9	224
124	116	ALL NIPPON AIRWAYS	JAPAN	AIR TRANSPORT	9,392.7	5.6	39.5	—	484
125	161	DDI CORP.	JAPAN	TELECOMMUNICATIONS	9,343.6	51.8	(240.5)	—	963
126	136	LG ELECTRONICS	SOUTH KOREA	CONSUMER ELECTRONICS	9,326.2	13.8	80.6	(18.2)	318
127	118	SUMITOMO CHEMICAL	JAPAN	CHEMICALS	9,299.5	6.3	197.4	15.9	155
128	171	SSANGYONG CORP.	SOUTH KOREA	GENERAL TRADING	9,161.9	40.5	3.5	(38.3)	824
129	117	TOKYO GAS	JAPAN	FUEL GAS	9,083.3	3.1	141.9	(7.9)	204
130	119	MARUHA CORP.	JAPAN	FISHERY	8,991.9	2.0	6.8	(46.6)	780
131	140	KOREA TELECOM	SOUTH KOREA	TELECOMMUNICATIONS	8,904.3	9.7	224.3	(56.8)	134
132	122	KINKI NIPPON RAILWAY	JAPAN	RAIL TRANSPORT	8,730.4	3.9	59.7	148.6	376
133	126	DAINIPPON INK & CHEM.	JAPAN	CHEMICALS, INK	8,696.2	8.9	79.0	24.6	319
134	125	FUJI ELECTRIC	JAPAN	INDUSTRIAL MACHINERY	8,690.8	6.2	75.3	39.5	328
135	123	UNY	JAPAN	DEPARTMENT STORES	8,541.9	9.4	90.6	(20.1)	298
136	137	TAIWAN POWER	TAIWAN	POWER GENERATION	8,510.3	5.6	1,247.9	(6.5)	13
137	325	RIO TINTO	AUSTRALIA	MINING	8,452.0	(10.1)	1,098.4	(19.2)	17
138	129	AISIN SEIKI	JAPAN	CAR PARTS	8,391.8	10.2	122.5	(11.4)	230
139	142	DAIHATSU MOTOR	JAPAN	CARS, CAR PARTS	8,361.5	14.6	181.3	167.5	168
140	128	KAO CORP.	JAPAN	HOUSEHOLD PRODUCTS	8,286.5	7.9	253.7	12.5	117
141	139	NISSEI SANGYO	JAPAN	EQUIPMENT TRADING	8,228.2	12.3	27.2	(25.6)	578
142	158	KIA MOTORS	SOUTH KOREA	CARS, TRUCKS	8,213.2	16.1	8.7	(38.7)	757
143	134	VICTOR CO. OF JAPAN	JAPAN	CONSUMER ELECTRONICS	8,185.1	10.4	42.2	5.6	466
144	143	FUJI XEROX	JAPAN	COPIERS	7,951.9	9.3	247.2	21.7	124
145	300	SHANGHAI AUTOMOTIVE	CHINA	CARS	7,889.4	22.9	801.6	21.8	26
146	141	DAIMARU	JAPAN	DEPARTMENT STORES	7,879.5	7.0	19.1	(68.9)	637
147	151	YAMAHA MOTOR	JAPAN	MOTORCYCLES	7,822.3	16.1	125.1	270.3	223
148	183	TATTERSALLS SWEEP	AUSTRALIA	GAMING	7,742.1	15.2	NA	—	—
149	138	TAKEDA CHEMICAL INDS.	JAPAN	PHARMACEUTICALS	7,711.2	4.7	656.2	19.3	38
150	146	OSAKA GAS	JAPAN	FUEL GAS	7,702.4	8.7	155.3	15.7	188

Company ranking by sales. Key to notes: All data are for fiscal years that ended between July 1997 and June 1998, except for companies with an asterisk (*) in the Notes column, which denotes data from the previous accounting period. The numbers refer to the month the fiscal year ended: 1 for January; 2 February; 3 March; 4 April; 5 May; 6 June; 7 July; 8 August; 9 September; 10 October; 11 November; 12 December. The letters denote publicly listed (L), unlisted (U), and state-controlled (S) companies. Financial results incorporate those of subsidiaries. Sales also refers to turnover, gross income, or revenue. Net profit is computed after deducting tax and minority interests while excluding extraordinary items. % Change is from the previous year's result in local currency. Sales per $1 Assets is equivalent to sales-to-assets ratio. Equity is the sum of paid-up capital, reserves, and retained

Asia's Largest Companies by Sales

121 to 150

ASSETS $ MILLION	RANK	SALES PER $1 ASSETS	EQUITY $ MILLION	RANK	EMPLOYEES NUMBER	RANK	PROFIT PER EMPLOYEE	MARKET CAP. ($M)	PROFIT AS % OF SALES	ASSETS	EQUITY	NOTES (Key Below)
27,083.6	37	0.35	4,264.0	88	11,325	255	22,103	5,872.7	2.6	0.9	5.9	3 L
5,598.8	249	1.70	690.8	519	10,784	263	—	1,726.7	—	—	—	2 L
13,111.6	106	0.72	2,205.3	183	16,500	171	7,577	4,118.4	1.3	0.0	5.7	3 L
11,653.9	130	0.81	1,266.4	334	14,700	187	2,688	7,085.7	0.4	0.3	3.1	3 L
9,704.7	149	0.96	1,613.9	257	2,796	644	—	6,532.6	—	—	—	3 L
8,504.0	167	1.0	1,854.1	224	34,525	70	2,335	1,345.2	0.9	0.9	4.3	12 L
12,485.4	114	0.74	2,599.3	154	6,294	381	31,357	5,821.3	2.1	1.6	7.6	3 L
612.5	871	14.96	150.4	811	935	880	3,769	26.9	0.0	0.6	2.3	12 L
16,290.0	76	0.56	3,814.2	103	16,002	177	8,865	6,373.1	1.6	0.9	3.7	3 L
4,163.2	336	2.16	189.4	793	1,541	806	4,426	489.5	0.1	0.2	3.6	3 L
18,076.3	65	—	6,214.4	55	60,067	34	3,734	—	2.5	1.2	3.6	12 U S
14,412.4	92	0.61	1,813.3	227	12,109	233	4,932	9,042.0	0.7	0.4	3.3	3 L
9,979.0	144	0.87	1,730.6	243	25,892	114	3,089	3,033.7	0.9	0.8	4.6	3 L
8,609.6	164	1.01	1,653.2	252	13,234	209	5,688	2,111.9	0.9	0.9	4.6	3 L
5,538.9	252	1.54	1,904.3	215	6,705	361	13,517	3,088.6	1.1	1.6	4.8	2 L
34,815.3	29	0.24	17,364.9	7	30,152	82	41,387	—	14.7	3.6	7.2	6 U S
17,108.7	68	0.49	7,442.3	42	51,000	42	21,537	7,796.6	12.0	6.4	14.8	12 L E
6,373.6	223	1.32	2,510.3	161	11,040	258	11,096	2,918.2	1.5	1.9	4.9	3 L
5,397.5	258	1.55	1,165.9	354	21,392	137	8,477	1,958.3	2.2	3.4	15.6	3 L
7,419.8	191	1.12	3,489.2	115	6,994	352	36,269	8,493.2	3.1	3.4	7.3	3 L
2,731.0	449	3.01	842.0	452	3,071	606	8,843	888.6	0.3	0.0	3.2	3 L
8,632.9	163	0.95	1,637.7	256	29,619	89	295	601.4	0.1	0.1	0.5	12 L F
5,551.8	251	1.47	2,302.1	173	28,540	92	1,477	2,488.9	0.5	0.8	1.8	3 L
6,336.2	224	1.26	2,575.4	157	27,670	103	8,934	—	3.1	3.9	9.6	10 U
6,634.2	218	—	2,498.3	162	60,981	33	13,144	—	10.2	12.1	32.1	12 U S G
3,931.8	352	2.00	665.3	530	6,238	383	3,064	1,003.1	0.2	0.5	2.9	2 L
6,019.8	235	1.30	1,109.7	368	26,074	111	4,799	1,816.9	1.6	2.1	11.3	3 L
NA	—	—	NA	—	315	963	—	—	—	—	—	6 U
11,222.4	134	0.69	6,960.3	47	16,586	170	39,564	25,065.8	8.5	5.8	9.4	3 L
11,028.9	137	0.70	3,427.9	117	10,238	271	15,168	5,610.2	2.0	1.4	4.5	3 L

earnings. Liabilities can be estimated by deducting equity from assets. Market Capitalization is the total value of all shares of listed firms as of **Nov. 5**. Profit as % of Sales is usually called net profit margin. Profit as % of Assets, return on assets; Profit as % of Equity, return on equity. All money values are in US$. Currency conversion uses average **1996** rates (except for Market Cap.); for Australia, A$1.2773 per $1; China, RMB8.3142; Hong Kong, HK$7.80; India, Rs35.433; Indonesia, Rp2,342.3; Japan, ¥108.78; Malaysia, RM2.5159; New Zealand, NZ$1.453; Pakistan, Rs36.079; Philippines, Pesos 26.216; Singapore, S$1.41; South Korea, Won 804.45; Taiwan, NT$27.50; Thailand, Baht 25.343. NA not available. Values less than $50,000 appear as $0.0; those less than 0.05% as 0.0%. Market Capitalization from Datastream. More notes on pages 84 and 85.

Asia's Largest Companies By Sales

RANK 1997	RANK 1996	COMPANY NAME	COUNTRY	MAIN BUSINESS	SALES $ MILLION	%CHANGE	NET PROFIT $ MILLION	%CHANGE	RANK
151	133	NIPPON MEAT PACKERS	JAPAN	MEAT PRODUCTS	7,653.5	2.0	26.8	(76.3)	581
152	132	TOSHOKU	JAPAN	FOOD TRADING	7,583.2	1.8	15.3	26.0	682
153	131	KOKUBU & CO.	JAPAN	FOOD TRADING	7,581.7	3.0	15.3	14.4	680
154	157	SUMITOMO FORESTRY	JAPAN	LUMBER, HOUSING	7,519.3	17.1	120.0	20.9	234
155	147	NIPPON SHUPPAN HANBAI	JAPAN	PUBLICATIONS DISTRIBUTION	7,508.9	7.3	14.8	12.3	686
156	187	MATSUSHITA COMM. INDL.	JAPAN	TELECOM. EQUIPMENT	7,486.3	36.8	263.7	299.7	114
157	160	CANON SALES	JAPAN	DISTRIBUTION	7,338.4	16.7	92.4	45.6	293
158	145	TOHAN	JAPAN	PUBLICATIONS DISTRIBUTION	7,328.7	3.3	30.4	12.3	544
159	168	HYUNDAI MOTOR SERVICE	SOUTH KOREA	CAR DEALERSHIP	7,272.1	10.4	39.6	(0.7)	483
160	148	AJINOMOTO	JAPAN	FOOD, SEASONING	7,247.7	5.0	140.9	46.2	207
161	163	MITSUI O.S.K. LINES	JAPAN	SHIPPING	7,151.1	17.5	55.8	29.6	390
162	245	FIRST PACIFIC	HONG KONG	TRADING, INVESTMENT	7,025.7	33.8	202.2	29.6	149
163	195	DAIRY FARM	HONG KONG	SUPERMARKETS, FOOD	6,968.4	11.8	41.5	(72.1)	474
164	156	FURUKAWA ELECTRIC	JAPAN	CABLES, WIRES	6,933.9	7.2	116.6	92.4	242
165	215	LG CALTEX OIL CORP.	SOUTH KOREA	OIL REFINING	6,920.3	24.9	15.2	(92.2)	683
166	154	FUJITA CORP.	JAPAN	CONSTRUCTION	6,867.9	4.2	5.0	(78.4)	792
167	149	OKI ELECTRIC INDUSTRY	JAPAN	INFORMATION EQUIPMENT	6,731.2	(2.2)	29.7	(86.9)	549
168	150	TOYO SEIKAN	JAPAN	CANS	6,721.5	(0.9)	152.1	(35.1)	194
169	153	NISHIMATSU CONSTRUCTION	JAPAN	CONSTRUCTION	6,691.8	0.8	115.5	(12.3)	247
170	166	KYOCERA CORP.	JAPAN	SEMICONDUCTOR PARTS	6,570.7	10.4	419.7	(44.7)	65
171	269	PETROLEUM AUTHORITY	THAILAND	OIL REFINING, DISTRIBUTION	6,538.8	35.1	327.5	10.3	88
172	178	NIPPON PETRO. REFINING	JAPAN	OIL REFINING	6,535.4	22.5	25.8	(71.1)	589
173	165	YAMATO TRANSPORT	JAPAN	TRUCKING	6,527.8	8.3	143.5	23.9	202
174	218	QANTAS	AUSTRALIA	AIR TRANSPORT	6,504.0	7.3	197.8	2.6	154
175	176	MOBIL SEKIYU	JAPAN	OIL DISTRIBUTION	6,473.7	13.3	25.9	(67.0)	587
176	254	DAEWOO HEAVY INDUSTRIES	SOUTH KOREA	SHIPBUILDING, MACHINERY	6,400.0	29.9	92.0	(42.2)	289
177	164	YUKIJIRUSHI ACCESS	JAPAN	FOOD TRADING	6,388.0	6.4	0.5	24.4	871
178	174	TODA CORP.	JAPAN	CONSTRUCTION	6,337.5	10.2	62.9	0.9	359
179	239	SEAGATE TECHNOLOGY INTL.	SINGAPORE	DISK DRIVES	6,242.6	16.3	797.2	75.6	27
180	173	YUASA TRADING	JAPAN	MACHINERY TRADING	6,237.9	7.9	(4.6)	—	894

Company ranking by sales. Key to notes: All data are for fiscal years that ended between July 1997 and June 1998, except for companies with an asterisk (*) in the Notes column, which denotes data from the previous accounting period. The numbers refer to the month the fiscal year ended: 1 for January; 2 February; 3 March; 4 April; 5 May; 6 June; 7 July; 8 August; 9 September; 10 October; 11 November; 12 December. The letters denote publicly listed (L), unlisted (U), and state-controlled (S) companies. Financial results incorporate those of subsidiaries. Sales also refers to turnover, gross income, or revenue. Net profit is computed after deducting tax and minority interests while excluding extraordinary items. % Change is from the previous year's result in local currency. Sales per $1 Assets is equivalent to sales-to-assets ratio. Equity is the sum of paid-up capital, reserves, and retained

Asia's Largest Companies by Sales

151 to 180

ASSETS $ MILLION	RANK	SALES PER $1 ASSETS	EQUITY $ MILLION	RANK	EMPLOYEES NUMBER	RANK	PROFIT PER EMPLOYEE	MARKET CAP. ($M)	PROFIT AS % OF SALES	ASSETS	EQUITY	NOTES (Key Below)
5,315.9	260	1.44	1,946.5	206	24,400	119	1,100	3,011.5	0.4	0.5	1.4	3 L
7,698.2	185	0.99	747.2	496	1,519	812	10,052	219.7	0.2	0.2	2.0	10 L
2,583.6	474	2.93	NA	—	1,900	765	8,066	—	0.2	0.6	—	12 U A
3,954.9	350	1.90	1,281.1	329	6,528	367	18,529	1,230.3	1.6	3.1	9.4	3 L
2,728.9	450	2.75	184.4	796	3,690	544	4,016	—	0.2	0.5	8.0	3 U
4,498.8	314	1.66	2,183.9	186	7,962	328	33,122	5,725.2	3.5	5.9	12.1	3 L
4,610.6	300	1.59	2,084.0	193	8,179	318	11,294	2,701.1	1.3	2.0	4.4	12 L
NA	—	—	NA	—	2,836	637	10,726	—	0.4	—	—	3 U A
5,222.8	265	1.39	644.4	540	14,959	185	2,644	210.2	0.5	0.8	6.1	12 L
7,355.5	194	0.99	3,499.9	113	5,319	435	26,498	6,040.1	1.9	1.9	4.0	3 L
10,947.5	138	0.65	1,187.5	351	15,000	184	3,721	1,761.1	0.8	0.5	4.7	3 L
8,491.8	168	0.83	1,449.6	289	52,880	41	3,824	1,861.1	2.9	2.4	13.9	12 L
3,121.3	413	2.23	1,247.4	341	49,900	44	832	1,588.2	0.6	1.3	3.3	12 L
8,483.5	169	0.82	1,861.3	223	9,554	286	12,201	3,164.1	1.7	1.4	6.3	3 L
6,814.1	208	1.02	1,412.7	299	2,364	696	6,427	—	0.2	0.2	1.1	12 U
14,061.6	96	0.49	1,916.0	210	5,442	425	1,100	346.9	0.1	0.0	0.3	3 L
7,522.1	189	0.89	1,957.2	205	21,355	138	1,391	1,633.2	0.4	0.4	1.5	3 L
6,658.7	214	1.01	3,973.3	98	6,505	369	23,374	3,493.8	2.3	2.3	3.8	3 L
8,057.8	174	0.83	1,441.4	291	5,856	406	19,723	1,364.0	1.7	1.4	8.0	3 L A
9,199.7	157	0.71	6,525.5	52	13,270	208	31,624	10,977.5	6.4	4.6	6.4	3 L
4,583.4	301	1.43	1,649.8	254	3,430	572	95,494	—	5.0	7.1	19.9	12 U S
4,830.1	288	1.35	1,074.1	377	1,640	787	15,712	—	0.4	0.5	2.4	12 U A
5,053.5	275	1.29	2,009.0	200	71,826	24	1,998	4,881.4	2.2	2.8	7.1	3 L
7,760.1	182	0.84	2,091.1	192	30,080	83	6,577	2,017.9	3.0	2.5	9.5	6 L
2,951.7	430	2.19	666.2	529	1,059	867	24,497	—	0.4	0.9	3.9	12 U A
11,099.3	135	0.58	3,515.2	111	20,320	143	4,575	2,332.5	1.5	0.8	2.6	12 L
1,401.7	717	4.56	81.2	863	3,405	574	151	—	0.0	0.0	0.6	3 U A
7,186.4	198	0.88	1,545.3	265	5,662	414	11,117	1,513.6	0.0	0.9	4.1	3 L A
1,843.0	611	3.39	1,373.8	307	19,528	150	40,822	—	12.8	43.2	58.0	6 U
4,216.7	330	1.48	285.8	737	1,539	808	—	227.9	—	—	—	3 L

earnings. Liabilities can be estimated by deducting equity from assets. Market Capitalization is the total value of all shares of listed firms as of **Nov. 5**. Profit as % of Sales is usually called net profit margin. Profit as % of Assets, return on assets; Profit as % of Equity, return on equity. All money values are in US$. Currency conversion uses average **1996** rates (except for Market Cap.); for Australia, A$1.2773 per $1; China, RMB8.3142; Hong Kong, HK$7.80; India, Rs35.433; Indonesia, Rp2,342.3; Japan, ¥108.78; Malaysia, RM2.5159; New Zealand, NZ$1.453; Pakistan, Rs36.079; Philippines, Pesos 26.216; Singapore, S$1.41; South Korea, Won 804.45; Taiwan, NT$27.50; Thailand, Baht 25.343. NA not available. Values less than $50,000 appear as $0.0; those less than 0.05% as 0.0%. Market Capitalization from Datastream. More notes on pages 84 and 85.

Asia's Largest Companies By Sales

RANK 1997	RANK 1996	COMPANY NAME	COUNTRY	MAIN BUSINESS	SALES $ MILLION	%CHANGE	NET PROFIT $ MILLION	%CHANGE	RANK
181	170	SUZUKEN	JAPAN	PHARMACEUTICALS TRADING	6,227.6	5.8	68.2	3.3	344
182	200	TOSTEM CORP.	JAPAN	BUILDING MATERIALS	6,225.3	18.3	173.5	(15.9)	175
183	181	CHORI	JAPAN	TEXTILE TRADING	6,208.9	11.8	22.7	—	608
184	162	SAPPORO BREWERIES	JAPAN	BEER	6,117.9	0.4	35.0	58.6	510
185	193	TONEN	JAPAN	OIL REFINING, DISTRIBUTION	6,116.2	13.4	92.3	(50.1)	294
186	169	YAMAZAKI BAKING	JAPAN	PASTRIES, BREAD	6,105.5	2.8	122.8	(1.6)	229
187	192	HANWA	JAPAN	STEEL TRADING	6,053.7	11.0	10.0	(8.0)	734
188	207	CHUNGHWA TELECOM	TAIWAN	TELECOMMUNICATIONS	6,036.9	5.5	1,998.3	20.4	6
189	216	BTR NYLEX	AUSTRALIA	PACKAGING, PLASTICS	6,006.5	(1.3)	(169.7)	—	961
190	189	HAKUHODO	JAPAN	ADVERTISING	5,991.7	9.0	43.0	86.8	463
191	194	IWATANI INTERNATIONAL	JAPAN	GENERAL TRADING	5,952.8	10.3	9.3	34.8	742
192	221	ACER	TAIWAN	COMPUTERS	5,893.0	4.0	188.0	(52.8)	162
193	263	HYUNDAI ENG. & CONST.	SOUTH KOREA	CONSTRUCTION	5,882.4	22.0	26.3	(8.3)	584
194	177	TEIJIN LTD.	JAPAN	TEXTILES	5,876.1	3.3	104.4	33.8	269
195	206	FLETCHER CHALLENGE	NEW ZEALAND	PAPER, BUILDING MATERIALS	5,861.9	(6.1)	114.1	(66.1)	249
196	185	HITACHI ZOSEN	JAPAN	HEAVY MACHINERY	5,839.6	6.3	107.8	31.4	263
197	338	HEWLETT-PACKARD	SINGAPORE	COMPUTERS	5,839.1	48.4	1,040.7	36.0	19
198	246	SUNKYONG LTD.	SOUTH KOREA	GENERAL TRADING, OIL	5,826.8	15.8	10.6	(9.0)	726
199	159	SATO KOGYO	JAPAN	CONSTRUCTION	5,825.7	(8.3)	(45.3)	—	940
200	259	HYUNDAI HEAVY INDS.	SOUTH KOREA	SHIPBUILDING, MACHINERY	5,824.4	19.8	17.4	(48.4)	656
201	180	RYOSHOKU	JAPAN	FOOD WHOLESALER	5,823.8	4.3	18.9	20.0	644
202	172	UBE INDUSTRIES	JAPAN	CHEMICALS, MATERIALS	5,821.7	0.5	93.3	102.2	288
203	316	SHANGHAI BAOSHAN IRON	CHINA	STEEL	5,820.0	40.8	290.1	(14.2)	100
204	—	EAST CHINA ELECTRIC POWER	CHINA	POWER GENERATION	5,817.1	20.3	221.3	29.3	137
205	186	HINO MOTORS	JAPAN	TRUCKS, BUSES	5,816.5	6.0	66.5	(32.6)	349
206	179	NIPPON LIGHT METAL	JAPAN	ALUMINUM PRODUCTS	5,761.0	2.0	(13.9)	—	910
207	198	SHIN-ETSU CHEMICAL	JAPAN	CHEMICALS, MATERIALS	5,740.1	8.6	373.4	7.4	76
208	182	SEIKO EPSON	JAPAN	WATCHES, ELECTRONICS	5,726.2	3.7	32.2	40.0	528
209	258	MATSUSHITA-KOTOBUKI	JAPAN	CONSUMER ELECTRONICS	5,713.6	30.3	193.5	212.7	158
210	217	TDK	JAPAN	MAGNETIC TAPE	5,705.0	14.6	554.3	117.7	49

Company ranking by sales. Key to notes: All data are for fiscal years that ended between July 1997 and June 1998, except for companies with an asterisk (*) in the Notes column, which denotes data from the previous accounting period. The numbers refer to the month the fiscal year ended: 1 for January; 2 February; 3 March; 4 April; 5 May; 6 June; 7 July; 8 August; 9 September; 10 October; 11 November; 12 December. The letters denote publicly listed (L), unlisted (U), and state-controlled (S) companies. Financial results incorporate those of subsidiaries. Sales also refers to turnover, gross income, or revenue. Net profit is computed after deducting tax and minority interests while excluding extraordinary items. % Change is from the previous year's result in local currency. Sales per $1 Assets is equivalent to sales-to-assets ratio. Equity is the sum of paid-up capital, reserves, and retained

Asia's Largest Companies by Sales

181 to 210

ASSETS $ MILLION	RANK	SALES PER $1 ASSETS	EQUITY $ MILLION	RANK	EMPLOYEES NUMBER	RANK	PROFIT PER EMPLOYEE	MARKET CAP. ($M)	PROFIT AS % OF SALES	ASSETS	EQUITY	NOTES (Key Below)
3,866.1	359	1.61	1,073.2	380	5,114	443	13,331	1,157.5	1.1	1.8	6.4	3 L
6,747.6	211	0.92	3,300.0	119	12,600	220	13,770	2,608.1	2.8	2.6	5.3	3 L
3,220.7	402	1.93	29.2	892	1,240	844	18,297	266.7	0.4	0.7	77.7	3 L
7,973.1	176	0.77	1,300.5	323	3,867	533	9,062	2,017.9	0.6	0.4	2.7	12 L
6,266.0	227	0.98	2,333.1	171	2,133	731	43,253	4,356.9	1.5	1.5	3.0	12 L
3,871.8	356	1.58	1,980.9	203	18,406	160	6,670	3,019.2	2.0	3.2	6.2	12 L
4,533.9	309	1.34	676.2	525	1,304	838	7,677	786.0	0.2	0.2	1.5	3 L
15,076.8	86	0.40	11,681.5	20	35,500	68	56,291	—	33.1	13.3	17.1	6 U S
7,218.7	197	0.83	2,906.8	139	30,000	84	—	—	—	—	—	12 U
2,319.7	518	2.58	393.8	674	3,550	558	12,119	—	0.7	1.9	10.9	11 U A
4,026.5	344	1.48	434.2	647	1,563	801	5,970	600.9	0.2	0.2	2.1	3 L
4,192.0	334	1.41	2,008.0	201	16,778	166	11,205	2,292.3	3.2	4.5	9.4	12 L
8,819.4	160	0.67	1,222.4	346	28,222	95	931	955.5	0.4	0.3	2.1	12 L
8,007.5	175	0.73	2,977.7	136	6,471	375	16,133	3,140.8	1.8	1.3	3.5	3 L
9,214.7	155	0.64	3,292.3	120	23,000	127	4,963	5,055.5	1.9	1.2	3.5	6 L
6,829.5	207	0.86	1,010.6	399	4,134	508	26,078	2,166.6	1.8	1.6	10.7	3 L
4,356.1	322	1.34	3,704.9	106	9,000	304	115,637	—	17.8	23.9	28.1	10 U
1,343.5	731	4.34	447.6	641	1,115	859	9,504	224.4	0.2	0.8	2.4	12 L
9,154.9	158	0.64	357.0	700	6,531	366	—	241.1	—	—	—	3 L
9,470.9	152	0.61	2,348.0	169	27,416	105	636	—	0.3	0.2	0.7	12 U
1,833.1	613	3.18	212.7	783	1,840	773	10,267	672.2	0.3	1.0	8.9	12 L
8,375.6	170	0.70	823.2	462	14,423	193	6,466	1,599.5	1.6	1.1	11.3	3 L
11,909.0	124	0.49	7,110.6	46	10,542	266	27,519	—	4.0	2.4	4.1	12 U S
11,842.1	125	0.49	5,957.4	59	200,000	8	1,106	—	3.8	1.9	3.7	12 U S
3,667.6	372	1.59	1,302.2	322	9,339	295	7,124	1,268.3	1.1	1.8	5.1	3 L
6,149.6	228	0.94	1,327.5	316	3,979	522	—	1,143.1	—	—	—	3 L
8,560.0	166	0.67	3,444.8	116	18,896	155	19,759	9,512.2	6.5	4.4	10.8	3 L
NA	—	—	NA	—	11,000	259	2,925	—	0.6	—	—	3 U A
3,561.3	381	1.60	1,863.4	222	10,742	264	18,015	4,657.5	3.4	5.4	10.4	3 L
6,029.4	234	0.95	4,359.2	87	28,055	99	19,758	12,712.4	9.7	9.2	12.7	3 L

earnings. Liabilities can be estimated by deducting equity from assets. Market Capitalization is the total value of all shares of listed firms as of **Nov. 5**. Profit as % of Sales is usually called net profit margin. Profit as % of Assets, return on assets; Profit as % of Equity, return on equity. All money values are in US$. Currency conversion uses average **1996** rates (except for Market Cap.); for Australia, A$1.2773 per $1; China, RMB8.3142; Hong Kong, HK$7.80; India, Rs35.433; Indonesia, Rp2.342.3; Japan, ¥108.78; Malaysia, RM2.5159; New Zealand, NZ$1.453; Pakistan, Rs36.079; Philippines, Pesos 26.216; Singapore, S$1.41; South Korea, Won 804.45; Taiwan, NT$27.50; Thailand, Baht 25.343. NA not available. Values less than $50,000 appear as $0.0; those less than 0.05% as 0.0%. Market Capitalization from Datastream. More notes on pages 84 and 85.

Asia's Largest Companies By Sales

RANK 1997	RANK 1996	COMPANY NAME	COUNTRY	MAIN BUSINESS	SALES $ MILLION	%CHANGE	NET PROFIT $ MILLION	%CHANGE	RANK
211	201	ISETAN	JAPAN	DEPARTMENT STORES	5,654.3	8.3	48.5	—	423
212	191	TOKYU CONSTRUCTION	JAPAN	CONSTRUCTION	5,629.3	4.1	(132.2)	—	957
213	202	NTT DATA CORP.	JAPAN	SYSTEM INTEGRATION	5,622.4	8.8	130.9	22.0	215
214	175	SEIBU DEPARTMENT STORES	JAPAN	DEPARTMENT STORES	5,602.3	(2.5)	28.4	1,218.8	565
215	188	KANEBO	JAPAN	TEXTILES, COSMETICS	5,591.9	2.3	(3.6)	—	889
216	240	SUMITOMO HEAVY INDS.	JAPAN	SHIPBUILDING	5,575.8	21.3	54.4	(1.7)	394
217	224	YAMAHA CORP.	JAPAN	MUSICAL INSTRUMENTS	5,559.3	13.8	129.3	49.2	217
218	220	ESSO SEKIYU	JAPAN	OIL DISTRIBUTION	5,549.4	12.2	19.8	(72.9)	631
219	293	SSANGYONG OIL REFINING	SOUTH KOREA	OIL REFINING	5,545.7	28.4	154.6	3.9	191
220	196	HAZAMA	JAPAN	CONSTRUCTION	5,545.1	3.8	(45.1)	—	939
221	184	SHIKOKU ELECTRIC POWER	JAPAN	POWER GENERATION	5,545.0	0.7	197.3	13.3	156
222	209	SANKYO CO.	JAPAN	PHARMACEUTICALS	5,484.6	7.1	468.5	15.7	61
223	197	OKAYA & CO.	JAPAN	STEEL TRADING	5,477.5	3.4	15.5	13.3	677
224	226	OMRON	JAPAN	ELECTRONIC COMPONENTS	5,462.0	13.1	144.7	7.9	199
225	204	NICHIREI	JAPAN	FOOD PRODUCTS	5,434.7	5.3	18.2	802.7	652
226	294	DAEWOO MOTOR	SOUTH KOREA	CARS, CAR PARTS	5,426.7	25.8	64.5	393.3	356
227	205	SHISEIDO	JAPAN	COSMETICS	5,410.7	4.9	176.1	9.4	173
228	199	ODAKYU ELECTRIC RAILWAY	JAPAN	RAIL TRANSPORT	5,371.0	1.9	34.2	10.1	516
229	222	SUMITOMO RUBBER INDS.	JAPAN	TIRES	5,353.6	9.2	43.1	922.5	462
230	228	GENERAL SEKIYU	JAPAN	OIL REFINING, DISTRIBUTION	5,334.5	11.6	44.2	(63.3)	454
231	237	KONICA	JAPAN	PHOTO MATERIALS	5,314.2	14.4	41.7	114.3	471
232	214	MEIJI MILK PRODUCTS	JAPAN	DAIRY PRODUCTS	5,309.5	5.6	22.5	(9.0)	610
233	304	SIME DARBY	MALAYSIA	TRADING, COMMODITIES	5,260.9	22.8	332.2	22.5	85
234	210	NAGASE & CO.	JAPAN	CHEMICALS TRADING	5,257.8	2.9	52.3	0.4	405
235	219	SHOWA DENKO	JAPAN	CHEMICALS	5,242.8	5.6	28.1	—	569
236	203	KINDEN	JAPAN	ELECTRICAL ENGINEERING	5,203.7	0.7	165.6	(11.2)	183
237	212	MITSUBISHI ESTATE	JAPAN	PROPERTY	5,139.9	1.4	352.6	—	81
238	241	TOYODA AUTOMATIC LOOM	JAPAN	INDUSTRIAL MACHINERY	5,127.7	11.7	164.8	32.3	184
239	272	SINGAPORE AIRLINES	SINGAPORE	AIR TRANSPORT	5,121.6	4.8	731.6	0.6	34
240	190	DAIKYO	JAPAN	CONSTRUCTION	5,083.4	(6.7)	(8.6)	—	903

Company ranking by sales. Key to notes: All data are for fiscal years that ended between July 1997 and June 1998, except for companies with an asterisk (*) in the Notes column, which denotes data from the previous accounting period. The numbers refer to the month the fiscal year ended: 1 for January; 2 February; 3 March; 4 April; 5 May; 6 June; 7 July; 8 August; 9 September; 10 October; 11 November; 12 December. The letters denote publicly listed (L), unlisted (U), and state-controlled (S) companies. Financial results incorporate those of subsidiaries. Sales also refers to turnover, gross income, or revenue. Net profit is computed after deducting tax and minority interests while excluding extraordinary items. % Change is from the previous year's result in local currency. Sales per $1 Assets is equivalent to sales-to-assets ratio. Equity is the sum of paid-up capital, reserves, and retained

Asia's Largest Companies by Sales

211 to 240

ASSETS $ MILLION	RANK	SALES PER $1 ASSETS	EQUITY $ MILLION	RANK	EMPLOYEES NUMBER	RANK	PROFIT PER EMPLOYEE	MARKET CAP. ($M)	PROFIT AS % OF SALES	ASSETS	EQUITY	NOTES (Key Below)
4,545.0	308	1.24	1,101.1	371	5,232	436	9,265	1,634.1	0.9	1.1	4.4	3 L
7,767.8	181	0.72	567.2	571	6,283	382	—	309.7	—	—	—	3 L
7,854.3	178	0.72	1,772.5	234	9,916	280	13,202	12,013.2	2.3	1.7	7.4	3 L
3,919.4	353	—	90.8	853	9,459	291	2,999	—	0.5	0.7	31.2	2 U A
6,701.4	213	0.83	(219.4)	909	4,526	481	—	569.0	—	—	—	3 L H
6,803.6	209	0.82	699.8	513	5,701	412	9,551	1,853.9	0.0	0.8	7.8	3 L
5,048.4	276	1.10	2,022.2	199	9,753	281	13,258	2,560.0	2.3	2.6	6.4	3 L
2,309.0	519	2.40	543.1	589	877	891	22,610	—	0.4	0.9	3.7	12 U A
4,813.0	289	1.15	1,360.8	310	2,215	719	69,778	795.2	2.8	3.2	11.4	12 L
9,207.7	156	0.60	722.4	504	5,012	449	—	353.6	—	—	—	3 L
13,474.5	103	0.41	3,229.8	127	10,502	268	18,789	4,433.7	3.6	1.5	6.1	3 L
7,031.6	202	0.78	4,035.1	96	11,914	241	39,326	1,326.0	8.5	6.7	11.6	3 L
2,070.1	573	2.65	325.5	720	930	881	16,686	—	0.3	0.7	4.8	2 L
5,427.0	257	1.01	2,969.5	137	23,244	125	6,225	4,533.2	2.6	2.7	4.9	3 L
3,572.5	379	1.52	863.2	443	2,785	646	6,526	951.0	0.3	0.5	2.1	3 L
6,554.1	220	0.83	956.9	414	17,243	163	3,741	—	1.2	0.0	6.7	12 U
5,608.9	248	0.96	3,568.2	108	22,045	133	7,986	5,698.8	3.3	3.1	4.9	3 L
10,135.8	143	0.53	1,268.9	333	4,140	507	8,254	3,485.8	0.6	0.3	2.7	3 L
5,789.9	244	0.92	827.0	460	24,000	121	1,794	1,157.5	0.8	0.7	5.2	12 L
3,605.6	376	1.48	1,135.6	362	1,240	845	35,667	2,127.1	0.8	1.2	3.9	3 L
5,451.3	256	0.97	1,519.3	275	4,774	468	8,744	1,695.3	0.8	0.8	2.7	3 L
2,641.4	466	2.01	669.6	528	5,607	417	4,010	866.4	0.4	0.9	3.4	3 L
15,242.5	83	0.35	2,286.6	177	37,000	66	8,979	3,714.8	6.3	2.2	14.5	6 L
3,039.0	422	1.73	1,093.2	372	1,210	849	43,214	722.7	0.0	1.7	4.8	3 L
6,703.0	212	0.78	879.7	429	8,860	305	3,175	1,761.5	0.5	0.4	3.2	12 L
5,730.9	246	0.91	2,532.8	160	9,151	301	18,093	3,364.3	3.2	2.9	6.5	3 L A
18,995.3	58	0.27	3,978.5	97	8,792	306	40,110	16,746.7	6.9	1.9	8.9	3 L
5,113.9	273	1.00	2,584.6	156	9,232	298	17,854	5,381.4	3.2	3.2	6.4	3 L
10,298.7	141	0.50	7,476.7	41	27,241	106	26,855	6,289.9	14.3	7.1	9.8	3 L S
13,763.6	99	0.37	1,186.0	352	2,250	715	—	315.0	—	—	—	3 L

earnings. Liabilities can be estimated by deducting equity from assets. Market Capitalization is the total value of all shares of listed firms as of **Nov. 5.** Profit as % of Sales is usually called net profit margin. Profit as % of Assets, return on assets; Profit as % of Equity, return on equity. All money values are in US$. Currency conversion uses average **1996** rates (except for Market Cap.); for Australia, A$1.2773 per $1; China, RMB8.3142; Hong Kong, HK$7.80; India, Rs35.433; Indonesia, Rp2.342.3; Japan, ¥108.78; Malaysia, RM2.5159; New Zealand, NZ$1.453; Pakistan, Rs36.079; Philippines, Pesos 26.216; Singapore, S$1.41; South Korea, Won 804.45; Taiwan, NT$27.50; Thailand, Baht 25.343. NA not available. Values less than $50,000 appear as $0.0; those less than 0.05% as 0.0%. Market Capitalization from Datastream. More notes on pages 84 and 85.

Asia's Largest Companies By Sales

RANK 1997	RANK 1996	COMPANY NAME	COUNTRY	MAIN BUSINESS	SALES $ MILLION	%CHANGE	NET PROFIT $ MILLION	%CHANGE	RANK
241	236	PIONEER ELECTRONIC	JAPAN	CONSUMER ELECTRONICS	5,079.8	9.1	23.1	—	606
242	208	PENTA-OCEAN CONST.	JAPAN	CIVIL ENGINEERING	5,062.5	(1.4)	34.0	(11.8)	511
243	279	CSR	AUSTRALIA	BUILDING MATERIALS, SUGAR	5,040.2	0.0	166.1	(35.9)	182
244	242	SHINSHO	JAPAN	STEEL TRADING	5,038.1	10.4	5.0	22.9	802
245	211	SEIBU RAILWAY	JAPAN	TOURISM, TRANSPORT	4,979.6	(2.4)	(15.0)	—	911
246	248	EBARA CORP.	JAPAN	INDUSTRIAL MACHINERY	4,974.1	10.2	90.5	22.4	299
247	227	MARUI	JAPAN	DEPARTMENT STORES	4,969.8	3.0	174.0	2.6	174
248	213	HOKKAIDO ELECTRIC POWER	JAPAN	POWER GENERATION	4,952.0	(1.9)	141.7	(11.3)	206
249	310	CHINA STATE CONST. ENG.	CHINA	CONSTRUCTION	4,951.8	16.7	55.1	(4.3)	393
250	247	YAZAKI CORP.	JAPAN	CAR PARTS	4,927.2	9.1	53.1	34.8	403
251	223	TOYOTA AUTO BODY	JAPAN	CAR ASSEMBLY	4,922.0	0.5	33.8	9.4	519
252	235	HITACHI CHEMICAL	JAPAN	CHEMICALS	4,920.4	5.5	71.4	37.2	337
253	278	AMCOR	AUSTRALIA	PACKAGING	4,918.3	(7.6)	(85.8)	—	950
254	167	SWIRE PACIFIC	HONG KONG	INVESTMENT, PROPERTY	4,917.4	(28.5)	981.3	18.6	21
255	229	MATSUZAKAYA	JAPAN	DEPARTMENT STORES	4,855.6	1.7	12.9	8,668.8	697
256	232	SUMITOMO METAL MINING	JAPAN	MINING	4,826.0	2.6	118.4	20.6	236
257	276	PACIFIC DUNLOP	AUSTRALIA	TRADING, BATTERIES	4,812.9	(12.8)	139.2	(233.0)	210
258	233	TOKYU DEPARTMENT STORE	JAPAN	DEPARTMENT STORES	4,808.0	2.4	(10.4)	—	905
259	265	MITSUI & CO. (AUSTRALIA)	AUSTRALIA	COMMODITY TRADING	4,802.7	(8.7)	8.8	(10.7)	754
260	231	KANDENKO	JAPAN	ELECTRICAL ENGINEERING	4,778.7	0.7	66.1	(6.3)	350
261	251	CHICHIBU ONODA CEMENT	JAPAN	CEMENT	4,759.3	6.3	89.3	1,084.8	303
262	244	MISAWA HOMES	JAPAN	CONSTRUCTION	4,704.6	3.6	26.5	8.3	583
263	295	HUTCHISON WHAMPOA	HONG KONG	RETAILING, TELECOM.	4,700.3	4.7	1,015.4	(10.1)	20
264	250	ASTRA INTERNATIONAL	INDONESIA	CAR ASSEMBLY, TRADING	4,688.0	(5.9)	200.4	26.6	152
265	249	NIPPON TRAVEL AGENCY	JAPAN	TRAVEL AGENCY	4,680.8	4.7	(2.5)	—	887
266	234	MEIDI-YA	JAPAN	FOOD & DRINK DISTRIBUTION	4,671.0	(0.0)	NA	—	—
267	374	BORAL	AUSTRALIA	BUILDING MATERIALS	4,624.5	18.1	315.8	96.1	92
268	267	MORINAGA MILK INDUSTRY	JAPAN	DAIRY PRODUCTS	4,615.0	7.8	30.3	7.8	546
269	230	MITSUI CHEMICALS	JAPAN	CHEMICALS	4,599.6	(3.4)	24.1	(43.7)	603
270	253	TOKYU CORP.	JAPAN	PROPERTY, RAIL TRANSPORT	4,584.9	3.0	282.7	1,437.5	104

Company ranking by sales. Key to notes: All data are for fiscal years that ended between July 1997 and June 1998, except for companies with an asterisk (*) in the Notes column, which denotes data from the previous accounting period. The numbers refer to the month the fiscal year ended: 1 for January; 2 February; 3 March; 4 April; 5 May; 6 June; 7 July; 8 August; 9 September; 10 October; 11 November; 12 December. The letters denote publicly listed (L), unlisted (U), and state-controlled (S) companies. Financial results incorporate those of subsidiaries. Sales also refers to turnover, gross income, or revenue. Net profit is computed after deducting tax and minority interests while excluding extraordinary items. % Change is from the previous year's result in local currency. Sales per $1 Assets is equivalent to sales-to-assets ratio. Equity is the sum of paid-up capital, reserves, and retained

Asia's Largest Companies by Sales

241 to 270

ASSETS $ MILLION	RANK	SALES PER $1 ASSETS	EQUITY $ MILLION	RANK	EMPLOYEES NUMBER	RANK	PROFIT PER EMPLOYEE	MARKET CAP. ($M)	PROFIT AS % OF SALES	PROFIT AS % OF ASSETS	PROFIT AS % OF EQUITY	NOTES (Key Below)
5,093.4	274	0.00	2,879.8	140	7,334	341	3,149	3,120.4	0.5	0.5	0.8	3 L
4,907.0	284	1.03	814.6	467	5,080	444	6,889	730.0	0.7	0.7	4.3	3 L A
6,101.1	232	0.83	2,736.2	145	23,300	124	7,130	3,551.4	3.3	2.7	6.1	3 L
2,649.9	463	1.90	74.3	866	865	893	5,813	147.5	0.1	0.2	6.8	3 L A
11,304.4	133	0.44	240.3	762	5,017	448	—	17,180.2	—	—	—	3 L
5,047.2	277	0.99	1,248.6	340	12,418	225	7,290	3,355.6	1.8	1.8	7.3	3 L
6,657.6	215	0.75	3,529.3	109	7,986	327	21,793	6,371.6	3.5	2.6	4.9	1 L
12,755.5	112	0.39	2,473.9	164	6,525	368	21,712	3,486.6	2.9	1.1	5.7	3 L
6,131.6	229	0.81	1,664.8	247	222,000	7	248	—	1.1	0.9	3.3	12 U S
2,651.9	462	1.86	613.8	551	12,700	217	4,179	—	1.1	2.0	8.6	6 U
1,916.3	596	2.57	561.5	578	8,216	316	4,119	693.5	0.7	1.8	6.0	3 L
4,033.8	343	1.22	865.5	441	4,594	478	15,534	1,649.1	1.5	1.8	8.2	3 L
5,496.8	255	0.89	2,714.6	146	25,088	116	—	3,155.8	—	—	—	6 L
16,197.2	78	0.30	12,921.5	12	56,000	39	17,523	8,280.7	19.0	6.1	7.6	12 L
2,515.6	486	1.93	753.9	491	5,944	399	2,170	734.6	0.3	0.5	1.7	2 L
5,395.7	259	0.89	2,188.4	184	3,606	552	32,846	2,785.3	2.5	2.2	5.4	3 L
4,378.7	320	1.10	1,445.9	290	38,148	61	3,650	2,213.6	2.9	3.2	9.6	6 L
4,093.9	341	1.17	818.3	463	3,966	524	—	587.2	—	—	—	1 L
767.9	846	6.25	58.4	876	142	975	62,141	—	0.2	1.1	15.1	12 U
4,163.4	335	1.15	1,483.7	282	10,122	273	6,535	1,373.3	1.4	1.6	4.5	3 L A
7,374.1	193	0.65	1,755.2	235	2,175	727	41,061	1,539.4	1.9	1.2	5.1	3 L
5,293.0	262	0.89	540.6	591	1,942	756	13,643	492.2	0.6	0.5	4.9	3 L
16,869.1	71	0.28	8,833.2	30	27,733	102	36,613	27,306.5	21.6	6.0	11.5	12 L
7,143.8	200	0.66	1,282.1	327	123,000	16	1,629	1,984.8	4.3	2.8	15.6	12 L
766.8	847	6.10	28.5	893	5,403	428	—	—	—	—	—	12 U A
NA	—	—	NA	—	2,334	701	—	—	—	—	—	2 U A
4,958.8	280	0.93	2,533.5	159	20,000	144	15,792	3,107.7	6.8	6.4	12.5	6 L
2,394.4	501	1.93	646.2	539	4,099	513	7,394	631.0	0.7	1.3	4.7	3 L
6,985.3	203	0.66	1,396.5	300	4,780	467	5,031	1,019.6	0.5	0.3	1.7	3 L I
14,624.9	91	0.31	2,288.0	176	18,698	158	15,119	4,632.7	6.2	1.9	12.4	3 L

earnings. Liabilities can be estimated by deducting equity from assets. Market Capitalization is the total value of all shares of listed firms as of **Nov. 5**. Profit as % of Sales is usually called net profit margin. Profit as % of Assets, return on assets; Profit as % of Equity, return on equity. All money values are in US$. Currency conversion uses average **1996** rates (except for Market Cap.); for Australia, A$1.2773 per $1; China, RMB8.3142; Hong Kong, HK$7.80; India, Rs35.433; Indonesia, Rp2,342.3; Japan, ¥108.78; Malaysia, RM2.5159; New Zealand, NZ$1.453; Pakistan, Rs36.079; Philippines, Pesos 26.216; Singapore, S$1.41; South Korea, Won 804.45; Taiwan, NT$27.50; Thailand, Baht 25.343. NA not available. Values less than $50,000 appear as $0.0; those less than 0.05% as 0.0%. Market Capitalization from Datastream. More notes on pages 84 and 85.

Asia's Largest Companies By Sales

RANK 1997	RANK 1996	COMPANY NAME	COUNTRY	MAIN BUSINESS	SALES $ MILLION	%CHANGE	NET PROFIT $ MILLION	%CHANGE	RANK
271	324	MITSUI ENG. & SHIPBUILDING	JAPAN	SHIPBUILDING, MACHINERY	4,569.0	30.6	(41.2)	—	935
272	298	KOREAN AIR	SOUTH KOREA	AIR TRANSPORT	4,555.4	8.4	(261.7)	—	966
273	238	HOKURIKU ELECTRIC POWER	JAPAN	POWER GENERATION	4,549.0	(2.0)	77.2	(33.6)	324
274	256	TOKYU LAND	JAPAN	PROPERTY	4,546.0	3.1	(80.8)	—	948
275	225	MAEDA CORP.	JAPAN	CONSTRUCTION	4,536.8	(6.3)	19.1	(31.0)	640
276	270	KAWASAKI KISEN	JAPAN	SHIPPING	4,530.7	6.6	57.9	122.3	381
277	282	KAMEI CORP.	JAPAN	OIL TRADING	4,522.7	10.5	32.8	29.0	524
278	268	OSAKA UOICHIBA	JAPAN	FISH WHOLESALER	4,515.1	5.8	16.4	24.9	668
279	326	MOBIL OIL AUSTRALIA	AUSTRALIA	OIL PRODUCTS	4,507.9	6.1	54.0	475.0	397
280	323	DAEWOO ELECTRONICS	SOUTH KOREA	CONSUMER ELECTRONICS	4,438.0	14.2	60.2	2.6	373
281	261	MATSUSHITA ELECTRONICS	JAPAN	SEMICONDUCTORS	4,430.9	1.4	66.6	(34.3)	348
282	281	NSK	JAPAN	BEARINGS	4,424.9	9.4	80.0	28.2	317
283	266	JAPAN PULP & PAPER	JAPAN	PAPER	4,377.0	1.8	18.5	(15.4)	649
284	271	TOYOBO	JAPAN	TEXTILES	4,367.9	3.0	36.3	12.5	505
285	275	TOTO	JAPAN	SANITARY WARES, FITTINGS	4,341.5	3.9	109.1	1.9	257
286	291	ASIA MATSUSHITA ELECTRIC	SINGAPORE	CONSUMER ELECTRONICS	4,336.2	(4.9)	44.7	(14.9)	449
287	344	ELEC. GENERATING AUTH.	THAILAND	POWER GENERATION	4,316.3	14.8	1,069.1	42.9	18
288	305	LG CHEMICAL	SOUTH KOREA	CHEMICALS	4,306.4	4.5	4.1	(96.4)	815
289	277	KEIO TEITO ELECTRIC RAIL.	JAPAN	RAIL TRANSPORT	4,289.7	3.8	57.5	17.1	385
290	264	NIPPON SUISAN	JAPAN	FISHING	4,284.1	(0.6)	46.2	(215.7)	438
291	257	ITOHAM FOODS	JAPAN	MEAT PRODUCTS	4,279.6	(2.6)	8.9	(68.8)	750
292	252	MITSUI CONSTRUCTION	JAPAN	CONSTRUCTION	4,257.7	(4.3)	3.1	6.2	829
293	386	SIAM CEMENT	THAILAND	CEMENT	4,232.8	7.8	267.8	10.1	111
294	262	HITACHI METALS	JAPAN	STEEL, MATERIALS	4,230.5	(2.8)	60.9	(67.8)	368
295	299	CASIO COMPUTER	JAPAN	CALCULATORS, WATCHES	4,220.5	11.5	34.0	432.4	517
296	373	NEW ZEALAND DAIRY BOARD	NEW ZEALAND	DAIRY PRODUCTS	4,214.7	15.3	7.8	(59.2)	763
297	274	NISSHIN STEEL	JAPAN	STEEL	4,211.4	0.6	47.5	(65.5)	430
298	285	NISSAN SHATAI	JAPAN	CAR ASSEMBLY	4,200.3	5.8	20.8	24.1	619
299	318	ALPS ELECTRIC	JAPAN	ELECTRONIC COMPONENTS	4,195.1	18.3	44.5	—	451
300	289	BHARAT PETROLEUM	INDIA	OIL REFINING	4,183.3	11.8	108.9	33.6	258

Company ranking by sales. Key to notes: All data are for fiscal years that ended between July 1997 and June 1998, except for companies with an asterisk (*) in the Notes column, which denotes data from the previous accounting period. The numbers refer to the month the fiscal year ended: 1 for January; 2 February; 3 March; 4 April; 5 May; 6 June; 7 July; 8 August; 9 September; 10 October; 11 November; 12 December. The letters denote publicly listed (L), unlisted (U), and state-controlled (S) companies. Financial results incorporate those of subsidiaries. Sales also refers to turnover, gross income, or revenue. Net profit is computed after deducting tax and minority interests while excluding extraordinary items. % Change is from the previous year's result in local currency. Sales per $1 Assets is equivalent to sales-to-assets ratio. Equity is the sum of paid-up capital, reserves, and retained

Asia's Largest Companies by Sales

271 to 300

ASSETS $ MILLION	RANK	SALES PER $1 ASSETS	EQUITY $ MILLION	RANK	EMPLOYEES NUMBER	RANK	PROFIT PER EMPLOYEE	MARKET CAP. ($M)	PROFIT AS % OF SALES	ASSETS	EQUITY	NOTES (Key Below)
6,123.3	230	0.75	800.9	474	5,356	432	—	962.7	—	—	—	3 L
8,250.2	171	0.55	1,158.2	357	16,407	172	—	440.4	—	—	—	12 L
13,725.5	101	0.33	2,655.4	151	5,772	410	13,367	3,433.3	1.7	0.6	2.9	3 L
9,594.9	150	0.47	700.2	512	772	906	—	1,119.1	—	—	—	3 L
5,970.2	239	0.76	1,534.4	270	4,305	500	4,431	711.0	0.4	0.3	1.2	3 L A
5,128.6	272	0.88	613.8	550	867	892	66,831	797.7	1.3	1.1	9.4	3 L
1,943.9	593	2.33	424.7	655	1,707	782	19,194	334.4	0.7	1.7	7.7	3 L
1,112.5	781	4.06	274.9	741	1,561	803	10,506	230.8	0.4	1.5	5.0	3 L
2,101.3	562	2.15	306.9	729	2,034	746	26,559	—	1.2	2.6	17.6	12 U
4,554.7	307	0.97	984.6	407	12,276	227	4,907	526.5	1.4	1.3	6.1	12 L
NA	—	—	NA	—	14,500	192	4,593	—	1.5	—	—	3 U A
6,468.7	221	0.68	2,182.7	187	9,331	296	8,680	2,303.3	1.8	1.3	3.7	3 L
2,298.0	522	1.90	514.8	609	1,468	819	12,593	528.8	0.4	0.8	3.6	3 L
5,199.3	267	0.84	990.3	404	5,989	398	6,062	1,195.1	0.8	0.7	3.7	3 L
4,712.9	293	0.92	2,370.2	168	11,483	252	9,499	3,365.7	2.5	2.3	4.6	3 L
1,009.2	805	4.30	274.5	742	636	919	70,253	—	1.0	4.4	16.3	3 U
11,678.8	129	0.37	4,609.7	79	32,867	78	32,527	—	24.8	9.2	23.2	9 U S
6,301.5	225	0.68	1,812.6	228	13,209	210	312	990.2	0.1	0.1	0.2	12 L
5,267.9	264	0.81	1,346.1	314	4,303	501	13,352	2,701.5	1.3	1.1	4.3	3 L
2,615.6	469	1.64	638.2	543	2,186	725	21,140	470.4	1.1	1.8	7.2	3 L
2,087.5	566	2.05	1,139.4	360	3,980	521	2,245	918.9	0.2	0.4	0.8	3 L
5,559.8	250	0.77	452.8	637	4,452	491	702	280.1	0.1	0.1	0.7	3 L
7,094.1	201	0.60	1,295.0	324	5,500	421	48,698	1,001.8	6.3	3.8	20.7	12 L
4,985.6	279	0.85	1,902.7	216	23,157	126	2,632	1,655.1	1.4	1.2	3.2	3 L
4,568.4	304	0.92	1,604.4	259	11,932	240	2,851	2,363.9	0.8	0.7	2.1	3 L
2,557.2	480	1.65	1,020.7	395	8,274	313	940	—	0.2	0.3	0.8	5 U
6,004.8	236	0.70	2,410.9	166	9,469	290	5,020	1,691.8	1.1	0.8	1.0	3 L
1,726.7	640	2.43	611.3	552	4,876	461	4,276	487.4	0.5	1.2	3.4	3 L
4,503.4	312	0.93	1,222.8	345	21,527	136	2,069	1,987.7	1.1	0.0	3.6	3 L
1,090.2	789	3.84	488.8	620	11,499	251	9,468	1,740.6	2.6	9.0	22.3	3 L S *

earnings. Liabilities can be estimated by deducting equity from assets. Market Capitalization is the total value of all shares of listed firms as of **Nov. 5**. Profit as % of Sales is usually called net profit margin. Profit as % of Assets, return on assets; Profit as % of Equity, return on equity. All money values are in US$. Currency conversion uses average **1996** rates (except for Market Cap.); for Australia, A$1.2773 per $1; China, RMB8.3142; Hong Kong, HK$7.80; India, Rs35.433; Indonesia, Rp2.342.3; Japan, ¥108.78; Malaysia, RM2.5159; New Zealand, NZ$1.453; Pakistan, Rs36.079; Philippines, Pesos 26.216; Singapore, S$1.41; South Korea, Won 804.45; Taiwan, NT$27.50; Thailand, Baht 25.343. NA not available. Values less than $50,000 appear as $0.0; those less than 0.05% as 0.0%. Market Capitalization from Datastream. More notes on pages 84 and 85.

Asia's Largest Companies By Sales

RANK 1997	RANK 1996	COMPANY NAME	COUNTRY	MAIN BUSINESS	SALES $ MILLION	%CHANGE	NET PROFIT $ MILLION	%CHANGE	RANK
301	297	YAMANOUCHI PHARM.	JAPAN	PHARMACEUTICALS	4,180.4	9.8	384.9	3.3	72
302	349	HONGKONG TELECOM	HONG KONG	TELECOMMUNICATIONS	4,176.6	10.8	1,433.0	12.5	9
303	360	SHELL AUSTRALIA	AUSTRALIA	OIL, CHEMICALS, METALS	4,165.6	3.7	232.1	(26.7)	132
304	292	DAIKIN INDUSTRIES	JAPAN	INDUSTRIAL AIR CON	4,161.4	6.6	61.1	(1.5)	367
305	339	CATHAY PACIFIC AIRWAYS	HONG KONG	AIR TRANSPORT	4,151.4	6.3	488.3	27.9	60
306	321	ELECTRIC POWER DEVT.	JAPAN	POWER GENERATION	4,146.9	2.5	50.9	13.0	412
307	288	TOBISHIMA	JAPAN	CONSTRUCTION	4,122.5	4.2	5.8	(77.9)	793
308	341	MINOLTA	JAPAN	OFFICE EQUIP., CAMERAS	4,119.1	22.5	94.6	142.5	285
309	308	KONOIKE CONSTRUCTION	JAPAN	CONSTRUCTION	4,116.8	10.0	19.3	(1.2)	635
310	314	CHIYODA CORP.	JAPAN	PLANT ENGINEERING	4,094.0	14.3	(490.2)	—	973
311	243	HASEKO	JAPAN	CONSTRUCTION	4,087.5	(10.2)	(438.4)	—	972
312	273	TOKYO SANGYO	JAPAN	MACHINERY TRADING	4,073.4	(2.8)	9.1	3.2	748
313	283	HANKYU DEPT. STORES	JAPAN	DEPARTMENT STORES	4,055.8	0.8	26.6	125.3	582
314	346	SAMSUNG HEAVY INDS.	SOUTH KOREA	SHIPBUILDING	4,047.1	11.5	(366.2)	—	968
315	347	KURAYA CORP.	JAPAN	PHARMACEUTICALS TRADING	4,042.0	23.8	24.9	25.3	599
316	363	PER. LISTRIK NEGARA (PLN)	INDONESIA	POWER GENERATION	4,020.9	16.1	498.1	14.4	57
317	446	DAVIDS	AUSTRALIA	FOOD & DRINK DISTRIBUTION	3,995.0	25.0	(188.1)	—	962
318	280	OKURA & CO.	JAPAN	GENERAL TRADING	3,993.6	(1.0)	(18.1)	—	913
319	301	YKK ARCH. PRODUCTS	JAPAN	BUILDING MATERIALS	3,986.5	6.3	29.2	13.8	558
320	320	SEGA ENTERPRISES	JAPAN	ELECTRONIC GAMES	3,978.9	12.5	18.7	(51.7)	648
321	309	TOKYO ELECTRON	JAPAN	ELECTRONICS TRADING	3,978.5	7.7	275.6	(3.2)	109
322	260	HYUNDAI ELECTRON. INDS.	SOUTH KOREA	CONSUMER ELECTRONICS	3,937.2	(18.8)	88.4	(91.5)	306
323	311	HANKYU CORP.	JAPAN	RAIL TRANSPORT	3,904.5	7.3	56.1	—	388
324	317	YANASE & CO.	JAPAN	CAR DEALERSHIP	3,891.2	9.5	11.6	20.6	710
325	492	YUKONG INTERNATIONAL (S)	SINGAPORE	OIL TRADING	3,875.8	40.4	13.0	93.5	694
326	329	MITSUBISHI AUSTRALIA	AUSTRALIA	GENERAL TRADING	3,868.0	(8.3)	1.9	(26.2)	846
327	296	IZUMIYA	JAPAN	SUPERMARKETS	3,849.7	0.5	61.8	0.6	366
328	350	NINTENDO	JAPAN	ELECTRONIC GAMES	3,844.6	18.1	601.0	9.4	45
329	303	ASAHI SHIMBUN PUBLISH.	JAPAN	NEWSPAPER PUBLISHING	3,842.1	2.9	31.2	3.8	537
330	284	NAGASAKIYA	JAPAN	CLOTHES RETAILING	3,830.5	(4.2)	33.7	—	520

Company ranking by sales. Key to notes: All data are for fiscal years that ended between July 1997 and June 1998, except for companies with an asterisk (*) in the Notes column, which denotes data from the previous accounting period. The numbers refer to the month the fiscal year ended: 1 for January; 2 February; 3 March; 4 April; 5 May; 6 June; 7 July; 8 August; 9 September; 10 October; 11 November; 12 December. The letters denote publicly listed (L), unlisted (U), and state-controlled (S) companies. Financial results incorporate those of subsidiaries. Sales also refers to turnover, gross income, or revenue. Net profit is computed after deducting tax and minority interests while excluding extraordinary items. % Change is from the previous year's result in local currency. Sales per $1 Assets is equivalent to sales-to-assets ratio. Equity is the sum of paid-up capital, reserves, and retained

Asia's Largest Companies by Sales

301 to 330

ASSETS $ MILLION	RANK	SALES PER $1 ASSETS	EQUITY $ MILLION	RANK	EMPLOYEES NUMBER	RANK	PROFIT PER EMPLOYEE	MARKET CAP. ($M)	PROFIT AS % OF SALES	ASSETS	EQUITY	NOTES (Key Below)
7,717.2	183	0.54	4,419.7	85	8,000	325	48,109	8,157.9	9.2	4.0	8.7	3 L
6,110.9	231	0.68	3,883.0	102	13,767	202	104,092	22,384.8	34.3	23.5	36.9	3 L
4,957.7	281	0.84	2,626.5	153	5,169	439	44,893	—	5.6	4.7	8.8	12 U
3,937.9	351	1.06	1,313.5	320	13,761	203	4,439	1,386.1	1.5	1.6	4.7	3 L
8,607.3	165	0.48	3,246.8	124	15,757	179	30,992	3,681.3	11.8	5.7	15.0	12 L
18,159.5	64	0.23	840.4	454	3,687	545	13,808	—	1.2	0.3	6.1	3 U A
4,708.5	294	0.88	285.1	738	3,394	576	1,723	193.9	0.1	0.1	2.1	3 L
3,717.8	369	1.11	607.4	554	4,658	474	20,308	1,367.1	2.3	2.5	15.6	3 L
4,561.1	306	0.90	322.9	721	4,909	457	3,933	—	0.5	0.4	5.0	9 U A
3,382.2	391	1.21	530.0	599	2,954	620	—	350.4	—	—	—	3 L
9,563.2	151	0.43	139.1	817	2,330	702	—	413.3	—	—	—	3 L
423.2	892	9.63	104.8	845	340	960	26,903	107.5	0.2	2.2	8.7	3 L A
3,544.0	384	1.14	938.9	418	5,485	422	4,857	1,453.3	0.7	0.8	2.8	3 L
6,641.5	216	0.61	1,011.5	398	12,589	222	—	678.6	—	—	—	12 U
2,507.8	488	1.61	377.8	687	3,469	567	7,179	339.5	0.6	0.0	6.6	9 L
22,449.6	45	0.18	12,479.8	15	56,476	38	8,821	—	12.4	2.2	3.0	12 U S
1,111.1	782	3.60	202.4	787	12,190	230	—	232.1	—	—	—	6 L
2,920.1	432	1.37	41.5	887	880	890	—	331.8	—	—	—	3 L
2,166.6	550	1.84	343.5	711	10,855	261	2,691	—	0.7	1.3	8.5	1 U
3,911.6	354	1.02	1,435.1	293	5,352	433	3,490	2,454.7	0.5	0.5	1.3	3 L
3,558.3	382	1.12	1,907.3	213	6,988	353	39,433	9,356.5	6.9	7.7	14.4	3 L
7,786.1	180	0.51	1,790.9	231	19,728	148	4,483	1,530.2	2.2	1.1	4.9	12 L
11,997.9	122	0.33	1,427.2	295	4,949	453	11,342	4,250.6	1.4	0.5	3.9	3 L
NA	—	—	NA	—	4,926	456	2,351	—	0.3	—	—	9 U A
622.0	869	6.22	4.6	902	12	988	1,086,934	—	0.3	2.1	284.6	9 L
158.3	911	24.44	34.1	891	107	978	18,007	—	0.1	1.2	5.6	12 U
2,695.1	453	1.43	1,311.1	321	4,092	515	15,110	897.5	1.6	2.3	4.7	2 L
6,762.5	210	0.57	5,182.2	66	980	873	614,243	12,943.0	15.7	8.9	11.6	3 L
NA	—	—	NA	—	7,774	333	4,016	—	0.8	—	—	3 U A
3,564.9	380	1.08	49.0	880	2,888	628	11,679	245.8	0.9	0.9	68.8	2 L

earnings. Liabilities can be estimated by deducting equity from assets. Market Capitalization is the total value of all shares of listed firms as of **Nov. 5**. Profit as % of Sales is usually called net profit margin. Profit as % of Assets, return on assets; Profit as % of Equity, return on equity. All money values are in US$. Currency conversion uses average **1996** rates (except for Market Cap.); for Australia, A$1.2773 per $1; China, RMB8.3142; Hong Kong, HK$7.80; India, Rs35.433; Indonesia, Rp2,342.3; Japan, ¥108.78; Malaysia, RM2.5159; New Zealand, NZ$1.453; Pakistan, Rs36.079; Philippines, Pesos 26.216; Singapore, S$1.41; South Korea, Won 804.45; Taiwan, NT$27.50; Thailand, Baht 25.343. NA not available. Values less than $50,000 appear as $0.0; those less than 0.05% as 0.0%. Market Capitalization from Datastream. More notes on pages 84 and 85.

Asia's Largest Companies By Sales

RANK 1997	RANK 1996	COMPANY NAME	COUNTRY	MAIN BUSINESS	SALES $ MILLION	%CHANGE	NET PROFIT $ MILLION	%CHANGE	RANK
331	302	DAIDO STEEL	JAPAN	STEEL PRODUCTS	3,764.2	0.8	23.6	(32.2)	605
332	340	ITOCHU FUEL	JAPAN	FUEL TRADING	3,763.9	11.5	16.2	(36.6)	670
333	312	OIL & N. GAS COMMISSION	INDIA	OIL, FUEL GAS	3,745.5	1.1	565.9	3.1	47
334	388	MATSUSHITA ELEC. COMP.	JAPAN	ELECTRONIC COMPONENTS	3,741.8	8.6	71.5	35.2	336
335	332	AOKI CORP.	JAPAN	CONSTRUCTION	3,716.1	7.9	(84.5)	—	949
336	322	HITACHI CABLE	JAPAN	CABLE, WIRE	3,713.4	5.6	86.2	0.2	308
337	447	SUN HUNG KAI PROPERTIES	HONG KONG	PROPERTY DEVELOPMENT	3,712.8	28.0	1,815.4	28.3	7
338	330	NAN YA PLASTICS	TAIWAN	PETROCHEMICALS	3,712.7	(3.5)	282.9	(2.0)	103
339	405	CITIC	CHINA	INVESTMENT	3,712.5	15.7	297.6	20.9	98
340	315	YOKOHAMA RUBBER	JAPAN	TIRES	3,701.5	3.4	34.5	566.6	513
341	423	KDD	JAPAN	TELECOMMUNICATIONS	3,688.4	39.7	118.2	(6.7)	237
342	382	NISSHO IWAI PETROLEUM	SINGAPORE	OIL TRADING	3,686.8	6.4	(0.8)	—	882
343	333	MITSUI MINING & SMELTING	JAPAN	METALS, MINING	3,680.4	8.1	49.8	(28.8)	416
344	313	MITSUI PETROCHEMICAL	JAPAN	CHEMICALS	3,672.0	1.9	106.3	42.4	266
345	331	KYOWA HAKKO KOGYO	JAPAN	PHARMACEUTICALS, FOOD	3,655.3	6.0	113.4	(20.0)	250
346	319	CITIZEN WATCH	JAPAN	WATCHES	3,612.1	2.1	89.8	29.8	302
347	290	STEEL AUTHORITY OF INDIA	INDIA	STEEL AND IRON	3,604.2	(4.1)	145.4	(60.9)	197
348	342	TOKYO TOBACCO SERVICE	JAPAN	CIGARETTE TRADING	3,590.5	8.3	(4.3)	—	892
349	336	TAIWAN TOBACCO & WINE	TAIWAN	TRADING, DISTRIBUTION	3,585.5	(2.8)	NA	—	—
350	307	NEC HOME ELECTRONICS	JAPAN	ELECTRONIC GAMES	3,584.4	(3.5)	NA	—	—
351	351	TOSOH CORP.	JAPAN	CHEMICALS	3,560.8	10.9	55.8	(41.8)	391
352	356	NIPPON HODO	JAPAN	CIVIL ENGINEERING	3,544.3	11.9	33.9	(1.2)	518
353	327	NAGOYA RAILROAD	JAPAN	RAIL TRANSPORT	3,543.3	1.9	48.3	14.4	424
354	286	HINDUSTAN PETROLEUM	INDIA	OIL REFINING, DISTRIBUTION	3,516.0	15.7	172.8	19.1	176
355	337	DAISHOWA PAPER MFG.	JAPAN	PAPER	3,502.4	3.3	69.0	—	341
356	361	SEIKO	JAPAN	WATCH SALES	3,496.0	11.2	8.7	—	758
357	334	CONSUMERS CO-OP. KOBE	JAPAN	SUPERMARKETS	3,488.0	2.6	27.8	5.7	573
358	366	NIKON	JAPAN	CAMERAS	3,484.9	13.9	183.3	7.3	166
359	463	KOREA HEAVY INDUSTRIES	SOUTH KOREA	ENGINEERING, MACHINERY	3,483.4	27.6	187.3	(13.1)	163
360	335	OTSUKA PHARMACEUTICAL	JAPAN	FOOD, PHARMACEUTICALS	3,475.0	2.3	124.4	1.6	227

Company ranking by sales. Key to notes: All data are for fiscal years that ended between July 1997 and June 1998, except for companies with an asterisk (*) in the Notes column, which denotes data from the previous accounting period. The numbers refer to the month the fiscal year ended: 1 for January; 2 February; 3 March; 4 April; 5 May; 6 June; 7 July; 8 August; 9 September; 10 October; 11 November; 12 December. The letters denote publicly listed (L), unlisted (U), and state-controlled (S) companies. Financial results incorporate those of subsidiaries. Sales also refers to turnover, gross income, or revenue. Net profit is computed after deducting tax and minority interests while excluding extraordinary items. % Change is from the previous year's result in local currency. Sales per $1 Assets is equivalent to sales-to-assets ratio. Equity is the sum of paid-up capital, reserves, and retained

Asia's Largest Companies by Sales

331 to 360

ASSETS $ MILLION	RANK	SALES PER $1 ASSETS	EQUITY $ MILLION	RANK	EMPLOYEES NUMBER	RANK	PROFIT PER EMPLOYEE	MARKET CAP. ($M)	PROFIT AS % OF SALES	ASSETS	EQUITY	NOTES (Key Below)
4,222.5	329	0.89	1,230.7	343	6,192	386	3,804	833.1	0.6	0.6	1.9	3 L
1,811.3	620	2.08	703.7	511	2,434	686	6,651	373.8	0.4	0.9	2.3	3 L
NA	—	—	NA	—	47,501	47	11,913	3,315.6	15.1	—	—	3 L S
2,419.2	497	—	847.5	451	13,612	204	5,256	—	1.9	2.0	8.4	3 U
7,671.2	186	0.48	691.1	518	6,100	391	—	201.4	—	—	—	3 L
3,681.2	371	1.01	1,698.4	244	12,592	221	6,846	2,333.9	2.3	2.3	5.1	3 L
24,068.5	42	0.15	17,270.4	8	13,000	214	139,645	17,617.3	48.9	7.5	10.5	6 L
4,830.2	287	0.77	1,932.9	207	16,370	173	17,283	4,250.4	7.6	5.9	14.6	12 L
23,028.0	44	0.16	2,565.8	158	29,754	87	10,003	—	8.0	1.3	11.6	12 U S
3,869.6	358	0.96	995.6	403	12,267	229	2,812	936.3	0.9	0.9	3.5	3 L
5,883.2	241	0.63	3,240.8	125	5,379	430	21,976	3,020.2	3.2	2.0	3.6	3 L
95.6	915	38.56	0.2	904	7	990	—	—	—	—	—	3 U
4,249.0	326	0.87	357.0	701	3,032	610	16,415	2,148.8	1.4	1.2	13.9	3 L
4,577.7	302	0.80	1,541.2	267	3,266	585	32,561	—	2.9	2.3	6.9	3 U
3,969.2	349	0.92	1,658.3	250	5,174	438	21,921	2,188.5	3.1	2.9	6.8	3 L
3,536.3	385	1.02	1,865.3	221	20,000	145	4,488	1,952.0	2.5	2.5	4.8	3 L
NA	—	—	NA	—	187,504	11	775	1,561.9	4.0	—	—	3 L S
NA	—	—	NA	—	1,257	843	—	—	—	—	—	3 U A
NA	—	—	NA	—	13,500	205	—	—	—	—	—	12 U S
NA	—	—	NA	—	3,091	602	—	—	—	—	—	3 U A
4,707.9	295	0.76	712.2	509	3,853	535	14,470	1,411.3	1.6	1.2	7.8	3 L
3,179.1	405	1.11	1,210.7	348	2,785	647	12,190	611.3	0.0	1.1	2.8	3 L
9,448.8	153	0.37	1,503.9	277	7,989	326	6,048	3,003.7	1.4	0.5	3.2	3 L
NA	—	—	NA	—	11,209	256	15,414	2,785.6	4.9	—	—	3 L S
5,768.4	245	0.61	411.2	661	5,741	411	12,190	1,264.1	1.0	1.2	17.0	3 L
3,824.7	360	0.91	166.2	807	9,357	293	934	515.2	0.3	0.2	5.3	3 L
1,857.6	606	—	737.7	498	15,461	182	1,796	—	0.8	1.5	3.8	3 U A
4,231.2	328	0.82	1,524.0	274	6,955	355	26,351	4,587.3	5.3	4.3	12.0	3 L
3,535.6	386	0.99	1,252.3	339	7,632	335	24,544	—	5.4	5.3	14.0	12 U
2,679.2	455	—	1,488.0	281	5,211	437	23,876	—	3.6	4.6	8.4	3 U A

earnings. Liabilities can be estimated by deducting equity from assets. Market Capitalization is the total value of all shares of listed firms as of **Nov. 5**. Profit as % of Sales is usually called net profit margin. Profit as % of Assets, return on assets; Profit as % of Equity, return on equity. All money values are in US$. Currency conversion uses average **1996** rates (except for Market Cap.); for Australia, A$1.2773 per $1; China, RMB8.3142; Hong Kong, HK$7.80; India, Rs35.433; Indonesia, Rp2.342.3; Japan, ¥108.78; Malaysia, RM2.5159; New Zealand, NZ$1.453; Pakistan, Rs36.079; Philippines, Pesos 26.216; Singapore, S$1.41; South Korea, Won 804.45; Taiwan, NT$27.50; Thailand, Baht 25.343. NA not available. Values less than $50,000 appear as $0.0; those less than 0.05% as 0.0%. Market Capitalization from Datastream. More notes on pages 84 and 85.

Asia's Largest Companies By Sales

RANK 1997	RANK 1996	COMPANY NAME	COUNTRY	MAIN BUSINESS	SALES $ MILLION	%CHANGE	NET PROFIT $ MILLION	%CHANGE	RANK
361	358	FUJIKURA	JAPAN	CABLE, WIRE	3,460.1	9.5	65.8	124.9	351
362	466	HONG LEONG INVESTMENT	SINGAPORE	INVESTMENT	3,457.8	20.9	244.1	34.6	125
363	364	JAPAN TELECOM	JAPAN	TELECOMMUNICATIONS	3,455.2	11.0	233.9	19.5	128
364	876	AUSTRALIAN WHEAT BOARD	AUSTRALIA	FOOD TRADING	3,432.1	119.9	2,389.4	163.8	3
365	394	HYOSUNG CORP.	SOUTH KOREA	GENERAL TRADING	3,431.7	8.3	2.1	15.2	844
366	345	SHIONOGI & CO.	JAPAN	PHARMACEUTICALS	3,402.4	2.0	122.9	12.9	228
367	365	AISIN AW	JAPAN	CAR PARTS	3,385.7	10.6	83.7	65.5	313
368	343	NIHON SHURUI HANBAI	JAPAN	FOOD AND LIQUOR	3,379.8	2.2	4.6	73.0	811
369	406	TNT	AUSTRALIA	CARGO TRANSPORT	3,372.1	17.1	7.7	(75.4)	765
370	353	NISSHIN FLOUR MILLING	JAPAN	FLOUR MILLING	3,345.0	4.8	57.7	(0.5)	384
371	354	MEIJI SEIKA	JAPAN	FOOD, PHARMACEUTICALS	3,318.8	4.0	41.0	13.0	477
372	348	TOBU RAILWAY	JAPAN	RAIL TRANSPORT	3,283.0	0.6	44.7	—	450
373	383	KOYO SEIKO	JAPAN	BEARINGS	3,275.1	10.4	50.5	54.8	414
374	421	SAN MIGUEL CORP.	PHILIPPINES	BEER, FOOD, BEVERAGES	3,242.6	11.1	232.3	4.4	131
375	494	TENAGA NASIONAL	MALAYSIA	POWER GENERATION	3,237.8	18.8	317.1	(35.8)	90
376	368	TOA CORP.	JAPAN	CIVIL ENGINEERING	3,230.1	6.2	31.0	10.9	532
377	567	SHIN CATERPIL'R MITSUBISHI	JAPAN	CONSTRUCTION MACHINERY	3,223.1	12.4	48.5	148.0	422
378	376	JAPAN AIR SYSTEM	JAPAN	AIR TRANSPORT	3,211.8	6.8	2.8	308.1	834
379	367	MITSUBISHI RAYON	JAPAN	TEXTILES	3,209.4	5.2	75.4	97.4	327
380	387	CHINA STEEL CORP.	TAIWAN	STEEL PRODUCTS	3,199.3	2.8	491.9	19.2	59
381	359	UNITIKA	JAPAN	TEXTILES	3,193.6	1.3	(36.9)	—	933
382	371	IDEMITSU PETROCHEMICAL	JAPAN	PETROCHEMICALS	3,189.6	5.4	10.1	27.0	733
383	379	ITOCHU SHOKUHIN	JAPAN	FOOD DISTRIBUTION	3,185.4	6.4	18.7	15.8	647
384	580	BP SINGAPORE	SINGAPORE	OIL TRADING, REFINING	3,182.4	34.9	59.3	61.3	378
385	355	OKUMURA CORP.	JAPAN	CONSTRUCTION	3,177.6	(0.1)	62.4	(19.3)	362
386	362	LION	JAPAN	HOUSEHOLD PRODUCTS	3,176.2	1.7	38.5	(1.2)	488
387	385	KYUSHU MATSUSHITA ELEC.	JAPAN	ELECTRONIC COMPONENTS	3,173.6	8.1	12.9	120.5	698
388	378	FOOD CORP. OF INDIA	INDIA	FOOD TRADING	3,171.6	24.5	(0.3)	—	878
389	370	NIPPON STEEL CHEMICAL	JAPAN	CHEMICALS	3,165.3	4.4	(392.9)	—	969
390	408	HITACHI ASIA	SINGAPORE	ELECTRONICS	3,164.5	(0.8)	3.5	(87.2)	822

Company ranking by sales. Key to notes: All data are for fiscal years that ended between July 1997 and June 1998, except for companies with an asterisk (*) in the Notes column, which denotes data from the previous accounting period. The numbers refer to the month the fiscal year ended: 1 for January; 2 February; 3 March; 4 April; 5 May; 6 June; 7 July; 8 August; 9 September; 10 October; 11 November; 12 December. The letters denote publicly listed (L), unlisted (U), and state-controlled (S) companies. Financial results incorporate those of subsidiaries. Sales also refers to turnover, gross income, or revenue. Net profit is computed after deducting tax and minority interests while excluding extraordinary items. % Change is from the previous year's result in local currency. Sales per $1 Assets is equivalent to sales-to-assets ratio. Equity is the sum of paid-up capital, reserves, and retained

Asia's Largest Companies by Sales — 361 to 390

ASSETS $ MILLION	RANK	SALES PER $1 ASSETS	EQUITY $ MILLION	RANK	EMPLOYEES NUMBER	RANK	PROFIT PER EMPLOYEE	MARKET CAP. ($M)	PROFIT AS % OF SALES	ASSETS	EQUITY	NOTES (Key Below)
4,203.6	331	0.82	1,161.1	356	34,101	71	1,930	2,302.2	1.9	1.6	5.7	3 L
12,887.9	110	0.27	3,958.3	99	30,000	85	8,136	—	7.1	1.9	6.2	12 U
4,328.8	324	0.80	2,680.8	147	2,891	627	80,901	5,519.1	6.8	5.4	8.7	3 L A
1,631.9	667	2.10	609.7	553	406	951	5,885,309	—	69.6	146.4	391.9	9 U S
822.3	837	4.17	83.8	859	1,358	829	1,518	33.3	0.1	0.3	2.5	12 L
3,647.5	374	0.93	2,070.3	195	9,486	288	12,951	2,091.2	3.6	3.4	5.9	3 L
NA	—	—	NA	—	5,778	409	14,478	—	2.5	—	—	12 U A
972.0	812	—	238.7	764	1,439	825	3,194	—	0.1	0.5	1.9	3 U A
2,088.0	565	1.61	589.5	562	36,336	67	212	—	0.2	0.4	1.3	6 U *
2,341.8	511	1.43	1,425.4	296	2,737	654	21,093	1,734.1	1.7	2.5	4.1	3 L
2,839.4	440	1.17	1,390.9	303	5,414	427	7,575	1,505.0	1.2	1.4	2.9	3 L
11,085.4	136	0.30	1,281.8	328	16,362	174	2,729	3,194.4	1.4	0.4	3.5	3 L
3,597.4	377	0.91	1,066.2	383	12,832	216	3,937	1,101.1	1.5	1.4	4.7	3 L
3,772.7	367	0.86	1,539.4	268	28,544	91	8,137	2,630.1	7.2	6.2	15.1	12 L
12,913.1	109	0.25	6,529.0	51	23,565	123	13,457	8,204.6	9.8	2.5	4.9	8 L
3,051.8	420	1.06	457.0	636	3,322	580	9,619	374.2	0.0	1.1	6.0	3 L
2,765.5	448	—	715.3	507	7,310	343	6,641	—	1.5	1.8	6.8	3 U
3,514.0	387	0.91	200.1	788	5,838	407	476	1,194.0	0.1	0.1	1.4	3 L
3,787.1	365	0.85	1,214.8	347	4,127	510	18,281	1,919.5	2.4	1.0	6.2	3 L
7,382.7	192	0.43	4,180.4	91	9,089	302	54,115	6,028.5	15.4	6.7	11.8	6 L
4,094.8	340	0.78	116.5	837	3,680	546	—	473.7	0.3	—	—	3 L
NA	—	—	NA	—	2,502	675	4,053	—	0.3	—	—	3 U A
720.0	854	4.42	94.7	850	900	886	20,827	—	0.6	2.6	19.8	9 U A J
1,191.4	758	2.67	306.7	730	450	946	131,831	—	1.9	4.0	19.3	12 U
4,646.9	297	0.68	1,380.2	305	3,603	553	17,314	1,142.9	1.0	1.3	4.5	3 L A
2,646.6	465	1.20	962.5	409	4,601	477	8,360	1,153.5	1.2	1.5	3.0	12 L
2,557.0	479	1.24	1,457.1	287	11,328	254	1,136	1,812.8	0.4	0.5	0.9	3 L
NA	—	—	NA	—	65,131	29	—	—	-0.0	—	—	3 U S *
4,077.5	342	0.78	86.3	857	1,913	764	—	473.2	—	—	—	3 L
890.1	826	3.56	97.9	848	792	903	4,477	—	0.1	0.4	3.6	3 U

earnings. Liabilities can be estimated by deducting equity from assets. Market Capitalization is the total value of all shares of listed firms as of **Nov. 5.** Profit as % of Sales is usually called net profit margin. Profit as % of Assets, return on assets; Profit as % of Equity, return on equity. All money values are in US$. Currency conversion uses average **1996** rates (except for Market Cap.); for Australia, A$1.2773 per $1; China, RMB8.3142; Hong Kong, HK$7.80; India, Rs35.433; Indonesia, Rp2.342.3; Japan, ¥108.78; Malaysia, RM2.5159; New Zealand, NZ$1.453; Pakistan, Rs36.079; Philippines, Pesos 26.216; Singapore, S$1.41; South Korea, Won 804.45; Taiwan, NT$27.50; Thailand, Baht 25.343. NA not available. Values less than $50,000 appear as $0.0; those less than 0.05% as 0.0%. Market Capitalization from Datastream. More notes on pages 84 and 85.

Asia's Largest Companies By Sales

RANK 1997	RANK 1996	COMPANY NAME	COUNTRY	MAIN BUSINESS	SALES $ MILLION	%CHANGE	NET PROFIT $ MILLION	%CHANGE	RANK
391	328	JDC CORP.	JAPAN	CONSTRUCTION	3,158.7	(8.8)	6.7	(28.7)	781
392	458	DONG-AH CONSTRUCTION	SOUTH KOREA	CONSTRUCTION	3,143.2	14.5	25.5	(37.6)	592
393	427	TOYO CONSTRUCTION	JAPAN	CIVIL ENGINEERING	3,142.2	20.4	9.6	(23.2)	738
394	409	RECRUIT	JAPAN	PUBLISHING	3,141.1	14.6	18.0	0.9	642
395	470	SINGAPORE TELECOM	SINGAPORE	TELECOMMUNICATIONS	3,135.4	10.6	1,176.2	11.6	15
396	380	SUMITOMO CONSTRUCTION	JAPAN	CONSTRUCTION	3,132.0	4.8	5.5	1.7	796
397	412	AIWA	JAPAN	CONSUMER ELECTRONICS	3,127.9	14.7	58.5	19.9	380
398	369	KURARAY	JAPAN	TEXTILES	3,126.6	2.8	107.9	6.3	261
399	375	NIHON CEMENT	JAPAN	CEMENT	3,124.4	3.9	1.7	(94.8)	849
400	407	KYGNUS SEKIYU	JAPAN	OIL TRADING	3,122.6	13.2	6.2	3.4	787
401	357	SUMITOMO REALTY & DEVT.	JAPAN	PROPERTY	3,116.2	(1.6)	(16.0)	—	912
402	393	Q.P. CORP.	JAPAN	FOOD	3,115.4	8.7	45.1	8.6	445
403	352	NISSAN DIESEL MOTOR	JAPAN	TRUCKS, BUSES	3,114.9	(2.9)	30.9	(11.8)	540
404	918	HYUNDAI OIL REFINERY	SOUTH KOREA	OIL REFINING	3,096.0	116.9	27.4	—	576
405	453	DAELIM INDUSTRIAL	SOUTH KOREA	CONSTRUCTION, CHEMICALS	3,079.6	11.7	28.5	9.9	564
406	443	THAI AIRWAYS INTL.	THAILAND	AIR TRANSPORT	3,078.6	7.2	133.5	4.6	212
407	389	KOKUYO	JAPAN	OFFICE FURNITURE, EQUIP.	3,073.8	6.5	100.1	15.1	277
408	396	KANTO AUTO WORKS	JAPAN	CAR ASSEMBLY	3,062.2	7.9	10.7	(30.1)	724
409	544	SAMSUNG DISPLAY DEVICES	SOUTH KOREA	ELECTRONIC PARTS	3,058.8	27.3	204.1	60.0	147
410	554	HANWHA ENERGY	SOUTH KOREA	OIL REFINING	3,048.5	28.4	7.1	(46.8)	774
411	526	HYUNDAI PRECISION & IND.	SOUTH KOREA	CONTAINERS	3,046.4	23.4	25.0	(13.4)	596
412	384	MURATA MFG.	JAPAN	ELECTRONIC COMPONENTS	3,039.3	2.7	299.6	(12.5)	96
413	891	TATUNG	TAIWAN	CONSUMER ELECTRONICS	3,039.0	(1.1)	269.4	25.8	110
414	391	MITSUBISHI GAS CHEMICAL	JAPAN	CHEMICALS	3,035.7	5.5	102.5	18.6	274
415	512	FRANKLINS	AUSTRALIA	SUPERMARKETS	3,034.2	7.0	(42.0)	—	937
416	400	NTN CORP.	JAPAN	BEARINGS	3,013.7	7.4	72.9	38.6	333
417	381	SANKYU	JAPAN	TRANSPORT, ENGINEERING	3,006.2	0.6	25.2	(13.2)	595
418	377	ZENITAKA	JAPAN	CONSTRUCTION	3,001.4	0.1	7.5	(1.7)	767
419	425	SUMISHO MACHINERY	JAPAN	MACHINERY TRADING	2,996.1	13.9	3.7	22.4	820
420	392	SEINO TRANSPORTATION	JAPAN	TRUCKING	2,981.3	3.8	79.1	18.3	321

Company ranking by sales. Key to notes: All data are for fiscal years that ended between July 1997 and June 1998, except for companies with an asterisk (*) in the Notes column, which denotes data from the previous accounting period. The numbers refer to the month the fiscal year ended: 1 for January; 2 February; 3 March; 4 April; 5 May; 6 June; 7 July; 8 August; 9 September; 10 October; 11 November; 12 December. The letters denote publicly listed (L), unlisted (U), and state-controlled (S) companies. Financial results incorporate those of subsidiaries. Sales also refers to turnover, gross income, or revenue. Net profit is computed after deducting tax and minority interests while excluding extraordinary items. % Change is from the previous year's result in local currency. Sales per $1 Assets is equivalent to sales-to-assets ratio. Equity is the sum of paid-up capital, reserves, and retained

Asia's Largest Companies by Sales

391 to 420

ASSETS $ MILLION	RANK	SALES PER $1 ASSETS	EQUITY $ MILLION	RANK	EMPLOYEES NUMBER	RANK	PROFIT PER EMPLOYEE	MARKET CAP. ($M)	PROFIT AS % OF SALES	ASSETS	EQUITY	NOTES (Key Below)
4,373.6	321	0.72	385.4	678	2,549	669	2,636	141.2	0.2	0.2	1.7	3 L
5,304.4	261	0.59	1,108.6	369	6,539	364	3,898	494.5	0.8	0.5	2.3	12 L
3,550.3	383	0.89	438.5	646	2,965	616	3,249	195.2	0.3	0.3	2.2	3 L
11,793.7	127	0.27	1,530.3	271	3,642	549	5,212	—	0.6	0.2	1.2	3 U A
7,701.4	184	0.41	4,617.2	78	10,388	269	113,224	25,349.9	37.5	15.3	25.5	3 L S
4,346.1	323	0.72	344.1	709	2,787	645	1,986	298.6	0.2	0.1	1.6	3 L A
1,731.5	638	1.81	488.6	621	10,013	277	5,845	1,471.3	1.9	3.4	11.0	3 L
4,726.7	292	0.66	1,917.9	209	6,606	363	16,337	3,020.5	3.5	2.3	5.6	3 L
4,643.1	298	0.67	1,362.4	309	2,031	747	846	926.1	0.1	0.0	0.1	3 L
NA	—	—	NA	—	265	970	23,242	—	0.2	—	—	3 U A
17,042.3	70	0.18	2,296.3	174	773	905	—	2,890.8	—	—	—	3 L
2,289.7	523	1.36	1,028.7	390	7,860	329	5,739	1,178.9	1.4	1.0	4.4	11 L
3,152.5	411	0.99	573.6	567	4,942	454	6,258	518.9	0.0	0.0	5.4	3 L A
3,061.9	418	1.01	338.8	714	1,528	810	17,940	—	0.9	0.9	8.1	12 U
4,748.1	291	0.65	1,023.1	394	4,513	483	6,308	224.2	0.9	0.6	2.8	12 L
5,197.3	268	0.59	1,188.3	350	22,136	132	6,031	1,729.8	4.3	2.6	11.2	9 L S
2,849.9	438	1.08	1,664.5	248	3,119	600	32,103	3,039.9	3.3	3.5	6.0	3 L
1,736.5	636	1.76	398.9	669	6,108	390	1,756	245.0	0.4	0.6	2.7	3 L
3,309.4	397	0.92	1,529.1	272	12,603	219	16,198	1,180.4	6.7	6.2	13.4	12 L
3,026.8	424	1.01	190.9	792	1,489	816	4,745	128.2	0.2	0.2	3.7	12 L
2,906.4	433	1.05	403.6	668	8,445	311	2,964	322.0	0.8	0.9	6.2	12 L
5,927.1	240	0.51	4,488.8	81	23,588	122	12,701	9,978.3	9.9	5.1	6.7	3 L
4,202.1	332	0.72	1,478.4	283	33,588	75	8,021	2,422.3	8.9	6.4	18.2	12 L
4,480.2	316	0.68	1,503.2	278	3,541	560	28,942	1,667.8	3.4	2.3	6.8	3 L
776.0	845	3.91	189.3	794	21,300	139	—	—	—	—	—	12 U
4,278.7	325	0.70	1,550.8	264	13,287	207	5,484	1,586.7	2.4	1.7	4.7	3 L
2,531.4	482	1.19	466.5	634	12,500	224	2,014	429.2	0.8	0.0	5.4	3 L
3,332.0	396	0.90	320.0	724	2,475	683	3,020	233.1	0.2	0.2	2.3	3 L A
NA	—	—	NA	—	402	952	9,261	—	0.1	—	—	3 U A
4,026.3	345	0.74	1,982.7	202	15,528	180	5,093	1,272.4	2.7	1.0	3.0	3 L

earnings. Liabilities can be estimated by deducting equity from assets. Market Capitalization is the total value of all shares of listed firms as of **Nov. 5**. Profit as % of Sales is usually called net profit margin. Profit as % of Assets, return on assets; Profit as % of Equity, return on equity. All money values are in US$. Currency conversion uses average **1996** rates (except for Market Cap.); for Australia, A$1.2773 per $1; China, RMB8.3142; Hong Kong, HK$7.80; India, Rs35.433; Indonesia, Rp2.342.3; Japan, ¥108.78; Malaysia, RM2.5159; New Zealand, NZ$1.453; Pakistan, Rs36.079; Philippines, Pesos 26.216; Singapore, S$1.41; South Korea, Won 804.45; Taiwan, NT$27.50; Thailand, Baht 25.343. NA not available. Values less than $50,000 appear as $0.0; those less than 0.05% as 0.0%. Market Capitalization from Datastream. More notes on pages 84 and 85.

Asia's Largest Companies By Sales

RANK 1997	RANK 1996	COMPANY NAME	COUNTRY	MAIN BUSINESS	SALES $ MILLION	%CHANGE	NET PROFIT $ MILLION	%CHANGE	RANK
421	—	SANYO LIFE ELECTRONICS	JAPAN	ELECTRONIC COMPONENTS	2,969.8	1.9	4.7	98.5	806
422	429	SHOUGANG CORP.	CHINA	STEEL	2,967.2	(1.9)	38.5	—	487
423	411	MARUETSU	JAPAN	SUPERMARKETS	2,946.6	7.8	21.0	(6.3)	613
424	435	GOODMAN FIELDER	AUSTRALIA	FOOD	2,943.3	(5.9)	89.8	290.1	301
425	403	KATO SANGYO	JAPAN	FOOD TRADING	2,937.0	5.3	18.4	16.9	650
426	437	MITSUI OIL & GAS	JAPAN	OIL, GAS	2,935.6	14.0	1.2	(73.9)	858
427	489	TAIYO OIL	JAPAN	OIL REFINING, DISTRIBUTION	2,934.7	23.2	9.3	38.4	743
428	887	TOYOTA MOTOR SALES AUST.	AUSTRALIA	CAR DEALERSHIP	2,934.3	85.2	(4.6)	—	895
429	476	OTSUKA SHOKAI	JAPAN	ELECTRONICS TRADING	2,933.4	21.1	249.3	47.0	123
430	413	KOTOBUKIYA	JAPAN	SUPERMARKETS	2,924.9	5.2	(32.1)	—	928
431	905	SHANGHAI VOLKSWAGEN	CHINA	CARS	2,923.5	31.9	331.1	NA	86
432	622	COCA-COLA AMATIL	AUSTRALIA	SOFT DRINKS	2,900.5	24.8	111.3	2.5	253
433	416	ITOCHU KENZAI	JAPAN	BUILDING MATERIALS	2,900.4	7.7	6.1	8.1	789
434	422	NIPPON ELECTRIC GLASS	JAPAN	CATHODE-RAY TUBE GLASS	2,897.0	9.5	120.0	7.8	233
435	395	DAIO PAPER	JAPAN	PAPER	2,891.5	1.4	46.6	(22.5)	435
436	402	HINO MOTOR SALES	JAPAN	TRUCK & BUS DEALERSHIP	2,889.3	3.1	3.9	(95.3)	818
437	398	TEXAS INSTRUMENTS SING.	SINGAPORE	SEMICONDUCTORS	2,887.7	(11.9)	48.0	4.7	418
438	460	FOODLAND ASSOCIATED	AUSTRALIA	FOOD TRADING	2,882.3	2.5	37.0	(10.1)	497
439	426	NICHIEI	JAPAN	WOOD TRADING	2,859.8	9.5	(93.7)	—	951
440	560	TATA ENG. & LOCOMOTIVE	INDIA	CARS, TRUCKS, MACHINERY	2,858.5	28.5	215.2	43.8	139
441	499	OLYMPUS OPTICAL	JAPAN	ENDOSCOPES, CAMERAS	2,854.2	21.2	21.3	13.8	617
442	496	TAB NEW SOUTH WALES	AUSTRALIA	GAMING	2,853.4	1.5	88.7	0.8	305
443	404	NISHI-NIPPON RAILROAD	JAPAN	BUS & RAIL TRANSPORT	2,853.1	2.4	28.1	(15.7)	568
444	410	NIHON UNISYS	JAPAN	COMPUTER SALES	2,839.3	3.6	21.2	12.5	618
445	436	YAMAZEN	JAPAN	MACHINERY TRADING	2,832.9	9.9	24.9	98.5	598
446	432	HITACHI CONST. MACHINERY	JAPAN	HYDRAULIC SHOVELS	2,829.0	9.2	30.3	48.8	545
447	420	TOKYU STORE CHAIN	JAPAN	SUPERMARKETS	2,829.7	6.2	20.1	25.1	628
448	428	KANEKA CORP.	JAPAN	CHEMICALS	2,827.5	8.5	60.3	97.1	372
449	441	TEKKEN	JAPAN	CONSTRUCTION	2,814.4	11.1	12.2	(52.3)	706
450	477	TOYO SUISAN	JAPAN	NOODLES	2,809.1	16.1	40.4	6.6	479

Company ranking by sales. Key to notes: All data are for fiscal years that ended between July 1997 and June 1998, except for companies with an asterisk (*) in the Notes column, which denotes data from the previous accounting period. The numbers refer to the month the fiscal year ended: 1 for January; 2 February; 3 March; 4 April; 5 May; 6 June; 7 July; 8 August; 9 September; 10 October; 11 November; 12 December. The letters denote publicly listed (L), unlisted (U), and state-controlled (S) companies. Financial results incorporate those of subsidiaries. Sales also refers to turnover, gross income, or revenue. Net profit is computed after deducting tax and minority interests while excluding extraordinary items. % Change is from the previous year's result in local currency. Sales per $1 Assets is equivalent to sales-to-assets ratio. Equity is the sum of paid-up capital, reserves, and retained

Asia's Largest Companies by Sales

421 to 450

ASSETS $MILLION	RANK	SALES PER $1 ASSETS	EQUITY $MILLION	RANK	EMPLOYEES NUMBER	RANK	PROFIT PER EMPLOYEE	MARKET CAP. ($M)	PROFIT AS % OF SALES	ASSETS	EQUITY	NOTES (Key Below)
NA	—	—	NA	—	2,370	694	1,994	—	0.2	—	—	3 U A K
5,038.4	278	0.59	2,423.6	165	229,819	6	167	—	1.3	0.8	1.6	12 U S
1,801.6	623	1.64	1,030.0	388	3,602	554	6,102	491.1	0.7	1.2	2.1	2 L
1,722.9	643	1.71	1,023.2	393	15,113	183	5,942	1,944.0	3.1	5.2	8.8	6 L
970.0	813	3.03	341.9	712	1,535	809	12,002	281.5	0.6	1.9	5.4	9 L A
NA	—	—	NA	—	647	916	1,918	—	0.0	—	—	12 U A
NA	—	—	NA	—	643	918	14,468	—	0.3	—	—	3 U A
1,149.1	773	2.55	491.3	618	4,000	520	—	—	—	—	—	6 U
15,309.8	82	0.19	2,160.4	188	6,350	380	39,259	—	8.5	1.6	11.5	12 U A
2,083.3	567	1.40	256.2	750	3,315	581	—	234.0	—	—	—	2 L
1,384.7	722	2.11	848.5	450	10,333	270	32,045	—	11.3	23.9	39.0	12 U S
4,769.2	290	0.61	2,042.9	197	29,898	86	3,721	7,165.8	3.8	2.3	5.4	12 L
NA	—	—	NA	—	364	958	16,820	—	0.2	—	—	3 U A
4,521.1	311	0.64	1,260.0	337	10,000	279	12,098	1,981.3	4.2	2.7	9.6	3 L
3,995.4	346	0.72	959.6	411	3,169	590	14,705	747.5	1.6	1.2	4.9	3 L A
1,686.6	650	1.71	157.2	808	366	957	10,625	—	0.1	0.2	2.5	3 U A
883.0	827	3.27	407.9	665	2,184	726	22,426	—	1.7	5.5	12.0	12 U
1,258.0	744	2.29	372.0	689	11,898	242	3,112	744.4	1.3	2.9	9.9	7 L
2,043.3	581	1.40	450.5	638	1,997	752	—	160.9	—	—	—	3 L
2,321.8	517	1.23	1,029.4	389	37,413	63	5,751	2,023.5	7.5	9.3	20.9	3 L
4,689.5	296	0.61	1,656.4	251	5,865	405	3,640	1,919.5	0.7	0.5	1.3	3 L
148.7	912	19.18	89.7	855	1,648	786	53,853	—	3.1	59.7	98.0	6 U S
3,820.1	361	0.75	653.1	533	6,883	358	4,087	1,126.6	0.0	0.7	4.3	3 L
2,526.4	484	1.12	684.7	522	7,800	330	2,713	826.6	0.7	0.8	3.1	3 L
1,903.4	599	1.49	127.4	829	2,067	740	12,061	237.3	0.9	1.3	19.6	3 L
3,077.2	417	0.92	776.6	484	4,457	489	6,806	714.2	1.1	0.0	3.9	3 L
1,387.7	721	2.04	391.3	676	3,083	604	6,533	383.5	0.7	1.5	5.1	2 L
3,095.8	416	0.91	1,331.2	315	6,535	365	9,229	2,007.1	2.1	1.9	4.5	3 L
2,879.5	435	0.98	503.6	614	2,739	653	4,464	296.9	0.4	0.4	2.4	3 L
2,058.3	578	1.36	863.5	442	1,930	761	20,948	1,003.4	1.4	1.0	4.7	3 L

earnings. Liabilities can be estimated by deducting equity from assets. Market Capitalization is the total value of all shares of listed firms as of **Nov. 5**. Profit as % of Sales is usually called net profit margin. Profit as % of Assets, return on assets; Profit as % of Equity, return on equity. All money values are in US$. Currency conversion uses average **1996** rates (except for Market Cap.); for Australia, A$1.2773 per $1; China, RMB8.3142; Hong Kong, HK$7.80; India, Rs35.433; Indonesia, Rp2,342.3; Japan, ¥108.78; Malaysia, RM2.5159; New Zealand, NZ$1.453; Pakistan, Rs36.079; Philippines, Pesos 26.216; Singapore, S$1.41; South Korea, Won 804.45; Taiwan, NT$27.50; Thailand, Baht 25.343. NA not available. Values less than $50,000 appear as $0.0; those less than 0.05% as 0.0%. Market Capitalization from Datastream. More notes on pages 84 and 85.

Asia's Largest Companies By Sales

RANK 1997	RANK 1996	COMPANY NAME	COUNTRY	MAIN BUSINESS	SALES $ MILLION	%CHANGE	NET PROFIT $ MILLION	%CHANGE	RANK
451	455	HEIWADO	JAPAN	SUPERMARKETS	2,808.9	13.1	36.2	(14.0)	506
452	473	ASANUMA	JAPAN	CONSTRUCTION	2,800.3	15.2	11.5	(28.7)	712
453	550	PT GUDANG GARAM	INDONESIA	CLOVE CIGARETTES	2,799.9	17.2	279.7	78.8	106
454	442	FUJI TELEVISION NETWORK	JAPAN	BROADCASTING	2,791.5	10.3	124.5	93.1	226
455	465	MITSUI HOME	JAPAN	CONSTRUCTION	2,790.7	13.4	48.2	23.4	426
456	514	TOYOTA MOTOR (THAILAND)	THAILAND	CAR ASSEMBLY, SALES	2,785.5	4.3	34.2	(35.1)	515
457	484	MINEBEA	JAPAN	ELECTRONIC PARTS, BEARINGS	2,784.4	16.3	81.5	20.5	315
458	457	NIPPON TELEVISION	JAPAN	BROADCASTING	2,784.1	12.4	176.9	39.4	171
459	712	MARUBENI INTL. PETROLEUM	SINGAPORE	OIL TRADING	2,782.1	57.9	13.2	549.8	693
460	414	DAI NIPPON CONSTRUCTION	JAPAN	CONSTRUCTION	2,781.1	2.4	(0.9)	—	883
461	605	EON	MALAYSIA	CAR DEALERSHIP	2,769.8	22.5	180.6	36.4	169
462	415	PRIMA MEAT PACKERS	JAPAN	MEAT PRODUCTS	2,756.8	2.2	(133.3)	—	959
463	450	NITTO DENKO	JAPAN	INDUSTRIAL TAPE	2,756.3	10.4	94.2	23.5	286
464	452	SECOM	JAPAN	SECURITY SYSTEMS	2,752.0	10.7	212.8	1.9	142
465	508	MCDONALD'S CO. (JAPAN)	JAPAN	RESTAURANTS	2,747.1	17.0	100.7	27.4	276
466	538	ICI AUSTRALIA	AUSTRALIA	CHEMICALS	2,746.1	2.8	154.3	(26.7)	192
467	417	ROHM	JAPAN	COMPUTER PARTS	2,737.5	1.9	418.6	19.2	66
468	399	TANAKA KIKINZOKU KOGYO	JAPAN	METAL PRODUCTS	2,726.6	(2.9)	28.0	27.6	559
469	503	MITSUMI ELECTRIC	JAPAN	ELECTRONIC PARTS	2,720.3	16.1	36.6	(25.0)	502
470	456	KEIHIN ELEC. EXPRESS RAIL.	JAPAN	RAIL TRANSPORT	2,716.9	9.6	6.9	(33.9)	777
471	419	DAIWA CAN	JAPAN	CANS	2,713.1	1.2	104.8	(2.3)	268
472	485	ZEXEL	JAPAN	CAR PARTS	2,709.5	1.3	43.2	29.1	460
473	418	DAIEI PAPERS	JAPAN	PAPER TRADING	2,707.1	0.8	9.2	(27.0)	746
474	372	DAEWOO MOTOR SALES	SOUTH KOREA	CAR PARTS	2,696.9	NA	25.9	NA	588
475	424	RENGO	JAPAN	PACKAGING	2,681.7	1.6	29.5	140.4	552
476	434	KINTETSU DEPT. STORE	JAPAN	DEPARTMENT STORES	2,676.7	3.4	9.2	(22.2)	745
477	585	MOBIL OIL SINGAPORE	SINGAPORE	OIL TRADING, REFINING	2,661.0	14.2	126.7	(48.1)	219
478	444	PARCO	JAPAN	FASHION STORES	2,658.7	4.0	12.7	(6.4)	701
479	591	AMPOL	AUSTRALIA	PETROLEUM REFINING	2,658.2	9.2	82.1	12.3	314
480	644	HYUNDAI MERCH. MARINE	SOUTH KOREA	SHIPPING	2,657.8	30.9	24.2	(30.7)	601

Company ranking by sales. Key to notes: All data are for fiscal years that ended between July 1997 and June 1998, except for companies with an asterisk (*) in the Notes column, which denotes data from the previous accounting period. The numbers refer to the month the fiscal year ended: 1 for January; 2 February; 3 March; 4 April; 5 May; 6 June; 7 July; 8 August; 9 September; 10 October; 11 November; 12 December. The letters denote publicly listed (L), unlisted (U), and state-controlled (S) companies. Financial results incorporate those of subsidiaries. Sales also refers to turnover, gross income, or revenue. Net profit is computed after deducting tax and minority interests while excluding extraordinary items. % Change is from the previous year's result in local currency. Sales per $1 Assets is equivalent to sales-to-assets ratio. Equity is the sum of paid-up capital, reserves, and retained

Asia's Largest Companies by Sales — 451 to 480

ASSETS $ MILLION	RANK	SALES PER $1 ASSETS	EQUITY $ MILLION	RANK	EMPLOYEES NUMBER	RANK	PROFIT PER EMPLOYEE	MARKET CAP. ($M)	PROFIT AS % OF SALES	ASSETS	EQUITY	NOTES (Key Below)
2,371.4	503	1.18	680.6	524	3,381	577	10,721	530.1	1.3	1.5	5.3	2 L
2,471.1	491	1.13	362.1	696	2,655	658	4,328	126.5	0.4	0.5	3.2	3 L A
1,841.9	612	1.52	1,087.1	375	45,000	55	6,216	5,924.6	9.0	15.2	25.7	12 L
3,423.0	390	0.82	1,283.7	326	1,450	822	85,893	—	4.5	3.6	9.7	3 L A
2,156.3	554	1.29	589.8	561	2,156	728	22,360	420.1	1.7	2.2	8.2	3 L
1,285.8	738	2.17	322.8	722	6,075	393	5,631	—	1.2	2.7	10.6	12 U
5,177.6	271	0.54	1,138.4	361	37,096	64	2,196	4,121.8	2.9	1.6	7.2	3 L
3,034.1	423	0.92	1,498.1	279	1,238	846	142,890	4,386.2	6.4	5.8	11.8	3 L
271.6	904	10.24	27.4	895	27	984	489,861	—	0.5	4.9	48.3	3 U
3,211.3	403	0.87	253.6	751	2,602	663	—	112.8	—	—	—	3 L
3,483.0	388	0.80	508.0	611	3,435	571	52,583	738.3	6.5	5.2	35.6	12 L
1,205.3	755	2.29	176.8	800	2,433	687	—	202.1	—	—	—	3 L
2,854.8	437	0.97	1,525.3	273	8,589	309	10,973	2,927.8	3.4	3.3	6.2	3 L
3,987.0	347	0.69	2,598.5	155	10,902	260	19,522	7,338.4	7.7	5.3	8.2	3 L
1,459.5	701	1.88	736.5	500	4,500	485	22,386	—	3.7	6.9	13.7	12 U A
2,226.1	537	1.23	1,186.6	353	9,200	299	16,773	2,062.3	5.6	6.9	13.0	9 L
4,406.1	317	0.62	3,114.3	132	12,659	218	33,071	12,268.1	15.3	9.5	13.4	3 L
1,013.2	803	2.69	394.4	673	1,000	871	28,958	—	1.1	2.9	7.3	3 U A
1,739.0	635	1.56	260.2	749	37,000	65	990	1,046.9	1.3	2.1	14.1	3 L L
7,270.4	196	0.37	875.3	435	4,632	475	1,498	1,906.1	0.3	0.1	0.8	3 L
2,402.4	499	1.13	2,097.6	190	2,253	714	46,511	—	3.9	4.4	4.0	3 U A
2,788.6	446	0.97	825.7	461	5,562	418	7,773	888.9	1.6	1.6	5.2	3 L
1,271.0	741	2.13	151.3	810	644	917	14,332	—	0.3	0.7	6.1	3 U
2,398.2	500	1.12	182.6	797	4,369	497	5,930	—	0.0	1.1	14.2	12 U M
2,685.5	454	0.00	861.4	445	5,912	401	4,987	768.8	1.1	1.1	3.4	3 L
1,529.4	680	—	113.0	841	4,100	512	2,253	—	0.3	0.6	8.1	2 U A
2,360.7	506	1.13	931.0	421	610	923	207,776	—	4.8	5.4	13.6	12 U
2,122.5	559	1.25	478.3	625	583	929	21,729	277.1	0.5	0.6	2.6	2 L
2,403.6	498	1.11	876.9	432	1,935	758	42,428	—	3.1	3.4	9.4	6 U
2,849.0	439	0.93	398.0	670	2,780	648	8,722	—	0.9	0.9	6.1	12 U

earnings. Liabilities can be estimated by deducting equity from assets. Market Capitalization is the total value of all shares of listed firms as of **Nov. 5.** Profit as % of Sales is usually called net profit margin. Profit as % of Assets, return on assets; Profit as % of Equity, return on equity. All money values are in US$. Currency conversion uses average **1996** rates (except for Market Cap.); for Australia, A$1.2773 per $1; China, RMB8.3142; Hong Kong, HK$7.80; India, Rs35.433; Indonesia, Rp2,342.3; Japan, ¥108.78; Malaysia, RM2.5159; New Zealand, NZ$1.453; Pakistan, Rs36.079; Philippines, Pesos 26.216; Singapore, S$1.41; South Korea, Won 804.45; Taiwan, NT$27.50; Thailand, Baht 25.343. NA not available. Values less than $50,000 appear as $0.0; those less than 0.05% as 0.0%. Market Capitalization from Datastream. More notes on pages 84 and 85.

Asia's Largest Companies By Sales

RANK 1997	RANK 1996	COMPANY NAME	COUNTRY	MAIN BUSINESS	SALES $ MILLION	%CHANGE	NET PROFIT $ MILLION	%CHANGE	RANK
481	553	FORD MOTOR CO. OF AUST.	AUSTRALIA	CARS	2,656.6	(0.2)	170.2	7.8	179
482	482	ASAHI FOOD	JAPAN	FOOD TRADING	2,655.0	10.4	4.0	140.6	803
483	519	BEST DENKI	JAPAN	ELECTRONICS RETAILING	2,655.2	16.6	44.4	92.6	452
484	467	DOWA MINING	JAPAN	COPPER, ZINC	2,653.8	8.1	88.0	327.0	304
485	440	NISSIN FOOD PRODUCTS	JAPAN	NOODLES	2,646.0	4.3	77.6	10.8	323
486	451	INABATA & CO.	JAPAN	CHEMICALS TRADING	2,627.4	5.5	20.3	(10.7)	627
487	486	AICHI MACHINE INDUSTRY	JAPAN	TRUCK ASSEMBLY	2,624.6	9.9	28.1	41.6	570
488	490	KYUSHU OIL	JAPAN	OIL REFINING	2,612.4	9.8	8.5	(49.0)	760
489	558	ANSETT HOLDINGS	AUSTRALIA	AIR TRANSPORT	2,611.6	1.0	(27.4)	—	921
490	501	KASHIMA OIL	JAPAN	OIL REFINING	2,605.3	11.1	41.9	(69.6)	469
491	469	FUJISAWA PHARM.	JAPAN	PHARMACEUTICALS	2,601.1	6.4	65.1	52.1	353
492	608	BP AUSTRALIA	AUSTRALIA	OIL REFINING	2,596.6	8.6	97.2	79.9	283
493	566	TAIKO TRADING	JAPAN	CONSTRUCTION, TRADING	2,594.3	23.9	1.5	20.0	855
494	481	KENWOOD	JAPAN	CONSUMER ELECTRONICS	2,590.9	7.7	(27.0)	—	923
495	445	EISAI	JAPAN	PHARMACEUTICALS	2,588.3	2.0	178.8	1.0	170
496	510	NATIONAL HOUSE INDL.	JAPAN	BUILDING MATERIALS	2,586.6	11.4	132.1	17.0	214
497	487	YOKOGAWA ELECTRIC	JAPAN	INDUSTRIAL INSTRUMENTS	2,577.9	8.1	35.4	111.2	508
498	599	MALAYSIAN AIRLINE SYS.	MALAYSIA	AIR TRANSPORT	2,577.6	13.5	132.3	42.9	213
499	461	HITACHI TRANSPORT SYS.	JAPAN	TRUCKING	2,577.5	4.3	31.2	16.8	536
500	430	INAX	JAPAN	BUILDING MATERIALS	2,571.3	(1.1)	47.2	(9.9)	431
501	505	JAPAN RADIO	JAPAN	TELECOM. EQUIPMENT	2,567.7	9.7	44.7	56.2	448
502	448	SANSEIDO	JAPAN	PHARMACEUTICALS TRADING	2,555.1	2.2	28.7	0.0	563
503	552	HANJIN SHIPPING	SOUTH KOREA	SHIPPING	2,550.4	7.1	11.2	(83.3)	718
504	649	TELEKOM MALAYSIA	MALAYSIA	TELECOMMUNICATIONS	2,550.3	22.2	747.8	19.4	31
505	572	PIONEER INTERNATIONAL	AUSTRALIA	BUILDING MATERIALS, OIL	2,547.3	1.7	168.3	(16.8)	180
506	474	NITTSU SHOJI	JAPAN	CARGO TRANSPORT	2,546.5	4.0	13.0	19.4	690
507	506	FUJI OIL	JAPAN	OIL REFINING	2,544.3	8.9	12.2	(45.9)	705
508	478	TOHO PHARMACEUTICAL	JAPAN	PHARMACEUTICALS TRADING	2,540.0	4.0	10.0	126.1	720
509	480	DAIICHI PHARMACEUTICAL	JAPAN	PHARMACEUTICALS	2,539.5	5.6	231.4	17.4	133
510	521	SKYLARK	JAPAN	RESTAURANTS	2,538.5	11.8	13.5	(51.9)	692

Company ranking by sales. Key to notes: All data are for fiscal years that ended between July 1997 and June 1998, except for companies with an asterisk (*) in the Notes column, which denotes data from the previous accounting period. The numbers refer to the month the fiscal year ended: 1 for January; 2 February; 3 March; 4 April; 5 May; 6 June; 7 July; 8 August; 9 September; 10 October; 11 November; 12 December. The letters denote publicly listed (L), unlisted (U), and state-controlled (S) companies. Financial results incorporate those of subsidiaries. Sales also refers to turnover, gross income, or revenue. Net profit is computed after deducting tax and minority interests while excluding extraordinary items. % Change is from the previous year's result in local currency. Sales per $1 Assets is equivalent to sales-to-assets ratio. Equity is the sum of paid-up capital, reserves, and retained

Asia's Largest Companies by Sales

481 to 510

ASSETS $ MILLION	RANK	SALES PER $1 ASSETS	EQUITY $ MILLION	RANK	EMPLOYEES NUMBER	RANK	PROFIT PER EMPLOYEE	MARKET CAP. ($M)	PROFIT AS % OF SALES	ASSETS	EQUITY	NOTES (Key Below)
1,247.5	746	2.13	579.3	566	6,500	370	26,177	—	6.4	13.6	29.4	12 U
935.7	819	—	82.7	860	3,500	562	1,416	—	0.2	0.5	5.0	3 U
2,058.1	579	1.29	939.2	417	2,398	691	18,528	849.1	1.7	2.2	4.7	2 L
3,136.3	412	0.85	445.0	643	1,736	778	51,265	861.9	3.4	2.8	19.0	3 L
2,655.1	460	0.00	1,777.8	233	1,566	800	49,545	3,100.3	2.9	2.9	4.4	3 L
1,667.1	653	1.58	326.9	719	568	931	35,817	289.6	0.8	1.2	6.2	3 L
1,368.9	726	1.92	472.8	629	3,654	548	7,676	324.7	1.1	2.1	5.9	3 L
1,720.0	645	1.52	533.7	595	739	908	11,532	—	0.3	0.5	1.6	3 U A
3,060.1	419	0.85	423.3	656	17,067	164	—	—	—	—	—	6 U
2,079.8	569	1.25	287.9	735	635	920	65,957	—	1.6	2.0	14.5	3 U A
4,398.3	319	0.59	2,186.8	185	7,600	336	8,564	2,828.8	2.5	1.5	2.0	3 L
2,203.9	543	1.18	NA	—	2,600	664	37,368	—	3.7	4.4	—	12 U
1,254.1	745	—	46.6	883	287	968	5,189	—	0.1	0.1	3.2	3 U A
1,899.1	602	1.36	251.9	753	2,828	639	—	448.3	—	—	—	3 L
4,197.9	333	0.62	2,338.9	170	7,000	349	25,536	4,084.7	6.9	4.3	7.6	3 L
2,639.6	467	0.98	1,423.6	297	3,772	540	35,017	1,825.8	5.1	5.0	9.3	3 L
3,897.5	355	0.66	1,659.1	249	6,371	379	5,560	1,565.4	1.4	0.9	2.1	3 L
5,822.0	243	0.44	1,783.5	232	22,545	129	5,869	1,077.5	5.1	2.3	7.4	3 L S
2,354.3	507	1.09	873.8	438	8,245	315	3,789	1,020.7	1.2	1.3	3.6	3 L
2,615.2	470	0.98	1,607.7	258	6,781	359	6,960	951.6	1.8	1.8	2.9	10 L
2,593.0	472	0.99	840.9	453	7,563	338	5,916	1,181.9	1.7	1.7	5.3	3 L
1,486.1	689	1.72	537.4	594	2,404	690	11,923	—	1.1	1.9	5.3	3 U A
3,051.7	421	0.84	355.4	702	2,317	705	4,821	—	0.4	0.4	3.1	12 L
7,946.7	177	0.32	4,796.9	73	27,516	104	27,177	9,126.0	29.3	9.4	15.6	12 L S
2,889.8	434	0.88	1,572.6	263	10,073	275	16,710	2,330.5	6.6	5.8	10.7	6 L
NA	—	—	NA	—	3,949	525	3,536	—	0.5	—	—	3 U A
1,743.1	634	—	225.4	772	591	926	20,703	496.9	0.5	0.7	5.4	3 U A
1,355.7	727	1.87	267.4	746	2,657	657	4,138	94.7	0.4	0.8	4.1	3 L
4,491.9	315	0.57	2,657.5	150	3,883	531	59,596	4,095.5	9.1	5.2	8.7	3 L
2,128.8	557	1.19	778.4	482	2,480	681	5,456	1,179.9	0.5	0.6	1.7	12 L

earnings. Liabilities can be estimated by deducting equity from assets. Market Capitalization is the total value of all shares of listed firms as of **Nov. 5**. Profit as % of Sales is usually called net profit margin. Profit as % of Assets, return on assets; Profit as % of Equity, return on equity. All money values are in US$. Currency conversion uses average **1996** rates (except for Market Cap.); for Australia, A$1.2773 per $1; China, RMB8.3142; Hong Kong, HK$7.80; India, Rs35.433; Indonesia, Rp2.342.3; Japan, ¥108.78; Malaysia, RM2.5159; New Zealand, NZ$1.453; Pakistan, Rs36.079; Philippines, Pesos 26.216; Singapore, S$1.41; South Korea, Won 804.45; Taiwan, NT$27.50; Thailand, Baht 25.343. NA not available. Values less than $50,000 appear as $0.0; those less than 0.05% as 0.0%. Market Capitalization from Datastream. More notes on pages 84 and 85.

Asia's Largest Companies By Sales

RANK 1997	RANK 1996	COMPANY NAME	COUNTRY	MAIN BUSINESS	SALES $ MILLION	%CHANGE	NET PROFIT $ MILLION	%CHANGE	RANK
511	462	FUKUYAMA TRANSPORTING	JAPAN	TRUCKING	2,538.2	2.8	64.7	10.3	355
512	495	SUNTORY FOODS	JAPAN	DRINKS	2,532.6	7.2	27.6	19.1	575
513	672	BERJAYA GROUP	MALAYSIA	DIVERSIFIED	2,524.6	24.1	32.3	—	527
514	438	RYOSAN	JAPAN	ELECTRONICS TRADING	2,524.3	(1.4)	51.5	(1.6)	410
515	479	HITACHI PLANT ENG. & CON.	JAPAN	FACTORY ENGINEERING	2,518.3	4.1	44.4	20.3	453
516	390	JGC CORP.	JAPAN	PLANT ENGINEERING	2,514.2	(12.7)	(128.6)	—	956
517	472	FUKUJIN	JAPAN	PHARMACEUTICALS TRADING	2,513.0	3.3	23.6	54.2	604
518	511	TEC CORPORATION	JAPAN	ELECTRONICS TRADING	2,512.2	8.7	37.0	—	498
519	468	SANKYO ALUMINIUM IND.	JAPAN	BUILDING MATERIALS	2,510.3	2.6	(11.8)	—	907
520	433	ANDO CORP.	JAPAN	CONSTRUCTION	2,508.5	(3.1)	7.4	(14.9)	768
521	504	KYUDENKO CORP.	JAPAN	ELECTRICAL ENGINEERING	2,504.5	6.9	41.3	(18.5)	475
522	636	LG OIL PRODUCTS SALES	SOUTH KOREA	PETROLEUM PRODUCTS	2,503.4	24.2	0.2	(86.4)	875
523	397	LG SEMICON	SOUTH KOREA	SEMICONDUCTORS	2,498.4	(20.1)	113.3	(88.3)	251
524	841	CHINA HUANENG GROUP	CHINA	POWER GENERATION	2,490.4	13.9	128.9	7.5	218
525	449	YORK-BENIMARU	JAPAN	RETAILING	2,488.4	1.1	71.1	(2.1)	340
526	582	PRESIDENT ENTERPRISES	TAIWAN	DRINKS, FOOD	2,480.2	10.1	116.6	17.5	241
527	459	EZAKI GLICO	JAPAN	CONFECTIONERY	2,477.5	0.1	63.3	87.8	358
528	527	THAI OIL	THAILAND	OIL REFINING	2,477.0	(2.1)	8.8	107.1	753
529	737	LEIGHTON HOLDINGS	AUSTRALIA	CONSTRUCTION	2,474.9	25.5	103.4	88.4	271
530	665	PROTON	MALAYSIA	CARS	2,473.2	20.4	297.9	108.9	97
531	509	TOHO GAS	JAPAN	FUEL GAS	2,467.1	6.1	30.2	(26.2)	547
532	551	RELIANCE INDUSTRIES	INDIA	TEXTILES, CHEMICALS	2,463.9	12.1	373.3	1.3	77
533	502	NIPPON SANSO	JAPAN	GASES	2,456.3	4.8	19.0	217.5	630
534	596	KYOKUTO PETROLEUM INDS.	JAPAN	OIL REFINING	2,455.8	23.6	15.7	95.1	676
535	507	TOYO TIRE & RUBBER	JAPAN	TIRES	2,444.3	4.9	9.9	—	735
536	698	HENDERSON LAND DEVT.	HONG KONG	PROPERTY	2,431.6	24.2	1,232.8	15.0	14
537	525	KEIHAN ELECTRIC RAILWAY	JAPAN	RAIL TRANSPORT	2,428.6	8.7	17.8	(49.9)	655
538	651	NATIONAL POWER CORP.	PHILIPPINES	POWER GENERATION	2,427.3	21.3	211.4	41.6	143
539	524	SANKI ENGINEERING	JAPAN	ENGINEERING	2,424.0	8.2	29.3	(4.3)	555
540	498	NIPPON SHEET GLASS	JAPAN	GLASS	2,419.3	2.7	4.7	(53.2)	808

Company ranking by sales. Key to notes: All data are for fiscal years that ended between July 1997 and June 1998, except for companies with an asterisk (*) in the Notes column, which denotes data from the previous accounting period. The numbers refer to the month the fiscal year ended: 1 for January; 2 February; 3 March; 4 April; 5 May; 6 June; 7 July; 8 August; 9 September; 10 October; 11 November; 12 December. The letters denote publicly listed (L), unlisted (U), and state-controlled (S) companies. Financial results incorporate those of subsidiaries. Sales also refers to turnover, gross income, or revenue. Net profit is computed after deducting tax and minority interests while excluding extraordinary items. % Change is from the previous year's result in local currency. Sales per $1 Assets is equivalent to sales-to-assets ratio. Equity is the sum of paid-up capital, reserves, and retained

Asia's Largest Companies by Sales

511 to 540

ASSETS $ MILLION	RANK	SALES PER $1 ASSETS	EQUITY $ MILLION	RANK	EMPLOYEES NUMBER	RANK	PROFIT PER EMPLOYEE	MARKET CAP. ($M)	PROFIT AS % OF SALES	ASSETS	EQUITY	NOTES (Key Below)
2,666.2	457	0.95	1,467.3	285	16,703	168	3,875	1,137.0	2.6	2.4	4.4	3 L
NA	—	—	NA	—	830	896	33,216	—	1.1	—	—	12 U A
4,954.7	282	0.51	772.0	485	22,500	130	1,434	404.2	1.3	0.7	4.2	4 L
1,351.5	729	1.87	794.2	476	1,122	858	45,907	782.6	2.0	3.8	6.5	3 L
1,973.0	590	1.28	517.7	607	3,307	582	13,424	373.9	1.8	2.2	8.6	3 L
3,254.6	399	0.77	934.9	419	2,527	671	—	542.5	—	—	—	3 L
1,208.9	753	2.08	172.6	804	2,152	729	10,983	—	0.9	1.0	13.7	3 U A
1,776.8	625	1.41	860.3	446	5,662	413	6,540	993.2	1.5	2.1	4.3	3 L
2,660.9	458	0.94	802.7	473	6,005	395	—	407.7	—	—	—	5 L
2,226.1	536	1.13	346.8	707	2,301	707	3,232	154.8	0.3	0.3	2.1	3 L
2,351.8	509	1.07	930.2	422	7,070	348	5,845	515.3	1.6	1.8	4.4	3 L
2,577.2	475	0.97	58.5	875	1,287	840	175	—	0.0	0.0	0.4	12 U
6,295.8	226	0.40	1,879.6	220	9,438	292	12,000	—	4.5	1.8	6.0	12 U
13,562.5	102	0.18	1,537.6	269	NA	—	—	—	5.2	0.0	8.4	12 U S
900.5	823	2.76	684.1	523	2,040	744	34,856	889.2	2.9	7.9	10.4	2 L
2,049.2	580	1.21	1,072.1	381	6,135	388	19,003	2,663.5	4.7	5.7	10.9	12 L
2,110.2	561	1.17	934.3	420	4,100	511	15,428	1,001.0	2.6	2.0	6.8	3 L
2,819.9	442	0.88	641.8	542	980	874	9,021	—	0.4	0.3	1.4	9 U S
1,270.5	742	1.95	425.0	654	12,160	231	8,506	1,076.8	4.2	8.1	24.3	6 L
1,849.6	610	1.34	956.4	415	5,400	429	55,168	1,354.6	12.1	16.1	31.1	3 L
3,738.8	368	0.66	920.4	425	3,500	565	8,615	1,025.0	1.2	0.8	3.3	3 L
5,513.5	254	0.45	2,390.7	167	16,778	167	22,249	4,720.0	15.2	6.8	15.6	3 L
2,972.0	428	0.83	816.8	466	1,847	771	10,810	890.7	0.8	0.7	2.4	3 L
1,189.7	759	2.06	137.6	820	419	950	37,495	—	0.6	1.3	11.4	12 U A
2,509.6	487	0.97	505.1	612	8,083	321	1,225	606.1	0.4	0.4	1.0	3 L
13,168.3	105	0.18	7,722.3	39	3,500	564	352,239	9,141.5	50.7	9.4	15.0	6 L
5,194.9	269	0.47	1,013.0	397	3,550	559	5,008	1,843.7	0.7	0.3	1.8	3 L
17,458.1	66	0.14	3,773.8	105	14,686	188	14,397	—	8.7	1.2	5.6	12 U S
2,241.6	532	1.08	648.5	537	2,367	695	12,378	744.6	1.2	1.3	4.5	3 L
3,641.9	375	0.66	1,326.4	317	2,487	680	1,881	960.9	0.2	0.1	0.4	3 L

earnings. Liabilities can be estimated by deducting equity from assets. Market Capitalization is the total value of all shares of listed firms as of **Nov. 5.** Profit as % of Sales is usually called net profit margin. Profit as % of Assets, return on assets; Profit as % of Equity, return on equity. All money values are in US$. Currency conversion uses average **1996** rates (except for Market Cap.); for Australia, A$1.2773 per $1; China, RMB8.3142; Hong Kong, HK$7.80; India, Rs35.433; Indonesia, Rp2.342.3; Japan, ¥108.78; Malaysia, RM2.5159; New Zealand, NZ$1.453; Pakistan, Rs36.079; Philippines, Pesos 26.216; Singapore, S$1.41; South Korea, Won 804.45; Taiwan, NT$27.50; Thailand, Baht 25.343. NA not available. Values less than $50,000 appear as $0.0; those less than 0.05% as 0.0%. Market Capitalization from Datastream. More notes on pages 84 and 85.

Asia's Largest Companies By Sales

RANK 1997	RANK 1996	COMPANY NAME	COUNTRY	MAIN BUSINESS	SALES $ MILLION	%CHANGE	NET PROFIT $ MILLION	%CHANGE	RANK
541	535	SEVEN-ELEVEN JAPAN	JAPAN	CONVENIENCE STORES	2,418.7	10.0	536.9	9.3	51
542	570	ARACO	JAPAN	CAR ASSEMBLY	2,413.6	16.5	27.3	21.8	577
543	536	SHINTOA CORP.	JAPAN	GENERAL TRADING	2,412.0	10.1	0.5	13.5	869
544	632	AUSTRALIA POST	AUSTRALIA	POSTAL SERVICES	2,412.9	7.6	182.6	(1.9)	167
545	666	CHEIL JEDANG	SOUTH KOREA	FOOD, ENTERTAINMENT	2,402.4	18.7	6.5	(80.7)	785
546	515	DAICEL CHEMICAL INDS.	JAPAN	CHEMICALS	2,398.3	4.0	28.9	(36.0)	561
547	683	NATIONAL THERMAL POWER	INDIA	POWER GENERATION	2,395.0	31.9	381.7	20.3	74
548	—	SGS-THOMSON MICROELECT. ASIA	SINGAPORE	SEMICONDUCTORS	2,390.8	14.1	31.6	(26.2)	534
549	626	CHINA LIGHT & POWER	HONG KONG	POWER GENERATION	2,387.2	9.1	620.0	10.2	43
550	563	TOYODA GOSEI	JAPAN	CAR PARTS	2,383.1	13.3	29.3	50.9	557
551	539	LIFE CORP.	JAPAN	SUPERMARKETS	2,381.8	12.7	10.5	9.5	728
552	483	TOENEC	JAPAN	ENGINEERING	2,377.6	(0.8)	25.2	(10.5)	594
553	688	WMC	AUSTRALIA	MINING	2,376.6	13.5	232.7	(23.1)	130
554	528	TAKASAGO THERMAL ENG.	JAPAN	AIRCONDITIONING WORKS	2,361.5	6.1	36.4	(17.7)	504
555	564	SUMITOMO OSAKA CEMENT	JAPAN	CEMENT	2,358.5	12.2	41.7	—	472
556	500	TEXAS INSTRUMENTS JAPAN	JAPAN	SEMICONDUCTORS	2,351.1	0.0	48.3	(66.0)	425
557	547	JOSHIN DENKI	JAPAN	ELECTRONICS RETAILING	2,350.4	8.8	27.0	104.6	571
558	618	GMH AUTOMOTIVE	AUSTRALIA	CARS	2,348.7	0.0	190.2	(6.5)	161
559	491	FUDO CONSTRUCTION	JAPAN	CONSTRUCTION	2,337.8	(1.7)	4.7	(52.2)	807
560	561	PERLIS PLANTATIONS	MALAYSIA	SUGAR, FLOUR, PROPERTY	2,336.5	(3.7)	71.2	(18.3)	339
561	—	FUTURIS	AUSTRALIA	FARM SERVS., BLDG. PRODS.	2,330.9	NA	46.1	NA	440
562	548	NGK INSULATORS	JAPAN	CAR PARTS	2,322.8	7.7	101.3	18.8	275
563	513	CHUO GYORUI	JAPAN	FISH WHOLESALER	2,320.2	0.8	4.6	11.5	810
564	529	YANMAR DIESEL ENGINE	JAPAN	DIESEL ENGINES	2,317.0	4.3	16.2	(16.9)	669
565	532	FUKUDA CORP.	JAPAN	CONSTRUCTION	2,316.4	5.0	20.5	(17.0)	623
566	522	MARUDAI FOOD	JAPAN	MEAT	2,313.4	2.5	(29.8)	—	925
567	475	MITSUI MINING	JAPAN	COAL, OIL, CEMENT	2,312.1	(4.6)	(4.3)	—	893
568	493	KINSHO-MATAICHI	JAPAN	METALS TRADING	2,308.1	(2.7)	(7.4)	—	900
569	889	WESTERN DIGITAL (SING.)	SINGAPORE	DISK DRIVES	2,296.5	19.9	111.3	89.2	252
570	639	HEWLETT-PACKARD JAPAN	JAPAN	COMPUTERS	2,296.4	23.7	92.8	26.2	292

Company ranking by sales. Key to notes: All data are for fiscal years that ended between July 1997 and June 1998, except for companies with an asterisk (*) in the Notes column, which denotes data from the previous accounting period. The numbers refer to the month the fiscal year ended: 1 for January; 2 February; 3 March; 4 April; 5 May; 6 June; 7 July; 8 August; 9 September; 10 October; 11 November; 12 December. The letters denote publicly listed (L), unlisted (U), and state-controlled (S) companies. Financial results incorporate those of subsidiaries. Sales also refers to turnover, gross income, or revenue. Net profit is computed after deducting tax and minority interests while excluding extraordinary items. % Change is from the previous year's result in local currency. Sales per $1 Assets is equivalent to sales-to-assets ratio. Equity is the sum of paid-up capital, reserves, and retained

Asia's Largest Companies by Sales 53

541 to 570

ASSETS $ MILLION	RANK	SALES PER $1 ASSETS	EQUITY $ MILLION	RANK	EMPLOYEES NUMBER	RANK	PROFIT PER EMPLOYEE	MARKET CAP. ($M)	PROFIT AS % OF SALES	ASSETS	EQUITY	NOTES (Key Below)
4,870.2	286	0.50	3,499.3	114	3,430	573	156,544	30,815.0	22.2	11.0	15.3	2 L
1,005.8	807	2.40	292.6	734	4,803	464	5,694	—	1.1	2.7	9.3	3 U A
673.0	860	3.58	23.1	897	541	937	1,003	—	0.0	0.1	2.4	3 U
2,026.6	583	1.19	669.8	527	31,111	81	5,868	—	7.6	9.0	27.3	6 U S
2,382.4	502	1.01	750.1	493	6,096	392	1,059	261.3	0.3	0.3	0.9	12 L
4,249.9	327	0.56	1,319.3	318	4,876	460	5,920	1,012.9	1.2	0.7	2.2	3 L
7,614.1	187	—	4,185.5	90	19,153	152	19,931	—	15.9	5.0	9.1	3 U S*
407.1	894	5.87	84.3	858	550	933	57,515	—	1.3	7.8	37.5	12 U
4,400.9	318	0.54	2,671.8	148	6,111	389	101,456	11,940.7	25.0	14.1	23.2	9 L
1,880.4	605	1.27	749.4	495	6,496	373	4,506	546.6	1.2	1.6	3.9	3 L
1,098.5	785	2.17	294.4	732	3,083	603	3,402	264.2	0.4	0.0	3.6	2 L
1,911.8	597	1.24	671.0	526	6,954	356	3,623	370.6	1.1	1.3	3.8	3 L A
6,004.8	237	0.40	3,502.9	112	3,860	534	60,279	4,154.0	9.8	3.9	6.6	6 L
2,573.4	477	0.92	697.3	514	1,735	779	20,961	1,210.4	1.5	1.4	5.2	3 L
3,813.2	362	0.62	1,073.7	378	1,824	774	22,876	906.6	1.8	1.1	3.9	3 L
1,424.0	713	1.65	712.9	508	5,000	451	9,658	—	2.1	3.4	6.8	12 U A
1,375.4	724	1.71	580.8	565	3,005	613	9,312	250.1	1.2	2.0	4.8	3 L
1,017.8	801	2.31	469.7	631	5,644	415	33,707	—	8.1	18.7	40.5	12 U
1,900.2	600	1.23	261.7	748	1,938	757	2,414	300.5	0.2	0.2	1.8	3 L
1,518.7	683	1.54	751.5	492	9,600	282	7,414	733.2	3.1	4.7	9.5	12 L
1,044.5	793	2.23	364.1	693	6,000	396	7,688	550.9	1.0	4.4	12.7	6 L
3,230.1	400	0.72	1,544.1	266	4,457	490	22,736	3,037.9	4.4	3.1	6.6	3 L
310.2	900	7.48	175.7	802	314	964	14,726	81.9	0.2	1.5	2.6	3 L
2,228.9	535	—	348.5	705	3,439	570	4,715	—	0.7	0.7	4.7	3 U A
2,100.2	563	1.10	433.5	648	1,481	817	13,861	168.8	0.9	0.0	4.7	12 L
1,468.2	696	1.58	874.9	436	2,972	615	—	351.0	—	—	—	3 L
2,576.9	476	0.90	262.4	747	1,192	853	—	199.9	—	—	—	3 L
1,316.5	735	1.75	70.2	869	592	925	—	47.4	—	—	—	3 L
662.4	864	3.47	385.1	679	4,731	470	23,536	—	4.8	16.8	28.9	6 U
1,092.1	787	2.10	248.2	757	3,900	529	23,807	—	4.0	8.5	37.4	10 U A

earnings. Liabilities can be estimated by deducting equity from assets. Market Capitalization is the total value of all shares of listed firms as of **Nov. 5**. Profit as % of Sales is usually called net profit margin. Profit as % of Assets, return on assets; Profit as % of Equity, return on equity. All money values are in US$. Currency conversion uses average **1996** rates (except for Market Cap.); for Australia, A$1.2773 per $1; China, RMB8.3142; Hong Kong, HK$7.80; India, Rs35.433; Indonesia, Rp2.342.3; Japan, ¥108.78; Malaysia, RM2.5159; New Zealand, NZ$1.453; Pakistan, Rs36.079; Philippines, Pesos 26.216; Singapore, S$1.41; South Korea, Won 804.45; Taiwan, NT$27.50; Thailand, Baht 25.343. NA not available. Values less than $50,000 appear as $0.0; those less than 0.05% as 0.0%. Market Capitalization from Datastream. More notes on pages 84 and 85.

Asia's Largest Companies By Sales

RANK 1997	RANK 1996	COMPANY NAME	COUNTRY	MAIN BUSINESS	SALES $ MILLION	%CHANGE	NET PROFIT $ MILLION	%CHANGE	RANK
571	471	MATSUSHITA BATTERY INDL.	JAPAN	BATTERIES	2,295.9	5.1	121.7	5.9	231
572	590	AMSTEEL CORP.	MALAYSIA	STEEL, RETAILING	2,295.7	40.2	50.9	1.6	413
573	533	NKK TRADING	JAPAN	STEEL-PRODUCTS TRADING	2,293.4	4.1	0.7	516.7	866
574	583	IZUMI	JAPAN	SUPERMARKETS	2,292.7	13.7	24.0	(36.9)	597
575	541	CALSONIC	JAPAN	CAR PARTS	2,291.4	5.4	36.8	(16.0)	500
576	729	TRI PETCH ISUZU SALES	THAILAND	CAR DEALERSHIP	2,290.7	23.8	22.6	46.5	609
577	540	NICHIRO CORP.	JAPAN	FISHING	2,284.9	5.1	10.2	—	731
578	542	TOKYO BROADCASTING	JAPAN	BROADCASTING	2,281.6	5.1	60.9	(15.3)	369
579	594	DIA KENSETSU	JAPAN	PROPERTY	2,279.4	14.5	0.6	(94.7)	867
580	714	LG CONSTRUCTION	SOUTH KOREA	CONSTRUCTION	2,277.2	24.1	19.1	(21.5)	636
581	557	DENKI KAGAKU KOGYO	JAPAN	CHEMICALS	2,276.1	7.3	9.3	(71.9)	744
582	431	KUOK OILS & GRAINS	SINGAPORE	COMMODITIES TRADING	2,275.0	(21.9)	6.6	(82.0)	783
583	574	YASKAWA ELECTRIC	JAPAN	ELECTRIC MOTORS	2,275.3	11.3	11.1	—	719
584	549	TOYO INK MFG.	JAPAN	INK	2,273.4	5.6	47.7	91.8	428
585	569	TOPY INDUSTRIES	JAPAN	STEEL PRODUCTS	2,265.3	9.3	28.9	133.7	560
586	752	LOTTE SHOPPING	SOUTH KOREA	DEPARTMENT STORES	2,264.1	28.8	45.1	1.5	444
587	530	NIIGATA ENGINEERING	JAPAN	HEAVY MACHINERY	2,261.5	2.0	(19.9)	—	916
588	518	SUMITOMO LIGHT METAL	JAPAN	ALUMINUM PRODUCTS	2,253.2	(1.1)	(6.4)	—	896
589	556	SHIN NIKKEI	JAPAN	BUILDING MATERIALS	2,251.0	5.7	(12.6)	—	908
590	747	MANILA ELECTRIC CO.	PHILIPPINES	ELECTRICITY DISTRIBUTION	2,247.1	23.6	193.2	14.8	159
591	678	SANWA SHUTTER	JAPAN	SHUTTERS, DOORS	2,246.0	29.0	76.1	47.4	325
592	534	TOKYO TOYOPET MOTOR	JAPAN	CAR DEALERSHIP	2,246.2	2.1	1.2	(20.0)	859
593	656	PHILIPS (SINGAPORE)	SINGAPORE	CONSUMER ELECTRONICS	2,244.1	6.9	24.2	(32.3)	602
594	531	MATSUMURA-GUMI CORP.	JAPAN	CONSTRUCTION	2,243.5	1.4	6.0	(27.7)	791
595	587	UNISIA JECS CORP.	JAPAN	CAR PARTS	2,228.9	8.4	32.7	69.2	525
596	705	SANSHIN ELECTRONICS	JAPAN	ELECTRONICS TRADING	2,228.9	33.1	31.2	72.1	538
597	603	NOMURA REAL ESTATE DEVT.	JAPAN	PROPERTY	2,221.6	12.0	5.8	21.1	794
598	617	MAYNE NICKLESS	AUSTRALIA	TRANSPORT, SECURITY	2,219.8	(2.8)	90.7	36.0	297
599	523	NESTLE JAPAN	JAPAN	FOOD	2,216.4	(1.6)	115.8	2.4	245
600	739	HUNG KUK SANG SA	SOUTH KOREA	GENERAL TRADING	2,202.1	22.0	0.3	50.0	872

Company ranking by sales. Key to notes: All data are for fiscal years that ended between July 1997 and June 1998, except for companies with an asterisk (*) in the Notes column, which denotes data from the previous accounting period. The numbers refer to the month the fiscal year ended: 1 for January; 2 February; 3 March; 4 April; 5 May; 6 June; 7 July; 8 August; 9 September; 10 October; 11 November; 12 December. The letters denote publicly listed (L), unlisted (U), and state-controlled (S) companies. Financial results incorporate those of subsidiaries. Sales also refers to turnover, gross income, or revenue. Net profit is computed after deducting tax and minority interests while excluding extraordinary items. % Change is from the previous year's result in local currency. Sales per $1 Assets is equivalent to sales-to-assets ratio. Equity is the sum of paid-up capital, reserves, and retained

Asia's Largest Companies by Sales

571 to 600

ASSETS $ MILLION	RANK	SALES PER $1 ASSETS	EQUITY $ MILLION	RANK	EMPLOYEES NUMBER	RANK	PROFIT PER EMPLOYEE	MARKET CAP. ($M)	PROFIT AS % OF SALES	ASSETS	EQUITY	NOTES (Key Below)
1,924.4	594	1.19	1,059.3	384	4,672	472	26,052	—	5.3	6.3	11.5	3 U
3,783.3	366	0.61	592.4	560	NA	—	—	505.6	2.2	1.3	8.6	6 L *
1,012.7	804	2.26	40.0	889	535	938	1,272	—	0.0	0.1	1.7	3 U A
1,773.6	629	1.29	697.3	515	5,865	404	4,259	516.6	1.1	1.4	3.6	2 L A
1,600.7	672	1.43	538.1	593	9,551	287	3,855	697.7	1.6	2.3	6.8	3 L
1,392.9	719	1.64	119.1	833	900	887	25,122	—	0.0	1.6	18.0	9 U
1,278.3	740	1.79	126.2	830	946	877	10,777	260.3	0.4	0.8	8.1	3 L
2,864.5	436	0.80	1,745.1	239	2,016	749	30,214	2,938.9	2.7	2.1	3.5	3 L
4,622.6	299	0.49	490.2	619	1,106	860	574	182.2	0.0	0.0	0.1	3 L
2,248.3	531	1.01	352.1	703	2,294	710	8,336	220.1	0.8	0.9	5.4	12 L
3,380.0	393	0.67	737.3	499	3,298	583	2,812	872.5	0.4	0.3	1.3	3 L
254.3	906	8.95	63.7	872	137	976	48,214	—	0.3	2.6	10.4	12 U
2,194.5	548	1.04	361.4	697	4,242	505	2,622	812.2	0.5	0.5	3.1	3 L
2,964.3	429	0.77	1,090.5	373	2,951	621	16,158	854.4	2.1	1.6	4.4	3 L
2,204.6	541	1.03	449.0	639	2,848	634	10,152	481.9	1.3	1.3	6.4	3 L
2,145.6	555	1.06	341.4	713	4,129	509	10,927	—	1.0	2.1	13.2	12 U
2,991.5	427	0.76	273.5	743	5,026	447	—	288.8	—	—	—	3 L
3,582.9	378	0.63	61.0	874	2,806	641	—	367.9	—	—	—	3 L
2,283.5	525	0.99	859.8	447	4,397	495	—	175.2	—	—	—	3 L
2,587.0	473	0.87	1,518.0	276	7,793	331	24,785	2,011.5	8.6	7.5	12.7	12 L
3,104.4	415	0.72	1,073.5	379	8,210	317	9,267	1,418.7	3.4	2.5	7.1	3 L
NA	—	—	NA	—	4,424	493	266	—	0.1	—	—	3 U A
801.3	842	2.80	196.4	790	8,000	323	3,030	—	1.1	3.0	12.3	12 U
2,201.3	544	1.02	222.4	775	2,092	736	2,869	118.0	0.3	0.3	2.7	3 L A
1,598.0	673	1.39	568.9	569	7,586	337	4,307	498.6	1.5	2.0	5.7	3 L N
1,145.0	774	1.95	369.2	691	939	879	33,227	479.6	1.4	2.7	8.5	3 L
NA	—	—	NA	—	1,362	828	4,225	—	0.3	—	—	3 U A
2,353.4	508	0.94	877.7	431	28,000	100	3,239	1,715.9	4.1	3.9	10.3	7 L
NA	—	—	NA	—	2,800	643	41,368	—	5.2	—	—	12 U A
1,137.7	776	1.94	132.4	825	690	913	476	—	0.0	0.0	0.2	12 U

earnings. Liabilities can be estimated by deducting equity from assets. Market Capitalization is the total value of all shares of listed firms as of **Nov. 5**. Profit as % of Sales is usually called net profit margin. Profit as % of Assets, return on assets; Profit as % of Equity, return on equity. All money values are in US$. Currency conversion uses average **1996** rates (except for Market Cap.); for Australia, A$1.2773 per $1; China, RMB8.3142; Hong Kong, HK$7.80; India, Rs35.433; Indonesia, Rp2.342.3; Japan, ¥108.78; Malaysia, RM2.5159; New Zealand, NZ$1.453; Pakistan, Rs36.079; Philippines, Pesos 26.216; Singapore, S$1.41; South Korea, Won 804.45; Taiwan, NT$27.50; Thailand, Baht 25.343. NA not available. Values less than $50,000 appear as $0.0; those less than 0.05% as 0.0%. Market Capitalization from Datastream. More notes on pages 84 and 85.

# Asia's Top 1000 Blue-Chip Companies

Asia's Largest Companies By Sales

RANK 1997	RANK 1996	COMPANY NAME	COUNTRY	MAIN BUSINESS	SALES $ MILLION	%CHANGE	NET PROFIT $ MILLION	%CHANGE	RANK
601	671	MARUBENI ENERGY	JAPAN	GAS & OIL TRADING	2,191.8	23.7	2.9	185.6	830
602	568	DAIKEN CORP.	JAPAN	BUILDING MATERIALS	2,187.9	5.0	36.8	19.3	501
603	546	YURTEC	JAPAN	ELECTRICAL ENGINEERING	2,186.3	1.1	51.9	(16.8)	408
604	579	TAISHO PHARMACEUTICAL	JAPAN	PHARMACEUTICALS	2,185.1	7.6	306.9	4.3	94
605	555	YANMAR AGRI. EQUIPMENT	JAPAN	AGRICULTURAL EQUIPMENT	2,179.4	1.9	3.3	66.0	827
606	573	NHK SPRING	JAPAN	SPRINGS	2,178.0	5.9	29.5	65.8	553
607	730	FOSTER'S BREWING	AUSTRALIA	BEER	2,176.4	9.6	196.1	(14.6)	157
608	588	MITANI CORP.	JAPAN	GENERAL TRADING	2,170.8	8.7	11.5	41.8	714
609	606	TELKOM	INDONESIA	TELECOMMUNICATIONS	2,167.0	(0.6)	641.8	65.8	42
610	589	MEIDENSHA	JAPAN	INDUSTRIAL MACHINERY	2,161.3	8.3	12.4	71.7	704
611	593	NISSHINBO INDUSTRIES	JAPAN	TEXTILES	2,153.6	8.1	21.7	7.5	614
612	592	BROTHER INDUSTRIES	JAPAN	OFFICE EQUIPMENT	2,150.5	7.9	18.4	(8.0)	651
613	612	NEW WORLD DEVELOPMENT	HONG KONG	PROPERTY, HOTELS	2,143.0	(4.2)	533.0	21.9	53
614	520	SAN-MIC CHIYODA	JAPAN	PAPER TRADING	2,140.3	(5.4)	1.6	(21.5)	854
615	623	YKK CORP.	JAPAN	BUILDING MAT'LS, ZIPPERS	2,138.3	12.5	103.0	28.9	270
616	654	TELECOM NEW ZEALAND	NEW ZEALAND	TELECOMMUNICATIONS	2,136.1	6.2	399.8	(18.9)	68
617	619	ITOCHU PETROLEUM	SINGAPORE	OIL TRADING	2,136.1	23.9	(0.4)	—	879
618	663	CYCLE & CARRIAGE	SINGAPORE	CARS, PROPERTY, FOOD	2,135.4	2.5	141.9	10.2	203
619	571	LOTTE	JAPAN	CHEWING GUM	2,128.1	2.9	NA	—	—
620	620	BENESSE CORP.	JAPAN	PUBLISHING	2,124.8	11.2	108.4	16.5	259
621	742	WESFARMERS	AUSTRALIA	CHEMICALS, RETAILING	2,121.3	7.8	109.3	50.4	256
622	689	KOA OIL	JAPAN	OIL REFINING	2,116.0	23.5	12.0	(55.0)	696
623	565	CHIYODA CO.	JAPAN	SHOE RETAILING	2,109.7	0.6	46.8	(2.1)	433
624	586	NIHON KEIZAI SHIMBUN	JAPAN	NEWSPAPER PUBLISHING	2,106.1	5.1	48.8	12.2	420
625	537	HOTAI MOTOR	TAIWAN	CAR DEALERSHIP	2,103.2	(7.0)	29.4	(9.6)	554
626	616	JAPAN SYNTHETIC RUBBER	JAPAN	SYNTHETIC RUBBER	2,100.9	8.0	90.5	136.1	300
627	577	MITSUBISHI PAPER MILLS	JAPAN	PAPER	2,093.7	2.0	40.0	(19.4)	481
628	692	DEODEO CORP.	JAPAN	ELECTRONICS RETAILING	2,093.2	22.8	30.4	16.6	543
629	621	BRAMBLES INDUSTRIES	AUSTRALIA	TRANSPORT SERVICES	2,088.8	(10.1)	190.4	13.1	160
630	659	ASIA MOTORS	SOUTH KOREA	TRUCKS, BUSES	2,086.8	4.5	(36.6)	—	932

Company ranking by sales. Key to notes: All data are for fiscal years that ended between July 1997 and June 1998, except for companies with an asterisk (*) in the Notes column, which denotes data from the previous accounting period. The numbers refer to the month the fiscal year ended: 1 for January; 2 February; 3 March; 4 April; 5 May; 6 June; 7 July; 8 August; 9 September; 10 October; 11 November; 12 December. The letters denote publicly listed (L), unlisted (U), and state-controlled (S) companies. Financial results incorporate those of subsidiaries. Sales also refers to turnover, gross income, or revenue. Net profit is computed after deducting tax and minority interests while excluding extraordinary items. % Change is from the previous year's result in local currency. Sales per $1 Assets is equivalent to sales-to-assets ratio. Equity is the sum of paid-up capital, reserves, and retained

Asia's Largest Companies by Sales

601 to 630

ASSETS $ MILLION	RANK	SALES PER $1 ASSETS	EQUITY $ MILLION	RANK	EMPLOYEES NUMBER	RANK	PROFIT PER EMPLOYEE	MARKET CAP. ($M)	PROFIT AS % OF SALES	ASSETS	EQUITY	NOTES (Key Below)
NA	—	—	NA	—	314	965	9,281	—	0.1	—	—	3 U A
1,593.9	675	1.37	561.6	577	2,912	624	12,631	498.9	1.7	2.3	6.5	3 L A
1,443.1	706	1.51	686.3	521	5,561	419	9,333	434.3	2.4	3.6	7.6	3 L
3,981.0	348	0.55	3,136.7	130	4,819	462	63,686	8,659.3	14.1	7.7	9.8	3 L A
1,221.4	749	—	95.3	849	1,495	815	2,177	—	0.1	0.3	3.4	12 U A
2,184.5	549	0.00	734.5	502	4,099	514	7,190	724.8	1.4	1.3	4.0	3 L
3,870.0	357	0.56	2,240.0	181	11,500	249	17,054	3,836.3	9.0	5.1	8.8	6 L
1,008.3	806	2.15	233.7	768	804	899	14,247	118.2	0.5	1.1	4.9	3 L
7,592.2	188	0.29	3,785.6	104	37,644	62	17,049	9,389.0	29.6	8.5	16.0	12 L S
2,252.3	529	0.96	557.3	583	5,009	450	2,474	655.0	0.6	0.6	2.2	3 L
3,019.2	425	0.71	1,827.2	225	5,145	440	4,215	1,521.0	1.0	0.7	1.2	3 L
2,606.3	471	0.83	1,042.0	387	10,814	262	1,701	701.5	0.9	0.7	1.8	11 L
12,302.1	115	0.17	6,571.8	50	45,000	56	11,845	6,614.4	24.9	4.3	8.1	6 L *
NA	—	—	NA	—	743	907	2,128	—	0.1	—	—	3 U
4,529.1	310	—	1,904.8	214	9,472	289	10,979	—	4.9	2.3	5.5	3 U A
3,175.6	407	0.67	1,129.5	364	8,710	307	45,899	10,160.3	18.7	12.6	35.4	3 L
274.2	903	7.79	4.0	901	22	987	—	—	—	—	—	12 U
1,629.4	668	1.31	957.2	413	5,141	441	27,605	1,176.6	6.6	8.7	14.8	12 L
NA	—	—	NA	—	2,100	733	—	—	—	—	—	3 U
2,440.2	495	0.87	1,163.0	355	1,334	835	81,227	2,659.0	5.1	4.4	9.3	3 L
1,611.1	671	1.32	792.3	477	12,000	238	9,105	2,107.6	5.2	6.8	13.8	6 L
2,069.7	575	1.02	446.6	642	832	895	15,601	677.6	0.6	0.6	2.9	3 L
1,373.6	725	1.54	569.6	568	3,503	561	13,352	430.3	2.2	3.4	8.2	2 L
2,236.7	534	0.94	805.5	471	4,222	506	11,549	—	2.3	2.2	6.1	12 U A
530.1	882	3.97	316.1	726	1,216	848	24,143	620.9	1.4	5.5	9.3	12 L
2,522.1	485	0.83	1,002.2	401	3,014	612	30,022	1,758.7	4.3	3.6	9.0	3 L
3,176.6	406	0.66	1,052.7	385	3,593	556	11,135	787.4	1.9	1.3	3.8	3 L
1,516.0	685	1.38	695.4	517	3,886	530	7,830	474.3	1.5	2.0	4.4	3 L O
2,456.4	493	0.85	1,130.9	363	19,000	154	10,021	4,419.5	9.1	7.8	16.8	6 L
3,335.3	394	0.63	544.9	586	9,180	300	—	171.6	—	—	—	12 L

earnings. Liabilities can be estimated by deducting equity from assets. Market Capitalization is the total value of all shares of listed firms as of **Nov. 5.** Profit as % of Sales is usually called net profit margin. Profit as % of Assets, return on assets; Profit as % of Equity, return on equity. All money values are in US$. Currency conversion uses average **1996** rates (except for Market Cap.); for Australia, A$1.2773 per $1; China, RMB8.3142; Hong Kong, HK$7.80; India, Rs35.433; Indonesia, Rp2,342.3; Japan, ¥108.78; Malaysia, RM2.5159; New Zealand, NZ$1.453; Pakistan, Rs36.079; Philippines, Pesos 26.216; Singapore, S$1.41; South Korea, Won 804.45; Taiwan, NT$27.50; Thailand, Baht 25.343. NA not available. Values less than $50,000 appear as $0.0; those less than 0.05% as 0.0%. Market Capitalization from Datastream. More notes on pages 84 and 85.

Asia's Top 1000 Blue-Chip Companies

Asia's Largest Companies By Sales

RANK 1997	RANK 1996	COMPANY NAME	COUNTRY	MAIN BUSINESS	SALES $ MILLION	%CHANGE	NET PROFIT $ MILLION	%CHANGE	RANK
631	642	DAITO TRUST CONS.	JAPAN	CONSTRUCTION	2,083.5	13.1	60.8	(7.8)	370
632	595	KIRIN BEVERAGE	JAPAN	DRINKS	2,076.1	4.4	41.8	12.8	470
633	630	NOK CORP.	JAPAN	CAR PARTS	2,062.8	9.9	57.9	25.3	382
634	682	HOUSING INDL. DEVT. & CONST.	SOUTH KOREA	CONSTRUCTION	2,062.2	7.3	29.5	(31.6)	551
635	637	DAINIPPON SCREEN MFG.	JAPAN	PRINTING EQUIPMENT	2,058.3	10.7	85.7	71.9	309
636	878	SINGAPORE POWER	SINGAPORE	POWER, WATER, FUEL GAS	2,056.7	NA	546.8	NA	50
637	543	NOMURA TRADING	JAPAN	GENERAL TRADING	2,055.7	(5.2)	1.8	—	848
638	578	TOHTO SUISAN	JAPAN	FISH WHOLESALER	2,055.1	1.2	0.5	—	870
639	657	ESSO STANDARD THAILAND	THAILAND	OIL REFINING, DISTRIBUTION	2,049.9	28.1	(54.9)	—	942
640	700	SOUTHCORP HOLDINGS	AUSTRALIA	FOOD, DRINKS, PACKAGING	2,049.8	(0.3)	105.9	9.6	267
641	810	KEPPEL CORP.	SINGAPORE	SHIP-REPAIRING, FINANCE	2,046.6	20.0	144.8	(4.7)	198
642	581	POLA COSMETICS	JAPAN	COSMETICS	2,043.8	1.1	NA	—	—
643	516	YAOHAN JAPAN CORP.	JAPAN	SUPERMARKETS, STORES	2,041.0	(7.7)	(246.8)	—	964
644	697	NIPPON COMSYS CORP.	JAPAN	TELECOM. ENGINEERING	2,037.5	20.1	62.8	64.3	360
645	798	PETRON CORP.	PHILIPPINES	OIL REFINING, DISTRIBUTION	2,037.4	19.7	161.7	5.4	186
646	611	RYODEN TRADING	JAPAN	MACHINERY TRADING	2,032.1	4.5	16.0	55.1	662
647	675	KOLON INTERNATIONAL	SOUTH KOREA	GENERAL TRADING	2,031.0	4.6	9.4	(16.2)	740
648	764	CHINA NATIONAL AGRI.	CHINA	AGRICULTURAL PRODUCTS	2,025.8	11.5	0.3	(69.9)	873
649	610	TOBU DEPARTMENT STORES	JAPAN	DEPARTMENT STORES	2,023.4	3.7	NA	—	—
650	677	CARTER HOLT HARVEY	NEW ZEALAND	WOOD, PAPER	2,022.0	(4.3)	172.6	(44.6)	177
651	609	KOITO MANUFACTURING	JAPAN	CAR PARTS	2,022.8	3.6	43.2	20.0	461
652	724	AIR NEW ZEALAND	NEW ZEALAND	AIR TRANSPORT	2,015.2	(2.3)	103.3	(33.3)	272
653	774	LG METALS	SOUTH KOREA	NON-FERROUS METALS	2,013.3	17.0	9.8	(81.2)	736
654	638	DAITO GYORUI	JAPAN	FISH WHOLESALER	2,011.5	8.3	2.7	—	835
655	625	TANABE SEIYAKU	JAPAN	PHARMACEUTICALS	2,009.1	6.2	60.5	42.2	371
656	740	JARDINE INTL. MOTORS	HONG KONG	CAR DEALERSHIP	2,007.4	7.5	68.7	8.7	343
657	629	NIPPON PAINT	JAPAN	PAINT	1,995.5	6.1	7.0	163.2	776
658	624	TAIHEI KOGYO	JAPAN	CONSTRUCTION, ENG.	1,995.1	5.4	1.4	(88.8)	856
659	777	FRASER & NEAVE	SINGAPORE	DRINKS, FOOD	1,993.9	11.0	154.9	18.2	190
660	650	TOKUYAMA CORP.	JAPAN	MATERIALS, CHEMICALS	1,991.8	9.8	19.1	(42.9)	639

Company ranking by sales. Key to notes: All data are for fiscal years that ended between July 1997 and June 1998, except for companies with an asterisk (*) in the Notes column, which denotes data from the previous accounting period. The numbers refer to the month the fiscal year ended: 1 for January; 2 February; 3 March; 4 April; 5 May; 6 June; 7 July; 8 August; 9 September; 10 October; 11 November; 12 December. The letters denote publicly listed (L), unlisted (U), and state-controlled (S) companies. Financial results incorporate those of subsidiaries. Sales also refers to turnover, gross income, or revenue. Net profit is computed after deducting tax and minority interests while excluding extraordinary items. % Change is from the previous year's result in local currency. Sales per $1 Assets is equivalent to sales-to-assets ratio. Equity is the sum of paid-up capital, reserves, and retained

Asia's Largest Companies by Sales

631 to 660

ASSETS $ MILLION	RANK	SALES PER $1 ASSETS	EQUITY $ MILLION	RANK	EMPLOYEES NUMBER	RANK	PROFIT PER EMPLOYEE	MARKET CAP. ($M)	PROFIT AS % OF SALES	ASSETS	EQUITY	NOTES (Key Below)
2,196.2	547	0.95	1,391.6	301	2,025	748	30,048	1,214.3	2.9	2.8	4.4	3 L
1,155.6	771	1.80	458.6	635	2,840	635	14,734	851.8	2.0	3.6	9.1	12 L
1,776.3	626	1.16	799.8	475	3,662	547	15,798	1,120.6	2.8	3.3	7.2	3 L
2,475.0	490	0.83	467.3	633	3,127	598	9,435	307.4	1.4	1.2	6.3	12 L P
2,618.8	468	0.79	615.1	549	4,666	473	18,368	1,395.1	4.2	3.3	13.9	3 L
7,787.2	179	0.26	4,829.8	72	4,500	487	121,513	—	26.6	7.0	11.3	3 U S Q
NA	—	—	NA	—	583	928	3,154	—	0.1	—	—	3 U A
309.7	901	6.64	135.6	821	299	967	1,814	88.7	0.0	0.2	0.4	3 L
1,530.5	678	1.34	NA	—	1,600	793	—	—	—	—	—	12 U *
2,224.1	538	0.92	1,090.2	374	13,000	213	8,149	2,076.2	5.2	4.8	9.7	6 L
13,382.9	104	0.15	2,288.3	175	14,320	194	10,108	2,469.9	7.1	1.1	6.3	12 L
NA	—	—	NA	—	966	875	—	—	—	—	—	12 U A
2,200.2	546	0.93	154.9	809	1,208	851	—	5.3	—	—	—	3 L R
1,460.2	699	1.40	634.1	545	3,788	539	16,575	1,556.2	3.1	4.3	9.9	3 L
1,827.5	616	1.11	654.0	532	1,267	842	127,590	1,092.6	7.9	8.8	24.7	12 L
951.8	817	2.14	311.4	728	1,185	855	14,344	223.3	0.8	1.8	5.5	3 L
974.8	811	2.08	271.8	744	2,758	650	3,405	75.6	0.5	0.0	3.5	12 L
652.0	865	3.10	41.3	888	2,344	699	133	—	0.0	0.1	0.8	12 U S
NA	—	—	NA	—	2,956	619	—	—	—	—	—	3 U
5,201.1	266	0.39	3,279.9	121	12,140	232	14,217	3,177.8	8.5	3.3	5.3	3 L
2,004.8	587	1.01	725.1	503	4,557	480	9,483	954.9	2.1	2.2	5.0	3 L
2,301.3	520	0.88	1,150.2	359	9,340	294	11,058	1,063.5	5.1	4.5	8.0	6 L
1,212.7	752	1.66	207.3	785	1,286	841	7,629	132.4	0.5	0.8	4.7	12 L
278.4	902	7.22	98.5	846	316	962	8,407	46.5	0.1	0.0	2.7	3 L
2,369.0	504	0.85	1,272.9	332	5,073	445	11,929	1,618.4	3.0	2.6	4.8	3 L
959.0	815	2.09	425.3	653	7,400	340	9,284	333.6	3.4	7.2	16.2	12 L
2,136.9	556	0.93	830.4	457	4,612	476	1,527	560.8	0.4	0.3	0.8	3 L
1,725.8	642	1.16	252.4	752	7,195	344	192	134.4	0.1	0.1	0.5	3 L
4,499.8	313	0.44	1,753.1	237	10,064	276	15,393	1,633.4	7.8	3.4	8.8	9 L
2,659.9	459	0.75	861.6	444	2,879	629	6,629	873.7	0.0	0.7	2.2	3 L

earnings. Liabilities can be estimated by deducting equity from assets. Market Capitalization is the total value of all shares of listed firms as of **Nov. 5**. Profit as % of Sales is usually called net profit margin. Profit as % of Assets, return on assets; Profit as % of Equity, return on equity. All money values are in US$. Currency conversion uses average **1996** rates (except for Market Cap.); for Australia, A$1.2773 per $1; China, RMB8.3142; Hong Kong, HK$7.80; India, Rs35.433; Indonesia, Rp2,342.3; Japan, ¥108.78; Malaysia, RM2.5159; New Zealand, NZ$1.453; Pakistan, Rs36.079; Philippines, Pesos 26.216; Singapore, S$1.41; South Korea, Won 804.45; Taiwan, NT$27.50; Thailand, Baht 25.343. NA not available. Values less than $50,000 appear as $0.0; those less than 0.05% as 0.0%. Market Capitalization from Datastream. More notes on pages 84 and 85.

Asia's Largest Companies By Sales

RANK 1997	RANK 1996	COMPANY NAME	COUNTRY	MAIN BUSINESS	SALES $ MILLION	%CHANGE	NET PROFIT $ MILLION	%CHANGE	RANK
661	614	MAEDA ROAD CONST.	JAPAN	CIVIL ENGINEERING	1,987.8	2.9	46.2	(8.2)	439
662	604	RENOWN	JAPAN	CLOTHING	1,984.1	1.0	(36.0)	—	934
663	694	SANDEN	JAPAN	CAR AIRCONDITIONERS	1,983.8	16.4	60.1	121.1	374
664	788	ALCOA OF AUSTRALIA	AUSTRALIA	METAL PRODUCTS	1,982.2	6.4	304.0	24.2	95
665	598	EAST JAPAN KIOSK	JAPAN	RETAILING	1,975.2	(0.3)	3.3	2.9	826
666	923	LG INDUSTRIES	SOUTH KOREA	MACHINERY	1,973.6	39.8	37.8	7.0	494
667	646	AUTOBACS SEVEN	JAPAN	CAR-RELATED RETAILING	1,971.6	8.2	92.0	2.4	295
668	635	ONWARD KASHIYAMA	JAPAN	APPAREL	1,970.6	5.6	99.9	24.5	278
669	706	SUMITOMO WIRING SYSTEMS	JAPAN	CAR PARTS	1,967.5	17.7	25.6	40.2	590
670	668	SHINRYO CORP.	JAPAN	AIRCONDITIONING WORKS	1,963.8	10.4	55.9	(16.5)	389
671	602	FUJISASH	JAPAN	BUILDING MATERIALS	1,961.8	(0.3)	(22.3)	—	918
672	948	OPTUS COMMUNICATIONS	AUSTRALIA	TELECOMMUNICATIONS	1,961.6	28.9	(322.3)	—	967
673	744	KYOWA EXEO CORP.	JAPAN	TELECOM. ENGINEERING	1,960.6	22.1	46.5	64.6	436
674	—	MOTOROLA ELECTRONIC (CHINA)	CHINA	COMMUNICATION PRODS.	1,960.5	NA	NA	—	—
675	601	ODAKYU DEPT. STORE	JAPAN	DEPARTMENT STORES	1,955.3	(0.7)	(6.7)	—	897
676	647	BEIJING YANSHAN PETROCHEM.	CHINA	CHEMICALS	1,953.8	(7.6)	62.3	(33.2)	363
677	640	JAPAN TRAVEL BUREAU	JAPAN	TRAVEL AGENCY	1,953.3	5.8	19.5	(32.8)	632
678	607	MORINAGA & CO.	JAPAN	CONFECTIONERY	1,952.6	(0.5)	(7.0)	—	901
679	842	TOSHIBA ELECTRON. ASIA (SING.)	SINGAPORE	SEMICONDUCTORS	1,951.8	(1.3)	(1.9)	—	886
680	726	AMWAY JAPAN	JAPAN	HOUSEHOLD-GOODS RETAIL	1,950.7	19.2	258.1	21.8	116
681	685	KAJIMA ROAD	JAPAN	CIVIL ENGINEERING	1,947.6	13.1	16.7	(21.5)	664
682	884	IDEMITSU INTL. (ASIA)	SINGAPORE	OIL TRADING	1,942.6	(17.5)	7.1	(50.0)	772
683	627	KOWA	JAPAN	TEXTILES, MACHINERY	1,933.6	2.0	51.4	(17.5)	411
684	711	JARDINE PACIFIC	HONG KONG	TRADING, SERVICES	1,929.0	6.9	93.5	(7.5)	287
685	628	INAGEYA	JAPAN	SUPERMARKETS	1,927.9	2.3	20.4	28.9	624
686	676	YAMAE HISANO	JAPAN	FOOD TRADING	1,917.2	9.7	12.7	30.1	700
687	664	CÉCILE	JAPAN	MAIL-ORDER SALES	1,916.4	7.1	11.5	2.9	713
688	718	DAI-DAN	JAPAN	ENGINEERING	1,915.9	16.1	26.9	(7.7)	580
689	735	NEC SYSTEM INTEGRATION	JAPAN	ELECTRICAL ENGINEERING	1,915.6	18.3	17.2	41.7	659
690	758	TOYO ENGINEERING	JAPAN	PLANT ENGINEERING	1,914.7	21.5	6.3	(61.4)	786

Company ranking by sales. Key to notes: All data are for fiscal years that ended between July 1997 and June 1998, except for companies with an asterisk (*) in the Notes column, which denotes data from the previous accounting period. The numbers refer to the month the fiscal year ended: 1 for January; 2 February; 3 March; 4 April; 5 May; 6 June; 7 July; 8 August; 9 September; 10 October; 11 November; 12 December. The letters denote publicly listed (L), unlisted (U), and state-controlled (S) companies. Financial results incorporate those of subsidiaries. Sales also refers to turnover, gross income, or revenue. Net profit is computed after deducting tax and minority interests while excluding extraordinary items. % Change is from the previous year's result in local currency. Sales per $1 Assets is equivalent to sales-to-assets ratio. Equity is the sum of paid-up capital, reserves, and retained

Asia's Largest Companies by Sales

661 to 690

ASSETS $ MILLION	RANK	SALES PER $1 ASSETS	EQUITY $ MILLION	RANK	EMPLOYEES NUMBER	RANK	PROFIT PER EMPLOYEE	MARKET CAP. ($M)	PROFIT AS % OF SALES	ASSETS	EQUITY	NOTES (Key Below)
1,431.6	710	1.39	946.7	416	1,894	767	24,385	581.8	2.3	3.2	4.9	3 L A
2,166.2	551	0.92	721.1	505	7,180	345	—	298.8	—	—	—	1 L
1,651.8	659	1.20	544.6	588	2,628	661	22,853	905.5	3.0	3.6	11.0	3 L
2,361.9	505	0.84	1,471.2	284	5,445	424	55,831	—	15.3	12.9	20.7	12 U
NA	—	—	NA	—	6,400	376	517	—	0.2	—	—	3 U A
2,076.1	571	0.95	407.0	664	10,207	272	3,705	302.2	1.9	1.8	9.3	12 L
1,472.0	694	1.34	1,078.9	376	1,679	785	54,812	1,956.7	4.7	6.2	8.5	3 L
2,451.4	494	0.80	1,580.2	262	2,686	656	37,182	2,586.3	5.1	4.1	6.3	2 L
1,142.1	775	1.72	271.2	745	16,999	165	1,504	245.2	1.3	2.2	9.4	3 L
2,009.2	586	0.98	643.8	541	2,550	668	21,919	—	2.8	2.8	8.7	9 U A
2,111.5	560	0.93	405.1	667	4,032	517	—	117.1	—	—	—	3 L
4,566.2	305	0.43	1,349.8	313	7,000	350	—	—	—	—	—	6 U
1,282.9	739	1.53	406.2	666	3,973	523	11,701	897.0	2.4	3.6	11.4	3 L
980.6	809	1.00	NA	—	NA	—	—	—	—	—	—	12 U
NA	—	—	NA	—	2,272	712	—	—	—	—	—	2 U A
1,448.8	705	1.35	832.6	456	47,571	46	1,310	—	3.2	4.3	7.5	12 U S
4,135.7	339	0.47	482.2	624	8,522	310	2,293	—	1.0	0.5	4.1	3 U A
1,766.2	630	1.11	411.8	659	2,507	673	—	409.7	—	—	—	3 L
522.2	884	3.74	118.9	834	523	939	—	—	—	—	—	3 U
1,067.0	791	1.83	587.1	564	1,044	868	247,265	3,919.3	13.2	24.2	43.0	8 L
NA	—	—	NA	—	1,857	770	8,975	—	0.9	—	—	3 U A
562.3	879	3.45	77.2	865	22	986	322,373	—	0.4	1.3	9.2	3 U
1,461.9	698	1.32	651.6	534	1,900	766	27,042	—	2.7	3.5	7.9	3 U A
1,850.0	609	1.04	664.8	531	73,000	23	1,281	—	4.8	5.1	14.1	12 U
796.8	843	2.42	346.1	708	1,846	772	11,055	405.1	1.1	2.6	5.9	3 L
647.6	866	2.96	107.0	843	964	876	13,217	147.3	0.7	1.0	11.9	3 L
1,087.9	790	1.76	423.3	657	2,122	732	5,407	393.7	0.6	1.1	2.7	3 L A
1,642.3	662	1.17	475.3	626	1,581	796	16,996	341.2	1.4	1.6	5.7	3 L A
1,188.5	761	1.61	370.1	690	3,174	589	5,416	783.3	0.9	1.4	4.6	3 L A
2,671.6	456	0.72	817.4	465	1,562	802	4,020	356.9	0.3	0.2	0.8	3 L

earnings. Liabilities can be estimated by deducting equity from assets. Market Capitalization is the total value of all shares of listed firms as of **Nov. 5**. Profit as % of Sales is usually called net profit margin. Profit as % of Assets, return on assets; Profit as % of Equity, return on equity. All money values are in US$. Currency conversion uses average **1996** rates (except for Market Cap.); for Australia, A$1.2773 per $1; China, RMB8.3142; Hong Kong, HK$7.80; India, Rs35.433; Indonesia, Rp2.342.3; Japan, ¥108.78; Malaysia, RM2.5159; New Zealand, NZ$1.453; Pakistan, Rs36.079; Philippines, Pesos 26.216; Singapore, S$1.41; South Korea, Won 804.45; Taiwan, NT$27.50; Thailand, Baht 25.343. NA not available. Values less than $50,000 appear as $0.0; those less than 0.05% as 0.0%. Market Capitalization from Datastream. More notes on pages 84 and 85.

Asia's Largest Companies By Sales

RANK 1997	RANK 1996	COMPANY NAME	COUNTRY	MAIN BUSINESS	SALES $ MILLION	%CHANGE	NET PROFIT $ MILLION	%CHANGE	RANK
691	655	RYOBI	JAPAN	METAL PRODUCTS	1,913.9	5.0	(34.7)	—	930
692	819	ARABIAN OIL	JAPAN	OIL EXPLORATION, REFINING	1,911.9	32.0	18.0	165.1	641
693	797	JAPAN OIL DEVELOPMENT	JAPAN	OIL DEVELOPMENT	1,908.8	26.8	17.2	—	658
694	643	NIPPON ROAD	JAPAN	CIVIL ENGINEERING	1,908.6	4.2	15.8	10.2	675
695	710	HANWHA CHEMICAL	SOUTH KOREA	PETROCHEMICALS	1,907.2	3.3	(31.9)	—	927
696	738	CHAIN STORE OKUWA	JAPAN	FOOD RETAILING	1,901.3	15.7	28.3	(9.9)	566
697	883	HOWARD SMITH	AUSTRALIA	TRANSPORT	1,895.2	12.0	99.8	47.9	279
698	721	MALAYSIA LNG	MALAYSIA	GAS	1,894.0	42.0	346.2	4.2	82
699	634	KIKKOMAN	JAPAN	SOY SAUCE	1,893.7	1.3	66.0	63.8	347
700	—	HINDUSTAN LEVER	INDIA	PERSONAL-CARE PRODUCTS	1,893.3	95.5	116.9	73.2	240
701	662	KAYABA INDUSTRY	JAPAN	HYDRAULIC EQUIPMENT	1,891.5	5.5	51.6	34.8	409
702	699	DUSKIN	JAPAN	HOUSEHOLD PRODUCTS	1,889.7	11.8	58.9	(2.3)	379
703	653	SONY MUSIC ENTERTAINMENT	JAPAN	SOFTWARE	1,886.7	4.3	117.8	27.3	238
704	673	MITSUBISHI ELECTRIC BLDG.	JAPAN	ELEVATOR MAINTENANCE	1,885.4	7.2	74.2	(20.8)	330
705	691	SHOWA SANGYO	JAPAN	FOOD PRODUCTS	1,883.1	10.2	(3.7)	—	890
706	690	FUJI CO.	JAPAN	SUPERMARKETS	1,882.5	9.9	14.0	15.8	684
707	669	TOKAI RIKA	JAPAN	CAR PARTS	1,882.5	5.9	20.0	6.1	629
708	821	ORIENT OVERSEAS	HONG KONG	SHIPPING	1,882.3	12.6	109.5	67.9	255
709	704	ASATSU	JAPAN	ADVERTISING	1,881.8	12.3	20.4	20.1	626
710	661	MATSUSHITA REFRIGN.	JAPAN	REFRIGERATORS	1,880.2	4.9	27.8	(18.7)	574
711	750	INCHON IRON & STEEL	SOUTH KOREA	STEEL	1,878.2	5.9	16.8	(42.7)	663
712	964	CITY DEVELOPMENTS	SINGAPORE	PROPERTY	1,874.9	34.1	379.7	33.8	75
713	720	SHELL CO. OF THAILAND	THAILAND	OIL REFINING, DISTRIBUTION	1,872.6	8.7	52.7	12.9	404
714	633	KODANSHA	JAPAN	PUBLISHING	1,866.8	(0.1)	49.7	(15.9)	417
715	660	NISSAN CONSTRUCTION	JAPAN	CONSTRUCTION	1,855.4	3.3	1.9	(80.1)	847
716	796	SAMSUNG ELECTRO-MECH.	SOUTH KOREA	ELECTRONIC PARTS	1,851.5	10.9	43.0	0.4	455
717	562	TOKAI KOGYO	JAPAN	CONSTRUCTION	1,849.2	(12.1)	(36.0)	—	931
718	696	SHIMADZU	JAPAN	SCIENTIFIC INSTRUMENTS	1,849.1	8.8	29.3	77.1	556
719	778	CHINA AIRLINES	TAIWAN	AIR TRANSPORT	1,845.3	7.5	57.8	29.7	383
720	645	GUNZE	JAPAN	UNDERGARMENTS	1,841.7	1.1	32.0	25.2	522

Company ranking by sales. Key to notes: All data are for fiscal years that ended between July 1997 and June 1998, except for companies with an asterisk (*) in the Notes column, which denotes data from the previous accounting period. The numbers refer to the month the fiscal year ended: 1 for January; 2 February; 3 March; 4 April; 5 May; 6 June; 7 July; 8 August; 9 September; 10 October; 11 November; 12 December. The letters denote publicly listed (L), unlisted (U), and state-controlled (S) companies. Financial results incorporate those of subsidiaries. Sales also refers to turnover, gross income, or revenue. Net profit is computed after deducting tax and minority interests while excluding extraordinary items. % Change is from the previous year's result in local currency. Sales per $1 Assets is equivalent to sales-to-assets ratio. Equity is the sum of paid-up capital, reserves, and retained

Asia's Largest Companies by Sales

691 to 720

ASSETS $ MILLION	RANK	SALES PER $1 ASSETS	EQUITY $ MILLION	RANK	EMPLOYEES NUMBER	RANK	PROFIT PER EMPLOYEE	MARKET CAP. ($M)	PROFIT AS % OF SALES	ASSETS	EQUITY	NOTES (Key Below)
2,073.0	572	0.92	337.0	715	9,264	297	—	501.5	—	—	—	3 L
1,163.4	769	1.64	502.7	615	2,318	704	8,190	1,213.7	0.0	1.6	3.8	12 L
3,455.5	389	0.55	228.1	771	204	972	84,403	—	0.9	0.5	7.5	12 U A
1,577.4	677	1.21	562.2	575	2,206	724	7,143	190.3	0.8	0.0	2.8	3 L
3,207.2	404	0.59	805.1	472	4,798	466	—	291.2	—	—	—	12 L
1,115.3	779	1.70	531.5	598	2,777	649	10,206	537.9	1.5	2.5	5.3	2 L
1,092.5	786	1.73	598.8	557	11,517	248	8,662	1,505.9	5.3	9.1	16.7	6 L
1,530.3	679	1.24	867.3	440	779	904	444,414	—	18.3	22.6	39.9	3 U *
2,002.6	588	0.95	926.3	423	2,963	617	22,605	1,206.6	3.5	3.3	7.2	12 L
NA	—	—	NA	—	12,000	235	9,744	5,341.7	6.2	—	—	12 L
1,518.3	684	1.25	618.5	547	4,297	502	12,010	618.2	2.7	3.4	8.3	3 L
1,459.5	700	1.29	789.5	479	2,068	739	28,499	—	3.1	4.0	7.5	3 U
2,701.8	452	0.70	2,133.1	189	1,708	781	68,984	3,817.0	6.2	4.4	5.5	3 L
2,081.4	568	—	874.9	437	7,169	347	10,348	—	3.9	3.6	8.5	3 U A
1,659.1	657	1.14	539.8	592	1,454	821	—	348.6	—	—	—	3 L
1,034.7	798	1.82	381.2	683	2,210	723	6,776	447.0	0.8	1.4	3.9	2 L A
1,437.2	707	1.31	503.7	613	6,142	387	3,261	319.5	1.1	1.4	3.0	3 L
1,734.7	637	1.09	689.8	520	4,030	518	27,160	317.7	5.8	6.3	15.9	12 L
1,102.6	784	1.71	648.5	536	1,638	788	12,437	686.7	1.1	1.8	3.1	12 L
1,688.6	649	1.11	777.7	483	4,513	484	6,150	743.4	1.5	1.6	3.6	3 L
1,718.0	646	1.09	558.7	581	3,148	594	5,324	301.9	0.9	0.0	2.0	12 L
5,873.8	242	0.32	1,883.5	219	13,200	211	28,767	3,740.9	20.3	6.5	20.2	12 L
573.2	876	3.27	NA	—	1,000	870	52,717	—	2.8	9.2	—	12 U *
NA	—	—	NA	—	1,179	856	42,136	—	2.7	—	—	11 U A
1,654.3	658	1.12	213.2	782	1,933	760	961	148.0	0.1	0.1	0.9	3 L
2,239.0	533	0.83	836.1	455	10,519	267	4,182	527.3	2.4	1.0	5.3	12 L
3,690.0	370	0.50	(57.1)	908	1,540	807	—	—	—	—	—	10 U H
2,326.5	514	0.79	879.6	430	6,900	357	4,246	974.0	1.6	1.3	3.3	3 L
2,795.4	444	0.66	1,152.0	358	8,251	314	7,007	1,670.0	3.1	2.1	5.0	12 L
1,982.7	589	0.93	1,255.9	338	3,494	566	9,432	718.3	1.8	1.7	2.6	3 L

earnings. Liabilities can be estimated by deducting equity from assets. Market Capitalization is the total value of all shares of listed firms as of **Nov. 5**. Profit as % of Sales is usually called net profit margin. Profit as % of Assets, return on assets; Profit as % of Equity, return on equity. All money values are in US$. Currency conversion uses average **1996** rates (except for Market Cap.); for Australia, A$1.2773 per $1; China, RMB8.3142; Hong Kong, HK$7.80; India, Rs35.433; Indonesia, Rp2,342.3; Japan, ¥108.78; Malaysia, RM2.5159; New Zealand, NZ$1.453; Pakistan, Rs36.079; Philippines, Pesos 26.216; Singapore, S$1.41; South Korea, Won 804.45; Taiwan, NT$27.50; Thailand, Baht 25.343. NA not available. Values less than $50,000 appear as $0.0; those less than 0.05% as 0.0%. Market Capitalization from Datastream. More notes on pages 84 and 85.

Asia's Largest Companies By Sales

RANK 1997	RANK 1996	COMPANY NAME	COUNTRY	MAIN BUSINESS	SALES $ MILLION	%CHANGE	NET PROFIT $ MILLION	%CHANGE	RANK
721	584	BANDAI	JAPAN	TOYS, GAMES	1,841.3	(8.2)	(73.3)	—	946
722	686	WORLD	JAPAN	CLOTHING	1,834.1	6.6	33.1	(17.3)	521
723	723	PALTAC CORP.	JAPAN	COSMETICS TRADING	1,830.9	10.7	11.8	(11.1)	709
724	709	SEIBU OIL	JAPAN	OIL REFINING	1,827.7	9.7	18.0	(7.0)	643
725	641	YAKULT HONSHA	JAPAN	DAIRY PRODUCTS	1,827.4	(1.0)	64.4	(17.3)	357
726	879	PILIPINAS SHELL PETRO.	PHILIPPINES	OIL REFINING, DISTRIBUTION	1,825.9	19.3	96.1	48.7	284
727	713	M.I.M. HOLDINGS	AUSTRALIA	COPPER, LEAD, ZINC	1,824.8	(21.7)	48.1	(66.8)	427
728	791	PT INDOCEMENT TUNGGAL	INDONESIA	CEMENT, PROPERTY	1,823.5	8.3	235.4	15.9	127
729	631	UCC UESHIMA COFFEE	JAPAN	SOFT DRINKS	1,819.6	(2.8)	NA	—	—
730	648	CHUDENKO	JAPAN	ENGINEERING	1,816.0	0.1	108.1	(19.6)	260
731	945	ITOCHU AUSTRALIA	AUSTRALIA	GENERAL TRADING	1,812.1	17.4	5.1	18.6	801
732	779	NGK SPARK PLUG	JAPAN	CAR PARTS	1,808.2	17.5	83.9	72.9	312
733	715	SHIN-IDEMITSU	JAPAN	OIL-PRODUCTS TRADING	1,806.1	9.2	2.9	(65.5)	831
734	761	MARUBENI AUSTRALIA	AUSTRALIA	GENERAL TRADING	1,802.7	(6.1)	(8.7)	—	904
735	806	FUJITSU BUSINESS SYSTEMS	JAPAN	ELECTRONICS TRADING	1,800.9	22.4	19.3	99.6	634
736	674	MIZUNO	JAPAN	SPORTS EQUIPMENT	1,800.7	2.6	13.0	(23.9)	695
737	652	TAKARA SHUZO	JAPAN	LIQUOR	1,794.0	(0.9)	38.1	(28.4)	492
738	845	TATA IRON & STEEL	INDIA	STEEL	1,792.5	8.5	97.7	(17.7)	282
739	701	CENTRAL GLASS	JAPAN	GLASS, CHEMICALS	1,792.1	6.5	28.7	(28.8)	562
740	575	RECRUIT COSMOS	JAPAN	PROPERTY	1,790.0	(12.4)	7.4	23.2	770
741	802	LG CABLE	SOUTH KOREA	CABLE, WIRE	1,788.5	8.9	25.9	112.5	586
742	731	YAMATAKE-HONEYWELL	JAPAN	INDUSTRIAL MACHINERY	1,788.1	10.1	46.4	4.9	437
743	670	ZENCHIKU	JAPAN	MEAT TRADING	1,787.8	0.8	2.8	204.0	833
744	749	TOKYU AGENCY	JAPAN	ADVERTISING	1,778.3	11.1	4.5	4.1	812
745	781	HOYA	JAPAN	OPTICAL GLASS	1,777.9	15.7	140.7	38.4	208
746	687	MEIWA TRADING	JAPAN	CHEMICALS TRADING	1,775.9	3.3	(1.0)	—	884
747	—	YULON MOTOR	TAIWAN	CARS	1,771.7	25.0	57.2	—	386
748	900	SSANGYONG ENG. & CONST.	SOUTH KOREA	CONSTRUCTION	1,767.8	20.6	6.1	(78.6)	788
749	—	QILU PETROCHEMICAL	CHINA	CHEMICALS	1,767.1	4.5	18.1	(29.7)	653
750	734	SHOWA ALUMINUM CORP.	JAPAN	ALUMINUM PRODUCTS	1,763.7	8.9	37.7	70.9	495

Company ranking by sales. Key to notes: All data are for fiscal years that ended between July 1997 and June 1998, except for companies with an asterisk (*) in the Notes column, which denotes data from the previous accounting period. The numbers refer to the month the fiscal year ended: 1 for January; 2 February; 3 March; 4 April; 5 May; 6 June; 7 July; 8 August; 9 September; 10 October; 11 November; 12 December. The letters denote publicly listed (L), unlisted (U), and state-controlled (S) companies. Financial results incorporate those of subsidiaries. Sales also refers to turnover, gross income, or revenue. Net profit is computed after deducting tax and minority interests while excluding extraordinary items. % Change is from the previous year's result in local currency. Sales per $1 Assets is equivalent to sales-to-assets ratio. Equity is the sum of paid-up capital, reserves, and retained

Asia's Largest Companies by Sales

721 to 750

ASSETS $ MILLION	RANK	SALES PER $1 ASSETS	EQUITY $ MILLION	RANK	EMPLOYEES NUMBER	RANK	PROFIT PER EMPLOYEE	MARKET CAP. ($M)	PROFIT AS % OF SALES	ASSETS	EQUITY	NOTES (Key Below)
2,275.4	526	0.81	876.6	433	924	882	—	758.4	—	—	—	3 L
2,325.4	515	0.79	1,279.4	331	2,395	692	13,841	1,416.0	1.8	1.4	2.6	3 L
582.4	874	3.14	144.7	813	1,085	863	10,887	102.9	0.6	2.0	8.2	9 L
1,149.1	772	1.59	230.8	769	499	942	38,043	—	1.0	1.7	8.2	3 U A
2,502.5	489	0.73	1,804.2	230	2,836	638	22,697	1,413.6	3.5	2.6	3.6	3 L
1,189.4	760	1.54	650.3	535	1,100	862	87,386	—	5.3	8.1	14.8	12 U
3,802.6	363	0.48	1,754.2	236	8,000	322	6,019	1,463.6	2.6	1.3	2.7	6 L
3,333.0	395	0.55	853.5	448	29,670	88	7,936	1,380.2	12.9	7.1	27.6	12 L
NA	—	—	NA	—	2,562	666	—	—	—	—	—	3 U A
2,423.3	496	0.75	1,599.2	260	5,817	408	18,585	1,615.9	5.0	4.5	6.8	3 L
269.7	905	6.72	46.1	884	83	981	61,123	—	0.3	1.9	11.0	3 U
3,016.9	426	0.60	1,291.1	325	5,372	431	15,617	1,479.5	4.6	2.8	6.5	3 L
821.8	839	—	NA	—	1,448	823	1,987	—	0.2	0.4	—	3 U A
238.8	908	7.55	5.4	900	93	979	—	—	—	—	—	3 U
1,170.3	766	1.54	527.8	601	3,719	542	5,191	732.3	1.1	1.6	3.7	3 L S
2,324.4	516	0.77	921.4	424	3,714	543	3,505	551.1	0.7	0.6	1.4	3 L
1,320.4	733	1.36	558.2	582	2,054	742	18,533	982.1	2.1	2.9	6.8	3 L
2,721.3	451	0.66	1,121.6	366	75,010	22	1,303	1,506.3	5.5	3.6	8.7	3 L
2,059.2	576	0.87	527.5	603	1,980	754	14,509	434.5	1.6	1.4	5.4	3 L
4,575.8	303	0.39	791.8	478	555	932	13,284	149.9	0.4	0.2	0.9	3 L
1,527.6	681	1.17	380.0	684	5,425	426	4,782	259.9	1.5	1.7	6.8	12 L
1,783.3	624	1.00	986.2	406	6,986	354	6,639	1,145.4	2.6	2.6	4.7	3 L
891.8	825	2.00	217.9	780	915	884	3,054	171.8	0.2	0.3	1.3	3 L
NA	—	—	NA	—	1,074	866	4,151	—	0.3	—	—	3 U A
2,161.2	552	0.82	1,317.8	319	9,588	284	14,669	3,874.7	7.9	6.5	10.7	3 L
963.7	814	1.84	73.7	867	464	944	—	119.3	—	—	—	3 L A
1,632.9	666	1.09	635.3	544	2,555	667	22,388	1,951.6	3.2	3.5	9.0	12 L
2,128.2	558	0.83	293.6	733	2,731	655	2,248	—	0.3	0.3	2.1	12 U
NA	—	—	1,227.0	344	50,577	43	357	—	1.0	—	1.5	12 USG
1,907.9	598	0.92	411.7	660	3,026	611	12,459	963.6	2.1	1.0	9.2	3 L

earnings. Liabilities can be estimated by deducting equity from assets. Market Capitalization is the total value of all shares of listed firms as of **Nov. 5**. Profit as % of Sales is usually called net profit margin. Profit as % of Assets, return on assets; Profit as % of Equity, return on equity. All money values are in US$. Currency conversion uses average **1996** rates (except for Market Cap.); for Australia, A$1.2773 per $1; China, RMB8.3142; Hong Kong, HK$7.80; India, Rs35.433; Indonesia, Rp2.342.3; Japan, ¥108.78; Malaysia, RM2.5159; New Zealand, NZ$1.453; Pakistan, Rs36.079; Philippines, Pesos 26.216; Singapore, S$1.41; South Korea, Won 804.45; Taiwan, NT$27.50; Thailand, Baht 25.343. NA not available. Values less than $50,000 appear as $0.0; those less than 0.05% as 0.0%. Market Capitalization from Datastream. More notes on pages 84 and 85.

Asia's Largest Companies By Sales

RANK 1997	RANK 1996	COMPANY NAME	COUNTRY	MAIN BUSINESS	SALES $ MILLION	%CHANGE	NET PROFIT $ MILLION	%CHANGE	RANK
751	805	PFU	JAPAN	COMPUTERS	1,760.2	19.3	11.5	20.4	711
752	783	SOGO	JAPAN	DEPARTMENT STORES	1,759.7	14.6	1.9	(95.9)	845
753	727	SENKO	JAPAN	TRUCKING	1,757.4	7.4	21.5	5.5	615
754	679	GARUDA INDONESIA	INDONESIA	AIR TRANSPORT	1,755.2	NA	1.7	NA	852
755	658	JAPAN FREIGHT RAILWAY	JAPAN	RAIL TRANSPORT	1,754.9	(2.7)	17.4	169.8	657
756	684	SUMITOMO BAKELITE	JAPAN	MATERIALS, CHEMICALS	1,750.8	1.4	59.4	2.5	377
757	753	OKAMURA CORP.	JAPAN	OFFICE FURNITURE	1,749.5	10.5	10.7	(28.7)	725
758	708	KOKUSAI ELECTRIC	JAPAN	INFORMATION EQUIPMENT	1,747.2	4.8	62.3	6.1	364
759	762	BRIERLEY INVESTMENTS	NEW ZEALAND	HOTELS, INVESTMENT	1,740.0	(12.2)	214.1	0.3	140
760	756	ASAHI NATL. BROADCAST.	JAPAN	BROADCASTING	1,739.1	10.3	59.9	58.3	375
761	751	TAKISADA & CO.	JAPAN	TEXTILE TRADING	1,735.4	8.0	30.5	3.2	542
762	873	EMAIL	AUSTRALIA	APPLIANCES, FURNITURE	1,732.5	4.4	43.3	0.2	459
763	736	MORITANI & CO.	JAPAN	MACHINERY TRADING	1,729.7	9.8	15.4	11.7	679
764	681	DAIDO KOGYO	JAPAN	STEEL TRADING	1,726.0	(0.4)	1.7	(60.6)	850
765	769	NIPPON FLOUR MILLS	JAPAN	FLOUR MILLING	1,723.6	10.6	17.1	(32.4)	660
766	910	WAKACHIKU CONSTRUCTION	JAPAN	CIVIL ENGINEERING	1,721.9	31.6	10.4	(17.7)	730
767	716	KANSAI PAINT	JAPAN	PAINT	1,720.0	4.2	36.8	35.2	499
768	733	MINERALS & METALS TRDG.	INDIA	METALS TRADING	1,717.9	15.4	16.1	(15.3)	671
769	984	ESSO AUSTRALIA	AUSTRALIA	OIL AND GAS PRODUCTS	1,714.6	19.0	497.1	47.7	58
770	824	SSANGYONG CEMENT INDL.	SOUTH KOREA	CEMENT, CONCRETE	1,713.6	7.2	2.6	(90.4)	838
771	667	NIPPON PETROCHEMICALS	JAPAN	CHEMICALS	1,712.0	(3.7)	8.1	(72.2)	761
772	746	SENSHUKAI CO.	JAPAN	RETAILING	1,712.6	6.8	6.7	(60.9)	782
773	702	KYOKUTO BOEKI	JAPAN	MACHINERY TRADING	1,712.0	2.1	5.5	(11.7)	797
774	816	MAKITA	JAPAN	POWER TOOLS	1,712.0	17.2	74.5	18.1	329
775	815	UNI-CHARM CORP.	JAPAN	SANITARY-CARE PRODUCTS	1,708.0	16.9	79.7	23.5	320
776	707	CHUGAI PHARMACEUTICAL	JAPAN	PHARMACEUTICALS	1,706.7	2.3	106.4	17.9	265
777	728	ASIA PULP & PAPER	SINGAPORE	PULP, PAPER	1,705.1	(10.2)	150.9	(32.7)	195
778	695	OKURA PULP & PAPER	JAPAN	PAPER TRADING	1,698.1	(0.2)	5.5	(6.5)	798
779	803	TAIKISHA	JAPAN	ENGINEERING	1,696.8	14.7	32.8	2.9	523
780	911	BURNS, PHILP & CO.	AUSTRALIA	FOOD	1,696.4	(6.1)	(683.7)	—	975

Company ranking by sales. Key to notes: All data are for fiscal years that ended between July 1997 and June 1998, except for companies with an asterisk (*) in the Notes column, which denotes data from the previous accounting period. The numbers refer to the month the fiscal year ended: 1 for January; 2 February; 3 March; 4 April; 5 May; 6 June; 7 July; 8 August; 9 September; 10 October; 11 November; 12 December. The letters denote publicly listed (L), unlisted (U), and state-controlled (S) companies. Financial results incorporate those of subsidiaries. Sales also refers to turnover, gross income, or revenue. Net profit is computed after deducting tax and minority interests while excluding extraordinary items. % Change is from the previous year's result in local currency. Sales per $1 Assets is equivalent to sales-to-assets ratio. Equity is the sum of paid-up capital, reserves, and retained

Asia's Largest Companies by Sales

751 to 780

ASSETS $ MILLION	RANK	SALES PER $1 ASSETS	EQUITY $ MILLION	RANK	EMPLOYEES NUMBER	RANK	PROFIT PER EMPLOYEE	MARKET CAP. ($M)	PROFIT AS % OF SALES	ASSETS	EQUITY	NOTES (Key Below)
877.0	829	2.01	441.2	644	2,865	632	4,014	—	0.7	1.3	2.6	3 U A
3,381.6	392	0.52	373.1	688	2,509	672	773	305.3	0.1	0.1	0.5	2 L
1,398.0	718	1.26	473.2	628	4,522	482	4,753	295.2	1.2	1.5	4.5	3 L
1,810.2	621	0.97	565.4	574	14,187	196	118	—	0.1	0.1	0.3	12 U
2,531.1	483	0.69	NA	—	11,864	243	1,468	—	0.0	0.7	—	3 U A
2,097.3	564	0.83	809.9	468	2,258	713	26,317	1,646.6	3.4	2.8	7.3	3 L
1,899.4	601	0.92	561.4	579	2,911	625	3,666	493.8	0.6	0.6	1.9	3 L
1,245.8	747	1.40	629.7	546	4,258	504	14,625	1,118.2	3.6	4.0	9.9	3 L
5,728.2	247	0.30	3,108.6	133	16,000	178	13,380	2,091.7	12.3	3.7	6.9	6 L
NA	—	—	NA	—	1,335	834	44,842	—	3.4	—	—	3 U A
1,500.6	687	1.16	541.5	590	1,345	831	22,651	—	1.8	2.0	5.6	1 U A
1,205.4	754	1.44	567.1	572	10,600	265	4,082	779.6	2.5	3.6	7.6	3 L
1,114.6	780	1.55	217.9	779	800	901	19,248	—	0.9	1.4	7.1	3 U
NA	—	—	NA	—	391	954	4,350	98.4	0.1	—	—	3 U
1,185.8	762	1.45	566.3	573	1,934	759	8,827	464.8	0.0	1.4	3.0	3 L
1,765.8	631	0.98	392.1	675	1,545	805	6,712	209.4	0.6	0.6	2.6	3 L A
1,650.9	660	1.04	755.0	490	2,958	618	12,453	794.7	2.1	2.2	4.9	3 L
NA	—	—	179.3	799	3,246	586	4,965	—	0.9	—	8.0	3 U S*
2,787.1	447	0.62	NA	—	1,187	854	418,823	—	28.0	17.8	—	12 U
4,149.0	337	0.41	1,585.4	261	4,058	516	638	217.9	0.2	0.1	0.2	12 L
1,811.6	619	—	133.5	823	1,570	798	5,159	—	0.5	0.4	6.1	3 U A
1,168.2	767	1.47	588.3	563	1,195	852	5,593	297.3	0.4	0.6	1.1	3 L
519.7	885	3.29	145.6	812	572	930	9,595	75.8	0.3	1.1	3.8	3 L
3,160.0	410	0.54	1,918.8	208	17,444	162	4,271	2,219.8	4.4	2.4	3.9	3 L
1,484.0	690	1.15	764.7	488	1,463	820	54,453	2,456.7	4.7	5.4	10.4	3 L
2,948.1	431	0.58	1,280.4	330	4,808	463	22,131	1,888.1	6.2	3.6	8.3	3 L
9,888.7	146	0.17	1,897.2	217	46,700	51	3,231	2,512.5	8.8	1.5	7.0	12 L
NA	—	—	NA	—	506	941	10,773	—	0.3	—	—	12 U A
1,480.7	692	1.15	447.6	640	1,955	755	16,763	495.8	1.9	2.2	7.3	3 L
1,722.7	644	0.98	239.9	763	10,093	274	—	145.5	—	—	—	6 L

earnings. Liabilities can be estimated by deducting equity from assets. Market Capitalization is the total value of all shares of listed firms as of **Nov. 5**. Profit as % of Sales is usually called net profit margin. Profit as % of Assets, return on assets; Profit as % of Equity, return on equity. All money values are in US$. Currency conversion uses average **1996** rates (except for Market Cap.); for Australia, A$1.2773 per $1; China, RMB8.3142; Hong Kong, HK$7.80; India, Rs35.433; Indonesia, Rp2.342.3; Japan, ¥108.78; Malaysia, RM2.5159; New Zealand, NZ$1.453; Pakistan, Rs36.079; Philippines, Pesos 26.216; Singapore, S$1.41; South Korea, Won 804.45; Taiwan, NT$27.50; Thailand, Baht 25.343. NA not available. Values less than $50,000 appear as $0.0; those less than 0.05% as 0.0%. Market Capitalization from Datastream. More notes on pages 84 and 85.

# Asia's Top 1000 Blue-Chip Companies

Asia's Largest Companies By Sales

RANK 1997	RANK 1996	COMPANY NAME	COUNTRY	MAIN BUSINESS	SALES $ MILLION	%CHANGE	NET PROFIT $ MILLION	%CHANGE	RANK
781	717	SAGAMI RAILWAY	JAPAN	PROPERTY, TRANSPORT	1,696.2	2.8	16.4	(17.1)	667
782	703	HOUSE FOODS	JAPAN	SPICES	1,695.6	1.2	72.8	(3.8)	334
783	804	TOYODA MACHINE WORKS	JAPAN	CAR PARTS, MACHINE TOOLS	1,695.1	14.9	37.8	34.5	493
784	885	CHEUNG KONG	HONG KONG	PROPERTY, INVESTMENT	1,692.6	7.3	1,570.6	10.1	8
785	789	NAKANO VINEGAR	JAPAN	VINEGAR, SEASONING	1,692.4	2.1	NA	—	—
786	767	FANUC	JAPAN	MACHINERY, ROBOTS	1,688.0	8.3	280.3	17.3	105
787	743	KYOKUYO	JAPAN	FISHING	1,688.2	4.8	2.2	—	843
788	—	CHINA NATIONAL OFFSHORE OIL	CHINA	OIL	1,680.7	68.2	382.5	270.7	73
789	771	MITSUBISHI PLASTICS	JAPAN	BUILDING MATERIALS	1,679.8	7.0	25.5	154.0	591
790	902	LEND LEASE	AUSTRALIA	PROPERTY, FINANCE	1,677.5	4.1	252.1	15.0	119
791	793	CLARION	JAPAN	CONSUMER ELECTRONICS	1,675.6	10.7	13.9	—	691
792	768	DAIKO ADVERTISING	JAPAN	ADVERTISING	1,673.4	7.3	2.4	392.3	841
793	760	SAN-AI OIL	JAPAN	OIL-PRODUCTS TRADING	1,670.9	6.1	0.2	(98.2)	876
794	—	EVERGREEN MARINE	TAIWAN	SHIPPING	1,667.6	9.0	117.0	1.4	239
795	831	HITACHI MAXELL	JAPAN	MAGNETIC TAPE, DISKS	1,664.4	16.8	52.3	23.8	406
796	757	ORIENTAL LAND	JAPAN	LEISURE-PARK OPERATOR	1,663.6	5.5	146.2	8.3	196
797	775	S X L	JAPAN	CONSTRUCTION	1,660.3	7.1	30.0	22.6	539
798	864	HITACHI BUILDING SYSTEMS	JAPAN	ELEVATORS	1,656.9	19.8	NA	—	—
799	722	TAISEI ROTEC	JAPAN	CONSTRUCTION	1,655.1	0.7	10.9	(26.2)	722
800	870	I.T.C.	INDIA	TOBACCO	1,654.6	14.6	97.9	32.9	281
801	898	KASHO	JAPAN	GENERAL TRADING	1,653.4	24.8	5.4	(7.6)	799
802	790	SUZUYO SHOJI	JAPAN	OIL-PRODUCTS TRADING	1,651.6	8.5	1.2	(51.9)	860
803	—	TELEPHONE ORGANIZATION	THAILAND	TELECOMMUNICATIONS	1,650.6	20.6	830.4	36.2	24
804	795	STANLEY ELECTRIC	JAPAN	CAR PARTS	1,647.6	9.3	20.7	146.4	620
805	818	NIPPON ZEON	JAPAN	SYNTHETIC RUBBER	1,645.6	12.9	42.2	39.9	465
806	745	YODOGAWA STEEL WORKS	JAPAN	STEEL SHEETS	1,641.8	2.3	45.2	(20.1)	442
807	597	DONGFENG MOTORS CORP.	CHINA	CARS	1,639.0	(28.9)	46.7	NA	434
808	933	SINGAPORE POOLS	SINGAPORE	LOTTERY	1,639.4	11.0	53.4	(21.5)	400
809	763	TOSHIBA LIGHTING & TECH.	JAPAN	APPLIANCES, ELECTRONICS	1,638.2	4.7	NA	—	—
810	968	CITIC PACIFIC	HONG KONG	TRADING, INFRASTRUCTURE	1,635.4	17.7	456.7	18.9	62

Company ranking by sales. Key to notes: All data are for fiscal years that ended between July 1997 and June 1998, except for companies with an asterisk (*) in the Notes column, which denotes data from the previous accounting period. The numbers refer to the month the fiscal year ended: 1 for January; 2 February; 3 March; 4 April; 5 May; 6 June; 7 July; 8 August; 9 September; 10 October; 11 November; 12 December. The letters denote publicly listed (L), unlisted (U), and state-controlled (S) companies. Financial results incorporate those of subsidiaries. Sales also refers to turnover, gross income, or revenue. Net profit is computed after deducting tax and minority interests while excluding extraordinary items. % Change is from the previous year's result in local currency. Sales per $1 Assets is equivalent to sales-to-assets ratio. Equity is the sum of paid-up capital, reserves, and retained

Asia's Largest Companies by Sales

781 to 810

ASSETS $ MILLION	RANK	SALES PER $1 ASSETS	EQUITY $ MILLION	RANK	EMPLOYEES NUMBER	RANK	PROFIT PER EMPLOYEE	MARKET CAP. ($M)	PROFIT AS % OF SALES	ASSETS	EQUITY	NOTES (Key Below)
4,875.9	285	0.35	606.2	555	2,362	697	6,963	1,170.3	0.0	0.3	2.7	3 L
2,011.2	585	0.84	1,391.3	302	3,054	607	23,843	1,922.1	4.3	3.6	5.2	3 L
1,681.3	652	1.01	871.6	439	4,381	496	8,639	1,210.7	2.2	2.3	4.3	3 L
12,283.8	117	0.14	8,790.1	31	3,820	536	411,163	15,899.0	92.8	12.8	17.9	12 L
NA	—	—	NA	—	2,500	677	—	—	—	—	—	11 U
5,191.1	270	0.33	4,652.1	77	2,143	730	130,802	9,553.9	16.6	5.4	6.0	3 L
605.7	873	2.79	89.9	854	729	910	2,976	194.1	0.1	0.4	2.4	3 L A
3,796.4	364	0.44	1,732.2	242	28,105	97	13,608	—	22.8	10.1	22.1	12 U S G
1,808.4	622	0.93	473.7	627	2,442	685	10,461	449.0	1.5	1.4	5.4	3 L
3,659.1	373	0.46	2,285.6	178	6,736	360	37,425	5,048.5	15.0	6.9	11.0	6 L
1,640.5	663	1.02	314.3	727	11,600	246	1,198	514.2	0.8	0.8	4.4	3 L
645.9	867	2.59	92.0	851	1,388	827	1,696	—	0.1	0.4	2.6	3 U
1,041.0	795	1.60	303.1	731	895	889	195	236.9	0.0	0.0	0.1	3 L
2,330.1	512	0.72	1,123.0	365	1,393	826	84,021	1,850.1	7.0	5.0	10.4	12 L
2,301.2	521	0.72	1,738.5	241	4,955	452	10,545	2,309.7	3.1	2.3	3.0	3 L
3,267.5	398	—	2,643.8	152	2,405	689	60,784	—	8.8	4.5	5.5	3 L A
2,569.7	478	0.65	765.0	487	2,279	711	13,598	305.7	1.9	1.2	4.1	3 L
1,829.5	615	0.91	46.9	882	5,480	423	—	—	—	—	—	3 U A
1,293.0	737	1.28	440.2	645	1,859	769	5,870	194.2	0.7	0.8	2.5	3 L A
860.2	831	1.92	383.6	681	12,000	236	8,159	3,741.1	5.9	11.4	25.5	3 L
701.1	856	2.36	91.0	852	455	945	11,961	300.0	0.3	0.8	5.9	3 L
NA	—	—	NA	—	545	936	2,142	—	0.1	—	—	8 U A
8,064.8	173	0.20	5,830.9	60	26,248	110	31,638	—	50.3	10.3	14.2	9 U S
1,743.5	633	0.94	913.8	426	17,910	161	1,155	731.3	1.3	1.2	2.3	3 L
1,949.2	592	0.84	521.1	606	3,456	568	12,199	853.1	2.6	2.2	8.1	3 L
2,156.7	553	0.76	1,234.7	342	1,920	762	23,557	1,201.6	2.8	2.1	3.7	3 L
NA	—	—	1,646.9	255	149,233	14	313	—	2.8	—	2.8	12 U S T
381.3	896	4.30	238.5	765	157	974	340,048	—	3.3	14.0	22.4	3 U
874.2	830	1.87	66.2	870	3,600	555	—	—	—	—	—	3 U A
6,405.0	222	0.26	4,683.1	75	11,750	245	38,865	9,436.4	27.9	7.1	9.8	12 L

earnings. Liabilities can be estimated by deducting equity from assets. Market Capitalization is the total value of all shares of listed firms as of **Nov. 5**. Profit as % of Sales is usually called net profit margin. Profit as % of Assets, return on assets; Profit as % of Equity, return on equity. All money values are in US$. Currency conversion uses average **1996** rates (except for Market Cap.); for Australia, A$1.2773 per $1; China, RMB8.3142; Hong Kong, HK$7.80; India, Rs35.433; Indonesia, Rp2.342.3; Japan, ¥108.78; Malaysia, RM2.5159; New Zealand, NZ$1.453; Pakistan, Rs36.079; Philippines, Pesos 26.216; Singapore, S$1.41; South Korea, Won 804.45; Taiwan, NT$27.50; Thailand, Baht 25.343. NA not available. Values less than $50,000 appear as $0.0; those less than 0.05% as 0.0%. Market Capitalization from Datastream. More notes on pages 84 and 85.

Asia's Largest Companies By Sales

RANK 1997	RANK 1996	COMPANY NAME	COUNTRY	MAIN BUSINESS	SALES $ MILLION	%CHANGE	NET PROFIT $ MILLION	%CHANGE	RANK
811	559	SEIKA	JAPAN	MACHINERY TRADING	1,632.2	(22.7)	12.2	41.4	707
812	765	CHUNICHI SHIMBUN	JAPAN	NEWSPAPER PUBLISHING	1,628.2	4.1	52.2	22.5	407
813	925	MARUTI UDYOG	INDIA	CARS	1,626.8	20.9	143.0	19.3	201
814	835	KATOKICHI	JAPAN	FROZEN FOODS	1,625.3	14.3	22.2	—	611
815	732	KYUSHU RAILWAY	JAPAN	RAIL TRANSPORT	1,624.7	0.1	9.2	133.9	747
816	958	MITSUBISHI MOTORS AUST.	AUSTRALIA	CAR ASSEMBLY, SALES	1,624.6	9.7	(51.5)	—	941
817	770	ARAI-GUMI	JAPAN	CONSTRUCTION	1,621.4	4.1	(3.8)	—	891
818	890	NEW ZEALAND DAIRY GROUP	NEW ZEALAND	DAIRY PRODUCTS	1,613.2	(0.2)	(0.0)	—	877
819	773	AICHI TOYOTA MOTOR	JAPAN	CAR DEALERSHIP	1,612.2	3.8	16.5	7.2	665
820	766	JS CORP.	JAPAN	PROPERTY	1,611.9	3.2	20.6	(51.1)	622
821	932	BHARAT HEAVY ELECTRICALS	INDIA	ENGINEERING	1,610.6	7.7	130.7	18.6	216
822	838	TOHOKU OIL	JAPAN	OIL REFINING	1,608.1	13.4	(2.7)	—	888
823	787	MAINICHI NEWSPAPERS	JAPAN	NEWSPAPER PUBLISHING	1,607.0	5.3	3.5	291.8	823
824	853	AUSTRALIAN NATIONAL IND.	AUSTRALIA	METAL PRODUCTS	1,606.6	4.2	24.4	—	600
825	772	SHOWA ELEC. WIRE & CABLE	JAPAN	CABLE, WIRE	1,606.4	3.4	(11.6)	—	906
826	748	NANKAI ELECTRIC RAILWAY	JAPAN	RAIL TRANSPORT	1,604.6	0.3	32.1	196.2	529
827	—	LI & FUNG	HONG KONG	TRADING	1,604.4	35.8	38.5	33.3	489
828	812	KURIMOTO	JAPAN	METAL PRODUCTS	1,600.5	9.2	41.3	(2.2)	476
829	693	JAPAN ATOMIC POWER	JAPAN	POWER GENERATION	1,598.8	(6.2)	9.7	(17.1)	737
830	938	ENERGYAUSTRALIA	AUSTRALIA	POWER GENERATION	1,598.7	(2.3)	155.0	—	189
831	830	FORMOSA PLASTICS	TAIWAN	PLASTICS	1,596.8	0.4	221.9	11.7	136
832	799	TOYOSHIMA & CO.	JAPAN	TEXTILE TRADING	1,590.3	6.2	7.4	34.4	769
833	915	MANDO MACHINERY	SOUTH KOREA	CAR PARTS	1,587.9	11.0	38.1	(22.7)	491
834	951	BMW JAPAN	JAPAN	CAR DEALERSHIP	1,586.7	3.7	NA	—	—
835	776	TONEN CHEMICAL	JAPAN	PETROCHEMICALS	1,586.3	2.3	11.5	(88.7)	715
836	928	IBM AUSTRALIA	AUSTRALIA	COMPUTERS	1,585.6	2.4	69.1	(1.8)	342
837	930	NATSTEEL	SINGAPORE	BUILDING MATERIALS	1,583.1	7.8	39.2	29.6	485
838	844	KURITA WATER INDUSTRIES	JAPAN	WATER-TREATMENT EQUIP.	1,577.4	11.9	116.3	1.7	243
839	897	QUEENSLAND SUGAR CORP.	AUSTRALIA	SUGAR	1,571.0	(2.8)	(7.3)	—	899
840	850	ASAHI KASEI HOMES	JAPAN	CONSTRUCTION	1,570.8	11.8	5.6	22.4	795

Company ranking by sales. Key to notes: All data are for fiscal years that ended between July 1997 and June 1998, except for companies with an asterisk (*) in the Notes column, which denotes data from the previous accounting period. The numbers refer to the month the fiscal year ended: 1 for January; 2 February; 3 March; 4 April; 5 May; 6 June; 7 July; 8 August; 9 September; 10 October; 11 November; 12 December. The letters denote publicly listed (L), unlisted (U), and state-controlled (S) companies. Financial results incorporate those of subsidiaries. Sales also refers to turnover, gross income, or revenue. Net profit is computed after deducting tax and minority interests while excluding extraordinary items. % Change is from the previous year's result in local currency. Sales per $1 Assets is equivalent to sales-to-assets ratio. Equity is the sum of paid-up capital, reserves, and retained

Asia's Largest Companies by Sales

811 to 840

ASSETS $ MILLION	RANK	SALES PER $1 ASSETS	EQUITY $ MILLION	RANK	EMPLOYEES NUMBER	RANK	PROFIT PER EMPLOYEE	MARKET CAP. ($M)	PROFIT AS % OF SALES	ASSETS	EQUITY	NOTES (Key Below)
667.1	863	2.45	176.5	801	349	959	34,901	193.0	0.7	1.8	6.9	3 L
1,424.3	714	1.14	379.4	685	3,870	532	13,476	—	3.2	3.7	13.7	3 U A
827.5	834	1.97	427.0	652	5,324	434	27,040	—	8.8	17.4	33.6	3 U S
2,211.0	540	0.74	807.1	470	4,315	499	5,151	819.6	1.4	1.0	2.8	11 L
NA	—	—	NA	—	13,020	212	707	—	0.6	—	—	3 U A
931.6	820	1.74	62.1	873	4,000	519	—	—	—	—	—	12 U
2,344.3	510	0.69	169.6	806	1,779	777	—	75.5	—	—	—	12 L
902.9	822	1.79	527.6	602	3,126	599	—	—	—	—	—	5 U
954.7	816	1.69	347.9	706	2,247	716	7,344	314.4	1.0	1.7	4.7	3 L A
NA	—	—	NA	—	2,087	737	9,862	—	1.3	—	—	3 U A
NA	—	—	NA	—	68,932	26	1,896	244.3	8.1	—	—	3 L S
NA	—	—	NA	—	385	956	—	—	—	—	—	3 U A
1,478.9	693	1.09	58.1	877	3,902	528	905	—	0.2	0.2	6.1	3 U A
1,215.5	751	1.32	532.5	596	7,500	339	3,257	814.9	1.5	2.0	4.6	6 L
1,856.5	607	0.87	559.5	580	2,507	674	—	473.0	—	—	—	3 L
6,079.4	233	0.26	1,103.5	370	4,690	471	6,839	2,323.4	1.0	0.5	2.9	3 L
373.2	898	4.30	116.9	836	2,300	709	16,722	738.5	2.4	10.3	32.9	12 L
2,078.1	570	0.77	1,004.8	400	3,141	596	13,150	800.7	2.6	1.0	4.1	3 L
NA	—	—	NA	—	1,599	794	6,037	—	0.6	—	—	3 U A
2,826.3	441	0.57	1,194.7	349	3,136	597	49,431	—	9.7	5.5	12.0	6 U S
2,534.1	481	0.63	1,456.6	288	3,449	569	64,349	4,443.2	13.9	8.8	15.2	12 L
NA	—	—	NA	—	425	949	17,499	—	0.5	—	—	6 U*A
1,693.8	648	0.94	334.0	717	8,091	320	4,715	204.8	2.4	2.3	11.4	12 L
NA	—	—	NA	—	670	915	—	—	—	—	—	12 U A
1,333.7	732	1.19	468.8	632	1,338	833	8,561	—	0.7	0.9	2.4	12 U A
985.9	808	1.61	222.9	774	2,800	642	24,675	—	4.4	7.0	30.0	12 U
1,467.2	697	1.08	492.6	617	15,501	181	2,532	617.8	2.5	2.7	7.0	12 L
1,527.6	682	1.03	905.3	427	1,481	818	78,552	2,275.2	7.4	7.6	12.9	3 L
518.0	886	3.03	278.8	740	209	971	—	—	—	—	—	6 U S*
NA	—	—	NA	—	2,628	660	2,123	—	0.4	—	—	3 U A

earnings. Liabilities can be estimated by deducting equity from assets. Market Capitalization is the total value of all shares of listed firms as of **Nov. 5**. Profit as % of Sales is usually called net profit margin. Profit as % of Assets, return on assets; Profit as % of Equity, return on equity. All money values are in US$. Currency conversion uses average **1996** rates (except for Market Cap.); for Australia, A$1.2773 per $1; China, RMB8.3142; Hong Kong, HK$7.80; India, Rs35.433; Indonesia, Rp2,342.3; Japan, ¥108.78; Malaysia, RM2.5159; New Zealand, NZ$1.453; Pakistan, Rs36.079; Philippines, Pesos 26.216; Singapore, S$1.41; South Korea, Won 804.45; Taiwan, NT$27.50; Thailand, Baht 25.343. NA not available. Values less than $50,000 appear as $0.0; those less than 0.05% as 0.0%. Market Capitalization from Datastream. More notes on pages 84 and 85.

Asia's Largest Companies By Sales

RANK 1997	RANK 1996	COMPANY NAME	COUNTRY	MAIN BUSINESS	SALES $ MILLION	%CHANGE	NET PROFIT $ MILLION	%CHANGE	RANK
841	808	SHINMAYWA INDUSTRIES	JAPAN	HEAVY VEHICLES, AIRCRAFT	1,570.6	6.9	15.5	(28.9)	678
842	680	MOTOROLA ELECTRONICS	SINGAPORE	COMMUNICATIONS	1,569.6	(22.2)	250.4	(13.0)	121
843	755	MARUTOMI GROUP	JAPAN	SHOE RETAILING	1,565.3	(0.8)	1.1	(73.5)	861
844	813	INABA DENKISANGYO	JAPAN	ELECTRICAL-EQUIP. TRADING	1,564.9	6.9	34.3	11.7	514
845	881	FUSHUN PETROCHEMICAL	CHINA	CHEMICALS	1,563.6	35.6	204.5	NA	145
846	825	DAIHO CORPORATION	JAPAN	CIVIL ENGINEERING	1,563.4	8.8	15.8	2.9	674
847	725	FUJITSU GENERAL	JAPAN	CONSUMER ELECTRONICS	1,559.6	(4.1)	30.0	(19.0)	548
848	786	AOYAMA TRADING	JAPAN	CLOTHES RETAILING	1,557.0	1.8	103.0	2.6	273
849	719	SHUEISHA	JAPAN	PUBLISHING	1,556.4	(5.5)	NA	—	—
850	817	FURUKAWA CO.	JAPAN	INDUSTRIAL MACHINERY	1,553.4	6.3	14.9	(79.2)	685
851	955	PETRONAS DAGANGAN	MALAYSIA	OIL MARKETING	1,549.3	10.2	62.7	1.2	361
852	814	WACOAL	JAPAN	UNDERGARMENTS	1,547.4	5.8	67.4	1.5	346
853	860	DAISUE CONSTRUCTION	JAPAN	CONSTRUCTION	1,546.9	11.2	(33.7)	—	929
854	801	AICHI STEEL WORKS	JAPAN	STEEL	1,539.7	3.3	10.9	38.5	721
855	754	DAIKUMA	JAPAN	DISCOUNT STORES	1,533.5	(3.1)	17.0	(21.0)	654
856	855	SUMITOMO AUSTRALIA	AUSTRALIA	GENERAL TRADING	1,526.7	(11.6)	2.2	—	842
857	784	OKAMOTO	JAPAN	PAPER TRADING	1,526.5	(0.5)	7.8	(40.3)	762
858	862	SUMITOMO COAL MINING	JAPAN	BUILDING MATERIALS, COAL	1,525.6	10.0	2.8	—	832
859	—	OHMOTO GUMI	JAPAN	CONSTRUCTION	1,522.0	32.4	36.6	37.2	503
860	794	MITSUBISHI LOGISTICS	JAPAN	TRANSPORT, PROPERTY	1,520.5	0.8	62.1	(5.1)	365
861	962	KUMHO TIRE	SOUTH KOREA	TIRES	1,518.2	13.1	7.7	—	764
862	903	FORMOSA CHEM. & FIBRE	TAIWAN	TEXTILES	1,517.4	3.2	125.6	3.1	221
863	834	SUMITOMO DENSETSU	JAPAN	ELECTRICAL ENGINEERING	1,512.0	6.3	3.8	(63.3)	819
864	800	TOKYO SEIKA	JAPAN	FOOD TRADING	1,511.5	1.4	7.3	(3.5)	771
865	972	MMC SITTIPOL	THAILAND	CAR ASSEMBLY, SALES	1,510.7	11.0	0.2	(97.6)	874
866	—	PACIFIC PETROLEUM & TRADING	JAPAN	OIL TRADING	1,506.3	155.5	0.6	—	868
867	782	SEIYU FOODS	JAPAN	SUPERMARKETS	1,504.7	(2.0)	1.0	(39.4)	863
868	839	SOGO KEIBI HOSHO	JAPAN	SECURITY SYSTEMS	1,501.4	6.1	39.9	16.5	482
869	854	TATEYAMA ALUMINIUM IND.	JAPAN	BUILDING MATERIALS	1,500.9	7.2	0.8	—	865
870	983	ASIANA AIRLINES	SOUTH KOREA	AIR TRANSPORT	1,498.5	14.4	(67.2)	—	944

Company ranking by sales. Key to notes: All data are for fiscal years that ended between July 1997 and June 1998, except for companies with an asterisk (*) in the Notes column, which denotes data from the previous accounting period. The numbers refer to the month the fiscal year ended: 1 for January; 2 February; 3 March; 4 April; 5 May; 6 June; 7 July; 8 August; 9 September; 10 October; 11 November; 12 December. The letters denote publicly listed (L), unlisted (U), and state-controlled (S) companies. Financial results incorporate those of subsidiaries. Sales also refers to turnover, gross income, or revenue. Net profit is computed after deducting tax and minority interests while excluding extraordinary items. % Change is from the previous year's result in local currency. Sales per $1 Assets is equivalent to sales-to-assets ratio. Equity is the sum of paid-up capital, reserves, and retained

Asia's Largest Companies by Sales

841 to 870

ASSETS $ MILLION	RANK	SALES PER $1 ASSETS	EQUITY $ MILLION	RANK	EMPLOYEES NUMBER	RANK	PROFIT PER EMPLOYEE	MARKET CAP. ($M)	PROFIT AS % OF SALES	ASSETS	EQUITY	NOTES (Key Below)
1,760.7	632	0.89	817.5	464	2,748	652	5,633	421.5	0.0	0.9	1.9	3 L
1,472.1	695	1.07	1,438.6	292	4,500	486	55,651	—	15.0	17.0	17.4	12 U
1,038.6	796	1.51	208.0	784	2,624	662	427	51.5	0.1	0.1	0.5	2 L A
1,014.3	802	1.54	409.2	663	1,020	869	33,590	319.8	2.2	3.4	8.4	3 L A
NA	—	—	NA	—	60,000	35	3,408	—	13.1	—	—	12 U S*
1,450.0	703	1.08	244.1	759	1,682	784	9,368	149.1	1.0	1.1	6.5	3 L A
1,167.4	768	1.34	122.2	831	6,500	371	4,618	449.8	1.9	2.6	24.6	3 L
3,162.2	409	0.49	1,974.5	204	3,294	584	31,276	2,012.0	6.6	3.3	5.2	3 L A
NA	—	—	NA	—	723	911	—	—	—	—	—	5 U* A
2,213.5	539	0.70	615.7	548	2,217	718	6,705	521.7	0.0	0.7	2.4	3 L
670.8	861	2.31	319.2	725	1,605	792	39,086	557.4	4.1	9.4	19.7	3 L
1,820.1	617	0.85	1,353.1	311	5,061	446	13,325	1,672.2	4.4	3.7	4.0	3 L
1,775.0	628	0.87	127.5	828	1,342	832	—	110.2	—	—	—	3 L A
1,620.2	669	0.95	894.2	428	3,222	587	3,390:	491.5	0.7	0.7	1.2	3 L
512.7	887	—	378.8	686	2,390	693	7,524	—	1.2	3.5	4.7	2 U A
142.1	913	10.75	13.9	899	45	983	48,453	—	0.1	1.5	15.6	12 U
621.2	870	2.46	117.4	835	506	940	15,497	—	0.5	1.3	6.7	4 U A
1,856.3	608	0.82	(43.8)	907	807	898	3,520	134.4	0.2	0.2	—	3 L H
1,430.9	711	1.06	486.1	623	1,446	824	25,315	—	2.4	2.6	7.5	3 L
2,649.2	464	0.57	990.3	405	2,757	651	22,524	1,800.2	4.1	2.3	6.3	3 L U
2,059.0	577	0.74	329.7	718	6,227	384	1,243	152.1	0.5	0.4	2.3	12 L
2,654.8	461	0.57	1,493.3	280	7,739	334	16,229	2,424.8	8.3	4.7	8.4	12 L
1,184.7	763	1.28	243.0	760	2,066	741	1,842	223.8	0.3	0.3	1.6	3 L
NA	—	—	NA	—	546	935	13,352	—	0.5	—	—	3 U A
1,129.9	777	1.34	77.9	864	2,500	676	92	—	0.0	0.0	0.3	12 U
248.7	907	6.06	72.2	868	27	985	21,450	—	0.0	0.2	0.8	12 U A V
NA	—	—	NA	—	2,095	735	478	—	0.1	—	—	2 U A
1,420.8	715	1.06	486.8	622	14,260	195	2,798	—	2.7	2.8	8.2	3 U A
1,352.5	728	1.11	203.7	786	3,357	579	225	241.3	0.1	0.1	0.4	3 L
2,801.9	443	0.53	25.2	896	6,211	385	—	—	—	—	—	12 U

earnings. Liabilities can be estimated by deducting equity from assets. Market Capitalization is the total value of all shares of listed firms as of **Nov. 5**. Profit as % of Sales is usually called net profit margin. Profit as % of Assets, return on assets; Profit as % of Equity, return on equity. All money values are in US$. Currency conversion uses average **1996** rates (except for Market Cap.); for Australia, A$1.2773 per $1; China, RMB8.3142; Hong Kong, HK$7.80; India, Rs35.433; Indonesia, Rp2,342.3; Japan, ¥108.78; Malaysia, RM2.5159; New Zealand, NZ$1.453; Pakistan, Rs36.079; Philippines, Pesos 26.216; Singapore, S$1.41; South Korea, Won 804.45; Taiwan, NT$27.50; Thailand, Baht 25.343. NA not available. Values less than $50,000 appear as $0.0; those less than 0.05% as 0.0%. Market Capitalization from Datastream. More notes on pages 84 and 85.

Asia's Largest Companies By Sales

RANK 1997	RANK 1996	COMPANY NAME	COUNTRY	MAIN BUSINESS	SALES $ MILLION	%CHANGE	NET PROFIT $ MILLION	%CHANGE	RANK
871	848	NITTO BOSEKI	JAPAN	BUILDING MATERIALS	1,498.5	6.6	41.0	33.5	467
872	811	MITSUBISHI PAPER SALES	JAPAN	PAPER TRADING	1,498.3	2.2	5.1	28.0	800
873	—	HYOSUNG T&C CO.	SOUTH KOREA	TEXTILES	1,491.9	13.8	43.9	40.1	456
874	837	CHUGAI BOYEKI	JAPAN	CHEMICALS TRADING	1,491.2	5.1	3.7	22.1	821
875	823	INOAC	JAPAN	CAR PARTS	1,488.9	3.2	30.5	(9.8)	541
876	822	MITSUBISHI CONSTRUCTION	JAPAN	CONSTRUCTION	1,482.1	2.7	(31.5)	—	926
877	780	FORD LIO HO MOTOR	TAIWAN	CARS	1,479.0	(14.1)	NA	—	—
878	866	MARUICHI	JAPAN	FOOD TRADING	1,476.2	7.2	(0.6)	—	880
879	792	FUJI DENKI REIKI	JAPAN	EQUIPMENT TRADING	1,476.1	(2.6)	10.5	(34.4)	727
880	875	GUNZE SANGYO	JAPAN	TEXTILE TRADING	1,475.2	8.7	(19.8)	(52.7)	915
881	867	KINKI COCA-COLA BOTTLING	JAPAN	SOFT DRINKS	1,475.1	7.8	14.3	61.2	689
882	920	PROGRESSIVE ENTERPRISES	NEW ZEALAND	FOOD	1,474.9	2.3	2.5	(81.2)	839
883	807	FEDERAL FLOUR MILLS	MALAYSIA	FLOUR, ANIMAL FEED	1,473.5	(12.0)	45.6	(20.0)	441
884	869	HITACHI KOKI	JAPAN	POWER TOOLS, PRINTERS	1,471.7	7.9	12.5	29.1	703
885	989	VIDESH SANCHAR NIGAM	INDIA	TELECOMMUNICATIONS	1,468.3	16.3	144.4	20.6	200
886	809	UCHIDA YOKO	JAPAN	OFFICE-EQUIPMENT TRDG.	1,467.6	9.5	7.7	(9.2)	766
887	886	TOKYO STEEL MFG.	JAPAN	STEEL	1,467.4	9.5	(103.6)	—	953
888	950	PAKISTAN STATE OIL	PAKISTAN	OIL REFINING, DISTRIBUTION	1,467.1	7.6	41.5	43.9	473
889	—	SHOGAKUKAN	JAPAN	BOOK PUBLISHING	1,466.2	5.2	53.1	7.2	402
890	—	NOVARTIS JAPAN	JAPAN	PHARMACEUTICALS	1,465.3	NA	NA	—	—
891	820	SEIKO INSTRUMENTS	JAPAN	WATCHES	1,465.1	1.3	NA	—	—
892	—	UMW HOLDINGS	MALAYSIA	VEHICLE ASSEMBLY	1,462.1	25.8	92.9	140.3	291
893	828	NAVIX LINE	JAPAN	SHIPPING	1,459.5	1.8	31.5	297.5	535
894	832	YAGI & CO.	JAPAN	TEXTILE TRADING	1,458.8	2.4	6.5	(1.4)	784
895	858	TOKAI DENPUN	JAPAN	FOOD TRADING	1,457.0	4.6	10.9	70.1	723
896	852	NIPPON SHOKUBAI	JAPAN	CHEMICALS	1,456.7	3.8	50.5	(2.0)	415
897	895	TOPPAN FORMS	JAPAN	PRINTING	1,456.1	9.6	43.5	243.4	458
898	829	ITOKIN	JAPAN	CLOTHING	1,454.7	1.5	18.9	44.1	646
899	—	CONAGRA HOLDINGS (AUST.)	AUSTRALIA	MEAT	1,450.7	(2.5)	(29.5)	—	924
900	846	TOAGOSEI	JAPAN	CHEMICALS	1,449.4	2.0	29.6	(5.3)	550

Company ranking by sales. Key to notes: All data are for fiscal years that ended between July 1997 and June 1998, except for companies with an asterisk (*) in the Notes column, which denotes data from the previous accounting period. The numbers refer to the month the fiscal year ended: 1 for January; 2 February; 3 March; 4 April; 5 May; 6 June; 7 July; 8 August; 9 September; 10 October; 11 November; 12 December. The letters denote publicly listed (L), unlisted (U), and state-controlled (S) companies. Financial results incorporate those of subsidiaries. Sales also refers to turnover, gross income, or revenue. Net profit is computed after deducting tax and minority interests while excluding extraordinary items. % Change is from the previous year's result in local currency. Sales per $1 Assets is equivalent to sales-to-assets ratio. Equity is the sum of paid-up capital, reserves, and retained

Asia's Largest Companies by Sales

871 to 900

ASSETS $ MILLION	RANK	SALES PER $1 ASSETS	EQUITY $ MILLION	RANK	EMPLOYEES NUMBER	RANK	PROFIT PER EMPLOYEE	MARKET CAP. ($M)	PROFIT AS % OF SALES	ASSETS	EQUITY	NOTES (Key Below)
1,633.7	664	0.92	515.6	608	4,405	494	9,531	660.7	2.8	2.6	8.1	3 L
NA	—	—	NA	—	437	948	11,612	—	0.3	—	—	3 U A
2,204.3	542	0.68	528.1	600	4,474	488	9,809	139.9	2.9	1.0	8.3	12 L W
822.9	836	1.81	66.1	871	441	947	8,422	—	0.2	0.5	5.6	3 U A
1,122.9	778	1.33	531.7	597	2,328	703	13,094	—	2.1	2.7	5.7	12 U A
1,350.5	730	1.0:	110.8	842	1,626	790	—	84.3	—	—	—	3 L
NA	—	—	NA	—	2,300	708	—	—	—	—	—	12 U
391.2	895	3.77	138.0	818	999	872	—	225.6	—	—	—	3 L
818.2	840	1.80	395.4	672	906	885	11,598	248.7	0.7	1.3	2.7	3 L
859.0	832	1.72	171.3	805	681	914	—	127.1	—	—	—	3 L
1,091.7	788	1.35	647.6	538	2,537	670	5,624	723.9	0.0	1.3	2.2	12 L
462.8	888	3.19	197.3	789	12,000	237	206	271.6	0.2	0.5	1.3	7 L
612.4	872	2.41	362.2	695	2,000	751	22,807	373.3	3.1	7.4	12.6	12 L
1,776.3	627	0.83	1,019.7	396	3,053	608	4,089	593.4	0.8	0.7	1.2	3 L
1,483.7	691	0.99	848.9	449	2,873	631	50,276	1,895.7	9.8	9.7	17.0	3 L S
1,218.1	750	1.20	286.0	736	2,652	659	2,888	158.2	0.5	0.6	2.7	7 L*
2,273.4	527	0.65	1,465.4	286	1,328	836	—	1,106.4	—	—	—	3 L A
422.1	893	3.48	115.0	839	2,895	626	14,344	2,180.9	2.8	9.8	36.1	6 L S*
NA	—	—	NA	—	840	894	63,245	—	3.6	—	—	2 U A
NA	—	—	NA	—	3,100	601	—	—	—	—	—	12 U A X
NA	—	—	NA	—	6,000	397	—	—	—	—	—	3 U A
974.8	810	1.50	395.5	671	6,500	372	14,291	329.7	6.4	9.5	23.5	12 L
2,019.3	584	0.72	181.3	798	943	878	33,437	491.7	2.2	1.6	17.4	3 L
759.1	850	1.92	133.3	824	610	924	10,715	89.8	0.4	0.9	4.9	10 L
319.9	899	4.56	174.2	803	590	927	18,417	—	0.7	3.4	6.2	6 U A
1,897.9	603	0.77	982.5	408	2,214	720	22,787	1,153.3	3.5	2.7	5.1	11 L
NA	—	—	NA	—	3,041	609	14,296	—	2.0	—	—	3 U A Y
1,172.3	765	—	511.4	610	7,176	346	2,627	—	1.3	1.6	3.7	1 U
379.2	897	3.83	115.1	838	3,500	563	—	—	—	—	—	5 U
1,730.5	639	0.84	789.3	480	3,164	592	9,356	600.9	2.0	1.7	3.8	12 L

earnings. Liabilities can be estimated by deducting equity from assets. Market Capitalization is the total value of all shares of listed firms as of **Nov. 5**. Profit as % of Sales is usually called net profit margin. Profit as % of Assets, return on assets; Profit as % of Equity, return on equity. All money values are in US$. Currency conversion uses average **1996** rates (except for Market Cap.); for Australia, A$1.2773 per $1; China, RMB8.3142; Hong Kong, HK$7.80; India, Rs35.433; Indonesia, Rp2.342.3; Japan, ¥108.78; Malaysia, RM2.5159; New Zealand, NZ$1.453; Pakistan, Rs36.079; Philippines, Pesos 26.216; Singapore, S$1.41; South Korea, Won 804.45; Taiwan, NT$27.50; Thailand, Baht 25.343. NA not available. Values less than $50,000 appear as $0.0; those less than 0.05% as 0.0%. Market Capitalization from Datastream. More notes on pages 84 and 85.

Asia's Largest Companies By Sales

RANK 1997	RANK 1996	COMPANY NAME	COUNTRY	MAIN BUSINESS	SALES $ MILLION	%CHANGE	NET PROFIT $ MILLION	%CHANGE	RANK
901	—	SEMI-TECH (GLOBAL)	HONG KONG	APPLIANCES, ELECTRONICS	1,448.3	31.3	44.9	35.7	447
902	894	NIPPON DENSETSU KOGYO	JAPAN	ELECTRICAL ENGINEERING	1,446.1	8.8	18.9	(15.3)	645
903	517	TOWA REAL ESTATE DEVT.	JAPAN	PROPERTY	1,444.0	(36.7)	20.4	—	625
904	865	SUMITOMO PHARM.	JAPAN	PHARMACEUTICALS	1,444.7	4.9	35.3	(10.4)	509
905	963	AMADA CO.	JAPAN	METALWORKING MACHINERY	1,439.0	19.2	53.8	54.4	398
906	—	NESTLE AUSTRALIA	AUSTRALIA	FOOD	1,438.0	14.2	6.8	(61.3)	779
907	—	NISSHO IWAI AUSTRALIA	AUSTRALIA	GENERAL TRADING	1,438.7	7.5	2.6	218.6	837
908	904	NACHI-FUJIKOSHI	JAPAN	BEARINGS	1,434.3	8.0	16.0	187.1	661
909	954	SHANGHAI PETROCHEMICAL	CHINA	CHEMICALS	1,431.4	0.6	121.3	(52.6)	232
910	—	NIP. HOECHST MARION ROUSSEL	JAPAN	PHARMACEUTICALS	1,430.4	NA	NA	—	—
911	836	KAMIGUMI	JAPAN	HARBOR TRANSPORT	1,423.8	0.2	72.6	6.0	335
912	871	MITSUBISHI CABLE INDS.	JAPAN	CABLE, WIRE	1,423.7	4.5	20.6	16.4	621
913	937	SAM YANG	SOUTH KOREA	TEXTILES, FERTILIZER, SUGAR	1,422.1	2.4	(24.6)	—	919
914	—	YACHIYO INDUSTRY	JAPAN	CAR PARTS	1,419.8	35.7	14.7	93.5	687
915	857	NOZAKI & CO.	JAPAN	GENERAL TRADING	1,419.5	1.6	(21.0)	—	917
916	868	KURABO INDUSTRIES	JAPAN	TEXTILES	1,419.5	3.7	9.4	(51.3)	741
917	906	SEIBU CONSTRUCTION	JAPAN	CONSTRUCTION	1,415.0	7.6	4.7	(53.4)	809
918	914	OBAYASHI ROAD CORP.	JAPAN	CONSTRUCTION	1,413.7	9.5	7.1	15.5	775
919	1000	TOYOTA MOTOR CORP. AUST.	AUSTRALIA	CARS, TRUCKS	1,406.3	0.3	(74.1)	—	947
920	—	LARSEN & TOUBRO	INDIA	INDUSTRIAL MACHINERY	1,406.1	24.9	116.1	5.9	244
921	851	NOKYO TOURIST CORP.	JAPAN	TRAVEL AGENCY	1,397.0	(0.4)	(1.1)	—	885
922	888	NAKAIZUMI	JAPAN	LIQUOR TRADING	1,396.9	4.6	3.2	7.1	828
923	—	GAS AUTHORITY	INDIA	FUEL GAS	1,395.5	8.3	171.3	17.7	178
924	—	DAIFUKU	JAPAN	INDUSTRIAL EQUIPMENT	1,387.5	21.7	22.2	15.6	612
925	978	NAGOYA TOYOPET CORP.	JAPAN	CAR DEALERSHIP	1,387.2	16.3	8.9	48.4	752
926	861	SEIKODO	JAPAN	DISKS	1,387.1	13.0	NA	—	—
927	908	DAINIPPON PHARM.	JAPAN	PHARMACEUTICALS	1,383.9	5.5	37.4	(19.0)	496
928	919	SHOKUSAN JUTAKU SOGO	JAPAN	CONSTRUCTION	1,383.6	8.1	(45.1)	—	938
929	877	NOF CORP.	JAPAN	CHEMICALS, COATINGS	1,383.4	2.5	27.0	36.4	572
930	827	TAKENAKA CIVIL ENG.	JAPAN	CIVIL ENGINEERING	1,383.1	(3.6)	19.4	(1.4)	633

Company ranking by sales. Key to notes: All data are for fiscal years that ended between July 1997 and June 1998, except for companies with an asterisk (*) in the Notes column, which denotes data from the previous accounting period. The numbers refer to the month the fiscal year ended: 1 for January; 2 February; 3 March; 4 April; 5 May; 6 June; 7 July; 8 August; 9 September; 10 October; 11 November; 12 December. The letters denote publicly listed (L), unlisted (U), and state-controlled (S) companies. Financial results incorporate those of subsidiaries. Sales also refers to turnover, gross income, or revenue. Net profit is computed after deducting tax and minority interests while excluding extraordinary items. % Change is from the previous year's result in local currency. Sales per $1 Assets is equivalent to sales-to-assets ratio. Equity is the sum of paid-up capital, reserves, and retained

Asia's Largest Companies by Sales

901 to 930

ASSETS $ MILLION	RANK	SALES PER $1 ASSETS	EQUITY $ MILLION	RANK	EMPLOYEES NUMBER	RANK	PROFIT PER EMPLOYEE	MARKET CAP. ($M)	PROFIT AS % OF SALES	ASSETS	EQUITY	NOTES (Key Below)
3,165.4	408	0.46	1,048.1	386	NA	—	—	324.0	3.1	1.4	4.3	1 L
1,427.9	712	1.01	501.2	616	3,077	605	6,134	313.1	1.3	1.3	3.8	3 L
5,980.1	238	0.24	87.7	856	716	912	28,465	73.1	1.4	0.3	23.2	3 L A
1,313.3	736	1.10	527.2	604	2,500	678	14,139	—	2.4	2.7	6.7	3 U A
3,221.0	401	0.45	2,205.0	182	2,464	684	21,822	1,466.3	3.7	1.7	2.4	3 L
1,103.4	783	1.30	217.5	781	5,500	420	1,243	—	0.5	0.6	3.1	12 U
195.2	910	7.37	14.4	898	78	982	33,544	—	0.2	1.3	18.2	3 U
1,501.6	686	0.96	217.9	778	3,805	537	4,467	446.7	1.2	1.1	7.8	11 L
2,285.8	524	0.63	1,414.3	298	40,000	58	3,032	3,039.9	8.5	5.3	8.6	12 L S
NA	—	—	NA	—	3,930	526	—	—	—	—	—	12 U
2,201.3	545	0.65	1,351.6	312	3,748	541	19,369	1,188.2	5.1	3.3	5.4	3 L
1,633.3	665	0.87	602.9	556	2,035	745	10,123	543.6	1.4	1.3	3.4	3 L
1,161.5	770	1.22	282.6	739	3,586	557	—	152.4	—	—	—	6 L
562.2	880	2.53	144.2	814	2,096	734	7,026	127.1	1.0	2.6	10.2	3 L
686.0	857	2.07	(8.7)	905	300	966	—	54.4	—	—	—	3 L H
1,683.7	651	0.84	741.3	497	2,477	682	3,782	458.0	0.7	0.6	1.3	3 L
NA	—	—	NA	—	1,559	804	2,984	—	0.3	—	—	3 U A
946.0	818	1.49	245.0	758	1,567	799	4,506	104.6	0.5	0.7	2.9	3 L A
823.4	835	1.71	98.1	847	3,800	538	—	—	-5.3	-9.0	-75.6	12 U * Z
1,953.6	591	0.72	876.2	434	24,350	120	4,768	354.3	8.3	5.9	13.3	3 L
NA	—	—	NA	—	1,300	839	—	—	-0.1	—	—	3 U A
NA	—	—	NA	—	634	921	5,017	—	0.2	—	—	3 U A
NA	—	—	NA	—	NA	—	—	—	12.3	—	—	3 U S
1,431.8	709	0.97	544.6	587	2,861	633	7,747	811.4	1.6	1.5	4.1	3 L
880.6	828	1.58	237.4	766	2,410	688	3,685	—	0.6	1.0	3.7	3 U A
NA	—	—	NA	—	897	888	—	—	—	—	—	6 U *
1,644.5	661	0.84	809.6	469	2,934	623	12,733	699.8	2.7	2.3	4.6	3 L
1,611.7	670	0.86	220.2	776	1,579	797	—	103.5	—	—	—	3 L
1,711.8	647	0.81	521.6	605	2,836	636	9,864	506.6	2.0	1.6	5.4	3 L
1,020.8	800	1.36	219.4	777	1,613	791	11,997	—	1.4	1.9	8.8	12 U A

earnings. Liabilities can be estimated by deducting equity from assets. Market Capitalization is the total value of all shares of listed firms as of **Nov. 5**. Profit as % of Sales is usually called net profit margin. Profit as % of Assets, return on assets; Profit as % of Equity, return on equity. All money values are in US$. Currency conversion uses average **1996** rates (except for Market Cap.); for Australia, A$1.2773 per $1; China, RMB8.3142; Hong Kong, HK$7.80; India, Rs35.433; Indonesia, Rp2,342.3; Japan, ¥108.78; Malaysia, RM2.5159; New Zealand, NZ$1.453; Pakistan, Rs36.079; Philippines, Pesos 26.216; Singapore, S$1.41; South Korea, Won 804.45; Taiwan, NT$27.50; Thailand, Baht 25.343. NA not available. Values less than $50,000 appear as $0.0; those less than 0.05% as 0.0%. Market Capitalization from Datastream. More notes on pages 84 and 85.

Asia's Largest Companies By Sales

RANK 1997	RANK 1996	COMPANY NAME	COUNTRY	MAIN BUSINESS	SALES $ MILLION	%CHANGE	NET PROFIT $ MILLION	%CHANGE	RANK
931	880	POLA CHEMICAL INDUSTRY	JAPAN	COSMETICS	1,382.6	2.5	NA	—	—
932	874	GAKKEN	JAPAN	PUBLISHING	1,380.0	1.7	(0.6)	—	881
933	907	KEIYO	JAPAN	HOUSEHOLD-GOODS RETAIL	1,373.9	4.5	11.3	—	717
934	899	TEIJIN SHOJI	JAPAN	TEXTILE TRADING	1,372.9	3.7	1.0	(76.2)	862
935	—	AIR CHINA	CHINA	AIR TRANSPORT	1,372.5	4.9	32.0	(35.5)	530
936	—	MITAC INTERNATIONAL CORP.	TAIWAN	COMPUTERS	1,370.0	33.0	4.9	(11.0)	805
937	—	ROTHMANS HOLDINGS	AUSTRALIA	CIGARETTES	1,370.6	5.9	74.2	116.1	331
938	—	NEPTUNE ORIENT LINES	SINGAPORE	SHIPPING	1,367.7	3.3	14.7	(54.2)	688
939	—	BOONRAWD TRADING	THAILAND	BEER & SOFT DRINK SALES	1,364.5	19.5	2.4	(12.5)	840
940	—	JAPAN STEEL WORKS	JAPAN	STEEL	1,362.1	25.7	4.4	—	813
941	909	MARUZEN	JAPAN	BOOK RETAILING	1,360.7	3.9	8.7	—	759
942	847	HITACHI ELEC. SERVICES	JAPAN	ELECTRICAL ENGINEERING	1,360.6	1.8	22.8	42.8	607
943	—	KINTETSU REAL ESTATE	JAPAN	PROPERTY	1,360.0	22.6	2.6	(3.4)	836
944	956	TOKAI RUBBER INDUSTRIES	JAPAN	RUBBER PRODUCTS	1,357.5	11.2	46.9	12.3	432
945	970	TOSHIBA MACHINE	JAPAN	MACHINE TOOLS	1,356.4	13.2	(8.4)	—	902
946	859	COMALCO	AUSTRALIA	METALS, MINING	1,355.8	(26.6)	(13.2)	—	909
947	—	SINOPEC DAQING PETROCHEM.	CHINA	OIL REFINING	1,355.8	5.1	6.0	(55.6)	790
948	—	COSMO OIL INTERNATIONAL	SINGAPORE	OIL TRADING	1,354.6	26.6	1.3	—	857
949	926	TAKARA STANDARD	JAPAN	KITCHEN EQUIPMENT	1,352.2	6.4	53.5	14.6	399
950	—	SINGAPORE PETROLEUM	SINGAPORE	OIL REFINING	1,351.6	5.5	19.1	1.5	638
951	741	MILX CORP.	JAPAN	BUILDING MATERIALS	1,351.5	(16.2)	15.9	3.1	673
952	940	SANYO SHOKAI	JAPAN	CLOTHING	1,350.6	7.9	16.5	—	666
953	826	ISEKI & CO.	JAPAN	AGRICULTURAL MACHINERY	1,348.5	(6.1)	40.5	(27.8)	478
954	843	CHIZAKI KOGYO	JAPAN	CONSTRUCTION	1,346.6	(4.5)	0.0	(52.7)	864
955	982	SIAM MOTORS	THAILAND	CAR ASSEMBLY, DISTRIBUTOR	1,346.2	32.8	38.9	174.9	486
956	—	EPSON HANBAI	JAPAN	COMPUTER TRADING	1,345.8	18.1	NA	—	—
957	—	F.H. FAULDING	AUSTRALIA	PHARMACEUTICALS	1,344.2	8.2	32.5	48.4	526
958	965	BANYU PHARMACEUTICAL	JAPAN	PHARMACEUTICALS	1,340.7	11.5	110.9	10.2	254
959	992	TADANO	JAPAN	CRANES	1,338.4	14.2	38.2	76.0	490
960	934	KOBAYASHI PHARM.	JAPAN	PHARMACEUTICALS	1,337.6	6.3	25.4	68.3	593

Company ranking by sales. Key to notes: All data are for fiscal years that ended between July 1997 and June 1998, except for companies with an asterisk (*) in the Notes column, which denotes data from the previous accounting period. The numbers refer to the month the fiscal year ended: 1 for January; 2 February; 3 March; 4 April; 5 May; 6 June; 7 July; 8 August; 9 September; 10 October; 11 November; 12 December. The letters denote publicly listed (L), unlisted (U), and state-controlled (S) companies. Financial results incorporate those of subsidiaries. Sales also refers to turnover, gross income, or revenue. Net profit is computed after deducting tax and minority interests while excluding extraordinary items. % Change is from the previous year's result in local currency. Sales per $1 Assets is equivalent to sales-to-assets ratio. Equity is the sum of paid-up capital, reserves, and retained

Asia's Largest Companies by Sales

931 to 960

ASSETS $ MILLION	RANK	SALES PER $1 ASSETS	EQUITY $ MILLION	RANK	EMPLOYEES NUMBER	RANK	PROFIT PER EMPLOYEE	MARKET CAP. ($M)	PROFIT AS % OF SALES	ASSETS	EQUITY	NOTES (Key Below)
NA	—	—	NA	—	813	897	—	—	—	—	—	12 U A
2,027.8	582	0.68	829.6	459	1,823	775	—	331.4	—	—	—	3 L
816.1	841	1.68	389.0	677	1,081	864	10,485	388.1	0.8	1.4	2.9	2 L
677.7	859	2.03	42.2	886	394	953	2,637	—	0.1	0.2	2.5	3 U A
2,328.0	513	0.59	1,434.2	294	NA	—	—	—	2.3	1.4	2.2	12 U S
453.4	889	3.02	235.8	767	3,636	550	1,355	396.8	0.4	1.1	2.1	12 L
567.6	878	2.41	225.3	773	3,370	578	22,007	654.3	5.4	13.1	32.9	3 L
2,251.3	530	0.61	760.1	489	4,800	465	3,055	469.2	1.1	0.7	1.9	12 L
130.9	914	10.42	4.1	903	NA	—	—	—	0.2	1.8	58.9	12 U
1,888.4	604	0.72	561.7	576	3,165	591	1,380	515.2	0.3	0.2	0.8	3 L
1,381.8	723	0.98	129.3	826	2,492	679	3,482	267.5	0.6	0.6	6.7	3 L
848.8	833	1.60	368.0	692	4,760	469	4,799	—	1.7	2.7	6.2	3 U A
NA	—	—	NA	—	490	943	5,366	—	0.2	—	—	3 U A
1,199.8	757	1.13	470.6	630	4,335	498	10,813	910.1	3.5	3.9	9.0	3 L
1,457.0	702	0.93	362.5	694	2,810	640	—	449.3	—	—	—	3 L
2,466.2	492	0.55	1,023.0	392	4,586	479	—	2,445.4	—	—	—	12 L
2,069.7	574	0.66	NA	—	39,452	59	153	—	0.4	0.3	—	12 U S
223.4	909	6.06	49.6	879	10	989	134,752	—	0.1	0.6	2.7	12 U
1,923.1	595	0.70	961.7	410	4,446	492	12,026	912.0	3.0	2.8	5.6	3 L
1,052.0	792	1.28	384.5	680	179	973	106,621	325.8	1.4	1.8	4.0	12 L S
NA	—	—	NA	—	334	961	47,478	—	1.2	—	—	3 U A
1,260.8	743	1.07	430.3	650	2,073	738	7,947	614.6	1.2	1.3	3.8	12 L
1,664.1	654	0.81	410.5	662	2,303	706	17,583	384.9	3.0	2.4	9.9	3 L
1,583.2	676	0.85	54.6	878	1,597	795	599	—	0.1	0.1	1.8	3 U A
581.5	875	2.32	134.6	822	6,683	362	5,828	—	2.9	6.7	28.9	12 U *
NA	—	—	NA	—	1,100	861	—	—	—	—	—	3 U A
739.8	852	1.82	361.2	698	3,141	595	10,359	704.2	2.4	4.4	9.0	6 L
2,254.9	528	0.59	1,751.5	238	3,163	593	35,074	3,812.1	8.3	4.9	6.3	3 L A
1,833.1	614	0.73	709.4	510	1,731	780	22,050	611.6	2.9	2.1	5.4	3 L
703.8	855	1.90	119.7	832	1,506	814	16,872	—	1.9	3.6	21.2	3 U A

earnings. Liabilities can be estimated by deducting equity from assets. Market Capitalization is the total value of all shares of listed firms as of **Nov. 5**. Profit as % of Sales is usually called net profit margin. Profit as % of Assets, return on assets; Profit as % of Equity, return on equity. All money values are in US$. Currency conversion uses average **1996** rates (except for Market Cap.); for Australia, A$1.2773 per $1; China, RMB8.3142; Hong Kong, HK$7.80; India, Rs35.433; Indonesia, Rp2.342.3; Japan, ¥108.78; Malaysia, RM2.5159; New Zealand, NZ$1.453; Pakistan, Rs36.079; Philippines, Pesos 26.216; Singapore, S$1.41; South Korea, Won 804.45; Taiwan, NT$27.50; Thailand, Baht 25.343. NA not available. Values less than $50,000 appear as $0.0; those less than 0.05% as 0.0%. Market Capitalization from Datastream. More notes on pages 84 and 85.

Asia's Largest Companies By Sales

RANK 1997	RANK 1996	COMPANY NAME	COUNTRY	MAIN BUSINESS	SALES $ MILLION	%CHANGE	NET PROFIT $ MILLION	%CHANGE	RANK
961	941	SANKEN ELECTRIC	JAPAN	SEMICONDUCTORS	1,334.8	6.7	42.6	14.2	464
962	—	C. P. POKPHAND	HONG KONG	ANIMAL FEEDS	1,332.2	70.0	7.1	(89.2)	773
963	892	WATANABE PIPE	JAPAN	WATER-TREATMENT EQUIP.	1,330.9	0.0	1.7	35.3	851
964	896	YOSHINO KOGYOSHO	JAPAN	SYNTHETIC RESIN	1,330.8	0.3	NA	—	—
965	—	DONG KUK STEEL MILL	SOUTH KOREA	STEEL	1,329.5	5.6	98.9	283.5	280
966	946	DAINICHISEIKA COLOR	JAPAN	PIGMENTS, INK	1,329.2	6.5	15.9	(12.0)	672
967	—	NIPPON PETROLEUM GAS	JAPAN	OIL, GASES	1,327.7	23.5	3.5	1.1	825
968	—	BOONRAWD BREWERY	THAILAND	BEER, SOFT DRINKS	1,325.1	20.2	44.9	70.3	446
969	929	NAGOYA MITSUKOSHI	JAPAN	DEPARTMENT STORES	1,318.5	4.2	8.8	2.4	756
970	840	KANDEN KOGYO	JAPAN	ENGINEERING	1,316.9	(6.9)	26.2	(37.5)	585
971	912	RINNAI	JAPAN	GAS APPLIANCES	1,314.2	1.1	54.4	4.7	395
972	976	KASUMI	JAPAN	SUPERMARKETS	1,311.0	9.9	8.8	(28.4)	755
973	924	SUMITOMO 3M	JAPAN	ADHESIVE TAPE	1,309.0	2.9	65.7	(12.8)	352
974	990	NISSHIN OIL MILLS	JAPAN	FOOD PRODUCTS	1,307.8	11.4	3.0	(76.1)	817
975	996	BANGCHAK PETROLEUM	THAILAND	OIL PRODUCTS	1,306.2	(0.8)	40.4	17.6	480
976	959	SAN YANG INDUSTRY	TAIWAN	CARS, MOTORCYCLES	1,304.6	(3.4)	47.6	(12.1)	429
977	952	NORITZ CORP.	JAPAN	WATER HEATERS	1,303.2	6.2	21.4	(22.7)	616
978	—	TEAC CORP.	JAPAN	CONSUMER ELECTRONICS	1,300.4	25.1	34.8	126.2	512
979	939	TOA STEEL	JAPAN	STEEL	1,298.1	3.6	(56.0)	—	943
980	991	TAE KWANG INDL.	SOUTH KOREA	TEXTILES, ELECTRONICS	1,294.1	(0.5)	36.2	62.5	507
981	916	SUN-S	JAPAN	PHARMACEUTICALS TRADING	1,289.0	0.0	8.9	11.9	751
982	893	NARASAKI SANGYO	JAPAN	MACHINERY TRADING	1,287.4	(3.2)	(24.9)	—	920
983	—	MARUZEN PETROCHEMICAL	JAPAN	PETROCHEMICALS	1,287.3	20.7	9.5	458.9	739
984	994	JATCO	JAPAN	CAR PARTS	1,285.8	10.5	NA	—	—
985	935	KYOKUYO CO.	JAPAN	PAPER TRADING	1,282.2	2.3	4.9	13.0	804
986	—	CALTEX (PHILIPPINES)	PHILIPPINES	OIL REFINING, DISTRIBUTION	1,281.5	7.0	28.2	(34.7)	567
987	931	ASMO	JAPAN	CAR PARTS	1,280.9	1.4	41.0	18.8	468
988	967	NISSIN CORP.	JAPAN	HARBOR TRANSPORT	1,279.5	6.4	12.8	10.2	699
989	—	SICHUAN CHANGHONG ELECT.	CHINA	TELEVISION	1,273.4	56.5	201.5	45.6	151
990	979	KINTETSU WORLD EXPRESS	JAPAN	AIR-CARGO	1,273.0	6.9	11.9	16.2	708

Company ranking by sales. Key to notes: All data are for fiscal years that ended between July 1997 and June 1998, except for companies with an asterisk (*) in the Notes column, which denotes data from the previous accounting period. The numbers refer to the month the fiscal year ended: 1 for January; 2 February; 3 March; 4 April; 5 May; 6 June; 7 July; 8 August; 9 September; 10 October; 11 November; 12 December. The letters denote publicly listed (L), unlisted (U), and state-controlled (S) companies. Financial results incorporate those of subsidiaries. Sales also refers to turnover, gross income, or revenue. Net profit is computed after deducting tax and minority interests while excluding extraordinary items. % Change is from the previous year's result in local currency. Sales per $1 Assets is equivalent to sales-to-assets ratio. Equity is the sum of paid-up capital, reserves, and retained

Asia's Largest Companies by Sales

961 to 990

ASSETS $ MILLION	RANK	SALES PER $1 ASSETS	EQUITY $ MILLION	RANK	EMPLOYEES NUMBER	RANK	PROFIT PER EMPLOYEE	MARKET CAP. ($M)	PROFIT AS % OF SALES	ASSETS	EQUITY	NOTES (Key Below)
1,409.3	716	0.95	552.0	584	8,000	324	5,320	884.0	3.2	3.0	7.7	3 L
1,662.8	656	0.80	336.6	716	NA	—	—	539.7	0.5	0.4	2.1	12 L
1,173.7	764	1.13	48.2	881	1,780	776	950	—	0.1	0.1	3.5	3 U A
NA	—	—	NA	—	5,900	402	—	—	—	—	—	3 U A
1,814.3	618	0.73	596.2	558	1,984	753	49,836	374.0	7.4	5.4	16.6	12 L
1,203.6	756	1.10	358.8	699	1,696	783	9,355	447.9	1.2	1.3	4.4	3 L
822.3	838	1.61	141.2	816	285	969	12,322	—	0.3	0.4	2.5	3 U A
533.8	881	2.48	241.3	761	2,213	721	20,309	—	3.4	8.4	18.6	12 U
NA	—	—	NA	—	2,001	750	4,378	—	0.7	—	—	2 U A
NA	—	—	NA	—	2,940	622	8,927	—	1.0	—	—	3 U A
1,317.8	734	0.00	772.9	486	3,617	551	15,036	923.8	4.1	4.1	7.0	3 L
906.2	821	1.45	321.1	723	4,895	458	1,790	256.8	0.7	0.0	2.7	2 L S
NA	—	—	NA	—	2,235	717	29,388	—	5.0	—	—	12 U A
1,449.2	704	0.90	779.1	481	2,053	743	1,925	425.7	0.3	0.3	0.5	3 L
1,027.9	799	1.27	383.5	682	801	900	50,444	132.3	3.1	3.9	10.5	12 L S
759.7	849	1.72	429.9	651	4,272	503	11,143	—	3.6	6.3	11.1	12 U
1,242.5	748	1.05	735.5	501	2,876	630	7,451	436.4	1.6	1.7	2.9	12 L
760.0	848	1.71	138.5	819	6,491	374	5,356	246.1	2.7	4.6	25.1	3 L
3,119.1	414	0.42	550.2	585	1,514	813	—	133.4	—	—	—	3 L
1,436.3	708	0.90	695.9	516	9,595	283	3,769	358.1	2.8	2.5	5.2	8 L
634.5	868	2.03	141.5	815	1,523	811	5,867	112.8	0.7	1.4	6.3	3 L A
792.5	844	1.62	39.0	890	548	934	—	53.0	—	—	—	3 L
1,043.9	794	1.23	251.5	754	797	902	11,927	—	0.7	0.9	3.8	3 U A
NA	—	—	NA	—	2,600	665	—	—	—	—	—	3 U A
744.9	851	1.72	45.4	885	385	955	12,846	—	0.4	0.7	10.9	11 U
683.1	858	1.88	248.4	756	916	883	30,829	—	2.2	4.1	11.4	12 U
NA	—	—	NA	—	5,134	442	8,176	—	3.3	—	—	3 U A
669.0	862	1.91	248.0	755	1,210	850	10,568	277.0	0.0	1.9	5.1	3 L
1,387.9	720	0.92	592.9	559	NA	—	—	—	15.8	14.5	33.0	12 L S
451.4	890	2.82	114.4	840	1,233	847	9,625	—	0.9	2.6	10.4	12 U A

earnings. Liabilities can be estimated by deducting equity from assets. Market Capitalization is the total value of all shares of listed firms as of **Nov. 5.** Profit as % of Sales is usually called net profit margin. Profit as % of Assets, return on assets; Profit as % of Equity, return on equity. All money values are in US$. Currency conversion uses average **1996** rates (except for Market Cap.); for Australia, A$1.2773 per $1; China, RMB8.3142; Hong Kong, HK$7.80; India, Rs35.433; Indonesia, Rp2.342.3; Japan, ¥108.78; Malaysia, RM2.5159; New Zealand, NZ$1.453; Pakistan, Rs36.079; Philippines, Pesos 26.216; Singapore, S$1.41; South Korea, Won 804.45; Taiwan, NT$27.50; Thailand, Baht 25.343. NA not available. Values less than $50,000 appear as $0.0; those less than 0.05% as 0.0%. Market Capitalization from Datastream. More notes on pages 84 and 85.

Asia's Largest Companies By Sales

RANK 1997	RANK 1996	COMPANY NAME	COUNTRY	MAIN BUSINESS	SALES $ MILLION	%CHANGE	NET PROFIT $ MILLION	%CHANGE	RANK
991	975	JAMES HARDIE INDUSTRIES	AUSTRALIA	CONSTRUCTION	1,272.0	(7.2)	64.0	157.8	354
992	943	SANKEI SHIMBUN	JAPAN	NEWSPAPER PUBLISHING	1,272.9	1.9	3.0	17.9	816
993	997	IKKO	JAPAN	OIL DISTRIBUTION	1,271.9	10.2	4.1	(69.8)	814
994	944	SHOWA PHARMACEUTICAL	JAPAN	PHARMACEUTICALS TRADING	1,268.4	1.6	9.1	12.3	749
995	—	HANKOOK TIRE MFG.	SOUTH KOREA	TIRES	1,267.0	16.3	12.6	1.1	702
996	—	HIKAWA SHOJI	JAPAN	PETROCHEMICALS	1,267.6	36.2	NA	—	—
997	—	STATE RAIL N.S.W.	AUSTRALIA	RAIL TRANSPORT	1,267.4	(2.2)	(584.1)	—	974
998	—	HANSHIN CONSTRUCTION	SOUTH KOREA	CONSTRUCTION	1,265.2	18.8	1.6	—	853
999	849	TOTTORI SANYO ELECTRIC	JAPAN	ELECTRONIC PARTS	1,264.5	(10.1)	10.2	21.6	732
1000	—	THOMSON MULTIMEDIA	SINGAPORE	CONSUMER ELECTRONICS	1,264.5	(2.5)	(42.1)	—	936

Company ranking by sales. Key to notes: All data are for fiscal years that ended between July 1996 and June 1997, except for companies with an asterisk (*) in the Notes column, which denotes data from the previous accounting period. The numbers refer to the month the fiscal year ended: 1 for January; 2 February; 3 March; 4 April; 5 May; 6 June; 7 July; 8 August; 9 September; 10 October; 11 November; 12 December. The letters denote publicly listed (L), unlisted (U), and state-controlled (S) companies. Financial results incorporate those of subsidiaries. Sales also refers to turnover, gross income, or revenue. Net profit is computed after deducting tax and minority interests while excluding extraordinary items. % Change is from the previous year's result in local currency. Sales per $1 Assets is equivalent to sales-to-assets ratio. Equity is the sum of paid-up capital, reserves, and retained

Asia's Largest Companies by Sales

991 to 1000

ASSETS $ MILLION	RANK	SALES PER $1 ASSETS	EQUITY $ MILLION	RANK	EMPLOYEES NUMBER	RANK	PROFIT PER EMPLOYEE	MARKET CAP. ($M)	PROFIT AS % OF SALES	ASSETS	EQUITY	NOTES (Key Below)
1,499.7	688	0.85	568.5	570	9,559	285	6,798	1,233.0	5.1	4.3	11.4	3 L
523.6	883	2.43	82.2	862	3,186	588	1,255	—	0.3	0.8	4.9	3 U A
NA	—	—	NA	—	1,166	857	3,532	—	0.3	—	—	3 U A
721.2	853	1.76	188.7	795	1,081	865	8,368	109.6	0.7	1.3	4.8	3 L A
1,663.5	655	0.76	343.7	710	6,379	378	1,981	147.0	0.0	0.8	3.7	12 L
NA	—	—	NA	—	133	977	—	—	—	—	—	3 U A
9,759.9	148	0.13	7,795.8	37	19,742	147	—	—	—	—	—	6 U S
1,594.5	674	0.79	228.3	770	1,867	768	852	11.3	0.1	0.1	0.7	12 L
895.9	824	1.41	128.2	827	3,000	614	3,386	—	0.8	1.1	7.9	3 U AAA
436.3	891	2.90	(26.2)	906	NA	—	—	—	—	—	—	12 U H

earnings. Liabilities can be estimated by deducting equity from assets. Market Capitalization is the total value of all shares of listed firms as of **Nov. 5**. Profit as % of Sales is usually called net profit margin. Profit as % of Assets, return on assets; Profit as % of Equity, return on equity. All money values are in US$. Currency conversion uses average **1996** rates (except for Market Cap.); for Australia, A$1.2773 per $1; China, RMB8.3142; Hong Kong, HK$7.80; India, Rs35.433; Indonesia, Rp2.342.3; Japan, ¥108.78; Malaysia, RM2.5159; New Zealand, NZ$1.453; Pakistan, Rs36.079; Philippines, Pesos 26.216; Singapore, S$1.41; South Korea, Won 804.45; Taiwan, NT$27.50; Thailand, Baht 25.343. NA not available. Values less than $50,000 appear as $0.0; those less than 0.05% as 0.0%. Market Capitalization from Datastream. More notes on pages 84 and 85.

ADDITIONAL NOTES

The *Asiaweek 1000* annual rankings are based on consolidated results provided or confirmed by the ranked companies. Many China enterprises reported only pre-tax profits. These notes refer to the main table:

A. Unconsolidated results for these Japan companies.

B. Sanyo Electric Co. changed its year-end from November to March. Fiscal 1995 results are for the year to November 1995.

C. Denso Corp was formerly Nippondenso Co. Ltd., renamed in October 1996.

D. Oji Paper Co. was established by merging New Oji Paper Co. Ltd. and Honshu Paper Co. Ltd in October 1966.

E. Rio Tinto Co. was formerly CRA; it was renamed in June 1997.

F. Kia Motors sought protection from receivership in early 1997, and was nationalised in October.

G. Total profits reported by these China companies.

H. Negative equity reported by these companies, Kanebo, Nozaki & Co. and Sumitomo Coal Mining are operating normally; they are expecting to restore positive equity in a few years. Tokai Kogyo went bankrupt in July 1997.

I. Mitsui Chemicals was formed by merging Mitsui Petrochemical Industries and Mitsui Toatsu Chemicals in October 1996.

J. Itochu Shokuhin was formerly Matsushita Suzuki Co. Ltd., renamed in November 1995.

K. Sanyo life Electronics' 1995 results are for the year to November 1995.

L. Mitsumi Electric Co. Ltd. changed its year-end from January to March; its results are for 14 months.

M. Daewoo Motor Sales Corp. was formerly Woori Auto Sales Co.; it was renamed in February 1997.

N. Unisia Jecs Corp. changed its year-end from February to March; its results are for 13 months.

O. Deodeo Corp. was formerly Daiich Corp.; it was renamed in April 1997.

P. Housing Industrial Development & Construction was formerly Hyundai Housing & Development Co. Ltd.; it was renamed in November 1996.

Q. Singapore Power was corporatized in October 1995 to take over power and gas operations from the Public Utilities Board.

R. Yaohan Japan sought protection from creditors in September 1997. It planned to sell assets in China, Malaysia and the US. Yaohan is also to sell 14 outlets for household electrical goods.

S. For Fujitsu Business Systems Ltd. and Kasumi Ltd., unconsolidated results are used in 1996.

T. Pre-tax profits were reported by these Chinese companies.

U. Mitsubishi Logistics Corp. was formerly Mitsubishi Warehouse & Transportation Co. Ltd.; it was renamed in July 1996.

V. Pacific Petroleum $ Trading Co. Ltd. was formerly Japan Indonesia Co. Ltd; it was renamed in January 1996.

W. Hyosung T&C Co. was formerly Tongyang Nylon; it was renamed in November 1996.

X. Novartis Japan was formed by the merger of local units of Ciba and Sandoz in December 1996.

Y. Toppan Forms Co. Ltd. was formerly Toppan Moore Co. Ltd.; it was renamed in April 1997.

Z. Toyota Motor Corp. Australia's sales and net profit results are annualised.

AA. Tottori Sanyo Electric Co. Ltd. changed its year-end from November to March; fiscal 1995 results are for the year to November 1995.

Market capitalization from Datastream. Australian data from IBIS Business Information, Melbourne. Thai data from Laurie Rosenthal.

Chapter Two

THE BEST AND THE BIGGEST

The Largest Profits

The boost in exports from the continuing weak yen, has ensured a dominance of Japanese companies in the profitability stakes. Toyota Motor Corp., which doubled earnings, heads the list. The Australian Wheat Board, riding on firm commodity prices, saw a 163.8% leap in profits to climb into contention. The surge in mobile telephone use, has meant that telecom companies across the region feature prominently in the list — not the least being Asiaweek 1000 newcomer Thailand's Telephone Organisation.

1 to 20

Rank	Company	Profit $ Million	1000 Rank
1	TOYOTA MOTOR CORP.	3,547.7	6
2	PETROLIAM NASIONAL	2,892.0	96
3	AUSTRALIAN WHEAT BOARD	2,389.4	364
4	NIPPON TELEGRAPH & TEL.	2,311.6	8
5	HONDA MOTOR	2,033.2	14
6	CHUNGHWA TELECOM	1,998.3	188
7	SUN HUNG KAI PROPERTIES	1,815.4	337
8	CHEUNG KONG	1,570.6	784
9	HONGKONG TELECOM	1,433.0	302
10	SONY CORP.	1,282.0	12
11	MATSUSHITA ELECTRIC INDL.	1,267.3	10
12	TELSTRA	1,265.0	82
13	TAIWAN POWER	1,247.9	136
14	HENDERSON LAND DEVT.	1,232.8	536
15	SINGAPORE TELECOM	1,176.2	395
16	MITSUBISHI HEAVY INDS.	1,136.3	26
17	RIO TINTO	1,098.4	137
18	ELEC. GENERATING AUTH.	1,069.1	287
19	HEWLETT-PACKARD, SINGAPORE	1,040.7	197
20	HUTCHISON WHAMPOA	1,015.4	263

21 to 40

Rank	Company	Profit $ Million	1000 Rank
21	SWIRE PACIFIC	981.3	254
22	CANON	865.8	34
23	NEC CORP.	841.9	17
24	TELEPHONE ORGANIZATION	830.4	803
25	HITACHI LTD.	812.0	9
26	SEAGATE TECHNOLOGY INTL.	797.2	179
27	JAPAN TOBACCO	794.7	20
28	FUJI PHOTO FILM	784.6	95
29	TOKYO ELECTRIC POWER	750.2	16
30	TELEKOM MALAYSIA	747.8	504
31	KOREA ELECTRIC POWER	742.8	65
32	POHANG IRON & STEEL	735.1	86
33	SINGAPORE AIRLINES	731.6	239
34	NISSAN MOTOR	714.7	11
35	ITO-YOKADO	683.3	28
36	CHINA PETROCHEMICAL CORP.	662.6	29
37	TAKEDA CHEMICAL INDS.	656.2	149
38	DENSO CORP.	656.2	61
39	EAST JAPAN RAILWAY	649.6	35
40	BRIDGESTONE CORP.	646.6	44

The Biggest Losses

Japanese companies also dominate the loss-leaders, although Australian companies, still struggling with a weak dollar and rising import prices, came in second with eight. Japan's reluctance to institute economic reforms and the limping yen should see Japan keeping up the numbers — now 27, up from 11 in 1996. South Korea's economic woes will see more South Korean companies joining Korean Air and Asiana — which were both also hit by the decline in tourism.

1 to 20

Rank	Company	Profit $ Million	1000 Rank
1	SUMITOMO CORP.	-1,338.6	5
2	BURNS, PHILP & CO.	-683.7	780
3	STATE RAIL N.S.W.	-584.1	997
4	CHIYODA CORP.	-490.2	310
5	HASEKO	-438.4	311
6	JAPAN ENERGY CORP.	-425.5	42
7	MITSUI FUDOSAN	-404.4	92
8	NIPPON STEEL CHEMICAL	-392.9	389
9	SAMSUNG HEAVY INDS.	-366.2	314
10	OPTUS COMMUNICATIONS	-322.3	672
11	KOREAN AIR	-261.7	272
12	KANEMATSU CORP.	-253.1	23
13	YAOHAN JAPAN CORP.	-246.8	643
14	DDI CORP.	-240.5	125
15	DAVIDS	-188.1	317
16	BTR NYLEX	-169.7	189
17	MAZDA MOTOR CORP.	-161.3	50
18	PRIMA MEAT PACKERS	-133.3	462
19	JAPAN AIRLINES	-133.1	64
20	TOKYU CONSTRUCTION	-132.2	212

21 to 40

Rank	Company	Profit $ Million	1000 Rank
21	JGC CORP.	-128.6	516
22	MITSUBISHI CHEMICAL CORP.	-110.1	58
23	DAIEI	-109.5	25
24	TOKYO STEEL MFG.	-103.6	887
25	MITSUBISHI OIL	-95.7	104
26	NICHIEI	-93.7	439
27	AMCOR	-85.8	253
28	AOKI CORP.	-84.5	335
29	TOKYU LAND	-80.8	274
30	TOYOTA MOTOR CORP. AUST.	-74.1	919
31	BANDAI	-73.3	721
32	KUMAGAI GUMI	-67.6	119
33	ASIANA AIRLINES	-67.2	870
34	TOA STEEL	-56.0	979
35	ESSO STANDARD THAILAND	-54.9	639
36	MITSUBISHI MOTORS AUST.	-51.5	816
37	SATO KOGYO	-45.3	199
38	HAZAMA	-45.1	220
39	SHOKUSAN JUTAKU SOGO	-45.1	928
40	FRANKLINS	-42.0	415

The Largest Assets

In spite of Japan's economic doldrums, all but six of the list are Japanese companies. Telecommunications giant Nippon Telegraph & Telephone moved to the top, displacing Tokyo Electric Power for the first time in four years. Only five of the listed companies recorded increased asset values, while there were three newcomers: Australia's News Corp and BHP, and Malaysia's state-owned Petroliam Nasional. The largest increase on 1996 figures was Korea Electric Power with 21%.

1 to 20

Rank	Company	Assets $ Million	1000 Rank
1	NIPPON TELEGRAPH & TEL.	151,453.3	8
2	TOKYO ELECTRIC POWER	130,844.0	16
3	TOYOTA MOTOR CORP.	116,793.8	6
4	HITACHI LTD.	91,604.2	9
5	MITSUBISHI CORP.	88,802.7	2
6	MATSUSHITA ELECTRIC INDL.	79,940.3	10
7	MITSUI & CO.	69,727.7	1
8	MARUBENI CORP.	69,409.3	4
9	NISSAN MOTOR	68,705.4	11
10	EAST JAPAN RAILWAY	67,884.4	35
11	ITOCHU CORP.	67,486.0	3
12	KANSAI ELECTRIC POWER	63,356.7	32
13	CHUBU ELECTRIC POWER	56,959.2	37
14	CENTRAL JAPAN RAILWAY	56,748.5	89
15	TOSHIBA CORP.	53,403.0	13
16	SONY CORP.	52,218.6	12
17	NISSHO IWAI CORP.	49,774.7	7
18	SUMITOMO CORP.	49,613.5	5
19	KOREA ELECTRIC POWER	44,334.1	65
20	NEC CORP.	44,118.1	17

21 to 40

Rank	Company	Assets $ Million	1000 Rank
21	FUJITSU LTD.	43,460.0	18
22	NIPPON STEEL CORP.	41,455.6	27
23	MITSUBISHI HEAVY INDS.	40,096.5	26
24	HONDA MOTOR	38,530.0	14
25	KYUSHU ELECTRIC POWER	38,265.2	77
26	CHINA PETROCHEMICAL CORP.	37,788.4	29
27	MITSUBISHI ELECTRIC CORP.	37,742.1	21
28	TOHOKU ELECTRIC POWER	35,539.2	71
29	TAIWAN POWER	34,815.3	136
30	NEWS CORP.	32,379.2	90
31	MITSUI FUDOSAN	29,864.5	92
32	MITSUBISHI MOTORS	29,722.7	22
33	BROKEN HILL PROPRIETARY	28,759.9	48
34	TAISEI CORP.	27,672.2	43
35	NIPPON OIL	27,194.3	31
36	PETROLIAM NASIONAL	27,090.1	96
37	CHUGOKU ELECTRIC POWER	27,083.6	121
38	KAJIMA CORP.	26,368.6	39
39	WEST JAPAN RAILWAY	24,545.6	103
40	NKK CORP.	24,226.2	51

The Most Employees

Although unemployment is on the increase throughout the region, the leading employers should maintain their positions. Not surprisingly, the most populous countries have the most populous companies. In the top slot is still China Petrochemical Corp, closely followed by Jiangsu Supply & Marketing Co-op. The worsening crisis in Indonesia and the drop in foreign investment, is likely to hit Astra International and Per. Listrik Negara (PLN) over the short term.

1 to 20

Rank	Company	Employees	1000 Rank
1	CHINA PETROCHEMICAL CORP.	650,000	29
2	JIANGSU SUP. & MKTG. CO-OP.	500,000	57
3	HITACHI LTD.	330,152	9
4	MATSUSHITA ELECTRIC INDL.	270,651	10
5	NIPPON TELEGRAPH & TEL.	230,000	8
6	SHOUGANG CORP.	229,819	422
7	CHINA STATE CONST. ENG.	222,000	249
8	EAST CHINA ELECTRIC POWER	200,000	204
9	JARDINE MATHESON	200,000	94
10	NEC CORP.	190,000	17
11	STEEL AUTHORITY OF INDIA	187,504	347
12	TOSHIBA CORP.	186,000	13
13	COLES MYER	152,744	67
14	DONGFENG MOTORS CORP.	149,233	807
15	NISSAN MOTOR	135,331	11
16	ASTRA INTERNATIONAL	123,000	264
17	ITO-YOKADO	104,190	28
18	WOOLWORTHS	100,000	79
19	BRIDGESTONE CORP.	92,458	44
20	EAST JAPAN RAILWAY	78,624	35

21 to 40

Rank	Company	Employees	1000 Rank
21	CANON	75,628	34
22	TATA IRON & STEEL	75,010	738
23	JARDINE PACIFIC	73,000	684
24	YAMATO TRANSPORT	71,826	173
25	TOYOTA MOTOR CORP.	70,561	6
26	BHARAT HEAVY ELECTRICALS	68,932	821
27	SANYO ELECTRIC CO.	67,827	52
28	MITSUBISHI HEAVY INDS.	67,117	26
29	FOOD CORP. OF INDIA	65,131	388
30	MARUBENI CORP.	65,000	4
31	TELSTRA	64,609	82
32	BROKEN HILL PROPRIETARY	61,000	48
33	SHANGHAI AUTOMOTIVE	60,981	145
34	KOREA TELECOM	60,067	131
35	FUSHUN PETROCHEMICAL	60,000	845
36	SAMSUNG ELECTRONICS	59,086	38
37	DENSO CORP.	56,961	61
38	PER. LISTRIK NEGARA (PLN)	56,476	316
39	SWIRE PACIFIC	56,000	254
40	SUMITOMO ELECTRIC INDS.	55,854	93

The Biggest Equity

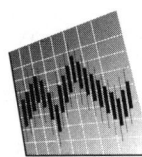

Compared with last year, there has not been much movement on the equity listing. The exception is Australia's media giant News Corp. Rupert Murdoch's flagship saw equity increase by 43%, moving the company up 13 places to No. 6. Hong Kong property companies are likely to slip on the 30-40% decline in property values, while China makes its first entry with China Petrochemical moving straight in at No.9.

1 to 20

Rank	Company	Equity $ Million	1000 Rank
1	TOYOTA MOTOR CORP.	52,186.3	6
2	NIPPON TELEGRAPH & TEL.	49,093.7	8
3	MATSUSHITA ELECTRIC INDL.	33,974.2	10
4	HITACHI LTD.	30,188.4	9
5	KOREA ELECTRIC POWER	21,010.7	65
6	NEWS CORP.	17,407.0	90
7	TAIWAN POWER	17,364.9	136
8	SUN HUNG KAI PROPERTIES	17,270.4	337
9	CHINA PETROCHEMICAL CORP.	15,418.3	29
10	TOKYO ELECTRIC POWER	13,741.2	16
11	SONY CORP.	13,416.3	12
12	SWIRE PACIFIC	12,921.5	254
13	HONDA MOTOR	12,763.7	14
14	BROKEN HILL PROPRIETARY	12,693.2	48
15	PER. LISTRIK NEGARA (PLN)	12,479.8	316
16	NISSAN MOTOR	12,466.4	11
17	JAPAN TOBACCO	12,436.1	20
18	MITSUBISHI HEAVY INDS.	12,386.4	26
19	FUJI PHOTO FILM	12,363.8	95
20	CHUNGHWA TELECOM	11,681.5	188

21 to 40

Rank	Company	Equity $ Million	1000 Rank
21	TOSHIBA CORP.	11,626.9	13
22	KANSAI ELECTRIC POWER	11,234.7	32
23	FUJITSU LTD.	10,861.3	18
24	PETROLIAM NASIONAL	10,857.3	96
25	MITSUBISHI CORP.	10,108.3	2
26	CHINESE PETROLEUM CORP.	9,473.3	85
27	NEC CORP.	9,223.9	17
28	CANON	9,026.2	34
29	DENSO CORP.	8,994.1	61
30	HUTCHISON WHAMPOA	8,833.2	263
31	CHEUNG KONG	8,790.1	784
32	CHUBU ELECTRIC POWER	8,679.8	37
33	SHARP	8,674.1	55
34	NIPPON STEEL CORP.	8,192.1	27
35	POHANG IRON & STEEL	8,115.8	86
36	ITO-YOKADO	8,101.3	28
37	STATE RAIL N.S.W.	7,795.8	997
38	TELSTRA	7,780.5	82
39	HENDERSON LAND DEVT.	7,722.3	536
40	DAI NIPPON PRINTING	7,641.7	83

The Highest Market Value

This listing is likely to see the one of the largest adjustments in the short- to medium-term. Japan, Seoul, Singapore and Hong Kong stock indices have slid 20-30% in 1998, and they are not expected to recover their former buoyancy for up to two years. However, Japanese manufacturers, with international market spread, continue to dominate the list. Pharmaceutical leader Takeda Chemical Industries recorded the biggest rise with 62%, followed by Canon with 28%.

1 to 20

Rank	Company	$ Millions	1000 Rank
1	NIPPON TELEGRAPH & TEL.	135,008.4	8
2	TOYOTA MOTOR CORP.	102,534.3	6
3	MATSUSHITA ELECTRIC INDL.	35,327.1	10
4	SONY CORP.	35,036.5	12
5	HONDA MOTOR	32,749.6	14
6	SEVEN-ELEVEN JAPAN	30,815.0	541
7	HUTCHISON WHAMPOA	27,306.5	263
8	HITACHI LTD.	25,951.8	9
9	SINGAPORE TELECOM	25,349.9	395
10	TOKYO ELECTRIC POWER	25,164.6	16
11	TAKEDA CHEMICAL INDS.	25,065.8	149
12	HONGKONG TELECOM	22,384.8	302
13	CANON	21,343.1	34
14	BROKEN HILL PROPRIETARY	20,565.1	48
15	ITO-YOKADO	20,336.8	28
16	FUJITSU LTD.	20,188.6	18
17	EAST JAPAN RAILWAY	18,764.2	35
18	FUJI PHOTO FILM	18,305.2	95
19	SUN HUNG KAI PROPERTIES	17,617.3	337
20	NEC CORP.	17,589.2	17

21 to 40

Rank	Company	$ Millions	1000 Rank
21	DENSO CORP.	17,419.3	61
22	SEIBU RAILWAY	17,180.2	245
23	KANSAI ELECTRIC POWER	16,926.1	32
24	BRIDGESTONE CORP.	16,884.3	44
25	MITSUBISHI ESTATE	16,746.7	237
26	CHEUNG KONG	15,899.0	783
27	MITSUBISHI HEAVY INDS.	15,822.0	26
28	JAPAN TOBACCO	15,794.6	20
29	DAI NIPPON PRINTING	14,684.6	83
30	NIPPON STEEL CORP.	14,333.6	27
31	TOSHIBA CORP.	14,233.8	13
32	NISSAN MOTOR	13,244.3	11
33	NINTENDO	12,943.0	328
34	TDK	12,712.4	210
35	MITSUBISHI CORP.	12,683.2	2
36	CHUBU ELECTRIC POWER	12,368.8	37
37	ROHM	12,268.1	467
38	NTT DATA CORP.	12,013.2	213
39	CHINA LIGHT & POWER	11,940.7	549
40	MITSUI & CO.	11,924.8	1

The Highest Growth in Sales

The global computer industry slump led to Taiwan's Acer dropping from the list. Samsung Electronics was similarly affected. Japan's Pacific Petroleum & Trading, which increased sales by 155%, moves into No.1, replacing Daewoo Heavy Industries, which the collapse of the South Korean economy help move out of the list altogether. Oil and oil product companies are well represented, but shrinking markets will affect the major players over the short term.

1 to 20

Rank	Company	% Change Over 1995	1000 Rank
1	PACIFIC PETROLEUM & TRADING	155.5	866
2	AUSTRALIAN WHEAT BOARD	119.9	364
3	HYUNDAI OIL REFINERY	116.9	404
4	HINDUSTAN LEVER	95.5	700
5	TOYOTA MOTOR SALES AUST.	85.2	428
6	C. P. POKPHAND	70.0	962
7	CHINA NATIONAL OFFSHORE OIL	68.2	788
8	MARUBENI INTL. PETROLEUM	57.9	459
9	SICHUAN CHANGHONG ELECT.	56.5	989
10	DDI CORP.	51.8	125
11	HEWLETT-PACKARD, SINGAPORE	48.4	197
12	MALAYSIA LNG	42.0	698
13	SHANGHAI BAOSHAN IRON	40.8	203
14	SSANGYONG CORP.	40.5	128
15	YUKONG INTERNATIONAL (S)	40.4	325
16	AMSTEEL CORP.	40.2	572
17	LG INDUSTRIES	39.8	666
18	KDD	39.7	341
19	OJI PAPER CO.	37.4	111
20	MATSUSHITA COMM. INDL.	36.8	156

21 to 40

Rank	Company	% Change Over 1995	1000 Rank
21	HIKAWA SHOJI	36.2	996
22	LI & FUNG	35.8	827
23	YACHIYO INDUSTRY	35.7	914
24	FUSHUN PETROCHEMICAL	35.6	845
25	PETROLEUM AUTHORITY	35.1	171
26	BP SINGAPORE	34.9	384
27	LG INTERNATIONAL CORP.	34.4	49
28	CITY DEVELOPMENTS	34.1	712
29	MITAC INTERNATIONAL CORP.	33.0	936
30	FIRST PACIFIC	33.8	162
31	SANSHIN ELECTRONICS	33.1	596
32	SIAM MOTORS	32.8	955
33	OHMOTO GUMI	32.4	859
34	INDIAN OIL	32.2	47
35	ARABIAN OIL	32.0	692
36	NATIONAL THERMAL POWER	31.9	547
37	SHANGHAI VOLKSWAGEN	31.9	431
38	WAKACHIKU CONSTRUCTION	31.6	766
39	SEMI-TECH (GLOBAL)	31.3	901
40	HYUNDAI MERCH. MARINE	30.9	480

The Highest Growth in Profits

Spectacular growth by Matsushita Electric Industrial, which saw a $604 million loss turned into a $1.27 billion profit, led the way. Any other year the Australian Wheat Board (from $858 million to $2.39 billion) and Honda Motor (from $752 million to $2.03 million) would normally have claimed the title. Nine state-controlled enterprises (energy and telecom industries) recorded modest growth. The falling buying power of Asian markets, likely to remain with us for sometime, will trim growth rates.

1 to 20

Rank	Company	Increase $ Million	1000 Rank
1	MATSUSHITA ELECTRIC INDL.*	1,790.1	10
2	HASEKO**	1,532.4	311
3	NISSAN MOTOR*	1,527.5	11
4	AUSTRALIAN WHEAT BOARD	1,483.8	364
5	HONDA MOTOR	1,382.3	14
6	MITSUBISHI ESTATE*	1,262.5	237
7	TOYOTA MOTOR CORP.	1,185.3	6
8	AOKI CORP.**	827.3	335
9	SONY CORP.	783.3	12
10	PETROLIAM NASIONAL	636.4	96
11	SUN HUNG KAI PROPERTIES	400.1	337
12	NISSHO IWAI CORP.*	372.0	7
13	CANON	359.8	34
14	SEAGATE TECHNOLOGY INTL.	343.3	179
15	ISETAN*	339.9	211
16	CHUNGHWA TELECOM	338.5	188
17	ELEC. GENERATING AUTH.	320.9	287
18	TDK	299.7	210
19	HEWLETT-PACKARD, SINGAPORE	280.8	197
20	CHINA NATIONAL OFFSHORE OIL	279.3	788

21 to 40

Rank	Company	Increase $ Million	1000 Rank
21	TOKYO ELECTRIC POWER	273.8	16
22	TOKYU CORP.	264.3	270
23	TELKOM	254.6	609
24	KANEBO**	249.4	215
25	PACIFIC DUNLOP*	243.2	257
26	TELEPHONE ORGANIZATION	220.8	803
27	PERTAMINA	214.2	40
28	DENSO CORP.	197.9	61
29	MATSUSHITA COMM. INDL.	197.7	156
30	NAGASAKIYA*	191.9	330
31	AUSTRALIAN NATIONAL IND.*	191.3	824
32	FUJI HEAVY INDUSTRIES	185.5	100
33	MITSUBISHI HEAVY INDS.	182.2	26
34	KENWOOD**	176.2	494
35	MARUZEN*	163.1	941
36	HENDERSON LAND DEVT.	160.8	536
37	ESSO AUSTRALIA	160.5	769
38	HONGKONG TELECOM	158.8	302
39	ENERGY AUSTRALIA*	156.6	830
40	PROTON	155.3	530

*Loss to profit **Reduced losses

The Biggest Profit Margins

Hong Kong's property companies have had a stranglehold at the top for sometime. At No.1, Cheung Kong soared with a margin of 93%. Now that Hong Kong's property market has lost up to 40% in value, with some analysts predicting further short-term falls, the situation is likely to change. Largely state-owned telecoms and power dominated the rest. Although debt-laden Malaysian, Thai and Indonesian telecoms will need to regroup to maintain their positions.

1 to 20

Rank	Company	Profit as % of sales	1000 Rank
1	CHEUNG KONG	92.8	784
2	AUSTRALIAN WHEAT BOARD	69.6	364
3	HENDERSON LAND DEVT.	50.7	536
4	TELEPHONE ORGANIZATION	50.3	803
5	SUN HUNG KAI PROPERTIES	48.9	337
6	SINGAPORE TELECOM	37.5	395
7	HONGKONG TELECOM	34.3	302
8	CHUNGHWA TELECOM	33.1	188
9	TELKOM	29.6	609
10	TELEKOM MALAYSIA	29.3	504
11	ESSO AUSTRALIA	28.0	769
12	CITIC PACIFIC	27.9	810
13	SINGAPORE POWER	26.6	636
14	CHINA LIGHT & POWER	25.0	549
15	PETROLIAM NASIONAL	25.2	96
16	NEW WORLD DEVELOPMENT	24.9	613
17	ELEC. GENERATING AUTH.	24.8	287
18	SEVEN-ELEVEN JAPAN	22.2	541
19	HUTCHISON WHAMPOA	21.6	263
20	CITY DEVELOPMENTS	20.3	712

21 to 40

Rank	Company	Profit as % of sales	1000 Rank
21	SWIRE PACIFIC	19.0	254
22	TELECOM NEW ZEALAND	18.7	616
23	MALAYSIA LNG	18.3	698
24	HEWLETT-PACKARD, SINGAPORE	17.8	197
25	FANUC	16.6	786
26	MOTOROLA ELECTRONICS	15.0	842
27	NATIONAL THERMAL POWER	15.9	547
28	SICHUAN CHANGHONG ELECT.	15.8	989
29	NINTENDO	15.7	328
30	CHINA STEEL CORP.	15.4	380
31	ALCOA OF AUSTRALIA	15.3	664
32	ROHM	15.3	467
33	RELIANCE INDUSTRIES	15.2	532
34	OIL & N. GAS COMMISSION	15.1	333
35	LEND LEASE	15.0	790
36	TAIWAN POWER	14.7	136
37	SINGAPORE AIRLINES	14.3	239
38	TAISHO PHARMACEUTICAL	14.1	604
39	FORMOSA PLASTICS	13.9	831
40	AMWAY JAPAN	13.2	680

The Highest Return on Assets

The Australian Wheat Board, riding high on bumper wheat crops and sales, moved to the top with a 146% return on assets. The six car manufacturing companies face stiffer competition as the Asian market stagnates on top of temporary oversupply. Telecommunications and information technology companies (12) put in a solid presence and are expected to remain in the top 40 — although companies like Motorola are savaging costs as a result of poorly performing Asian markets.

1 to 20

Rank	Company	Profit as % of assets	1000 Rank
1	AUSTRALIAN WHEAT BOARD	146.4	364
2	TAB NEW SOUTH WALES	59.7	442
3	SEAGATE TECHNOLOGY INTL.	43.2	179
4	AMWAY JAPAN	24.2	680
5	SHANGHAI VOLKSWAGEN	23.9	431
6	HEWLETT-PACKARD, SINGAPORE	23.9	197
7	HONGKONG TELECOM	23.5	302
8	MALAYSIA LNG	22.6	698
9	GMH AUTOMOTIVE	18.7	558
10	ESSO AUSTRALIA	17.8	769
11	MARUTI UDYOG	17.4	813
12	MOTOROLA ELECTRONICS	17.0	842
13	WESTERN DIGITAL (SING.)	16.8	569
14	PROTON	16.1	530
15	SINGAPORE TELECOM	15.3	395
16	GUDANG GARAM	15.2	453
17	SICHUAN CHANGHONG ELECT.	14.5	989
18	CHINA LIGHT & POWER	14.1	549
19	SINGAPORE POOLS	14.0	808
20	FORD MOTOR CO. OF AUST.	13.6	481

21 to 40

Rank	Company	Profit as % of assets	1000 Rank
21	CHUNGHWA TELECOM	13.3	188
22	ROTHMANS HOLDINGS	13.1	937
23	ALCOA OF AUSTRALIA	12.9	664
24	CHEUNG KONG	12.8	784
25	TELECOM NEW ZEALAND	12.6	617
26	I.T.C.	11.4	800
27	SEVEN-ELEVEN JAPAN	11.0	541
28	PETROLIAM NASIONAL	10.7	96
29	LI & FUNG	10.3	827
30	TELEPHONE ORGANIZATION	10.3	802
31	BHARAT PETROLEUM	9.0	300
32	PAKISTAN STATE OIL	9.8	888
33	VIDESH SANCHAR NIGAM	9.7	885
34	UMW HOLDINGS	9.5	892
35	ROHM	9.5	467
36	TELEKOM MALAYSIA	9.4	504
37	HENDERSON LAND DEVT.	9.4	536
38	PETRONAS DAGANGAN	9.4	851
39	TATA ENG. & LOCOMOTIVE	9.3	440
40	SHELL CO. OF THAILAND	9.2	713

The Highest Return on Equity

The list most likely to change. Already India's Reliance Industries, last year's No.1, has fallen off the map because of flat results. Japan's Chori, after forecasting losses will soon follow. Increased competition in drastically smaller markets should see Malaysian and Indonesian companies slipping on the list. Two newcomers are Shanghai Volkswagen and television manufacturer Sichuan Changhong Electronic. The Australian Wheat Board (392%) and Yukong International (285%) at the top were well ahead of the rest of the list.

1 to 20

Rank	Company	Profit as % of equity	1000 Rank
1	AUSTRALIAN WHEAT BOARD	391.9	364
2	YUKONG INTERNATIONAL (S)	284.6	325
3	TAB NEW SOUTH WALES	98.0	442
4	CHORI	77.7	183
5	NAGASAKIYA	68.8	330
6	BOONRAWD TRADING	58.9	939
7	SEAGATE TECHNOLOGY INTL.	58.0	179
8	MARUBENI INTL. PETROLEUM	48.3	459
9	AMWAY JAPAN	43.0	680
10	GMH AUTOMOTIVE	40.5	558
11	MALAYSIA LNG	39.9	698
12	SHANGHAI VOLKSWAGEN	39.0	431
13	SGS-THOMSON MICROELEC. ASIA	37.5	548
14	HEWLETT-PACKARD JAPAN	37.4	570
15	HONGKONG TELECOM	36.9	302
16	PAKISTAN STATE OIL	36.1	888
17	EON	35.6	462
18	TELECOM NEW ZEALAND	35.4	616
19	SICHUAN CHANGHONG ELECT.	33.0	989
20	MARUTI UDYOG	33.6	813

21 to 40

Rank	Company	Profit as % of equity	1000 Rank
21	ROTHMANS HOLDINGS	32.9	937
22	LI & FUNG	32.9	827
23	SEIBU DEPARTMENT STORES	31.2	214
24	PROTON	31.1	530
25	IBM AUSTRALIA	30.0	836
26	FORD MOTOR CO. OF AUST.	29.4	481
27	SIAM MOTORS	28.9	955
28	WESTERN DIGITAL (SING.)	28.9	569
29	HEWLETT-PACKARD, SINGAPORE	28.1	197
30	INDOCEMENT TUNGGAL	27.6	728
31	AUSTRALIA POST	27.3	544
32	PETROLIAM NASIONAL	26.6	96
33	FUJI HEAVY INDUSTRIES	26.4	100
34	GUDANG GARAM	25.7	453
35	I.T.C.	25.5	800
36	SINGAPORE TELECOM	25.5	395
37	TEAC CORP.	25.1	978
38	PETRON CORP.	24.7	645
39	FUJITSU GENERAL	24.6	847
40	LEIGHTON HOLDINGS	24.3	529

The Most Profit per Employee

Energy companies dominate the list. How much longer depends on the fallout of the oil price war. Economic adversity seems to be the spur for Japan (13) and Singapore (12). The disproportionate number of Singapore companies comes as no surprise, although seven of them are oil or petroleum companies. While the Japanese companies come from a wide range of industries: from computer games and robots to water treatment.

1 to 20

Rank	Company	$ per employee	1000 Rank
1	AUSTRALIAN WHEAT BOARD	5,885,309	364
2	YUKONG INTERNATIONAL (S)	1,086,934	325
3	NINTENDO	614,243	328
4	MARUBENI INTL. PETROLEUM	489,861	459
5	MALAYSIA LNG	444,414	698
6	ESSO AUSTRALIA	418,823	769
7	CHEUNG KONG	411,163	784
8	HENDERSON LAND DEVT.	352,239	536
9	SINGAPORE POOLS	340,048	808
10	IDEMITSU INTL. (ASIA)	322,373	682
11	AMWAY JAPAN	247,265	680
12	MOBIL OIL SINGAPORE	207,776	477
13	PETROLIAM NASIONAL	205,194	96
14	SEVEN-ELEVEN JAPAN	156,544	541
15	NIPPON TELEVISION	142,890	458
16	SUN HUNG KAI PROPERTIES	139,645	337
17	COSMO OIL INTERNATIONAL	134,752	948
18	BP SINGAPORE	131,831	384
19	FANUC	130,802	786
20	PETRON CORP.	127,590	645

21 to 40

Rank	Company	$ per employee	1000 Rank
21	CALTEX TRADING	124,738	116
22	SINGAPORE POWER	121,513	636
23	HEWLETT-PACKARD, SINGAPORE	115,637	197
24	SINGAPORE TELECOM	113,224	395
25	SINGAPORE PETROLEUM	106,621	950
26	HONGKONG TELECOM	104,092	302
27	CHINA LIGHT & POWER	101,456	549
28	PETROLEUM AUTHORITY	95,494	171
29	PILIPINAS SHELL PETRO.	87,386	726
30	FUJI TELEVISION NETWORK	85,893	454
31	JAPAN OIL DEVELOPMENT	84,403	693
32	EVERGREEN MARINE	84,021	794
33	BENESSE CORP.	81,227	620
34	JAPAN TELECOM	80,901	363
35	KURITA WATER INDUSTRIES	78,552	838
36	HONDA MOTOR	71,585	14
37	ASIA MATSUSHITA ELECTRIC	70,253	286
38	SSANGYONG OIL REFINING	69,778	219
39	SONY MUSIC ENTERTAINMENT	68,984	703
40	KAWASAKI KISEN	66,831	276

Chapter Three

THE LARGEST COMPANIES OUTSIDE JAPAN

One of the first things you notice about the *Asiaweek* 1000 list of Megacompanies in Asia is how top-heavy the roster is with Japanese enterprises. Japan accounts for 80.2% of the combined sales of the 1000. That share is way ahead of South Korea, the country with the second highest number of companies in the ranking, which has just 6.2% of the total turnover. Not surprisingly, the table of the 50 largest companies outside Japan ranked by sales is dominated by South Korea, though China, Australia, Taiwan, Malaysia, Singapore, Hong Kong, Thailand, New Zealand, and India are also represented. Most of those that make the grade are large conglomerates such as the Korean *chaebol*, including Samsung, Hyundai, and Daewoo. There are the big state petroleum firms, including Indian Oil, Thailand's Petroleum Authority, Taiwan's Chinese Petroleum Corp., and Malaysia's Petroliam Nasional or Petronas. Utilities and telecommunications giants also rate. These include Australia's Telstra, Korea Electric Power, and Chunghwa Telecom of Taiwan. Automakers are also big. Among them: Hyundai Motor, Shanghai Automotive, and Kia Motors. The remaining places are filled by the region's big diversified trading and investment groups, including Hong Kong's Jardine Matheson and First Pacific, as well as by other large companies including Rupert Murdoch's News Corp., the Australian airline Qantas, and Taiwan computer-maker Acer.

Don't expect this list to stay static in coming years. Korean groups, in particular, are in for a fall. Even before the crisis, Korean companies, including Kia Motors, were in deep trouble. Amid the crisis, many of the *chaebol* will have to streamline operations and limit the number of businesses they are in. Not that the *chaebol* will suddenly turn them into baby enterprises. Still, restructuring will cut them down to size. Instead of 40 or 50 companies in the typical conglomerate, after reform, perhaps only 10 may be left in each stable. The same may happen to state enterprises that are privatized or rationalized as Asian economies such as China seek to reform loss-making public-sector giants. For example, in recent years, Australia's Telstra, which was listed last year, has been reshaped into a more dynamic and productive enterprise.

Corporate renovation across the region, particularly after the crisis, will result in major changes in the rankings in coming years. It doesn't follow, though, that a big company's position on the list will drop as a result of restructuring. The goal for most enterprises is to improve productivity and competitiveness. If this is achieved, ideally sales will grow and a company could rise in the rankings. Take Taiwan's Acer, which founding chairman Stan Shih reorganized two years ago, introducing a decentralized management system. Shih's intention was to give managers of each of the group's units wider autonomy and to encourage entrepreneurship among them. Since then, Acer has continued its rise up the global personal computer sales league to become one of the top 10 PC producers in the world.

For now, it is almost impossible to predict just how East Asia's corporate landscape will look after the crisis is history and recovery takes hold. The betting, though, is that Asia's enterprises will be leaner, more competitive, and more productive. The next two tough years will prove to

The Largest Companies outside Japan

1 to 25

Rank	Company	Country	Sales $ Millions	Profit $ Millions	Profit as % of sales	Assets $ Millions	Work Force	1000 Rank
1	SAMSUNG CO.	SOUTH KOREA	29,997.8	54.1	0.2	7,448.4	9,049	24
2	CHINA PETROCHEMICAL CORP.	CHINA	26,874.5	662.6	2.5	37,788.4	650,000	29
3	HYUNDAI CORP.	SOUTH KOREA	25,548.9	15.3	0.1	572.6	614	30
4	DAEWOO CORP.	SOUTH KOREA	23,633.9	90.7	0.4	11,500.1	12,274	33
5	SAMSUNG ELECTRONICS	SOUTH KOREA	19,733.4	204.1	1.0	19,688.6	59,086	38
6	PERTAMINA	INDONESIA	19,276.5	578.1	2.0	14,205.5	33,333	40
7	SINOCHEM	CHINA	17,953.0	71.3	0.4	6,600.0	1,322	45
8	INDIAN OIL	INDIA	17,615.6	393.1	2.2	NA	33,915	47
9	BROKEN HILL PROPRIETARY	AUSTRALIA	17,474.4	320.0	1.8	28,759.9	61,000	48
10	LG INTERNATIONAL CORP.	SOUTH KOREA	17,454.3	26.9	0.2	1,726.0	1,352	49
11	JIANGSU SUP. & MKTG. CO-OP.	CHINA	16,303.3	185.9	1.1	6,635.9	500,000	57
12	KOREA ELECTRIC POWER	SOUTH KOREA	14,393.4	742.8	5.2	44,334.1	31,895	65
13	HYUNDAI MOTOR	SOUTH KOREA	14,282.8	107.9	0.8	9,943.0	47,174	66
14	COLES MYER	AUSTRALIA	14,229.2	219.5	1.5	5,534.9	152,744	67
15	WOOLWORTHS	AUSTRALIA	12,446.6	201.0	1.6	2,789.9	100,000	79
16	TELSTRA	AUSTRALIA	12,084.9	1,265.0	10.5	20,244.3	64,609	82
17	COFCO	CHINA	12,021.9	92.9	0.8	4,142.0	26,000	84
18	CHINESE PETROLEUM CORP.	TAIWAN	12,019.4	276.4	2.3	19,079.1	20,322	85
19	POHANG IRON & STEEL	SOUTH KOREA	11,989.7	735.1	6.1	19,524.1	28,093	86
20	NEWS CORP.	AUSTRALIA	11,716.9	563.7	4.8	32,379.2	28,200	90
21	JARDINE MATHESON	HONG KONG	11,605.0	536.1	4.6	14,285.4	200,000	94
22	PETROLIAM NASIONAL	MALAYSIA	11,480.0	2,892.0	25.2	27,090.1	14,094	96
23	YUKONG LTD.	SOUTH KOREA	10,345.1	84.8	0.8	12,104.5	6,022	112
24	CALTEX TRADING	SINGAPORE	9,872.6	10.5	0.1	1,037.4	84	116
25	LG ELECTRONICS	SOUTH KOREA	9,326.2	80.6	0.9	8,504.0	34,525	126

be more than a hiccup, but far less than a fatal blow. In the long run, Asia's economies will rebound and continue to expand. After a period of necessary consolidation, so will the region's corporations. In no time, they will be back in fighting form.

The Largest Companies outside Japan

26 to 50

Rank	Company	Country	Sales $ Millions	Profit $ Millions	Profit as % of sales	Assets $ Millions	Work Force	1000 Rank
26	SSANGYONG CORP.	SOUTH KOREA	9,161.9	3.5	0.0	612.5	935	128
27	KOREA TELECOM	SOUTH KOREA	8,904.3	224.3	2.5	18,076.3	60,067	131
28	TAIWAN POWER	TAIWAN	8,510.3	1,247.9	14.7	34,815.3	30,152	136
29	RIO TINTO	AUSTRALIA	8,452.0	1,098.4	12.0	17,108.7	51,000	137
30	KIA MOTORS	SOUTH KOREA	8,213.2	8.7	0.1	8,632.9	29,619	142
31	SHANGHAI AUTOMOTIVE	CHINA	7,889.4	801.6	10.2	6,634.2	60,981	145
32	TATTERSALLS SWEEP	AUSTRALIA	7,742.1	NA	—	NA	315	148
33	HYUNDAI MOTOR SERVICE	SOUTH KOREA	7,272.1	39.6	0.5	5,222.8	14,959	159
34	FIRST PACIFIC	HONG KONG	7,025.7	202.2	2.9	8,491.8	52,880	162
35	DAIRY FARM	HONG KONG	6,968.4	41.5	0.6	3,121.3	49,900	163
36	LG CALTEX OIL CORP.	SOUTH KOREA	6,920.3	15.2	0.2	6,814.1	2,364	165
37	PETROLEUM AUTHORITY	THAILAND	6,538.8	327.5	5.0	4,583.4	3,430	171
38	QANTAS	AUSTRALIA	6,504.0	197.8	3.0	7,760.1	30,080	174
39	DAEWOO HEAVY INDUSTRIES	SOUTH KOREA	6,400.0	92.0	1.5	11,099.3	20,320	176
40	SEAGATE TECHNOLOGY INTL.	SINGAPORE	6,242.6	797.2	12.8	1,843.0	19,528	179
41	CHUNGHWA TELECOM	TAIWAN	6,036.9	1,998.3	33.1	15,076.8	35,500	188
42	BTR NYLEX	AUSTRALIA	6,006.5	-169.7	—	7,218.7	30,000	189
43	ACER	TAIWAN	5,893.0	188.0	3.2	4,192.0	16,778	192
44	HYUNDAI ENG. & CONST.	SOUTH KOREA	5,882.4	26.3	0.4	8,819.4	28,222	193
45	FLETCHER CHALLENGE	NEW ZEALAND	5,861.9	114.1	1.9	9,214.7	23,000	195
46	HEWLETT-PACKARD	SINGAPORE	5,839.1	1,040.7	17.8	4,356.1	9,000	197
47	SUNKYONG LTD.	SOUTH KOREA	5,826.8	10.6	0.2	1,343.5	1,115	198
48	HYUNDAI HEAVY INDS.	SOUTH KOREA	5,824.4	17.4	0.3	9,470.9	27,416	200
49	SHANGHAI BAOSHAN IRON	CHINA	5,820.0	290.1	4.0	11,909.0	10,542	203
50	EAST CHINA ELECTRIC POWER	CHINA	5,817.1	221.3	3.8	11,842.1	200,000	204

Chapter Four

TOP ENTERPRISES BY COUNTRY

 Australia and New Zealand: Crisis Victims

In recent years, Australia and New Zealand have looked to their dynamic neighbors to revive their weak economies. Both countries sought to plug into the Asian grid and benefit from the region's fast growth and opening markets. Australia, in particular, has been an enthusiastic backer of such initiatives as the Asia-Pacific Economic Cooperation forum, building deep commercial links with the ASEAN nations who form a core within APEC.

Ironically, the effect the East Asian crisis has had on them is a measure of just how plugged-in Australia and New Zealand now are. External forces are ganging up on the pair. Tourism, property investment, university enrollment — the Asian turmoil is taking its toll. Take property in Australia. Asians have been big investors in inner city apartments in Sydney, Melbourne, Perth, and Brisbane, as well as all along the Gold Coast. Due to the Asian recession, sales are down sharply, and prices have plummeted 10–20% in the first quarter of 1998. Rentals are falling too. New projects are being delayed or canceled.

Tourism is also slumping. The number of Asian visitors to Australia has plunged. Year-on-year arrivals from Korea are down about 70%, from Japan down 15–20%, Malaysia down 30–40%, and Thailand down over 50% since devaluations began. This is hurting hotels, tour operators, airlines, resorts, tourist attractions that rely on tourist ticket sales, retailers, and duty free shops. In places like Cairns and the Gold Coast, duty free sales in March 1998 were down 40% year-on-year. Australian commodity exports to Asia including Japan, from wool and iron ore to wheat and meat, have fallen.

The Asian recession has slowed Australia's output. Most analysts have shaved off 1–1.5% from Australian GDP growth, which is forecast to come in under 3% this year from 3.75% in 1997. Falling exports to Asia, larger imports due to robust domestic demand, and a lower Australian dollar are likely to lead to a huge current account blowout. Some are predicting that the current account deficit for 1998 could reach 6.5–7% of GDP. A rising current account deficit and high unemployment — still at 8.5% of the workforce — have increased the pressure on the Australian dollar.

With the government wanting to decrease unemployment, one route available is to cut interest rates further. That could mean more pressure on the currency. The banking sector, coming off a year of record profits, will be sluggish, due partly to Asian exposure, and non-performing loans are slowly increasing. There is some good news for the Lucky Country. Inflation is at its lowest in decades. The government last year recorded a budget surplus due to the sale of state enterprises such as the Telstra telecommunications giant.

The story is similar in New Zealand, where a new leadership under conservative Jenny Shipley took over the governing coalition late last year. In March, Reserve Bank governor Don Brash sharply eased interest rates in a surprise effort to reinvigorate the economy and boost consumer confidence which has been battered by the Asian crisis. Brash said it was preferable to tolerate a rise in inflation from the current 1.6% than to risk letting the economy slow down dramatically. Growth for 1998 remains forecast at between 2.5% and 4%, but as with its larger neighbor, the figure will likely fall below 3%. While interest rates are expected to be volatile, inflation is set to remain below 2%. The local dollar is likely to continue to weaken. In March, an extended power blackout hit the central business district of Auckland, raising questions about the infrastructure standards of the city, New Zealand's commercial center.

Another area where both Australia and New Zealand are hurting as a result of the Asian economic turmoil is in university enrollment. Asian intake in educational institutions is down for the first time in recent memory. Only the numbers of students from Singapore and Hong Kong are holding up, while the figures from elsewhere in East Asia are down sharply. In a way, this could be a major setback to the integration of Australia and New Zealand with Asia.

Table I: Australia and New Zealand's Top Enterprises

Rank	Company	Main Business	Sales $ Millions	Profit $ Millions	Profit as % of sales	1000 Rank
1	BROKEN HILL PROPRIETARY	Steel, mining, oil	17,474.4	320.0	1.8	48
2	COLES MYER	Retailing	14,229.2	219.5	1.5	67
3	WOOLWORTHS	Retailing	12,446.6	201.0	1.6	79
4	TELSTRA	Telecommunications	12,084.9	1,265.0	10.5	82
5	NEWS CORP.	Publishing, broadcasting	11,716.9	563.7	4.8	90
6	RIO TINTO	Mining	8,452.0	1,098.4	12.0	137
7	TATTERSALLS SWEEP	Gaming	7,742.1	NA	—	148
8	QANTAS	Air transport	6,504.0	197.8	3.0	174
9	BTR NYLEX	Packaging, plastics	6,006.5	(169.7)	—	189
10	FLETCHER CHALLENGE*	Paper, building materials	5,861.9	114.1	1.9	195
11	CSR	Building materials, sugar	5,040.2	166.1	3.3	243
12	AMCOR	Packaging	4,918.3	(85.8)	—	253
13	PACIFIC DUNLOP	Trading, batteries	4,812.9	139.2	2.9	257
14	MITSUI & CO. (AUSTRALIA)	Commodity trading	4,802.7	8.8	0.2	259
15	BORAL	Building materials	4,624.5	315.8	6.8	267
16	MOBIL OIL AUSTRALIA	Oil products	4,507.9	54.0	1.2	279
17	NEW ZEALAND DAIRY BOARD*	Dairy products	4,214.7	7.8	0.2	296
18	SHELL AUSTRALIA	Oil, chemicals, metals	4,165.6	232.1	5.6	303
19	DAVIDS	Food & drink distribution	3,995.0	(188.1)	—	317
20	MITSUBISHI AUSTRALIA	General trading	3,868.0	1.9	0.1	326

*New Zealand

INVESTOR TIPS

Asian immigration and wider commercial exchange with their neighbors have made Australia and New Zealand significantly more cosmopolitan societies in recent years. Canberra's moves to abolish links to the British Crown and establish a republic are symbolic of the country's evolving identity. Though its population is only about the size of Taiwan's, Australia is a vast country, rich in resources. With the Sydney Olympics coming up in 2000, a new, more dynamic Australia will be making its international debut.

In the short term:

- Remember that some things have yet to change. The recent dockworkers strike shows that the union movement is alive and well in Australia. Investors should be sensitive to the strength of labor in shaping their plans.

- These days, a company dependent on Asian business may not be such an attractive option. But when Asia recovers, an enterprise that is already in the game could be a winner.

- Think carefully about your objectives if you are looking to establish a base in Australia or New Zealand. Some companies in expensive Asian cities have shifted backroom operations to Australia. But geographic distance and logistical factors may make the Southern Hemisphere impractical.

In the long term:

- Australia and New Zealand are reinventing themselves gradually. In Australia, the privatization of state firms is going to energize the economy over the long term. Both economies, with their traditional links to the West and the deepening contacts with Asia, will increasingly be interesting arenas for investment.

COMPANIES TO WATCH

- **Brierley Investments**

This New Zealand-based investment company, which used to be owned by Ronald Brierley, who heads the Guinness Peat Group, has controlling stakes in companies including Air New Zealand, John Fairfax (the Australian newspaper publisher), and Britain's Thistle Hotels. Despite its high-profile purchases, BIL has not profited much from them. The East Asian crisis has hit some of its largest interests hard. Recent turmoil in the boardroom has led to speculation that the company might be broken up or that it may sell off some of its assets.

- **News Corp.**

Rupert Murdoch's Australian-based holding company. Cash rich from half a billion in profits that are expected to roll in from just one movie, *Titanic*. Even before that blockbuster, Murdoch was cashed like never before and hasn't made any big purchases in a long while. The legendary tycoon is giving his children, particularly son Lachlan, greater responsibilities in running the group.

- **Telstra**

Australia's main telecom company which was listed late last year and has increased profits and efficiency by leaps and bounds in recent years. Its rivals such as Optus (half owned by Cable & Wireless) are still far behind with minuscule market share. Telstra also has hoards of cash and is looking for acquisitions in Asia and around the world. The company is led by blunt-talking American Frank Blount, who has downsized the once state-owned monopoly and made it an efficient, lean, dynamic company.

China: Steady and Stable

With China's neighbors in economic turmoil since the middle of 1997, all eyes have been on the mainland and how its leaders manage through the crisis. 'The most pressing threat is that China may have to devalue [the renminbi],' Philippines' president Fidel Ramos warned early this year. If Beijing were to allow the yuan to slip, that would almost certainly put the rest of the region through another wrenching round of plunging currencies. Hong Kong would likely have to jack up already high interest rates even higher to shore up its dollar's peg to the greenback. By most accounts, pledges from Chinese leaders, particularly economic czar Zhu Rongji who became premier in March, put to rest lingering doubts. 'They are pretty adamant that in the interests not only of Hong Kong and China but [also] of all of Asia, the renminbi should maintain the present level,' Donald Tsang Yam, Hong Kong's financial secretary, said in February.

The Asian economic crisis has been something of a debut for a new China, a China that behaves. The mainland has sailed through the rough East Asian waters, buffeted but hardly heading the *Titanic's* way. And Beijing has acted responsibly. Zhu repeated his vow to stick to his guns and keep the renminbi steady so often that he was in danger of sounding too insistent to be credible. But since the newly minted premier's star turn in London during the second Asia-Europe Meeting (ASEM) summit in April, the ranks of the believers have grown. China knows its economic stability is just what Asia and the rest of the world need right now and it is delivering just that. Make no mistake, China is not being charitable. By acting responsibly in the midst of the crisis, Beijing is ensuring that its own economy does not get pulled into the East Asian maelstrom.

To be sure, China is not Japan. Southeast Asia is looking to Tokyo to help pull its battered economies out of the turmoil. Its neighbors are simply counting on the mainland to remain steady. That will not be easy. With China treading a minefield of state-enterprise reform, rising unemployment, and a major banking overhaul, anything can go wrong. 'It is going to be very tricky but there is a good chance that China will go through the process well,' says Edward Tse Cho-che, vice president at Booz-Allen & Hamilton in Hong Kong, who oversees the multinational consulting firm's China practice. 'But if it runs into problems, gets pressured, and has to do a number of things including devalue the renminbi, then the rest of Asia will really be sucked into the whole swirl.'

The immense task ahead for China cannot be underestimated. Zhu's agenda is a long one. The problems of East Asia have demonstrated to the Chinese leadership that they cannot hold back on reforms. The government has set a growth target for 1998 of 8%, a goal some believe would be difficult to achieve. That might be too ambitious. In April, the International Monetary Fund (IMF) forecast 7% growth this year. The centerpiece of Zhu's plans is revamping the bloated, loss-making state-owned enterprise (SOE) sector. Zhu is also aiming to make heavy cuts in the government payroll and to turn the country's banks into true commercial institutions. Though its savings are high and its reserves are among the world's largest, China needs fresh capital to recapitalize state-owned banks. Zhu also wants to create a housing market on the mainland, with average Chinese owning their own homes. He calls it China's "New Deal". By providing housing, the government hopes to convince people to spend some of their enormous hoard of cash — much of it held outside the banking system — to stimulate the economy.

'It is common sense to say that China is faced with a tremendous challenge in its transformation and reforms,' says Jean-Michel Severino, the World Bank's vice president for East Asia and the Pacific. 'They will face a lot of difficulties in the process. But you can see the motivation and determination of the new government, so they have the assets to handle all these problems.' Among the most pressing issues: rising unemployment. Though official figures put urban joblessness at only around 2%, the real figure is probably higher, particularly in heavy industrial areas. The numbers will get worse once reforms of the 305,000 SOEs start kicking in.

These firms add little value to the economy, employing 110 million workers or about 70% of the urban workforce. They account for 80% of the banking system's outstanding loans. Tellingly, SOEs produce just 30% of China's industrial output. Across the board, the companies are saddled with sub-standard technology, constant interference from government bureaucrats, and poor management made worse by lax governance and a lack of transparency.

Beijing hopes that massive investment in infrastructure will alleviate the unemployment situation. Reflating the economy through a domestic stimulus package will also cushion the mainland from the effects of the East Asian crisis. 'The decision [on massive domestic investments] was made based on what has happened in Southeast Asia, particularly the possible slowdown of China's exports for next year because everybody is more competitive and is cutting imports from China,' says Fan Gang, director of the National Economic Research Institute in Beijing. By focusing on internal growth, the Chinese are signaling their resolve not to out-export their neighbors. If that happened, the region could find itself in a cycle of destabilizing competitive devaluations.

Yet China will also have to move to boost foreign direct investment by opening up markets even more, particularly with U.S. and European investors now hungrily buying up cheap assets in Southeast Asia and Korea. 'One of the ways to create jobs is to continue attracting foreign investment,' says Tse. 'If China wants to maintain economic stability, then it will have to do that.' Beijing will need to iron out problems investors — even well-connected ones — have been complaining about for years. On a recent trip to China to inspect a troubled Singapore township project in Suzhou, near Shanghai, Singapore senior minister Lee Kuan Yew spoke bluntly to officials about the difficulties the Lion City's flagship investment had encountered, especially infighting between the central government and Suzhou authorities.

Many foreign ventures in China have complained about difficulties in training and retaining local staff. Many investors now make it a point as far as possible to recruit Chinese. 'We hire about 20 local graduates a year,' says one regional boss in Hong Kong. 'These guys are world-class. All they need is some basic training in marketing, which does not take too long. They are better than someone just out of the U.S. You only need to invest in about two years of training.' But often, as soon as a qualified manager learns the ropes, he gets lured away to another company. Some firms have reported instances of ex-staff rejoining at the same position at three times the original salary after three years floating from one job to another. 'We're paying more money for

Table 2: China's Top Enterprises

Rank	Company	Main Business	Sales $ Millions	Profit $ Millions	Profit as % of sales	1000 Rank
1	CHINA PETROCHEMICAL CORP.	Chemicals	26,874.5	662.6	2.5	29
2	SINOCHEM	Chemicals trading	17,953.0	71.3	0.4	45
3	JIANGSU SUP. & MKTG. CO-OP.	Food processing, trading	16,303.3	185.9	1.1	57
4	COFCO	Food trading	12,021.9	92.9	0.8	84
5	SHANGHAI AUTOMOTIVE	Cars	7,889.4	801.6	**	10.2
6	SHANGHAI BAOSHAN IRON	Steel	5,820.0	290.1	4.0	203
7	EAST CHINA ELECTRIC POWER	Power generation	5,817.1	221.3	3.8	204
8	CHINA STATE CONST. ENG.	Construction	4,951.8	55.1	1.1	249
9	CITIC	Investment	3,712.5	297.6	8.0	339
10	SHOUGANG CORP.	Steel	2,967.2	38.5	1.3	422
11	SHANGHAI VOLKSWAGEN	Cars	2,923.5	331.1	11.3	431
12	CHINA HUANENG GROUP	Power generation	2,490.4	128.9	5.2	524
13	CHINA NATIONAL AGRI.	Agricultural products	2,025.8	0.3	0.0	648
14	MOTOROLA ELECTRONIC (CHINA)	Communication prods.	1,960.5	NA	—	674
15	BEIJING YANSHAN PETROCHEM.	Chemicals	1,953.8	62.3	3.2	676
16	QILU PETROCHEMICAL	Chemicals	1,767.1	18.1	**	1.0
17	CHINA NATIONAL OFFSHORE OIL	Oil	1,680.7	382.5	22.8	788
18	DONGFENG MOTORS CORP.	Cars	1,639.0	46.7	*	2.8
19	FUSHUN PETROCHEMICAL	Chemicals	1,563.6	204.5	13.1	845
20	SHANGHAI PETROCHEMICAL	Chemicals	1,431.4	121.3	8.5	909

*Pre-tax profit
**total profit

less talent,' complains one Hong Kong-based executive with a large multinational. 'You can talk about training all you want, but you are asking companies to compress 15 years of training into six months and then put someone in charge.' Many local MBA graduates, CEOs say, think that as soon as they join, they are qualified to run the company.

The new China that has emerged after the East Asian crisis is likely to attract another wave of foreign investors encouraged by what they have seen in recent months. Amid the turmoil, 'while Japan has failed to rise to the occasion, its rival for regional leadership has been making all the right moves,' says Robert Lees, secretary-general of the Pacific Basin Economic Council, a private-sector group of more than 1200 member companies in Asia and the Americas. 'Beijing has accepted the realities and responsibilities of being a full player in the global economy.' While that means China is becoming a much more predictable country, it must surely also mean that, for investors and people doing business there, the mainland has become a much more exciting place to be.

INVESTOR TIPS

The list of top Chinese enterprises includes mainly large state enterprises. Once SOE reforms take hold, China's corporate scene will change. Investors typically enter joint ventures with a local entity, but increasingly, some of the more savvy have found that setting up a wholly owned operation (Yes, it is possible!) has its advantages.

In the short term:

- Look for opportunities that may arise from coming developments such as the rationalization of state enterprises, the infrastructure investment program, and the housing initiative.

- The biggest headache for many investors is staffing. You train them, you lose them. Work hard to encourage loyalty among employees, but don't be surprised if your venture suffers from high turnover.

- Needless to say, do your homework. Despite what the pundits say about post-crisis Asia, *guanxi* — or networking — is still the name of the game.

Remember, it is often not the top officials or corporate chiefs whom you should be courting, but behind-the-scenes senior figures, normally retired ministers or bureaucrats. Their recommendation for your project will count more toward approval. Many foreign companies make the mistake of bringing their company chairman to Beijing or Shanghai for a round of audiences with the president and the premier and then sitting back. Sipping tea with Jiang Zemin may not be enough to seal a deal.

In the long term:

China is a long-run play. Anecdotal evidence suggests that few investors are making the loads of profits they may have hoped for when they first considered a move on the mainland. Stay the course. And don't look on the country as one big market that requires a full-frontal assault. One province, even one large municipality, could be the size of France. Success belongs to those who start modestly.

COMPANIES TO WATCH

- **Shanghai Volkswagen**

Reputed to be one of the most successful joint ventures in China. Most of Shanghai's taxicabs are VWs. The company is poised to grow along with the demand for automobiles. It enjoys one of the highest returns on equity of Asia's megacompanies.

- **CITIC**

The investment arm of the central government. Its Hong Kong operation is one of the special administrative region's major enterprises. CITIC is growing into a key player in the region.

- **Shanghai Petrochemical**

China's petrochemical industry is likely to continue to be a key sector. Shanghai Petrochemical is expected to benefit from industrial growth in the Shanghai area.

Hong Kong: Tiger's Misfortune

When British rule over Hong Kong ended on July 1, 1997, the handover to China turned out to be something of an anti-climax. Not surprising. The territory's 6 million people had more than a dozen years to get used to the idea, following the signing in 1984 of the crucial Sino-British Joint Declaration on the transfer. The wait had been marked by moments of high tension — the collapse of confidence following the June 1989 military crackdown in Beijing's Tiananmen Square, for example. There was also the last five years of British administration under the governorship of Chris Patten, who riled the mainland leadership by pushing through electoral reforms in the territory. That period saw Britain and China locked in bitter prolonged negotiations over almost all aspects of the transition.

But despite the political storms swirling over Hong Kong, economically, the territory thrived. Economic integration with the mainland, particularly with southern China and coastal areas, had pushed Hong Kong to a new level. The city secured its position as the region's finance and services hub and China's premier gateway to the world. By the time the handover came around, there was really only one question on people's minds: Would Beijing keep its hands off this smoothly purring money machine? For the most part, it has. Confounding their critics, Chinese leaders have taken pains to steer clear. Even behind the scenes, there is little evidence of interference. In October 1997, when currency traders put enormous pressure on the local dollar, leading to speculation that the peg to the greenback would be broken, Beijing remained on the sidelines, with officials expressing total support for Hong Kong's monetary authorities.

The Chinese did what they had to do, holding the line on the renminbi. Had they not done so, there is no question that confidence in Hong Kong would have taken a bad beating, whether or not the special administrative region (SAR) deserved it. As it was, even prior to the handover, Hong Kong had been burdened by far more than its fair share of troubles, many of them unrelated to the regional crisis and beyond the SAR's control. A serious retail slump was made worse last year by flagging tourism during and after the handover. The avian influenza crisis cut further into the travel trade. After most of East Asia's currencies depreciated dramatically following the flotation of the Thai baht in July, the betting was that expensive Hong Kong would have to adjust to stay competitive. Monetary authorities had to raise inter-bank lending rates to stave off speculation against the local dollar. Banks were forced to raise mortgage rates, choking off demand in the overheated real-estate sector and sending the property-heavy stock market plummeting. Property values plunged 30–35% in a matter of months.

Hong Kong's woes have deepened. Unemployment has started creeping up. It rose to 3.5% for the first quarter of 1998 and could top 4% (almost unimaginable for the territory) by the end of the year. Lay-offs in the financial, retail, and tourism sectors have been heavy. And companies have gone bankrupt. Among them: high-flying investment house Peregrine, which came undone by exposure to an Indonesian transport company. Though it had weathered the crisis reasonably well, by the fourth quarter of 1997, the SAR was clearly in a funk. Critics blamed the government of Chief Executive Tung Chee-hwa for the malaise, accusing it of incompetently handling everything from last year's bird flu outbreak and the red tide that decimated the territory's fishing industry in April to the preparations for the May 24 Legislative Council polls. Democracy groups have alleged that official policies since the handover have undermined the rule of law and stacked the political deck in favor of the pro-China business elite. Some investors have warned that Hong Kong needs to tackle the problem of high costs if the city is to remain competitive.

Financial Secretary Donald Tsang argues that Hong Kong is adjusting. He and other officials say there is no question of eliminating or altering the dollar peg. As for competitiveness, the SAR was reacting in its usual way through asset price deflation. The property market's correction, he reckons, has been significant by any measure. Says Tsang: 'In terms of attracting multinationals to establish a base here and in terms of rendering a decent profit to investment, we are very competitive. Also, we provide a return in a stable, hard currency. We are just as competitive as New York, London, Tokyo, or Singapore. We are certainly not as cheap as Jakarta, but we are talking about places in a different league.'

That is very much the point. The Asian crisis has separated the economic men from the boys. Hong Kong, Taiwan, and Singapore all took a hit and survived in good shape. China shares many of the problems plaguing its Southeast Asian neighbors, but its more closed economy has ironically been its saving grace. Hong Kong has proved its mettle. But for the SAR to retain its position, it will have to change. Property prices cannot be allowed to spiral, driven by speculative buying. More needs to be done to improve education and the sophistication of services.

The opening of the new international airport in July is set to underscore that few are able to deliver what Hong Kong can. With its infrastructure, low taxation, well-developed legal and financial systems, and relatively free society, the SAR remains ahead of any Chinese city, including Shanghai, and competitive with its Southeast Asian rival, Singapore. And with China turning its attention to reforming its state-owned enterprises and launching a massive domestic investment program, Hong Kong is likely to benefit even more. The biggest investor on the mainland, the SAR is poised to reach new heights as China's economy zooms forward. 'Whenever China moves, we take advantage,' says Tsang. 'We are near; we are well connected; we are part of the nation.'

It stands to reason then that when it comes to picking investments in Hong Kong, the China factor is the obvious key consideration. Nearly every one of the SAR's top enterprises on the *Asiaweek* 1000 list has a mainland mission which forms the backbone of its future plans. Even the old British trading houses, or *hongs*, such as Swire and Jardines are investing in the mainland. And the roster of Hong Kong megacompanies includes CITIC Pacific, the local investment arm of the Chinese central government. In coming years, more such Chinese firms will likely join the ranks of the SAR's biggest and best, particularly with the arrival in recent years of the so-called red chips, or Hong Kong-listed Chinese holding companies stocked with valuable mainland assets. The China play is a long-term strategy. No sure thing, by any means, but the mainland's track record so far suggests that the odds are in its favor. And that can only be good news for punters who take a bet on Hong Kong.

Table 3: Hong Kong's Top Enterprises

Rank	Company	Main Business	Sales $ Millions	Profit $ Millions	Profit as % of sales	1000 Rank
1	JARDINE MATHESON	General trading	11,605.0	536.1	4.6	94
2	FIRST PACIFIC	Trading, investment	7,025.7	202.2	2.9	162
3	DAIRY FARM	Supermarkets, food	6,968.4	41.5	0.6	163
4	SWIRE PACIFIC	Investment, property	4,917.4	981.3	19.0	254
5	HUTCHISON WHAMPOA	Retailing, telecom.	4,700.3	1,015.4	21.6	263
6	HONGKONG TELECOM	Telecommunications	4,176.6	1,433.0	34.3	302
7	CATHAY PACIFIC AIRWAYS	Air transport	4,151.4	488.3	11.8	305
8	SUN HUNG KAI PROPERTIES	Property development	3,712.8	1,815.4	48.9	337
9	HENDERSON LAND DEVT.	Property	2,431.6	1,232.8	50.7	536
10	CHINA LIGHT & POWER	Power generation	2,387.2	620.0	25.0	549
11	NEW WORLD DEVELOPMENT	Property, hotels	2,143.0	533.0	24.9	613
12	JARDINE INTL. MOTORS	Car dealership	2,007.4	68.7	3.4	656
13	JARDINE PACIFIC	Trading, services	1,929.0	93.5	4.8	684
14	ORIENT OVERSEAS	Shipping	1,882.3	109.5	5.8	708
15	CHEUNG KONG	Property, investment	1,692.6	1,570.6	92.8	784
16	CITIC PACIFIC	Trading, infrastructure	1,635.4	456.7	27.9	810
17	LI & FUNG	Trading	1,604.4	38.5	2.4	827
18	SEMI-TECH (GLOBAL)	Appliances, electronics	1,448.3	44.9	3.1	901
19	C. P. POKPHAND	Animal feeds	1,332.2	7.1	0.5	962
20	SIME DARBY HK	Car dealership	1,126.5	48.1	4.3	—

INVESTOR TIPS

Hong Kong is possibly the easiest place in Asia to do business. Setting up a company is easy, and the legal system is efficient. The city, in recent years, has become increasingly cosmopolitan. The big problem: costs. The crisis has improved the situation. Rents and property values are down, and inflation is moderating. But investors scouting around for the right place to set up their operations will want to consider other options. Still, if it is China you are looking at, Hong Kong is probably your best choice.

In the short term:

- Don't be put off by what you have heard about Hong Kong's high costs. Look at the big picture. Sure, running an office in Singapore or Kuala Lumpur may be easier on the budget, but if your primary target market is the mainland, the SAR may be the better base. Consider other factors such as the availability of skilled managers, the infrastructure, legal system, and access to banking services. And you may not need a flashy office in Central, but can make do with more modest facilities in cheaper precincts such as Quarry Bay or Kowloon. But Hong Kong is certainly no longer a city of cheap labor. Expect to pay top dollar to recruit and retain the best staff.

- Think regionally. Hong Kong can serve as your front office, the CEO's base, the boardroom with leather chairs and wood paneling, the executive housing and amenities. But consider locating back-room operations elsewhere. Some companies have transferred data-entry and processing divisions to China, India, the Philippines, and even Australia.

- If you are looking to set up a regional office in Hong Kong, hire locally as much as possible. Hong Kong boasts a high level of management expertise, with many executives trained in the West. Hong Kong people who left the territory prior to 1997 are returning, providing a substantial pool of competent management talent. Hiring locally will keep costs down. To keep staff loyal, pay attention to pay package levels in your industry and offer employees attractive benefits.

In the long term:

Is Hong Kong's long-term future secure? Shanghai, the argument goes, will eventually eclipse the SAR as China's premier financial center. Don't worry about this old chestnut now. Hong Kong is still way ahead. But be prepared for change. Hong Kong may not keep its substantial lead forever.

COMPANIES TO WATCH

- **First Pacific**

A major conglomerate controlled by Indonesia's Salim Group. It is selling a cash-making European division to clear out debts and prime itself to make substantial investments in Asia.

- **Cheung Kong**

The flagship of Li Ka-shing, one of Hong Kong's wealthiest tycoons, who controls Hutchison Whampoa, a major conglomerate. 'Superman Li' is handing over the day-to-day management to eldest son Victor. Hong Kong's property business may no longer be as lucrative as in K.S.'s heyday, but the Li family have diversified their interests. Younger son Richard is growing his own investment group, Pacific Century, which has stakes in property, finance, and information technology.

- **Li & Fung**

A global trading and distribution company with an impressive China network and a growing presence in emerging markets such as India. Headed by imaginative brothers Victor and William Fung, whose father moved the company to Hong Kong from China.

India: New Leadership, Old Problems

Ever since India accelerated economic reform in 1991, a succession of governments has struggled over how to embrace change in the face of intense, entrenched resistance. In March 1998 came an unlikely savior. The Bharatiya Janata Party (BJP), elected in large part because of its appeal to Hindu nationalism, heads a coalition government with the challenge of jump-starting an economy that is stuck in neutral. In the BJP's 'national agenda' released on the eve of Prime Minister Atal Behari Vajpayee's taking office, the party said it would continue with the reform process but would give it a 'strong *swadeshi* (self-reliance) thrust to ensure that the economy grows on the principle that India shall be built by Indians.' That is in line with the BJP's campaign pledge to allow foreign investment in 'core' areas like infrastructure and discourage it in 'non-priority areas' such as consumer goods. During the election campaign, the BJP boiled down its position to a catchy but not original phrase: 'computer chips, not potato chips.'

Does the BJP in government represent the end, at least for the time being, of India's economic liberalization? Certainly, supporters of the BJP victory would like to roll back at least pieces of the reforms. And every Indian government since the nation began liberalizing in the 1980s has faced public pressure to continue socialist policies aimed at providing cheap food and abundant employment. Still, BJP president Lal Krishna Advani has sought to reassure foreign investors nervous about the party's enthusiastic commitment to economic nationalism. 'Don't go by the connotation of the word *swadeshi*, which indicates a xenophobic attitude,' he says. 'There is no question of India going into a shell.'

Not that it could, even if it wanted to. In an era of free markets and globalization, every major political party in India agrees that the reforms undertaken so far, and the foreign investment attracted at the same time, are irreversible. The pace of reform, on the other hand, is most certainly in doubt. Any moves to restrict foreign competitors, raise tariff walls on imports, give India's own companies greater flexibility to hire and fire, and provide access to cheap financing would be popular with some of the key financial contributors to the BJP. The party is known to have spent at least $300 million on campaigning, much of it bankrolled by Indian businessmen. The list of contributors includes some of the nation's biggest companies, including the Tata Group and Reliance Industries. Already, the BJP has said it will offer tariff protection to some sectors such as cement, steel, chemicals, and pharmaceuticals beyond a 2004 deadline from the World Trade Organization to remove such import levies.

Just a few weeks after his party's election victory, Vajpayee told the Indian Parliament: 'This is the last time I am going to contest an election. In recent years, the cost of contesting has gone up [many times], making politicians more and more dependent on industrialists for funding.' Vajpayee's party fell just shy of an outright majority in the 545-member lower house of the legislature. Nevertheless, it and its close allies won 264 seats, which was close enough to a majority that it could assemble the coalition it needed. There is sure to be a payback.

'We are most concerned about finished goods that will be imported,' says Subodh Bhargava, chief executive of Eicher Goodearth, one of India's largest manufacturers of tractors and heavy vehicles. 'Multinationals have a number of advantages over us.' He offers these examples: 'I would like to have three-day inventories like my foreign competitors, but I can't. I have to keep 30-day inventories because any number of things like police checkpoints or breakdowns can hold up deliveries. We have to provide standby power generating systems. My competitors in Hong Kong, Osaka, and Kuala Lumpur don't have to worry about that at all.' Indian corporations

Table 4: India's Top Enterprises

Rank	Company	Main Business	Sales $ Millions	Profit $ Millions	Profit as % of sales	1000 Rank
1	INDIAN OIL	Oil refining	17,615.6	393.1	2.2	47
2	BHARAT PETROLEUM	Oil refining	4,183.3	108.9	2.6	300
3	OIL & N. GAS COMMISSION	Oil, fuel gas	3,745.5	565.9	15.1	333
4	STEEL AUTHORITY OF INDIA	Steel and iron	3,604.2	145.4	4.0	347
5	HINDUSTAN PETROLEUM	Oil refining, distribution	3,516.0	172.8	4.9	354
6	FOOD CORP. OF INDIA	Food trading	3,171.6	-0.3	-0.0	388
7	TATA ENG. & LOCOMOTIVE	Cars, trucks, machinery	2,858.5	215.2	7.5	440
8	RELIANCE INDUSTRIES	Textiles, chemicals	2,463.9	373.3	15.2	532
9	NATIONAL THERMAL POWER	Power generation	2,395.0	381.7	15.9	547
10	HINDUSTAN LEVER	Personal-care products	1,893.3	116.9	6.2	700
11	TATA IRON & STEEL	Steel	1,792.5	97.7	5.5	738
12	MINERALS & METALS TRDG.	Metals trading	1,717.9	16.1	0.9	768
13	I.T.C.	Tobacco	1,654.6	97.9	5.9	800
14	MARUTI UDYOG	Cars	1,626.8	143.0	8.8	813
15	BHARAT HEAVY ELECTRICALS	Engineering	1,610.6	130.7	8.1	821
16	VIDESH SANCHAR NIGAM	Telecommunications	1,468.3	144.4	9.8	885
17	LARSEN & TOUBRO	Industrial machinery	1,406.1	116.1	8.3	920
18	GAS AUTHORITY	Fuel gas	1,395.5	171.3	12.3	923
19	MAHANAGAR TELEPHONE	Telecommunications	1,136.4	250.4	22.0	—
20	COCHIN REFINERIES	Oil refining	1,105.7	26.2	2.4	—

also complain of difficulties in raising credit. Interest rates for entrepreneurs borrowing from Indian banks easily run up to 21%, three times the 7% rate that foreign investors are typically charged by their banks. Local businessmen have also been demanding an anti-dumping mechanism that would prevent surplus, low-cost products from abroad flooding India. 'We need help,' says automotive-and-steel tycoon Rahul Bajaj. 'Call it protectionism, call it anything you will.'

The BJP intends to help. Perhaps foremost, it wants to discourage foreign investment in consumer goods and attract foreign money into infrastructure development. Currently, about 53% of foreign direct investment goes to the consumer sector. Meanwhile, the need for international money for infrastructure is great. Over the next decade, India will require some $350 billion for roads, ports, power plants, and telecommunications services.

Consider the problems in Bangalore, which is called India's Silicon Valley. Roads there are in such disrepair that it takes about 45 minutes to cover the 4 km from the city's center to the Bangalore Information and Technology Park, home to a consortium of Singapore firms. The city suffers from an erratic supply of power and serious overcrowding because existing infrastructure is completely inadequate to handle a huge influx of migrant workers. The mighty Tata Group has proposed building a new airport to replace one that is decades old. Although the local government favors the plan and Tata says it will build the facility with private money from foreign partners, New Delhi has repeatedly delayed approval, although it now appears set to go ahead.

Identifying the problem is easy, however. Fixing it is tougher. For one thing, foreigners may be reluctant partners. At least some were put off by the experience of Enron Corp., a U.S. energy conglomerate. In 1995, a state government that was run by a BJP-aligned legislature canceled Enron's $2.9 billion power plant, India's biggest-ever foreign-funded project, to be built near Mumbai. The project was eventually revived after torturous negotiations, though the incident certainly tainted India's and the BJP's reputation. Clearly, India's new dominant political party has an image problem, at least with potential foreign investors. And that group represents just one of many different constituencies clamoring for attention.

In the end, though, the barometer of the party's success will be simple: economic performance. Hopes are high. In part that's because the BJP represents relative stability. After nearly two years of political and economic instability under the fractious United Front government, India is now led by a party whose leaders are relatively more united and have a shared perspective on the nation's problems. They have their work cut out. Industrial output, while still growing, has lost some of its verve. Growth was almost seven percentage points lower last year than in 1995. Meanwhile, GDP growth fell from 7.1% in 1995 to 5.5% last year. State revenues are projected to be $3.5 billion below earlier estimates this year. In an attempt to revive industry, the previous administration cut taxes and reduced interest rates last November, with little result.

Earlier this year, ratings agency Moody's Investors Service criticized the former government for caving in to demands to increase trade protection for Indian businesses. What Moody's failed to appreciate is that the forces in favor of shielding domestic Indian businesses from foreign competition have been strong for as long as there has been a debate about economic reform.

Meanwhile, away from the glare of international credit monitoring or domestic politics, the BJP is quietly pursuing reform in a neglected sector: agriculture. The party has said that as much as 60% of the government's planned spending will go toward agriculture and rural development. Not a bad goal. India is the world's second largest producer of food. Two-thirds of its workers toil in the fields and the spending is needed. A study commissioned by the Confederation of Indian Industry reveals that over the next decade, the agriculture sector will require $40 billion. The emphasis is significant for social as well as economic reasons. As Finance Minister Yashwant Sinha put it recently: 'We cannot have a society where we have islands of very high consumption and vast seas of deprivation and poverty.' Sinha's party fears that a reliance on foreign investment could turn India into a so-called 'dependent economy' whose survival increasingly is determined by foreign capital and technology.

Since 1991, three different Indian governments prior to the BJP have pursued foreign investment almost as if it were a holy grail, says Jay Dubashi, a former professor at the London School of Economics and now a key member of the BJP's economic planning committee. 'We believe that foreign investment alone cannot move the economy of a country as huge as ours.' The coming months will reveal what the BJP sees as the alternative. By the end of June, the government was to present its first annual budget. Undoubtedly, at that time and as long as this government lasts, the BJP's commitment to spend billions on such things as agricultural development and infrastructure, even if that means less for the kind of federal spending that repays past favors, will be put to the test.

INVESTOR TIPS

With the new government in place, investors should consider their moves carefully. India can be a trial. While it has a common law-based legal system, justice moves slowly. The country is renowned for its abundance of skilled computer programmers and technicians, but across the country, it is in dire need of infrastructure development. Don't approach India as you would Hong Kong or Singapore. India requires patience.

In the short term:

- Pay attention. Watch out for developments in foreign investment regulations. The BJP-led government, for example, is working on guidelines to restrict foreign investment for consumer goods. The Foreign Investment Promotion Council could also be abolished.

- Consider the best strategy. In the current climate, investment in infrastructure or in an infrastructure-related venture may make more sense than going into a consumer goods operation. Think of how you can invest in India's long-term growth through a local partnership or using a local vehicle.

- Don't get too bogged down by the politics. The reforms in India are irreversible. Don't let political rhetoric spook you. Be pragmatic. Look at the fundamentals, the regulations, and your partners; then make the appropriate move.

In the long term:

- Governments come and go. India, with nearly a billion people, is destined to become one of the great economies in the world. It will take a long time. There will be a lot of opportunities for foreign investors even if major sectors are kept closed. Don't be overwhelmed by the size of the market or the vastness of the country. A modest start can lead to bigger things.

COMPANIES TO WATCH

- **Bharat Petroleum and Hindustan Petroleum**

While they each have only a 20% share of India's refining business, against 55% for giant Indian Oil Corp., Hindustan Petroleum and Bharat Petroleum have entrenched retail distribution networks that give them the edge.

- **Maruti Udyog**

This state-funded car-making giant was founded in the 1970s by Sanjay Gandhi, a son of then-prime minister Indira Gandhi. Maruti dominates the auto market, chalking up hefty profits in 1997.

- **Tata Engineering & Locomotive and Tata Iron & Steel**

Parts of the Mumbai-based Tata Group, the country's biggest industrial conglomerate which is run by Ratan Tata, possibly India's best known tycoon. He has forged joint ventures with foreign multinationals such as IBM and AT&T.

Indonesia: Crisis Ground Zero

Sooner or later, most experts you talk to about recovery in East Asia will come to the point when they roll their eyes and note The Exception, the ticking-bomb economy that could derail the region's confidence train just as it has started to chug along. Indonesia is ground zero, where the crater from the currency meltdown is deepest. It is the country that will continue to make crisis-watchers cringe in horror well into 1999. 'Indonesia scares the daylights out of me and everyone else,' said economist Paul Krugman at a conference in Hong Kong in March 1998. "The mix of corrupt autocracy, susceptibility to economic snake-oil salesmen, ethnic tensions, and fumbles by the International Monetary Fund (IMF) have created the potential for a catastrophe of immense dimensions.' It is hard enough to say with reasonable conviction that the likes of Thailand or Korea will begin to recover by sometime next year. For Indonesia, the misery is set to last much longer.

To be fair, the depth of the despair Indonesia has fallen into is not all Jakarta's doing. Even the specialists at the IMF would probably agree that the Fund's initial off-the-shelf, cruel-to-be-kind rescue program was not exactly right for the biggest economy in Southeast Asia. It took nearly six months from when Indonesia first called the IMF in, but finally the program hammered out in three attempts has given some priority to the tens of billions of dollars in short-term foreign loans largely to the private sector. Such debt has been the central concern undermining the rupiah (not to mention the baht and the won) since the Asian crisis broke last year. The latest IMF deal, which was announced in April, includes an appendix on the restructuring of overseas loans to Indonesian banks and companies. It urged, among other measures, that 'negotiations between debtors and creditors begin as quickly as possible.'

Representatives of the two groups wasted little time, meeting in New York in mid-April. Private-sector foreign debt was estimated at $73.9 billion at the end of 1997, but $20 billion is set to be added to the figure under a new tally being done by the central bank as part of the third IMF package. The rupiah value of those IOUs is up more than three-fold since July 1997, wiping out the assets of most debtors and rendering them technically bankrupt. The chairman of the Indonesian Chamber of Commerce and Industry, Aburizal Bakrie, whose own family-owned group is reportedly struggling with half a billion dollars in debt, sees two options: 'Creditors needing quick cash might agree to debt reduction of up to 50%, but some could wait and expect nearly full repayment.'

Efforts to address Indonesia's debt problem have been slow; the first meeting between lenders and private-sector borrowers was in late February, several months after Jakarta's first IMF program was instituted. South Korea, on the other hand, got a debt moratorium within weeks of its bailout in December. Admittedly, it helped Korea's situation that most of its loans were owed by a small number of state-controlled financial institutions. Still, Indonesia's second Fund deal, signed in January, was criticized for largely ignoring the most pressing problems of rupiah-free fall and crushing foreign debt, which by then were dragging down banks and firms.

That previous agreement was sweeping and grand, with lots of policy but little detail. It was a laundry list of reforms long advocated by the World Bank and the IMF. The April plan addresses debt and banking problems directly with specific action. It provides for state financial support to debt restructuring, up to a limit. While the January package referred vaguely to 'strengthening the legal and supervisory framework for banking,' the new deal sets minimum capital of 250 billion rupiah and makes loan-loss provisions tax-deductible. The latest program also seems to have a more realistic timeframe, stretching to the end of 1999, compared to the end of April for many of the January prescriptions.

Like all plans, particularly one so expansive, the devil is in the implementation. Of the new prescriptions ex-President Suharto has said: 'We will carry them out consistently.' His government probably realizes that if it fails a third time, confidence may never come back. As of mid-May, Jakarta seemed to be keeping its end of the new bargain, moving on its pledges to eliminate subsidies on fuel and electricity, lift the export ban on crude palm oil, and break up key monopolies such as the clove market. On May 4, the IMF approved the immediate release of nearly $1 billion for Indonesia, adding that $2 billion could be available in the period to July pending monthly reviews. The funds are part of a $40 billion international rescue package for the economy. After an initial disbursement of $3 billion, the IMF had delayed the second tranche of the same amount because it had judged that Jakarta had failed to implement reforms it had agreed to earlier.

Peace with the IMF, assuming it lasts, is not likely to bring peace to Indonesia. Social unrest sparked by rising unemployment and massive price increases has been on the rise. Students and political activists have been protesting. Unprecedented demonstrations were held in urban areas against the re-election in March of former-President Suharto. In May, he angered his critics when he was reported to have dismissed the possibility of political reforms until after 2003, the year his latest term would have ended. In the event, later in May – following riots, looting and killing - Suharto stood down. He was replaced by Vice-President B. J. Habibie. Since then President Habibie has astutely shored up his political image, although he has been unable to provide, understandably, an economic quick-fix. IMF chief Michel Camdessus has said he is concerned about the turbulence, noting that the Fund has introduced 'social safety nets' to cushion its impact.

The mix of economic depression and social upheaval is already a volatile combination. Throw into the cocktail an influential, interventionist military, a growing Muslim grassroots movement, and byzantine behind-the-scenes maneuvering by a host of political players, and investors will want to consider any move in Indonesia with utmost caution. The immediate future for the country is decidedly bleak. The economic pain Indonesians will feel across all classes is undeniable. The IMF forecasts a 5% contraction in GDP this year, way down from 5% growth in 1997. Inflation is projected to rise from last year's 6.6% to 44.3%. With fuel prices expected to jump by nearly 75%, all sectors of the economy will be squeezed. The banking sector is in dire need of a massive overhaul that will require huge amounts of new capital. And the question remains whether the government will push through the reforms it has to implement even if they should threaten the business interests of members of Suharto's family. Consider Indonesia under extended probation. Any deviation now could cost it dearly.

Table 5: Indonesia's Top Enterprises

Rank	Company	Main Business	Sales $ Millions	Profit $ Millions	Profit as % of sales	1000 Rank
1	PERTAMINA	Oil exploration, refining	19276.5	578.1	2.0	40
2	ASTRA INTERNATIONAL	Car assembly, trading	4,688.0	200.4	4.3	264
3	PER. LISTRIK NEGARA (PLN)	Power generation	4,020.9	498.1	12.4	316
4	GUDANG GARAM	Clove cigarettes	2,799.9	279.7	9.0	453
5	TELKOM	Telecommunications	2,167.0	641.8	29.6	609
6	INDOCEMENT TUNGGAL	Cement, property	1,823.5	235.4	12.9	728
7	GARUDA INDONESIA	Air transport	1,755.2	1.7	0.1	754
8	INDOFOOD SUKSES MAKMUR	Food	1,206.4	149.0	12.4	—
9	H.M. SAMPOERNA	Cigarettes	1,010.3	169.3	16.8	—
10	UNITED TRACTORS	Heavy equipment	845.2	31.3	3.7	—
11	MATAHARI PUTRA PRIMA	Department stores	806.9	6.6	0.8	—
12	INDAH KIAT PULP & PAPER	Paper, pulp	773.8	112.0	14.6	—
13	UNILEVER INDONESIA	Personal care, food	702.3	54.2	7.7	—
14	BAKRIE & BROTHERS	Steel, pipe, car parts	671.1	79.9	11.9	—
15	POLYSINDO EKA PERKASA	Textiles	600.3	72.5	12.1	—
16	PABRIK KERTAS TJIWI KIMIA	Paper	593.9	61.9	10.4	—
17	CHAROEN POKPHAND INDONESIA	Poultry feed	535.3	21.6	4.0	—
18	INDOSAT	Telecommunications	522.1	222.7	42.7	—
19	JAPFA COMFEED	Animal feed, poultry	426.0	13.3	3.1	—
20	GADJAH TUNGGAL	Tires	421.3	57.2	13.6	—

INVESTOR TIPS

For all the gloom, there are reports of direct investors scouring Indonesia for bargains of a lifetime. One European fund manager in Hong Kong says he has started taking small positions under 10% in bombed-out listed companies that are going for a song. Indonesia today is a gamble, but it could also turn out to be the mother of all recovery plays. The April settlement with the IMF, if it holds, will boost confidence and could result in a similar return of investment that Thailand and Korea started seeing in the first quarter of 1998.

In the short term:

- Take a realistic attitude. This is the most battered of economies. Is placing a few spare million into the cauldron with the chance of achieving a fabulous triple-digit return in just a few years such a bad idea? If you won't miss the money if you lost it all, then why not?

- Even the best auditors would have trouble carrying out due diligence on an Indonesian company under current conditions. The dust should clear a bit once the debt situation is resolved. But it will always pay to seek out the best of the worst.

- Don't behave like a carpetbagger. It's tempting, but sensitivity will have its rewards. Foreigners will be able to participate in sectors in which they were previously barred. Unless you are an investor just out to flip an asset after a few years, take the high road and think of your long-term reputation.

In the long term:

- Take in the big picture. Indonesia is a big market with lots of potential. If you are planning a long-term presence, then the political risk should mean little to you. It is having your foot in the door that counts. Under President Habibie, privatization is accelerating and the private sector is opening up, so bargains abound. Buy now, and years down the road you will be congratulating yourself for having the courage and the foresight to plunge in. If you can't take the stress, then don't bother.

COMPANIES TO WATCH

- **Gudang Garam**

This clove cigarette maker is said to be weathering the crisis well, benefiting from lower costs and healthy export revenues.

- **H.M. Sampoerna**

Another clove cigarette maker that is reported to be enduring the turmoil in reasonably good form. Boss Putera Sampoerna spends much of his time in Singapore, where he has doubtless parked much of his personal wealth.

- **Indah Kiat Pulp & Paper**

Part of the Sinar Mas group of companies of ethnic Chinese tycoon Eka Tjipta Widjaja. Pulp and paper exporters should be able to ride the crisis well, so long as they are not saddled with huge debts. Sinar Mas, one of Indonesia's top business groups, owns one of the country's better-managed banks.

● Japan: On the Brink, But of What?

These days, most people are ready to bury Japan, not praise it. So it was something of a revelation when, in a packed Tokyo auditorium in April, Winthrop Smith spoke to some 2000 men and women, refugees from the recent collapse of Yamaichi Securities, which had been Japan's No. 4 brokerage. After the company went bankrupt, U.S. stockbroking giant Merrill Lynch stepped in and took over 33 branches of the failed enterprise, along with their staff. Smith, chairman of the New York-based multinational, wanted to tell his audience of the firm's plans to launch a nationwide retail brokerage operation in Japan later this year. The new troops were thrilled. 'We at Merrill Lynch are very, very bullish on Japan,' Smith declared. 'We do not underestimate this challenge. But there is no doubt in my mind that, working together, we can meet it. In the process, we can set an important example for the new Japan, and contribute in a meaningful way to the restoration of Japan to its rightful place of leadership in the global economy.'

Bullish on Japan? Leadership in the global economy? Longtime watchers of Japan's slow-motion meltdown could be forgiven for asking what the Merrill Lynch chief was on. After seven years in a sticky slump, the nation once held up as a paragon of financial prowess is sinking into recession. Its banks groan under the weight of bad loans, its financial markets are flaccid with little hope of recovery, its consumers shudder at the threat of job losses, its policy makers wallow in impotence. Indeed, pessimism is the order of the day, inside and outside Japan. 'The next epicenter of bankruptcy: eastern Japan contractors and banks of the west,' the weekly *Shukan Bunshun* blared in a recent lead story. Critics have dismissed Prime Minister Keizo Obuchi's new mammoth package of spending and tax cuts as too little too late. 'Incompetent politicians fiddle while Japan burns,' Yomiuri Research Institute deputy director Shibata Yasuhiko raged in a press commentary.

Week after week, statistics seem to show that Japan's economy is edging closer to the point of no return, threatening to drag the region and perhaps the world down with it. The worst-case scenario: a depression crushes major banks and companies, further contracting trade and the economy. That could lead Japan to pull in hundreds of billions of dollars in foreign assets, jacking up interest rates worldwide and exporting the slump not just to already-hurting Asia, but around the globe.

Yet soon after the global rash of collapsing-Japan statements and stories in March and April, a hopeful, if still gloomy, view of the world's second-largest economy is emerging. For starters, the Organization for Economic Cooperation and Development (OECD), the rich nations' club, has said that Japan is reforming its debt-ridden, regulation-strapped economy, although it should move faster. Indeed, there are signs that, after crippling its economy in a super-speculative blowout and then drifting aimlessly in a financial Bermuda Triangle, Japan is finally starting to learn to paddle. Says Richard Koo, chief economist at the Nomura Research Institute: 'I have become optimistic on Japan for the first time in nearly 10 years.'

Even more telling, some foreign institutions and enterprises are actually investing in the OECD economy from hell. Merrill Lynch's Tokyo launching is but the latest and most high-profile *gaijin* foray into Japan. American banks and so-called vulture funds are hunting for bargains in the depressed property sector, including loans that have been marked down and bundled into securities. The Pacific Century Group of Hong Kong-based junior tycoon Richard Li, son of the legendary property magnate Li Ka-shing, has recently made high-profile purchases

Table 6: Japan's Top Enterprises

Rank	Company	Main Business	Sales $ Millions	Profit $ Millions	Profit as % of sales	1000 Rank
1	MITSUBISHI CORP.	General trading	189,187.0	355.2	0.2	95
2	MITSUI & CO	General trading	186,266.0	323.0	0.2	104
3	ITOCHU CORP.	General trading	173.588.9	124.3	0.1	261
4	SUMITOMO CORP.	General trading	171,912.2	216.0	0.1	164
5	MARUBENI CORP.	General trading	165,269.6	160.7	0.1	210
6	TOYOTA MOTOR CORP.	Car, trucks	113,956.4	2,732.0	2.4	2
7	NISSHO IWAI CORP.	General trading	100,956.4	-266.3	—	970
8	HITACHI LTD.	Electronics, machinery	86,368.4	1,507.2	1.7	10
9	NIPPON TELEGRAPH & TEL.	Telecommunications	84,368.4	2,266.9	2.7	5
10	MATSUSHITA ELECTRIC INDL.	Appliances, electronics	72,239.5	-604.6	—	973
11	TOMEN CORP.	General trading	69,527.8	47.5	0.1	453
12	NISSAN MOTOR	Cars, car parts	64,204.8	-940.0	—	974
13	TOSHIBA CORP.	Electronics, machinery	54,434.3	961.0	1.8	23
14	TOKYO ELECTRIC POWER	Power generation	53,730.9	550.9	1.0	57
15	NICHIMEN CORP.	General trading	52,171.6	45.5	0.1	469
16	KANEMATSU CORP.	General trading	51,141.9	3.6	0.0	836
17	SONY CORP.	Electronics, entertainment	48,825.9	576.8	1.2	51
18	NEC CORP.	Electronics, computers	46,748.8	820.4	1.8	29
19	HONDA MOTOR	Car, motocycles	45,207.0	752.7	1.7	36
20	FUJITSU LTD	Computer	39,995.4	671.0	1.7	40

of Tokyo land. 'Despite all of the macro gloom-and-doom stories, at the micro level, in terms of the activity of American companies, there is actually more now than we've seen in quite some time,' says Glen Fukushima, president of the American Chamber of Commerce in Japan. 'The behavior of quite a few of these firms seems to indicate that they think the future of the Japanese economy is pretty good.'

So has the doomsday diatribe against Japan been overdone? Certainly, the bad news is real enough. The economy's wounds are staggering. Worst of all is the mountain of doubtful loans held by Japanese financial institutions, which is close to $600 billion, almost one-sixth of GDP. It has made banks reluctant to lend; despite record-low loan rates, more and more companies are issuing bonds or simply starving for funds. Tax cut or no tax cut, consumer spending, which accounts for 60% of GDP, isn't likely to revive much. The reason: the precarious state of companies in almost every major industry, from construction to airlines, makes unemployment a real possibility. Households are squirreling away savings just in case the breadwinners lose their jobs to retrenchment or bankruptcy. 'I cannot count on my husband's salary going up or even on job stability anymore,' says Kitagawa Kazuko of Saitama, north of Tokyo. The 45-year-old housewife and mother of three teenagers makes it a rule now to shop only two days a week and to buy just the items on her carefully prepared shopping list.

More important, while government stimulus measures may keep the economy going for another year, only sweeping fundamental restructuring can launch a self-sustaining recovery. And it looks like change will continue to be far too slow in coming. The potential pain involved, in pink slips, red ink, and black moods, has so far proved simply too daunting for the powers that be, whether bankers, chief executives, bureaucrats, or politicians. Instead, they have preferred to let lenders, companies, and the government get deeper and deeper into debt just to avoid owning up to and taking the rap for losses stored up since the late-1980s' 'bubble economy' burst. But constantly putting off financial Armageddon has only kept investors and consumers fearful of the future and unwilling to spend, whatever stimulus packages are lavished on them.

So what's the good news? First, Japan won't collapse, at least not for a long while and not with thousands of trillions of yen in savings and hundreds of billions of dollars in foreign assets to bank on. This year, the government's $123 billion fiscal stimulus package, the largest in yen terms, will stave off a sharp downturn and may even spur slight growth. 'It will clearly have an impact, it's too big not to,' says economist Ron Bevacqua at Merrill Lynch Japan. He estimates it will add one percentage point or more to GDP growth, which various forecasters have projected at between -2% and 1% for 1998. And it may well do better than past pump-priming outlays, which the Finance Ministry had often offset with tax hikes intended to contain the ballooning budget deficit. Those added levies are one major reason why some $800 billion in stimulus spending since 1992 has done little for the economy.

ING Barings strategist Pelham Smithers thinks the current spending measures and, yes, tax cuts 'appear more than sufficient for sustainable growth, much as the package in 1995 was.' That earlier outlay, he explains, lifted growth to 3.2% in fiscal 1996, but the sales tax hike in April 1997 (from 3% to 5%) squelched the incipient recovery. The International Monetary Fund (IMF) is forecasting growth of 1.3% next year. And this time, Japanese politicians appear to have taken the budget reins and, under public and international pressure, seem willing so far to set aside fiscal conservatism in favor of resolute action to spur growth and, under a new law, recapitalize lenders that write off hefty bad debts.

Now for the big question: Will Japan restructure far and fast enough? For businesses to begin clawing their way back into the black, they need such reforms as more transparent and realistic accounting, better provisions for loan losses, and a management approach that puts greater emphasis on raising profitability and efficiency, rather than simply keeping people on the payroll. Moreover, companies and consumers will resume serious spending only when the downside of future losses and pain has been fully acknowledged and discounted. And that is exactly what many reforms, particularly those dealing with transparency and financial restructuring, are supposed to do.

Of particular urgency is fixing the banks. Their reluctance to lend, due to bad loans burdening their balance sheets, is a major cause of the economic slump. Moreover, the support given by financial institutions to affiliated companies and favored clients has in turn enabled those debtors to avoid restructuring. Well, the good news is that Tokyo seems to be finally getting serious about prodding banks to make provisions for bad loans, so they can finally get them off their books. Jolted by the fall of Yamaichi Securities and 10th-ranked Hokkaido Takushoku Bank, the government announced last December a $230 billion outlay for the purpose, including $130 billion for deposit insurance. Moreover, the top 20 banks have set aside more than $200 billion since 1994 to cover dud assets, which they have also been selling.

The cash infusion into the deposit insurance system, technically bankrupt for years, is crucial. Unable to compensate savers, regulators could not close banks or even ask them to reveal all their soured loans, says Nomura's Koo. 'Now regulators are saying, we've got the safety net, so you've got to disclose your bad debts.' It is no coincidence, he adds, that the banks association head has said members would start calculating non-performing loans under stricter U.S. standards.

Owning up to past business mistakes is one big task; avoiding future ones is the other. That will require changes not just in the way the Japanese do business, but even in their idea of what business is all about. While Japan has undertaken many reforms through the years, it is financial-sector liberalization, given new impetus in the 'Big Bang' program begun in April, that may instigate the most fundamental changes. If implemented as envisioned, the reforms will redirect much of the 1200 trillion yen held by Japanese savers in near-zero-interest bank accounts into investments chosen for the best returns. Fund managers, local and foreign, will compete for all that yen and funnel it into ventures that are financially sound and transparent, well-managed and efficient, and, of course, highly profitable. 'That's changing Japanese capitalism from ground zero,' says Koo.

Corporations will eventually be less and less able to raise money on the basis of corporate, personal, or political connections. Increasingly, they will have to offer attractive returns, and that means they will have to rethink such old habits as chasing market share at any cost and keeping unproductive staff on the payroll. Nor can firms ignore small shareholders, especially if they wield the collective clout of millions of yield-hungry savers. Moreover, as foreign firms move into the liberalized fund-management industry, they will demand international standards of accounting, disclosure, and investor relations.

Launched on April 1, the Big Bang starts modestly, letting stockbrokers set different fees, and scrapping restrictions on foreign exchange transactions. Future reforms until 2001 aim to make Japan's banks, brokers, insurers, and investment managers more competitive by breaking down barriers between their lines of business, relaxing more restrictions, and allowing unbridled foreign competition. Half of Japan's 19 nationwide banks and three-fifths of the 130 regional lenders could go. 'Competition is getting fierce, notably in overseas trust funds, and a tough period will last for a while,' says Imagawa Tatsunori, a managing director of the Bank of Tokyo-Mitsubishi, Japan's No. 1. Domestic institutions will have to get bigger, more efficient, sound, and profitable.

As more and more Japanese demand international-level returns, billions of dollars will shift. Fidelity Investments Japan boss Bill Wilder says his company went from managing $300 million for one pension fund in 1996 to $3 billion for 30 funds today. When it began a phone-in advice service for investors in April, the number of calls was triple the forecast. Even small savers are much more aware of wider opportunities. Tanabe Yasuko, 32, a publishing company employee, recently transferred half of her savings, about $23,000, to a U.S. dollar time deposit at Citibank. 'Even with the risk of currency fluctuations, the interest of 4% to 5% a year is very attractive,' she says. 'This kind of choice we were not given before.' Both financial packages and structural reform depend on one key issue that divides optimists and pessimists: Does Japan have the political leadership to take the hard choices and see them through? The government has been criticized for policy flip-flops, most recently for its initial reluctance to cut taxes. 'Because the political leadership is everyday more fragile, it's taken them a year to start to change course,' fumes Kenneth Courtis, chief economist at Deutsche Bank Group Asia Pacific. 'Political leadership — that is the fundamental issue.' Meiji University economist-professor Takagi Masaru says: 'The government is still making a list of 642 items to deregulate 15 years after they started talking about them. Why? Many people in the ruling party and the bureaucracy are reluctant to have vested interests disappear.'

Optimists argue that political leadership is awakening. Though they were slow, the prime minister and his Liberal Democratic Party (LDP) did push aside the Finance Ministry, guardian of the budget and traditional architect of economic policy. 'When the Prime Minister returned from Malaysia in December and announced a 2-trillion-yen tax cut, (a senior Finance official) said no bureaucrat had known about that plan until 10 that morning,' says ING's Smithers. After Hokkaido Takushoku's collapse, politicians put together the $230 billion bank support package in two months. 'Pretty fast by anyone's standard,' says Koo. Plainly, when faced with heavy-duty disaster, even the hidebound LDP stirs. Which is why even a recession, if it happens, could be a blessing. For one thing, the tsunami of red ink from a much deeper slump would make it impossible for many creditors not to cut off defaulted borrowers, and firms not to lay off excess workers. Moreover, the resulting distress and desperation may finally make the agonies of sweeping reform palatable to the Japanese and their business and political chiefs.

In sum, just as the Asian currency crisis has pushed Korean and ASEAN economies to undertake structural change, a full-fledged downturn in Japan, complete with headline-grabbing bankruptcies and layoffs, may yet generate the political will and public determination, if not desperation, to see reform through. But let's hope Japan's leaders don't wait for that.

The Road is Paved

- Bankruptcies sink 17,439 companies in the fiscal year ended March 1998, the largest number since 1985, with a record $116 billion in liabilities.

- Unemployment rate hits 3.6% in February, the highest rate since data compilation began in 1953.

- One-third of 200 top firms in a newspaper survey plan to cut the number of new graduate hires. Only 29 plan to boost their intake.

- Household income edges down 1% in real terms in February year on year, while household spending falls 4.5%.

- Tokyo department store sales dive 21.4% in March year on year.

- Land prices fall for the seventh straight year in 1997, with commercial land losing 6.1% on average and residential land 1.4%.

- Private-sector machinery orders in February fall 17.9% year on year, and capital spending in the coming year is expected to drop 1.6%.

- Industrial output in February falls 3.3% month on month.

- Japanese companies see the economy growing 1.4% per year to 2001, the lowest expectations since surveys began in 1993.

With Good Intentions

1991 Full year GDP growth rate 3.8%, slowing from 5.1% in 1990.

1992 **Stimulus** The first stimulus package totaled $84.5b. with $40.3b. in 'real water,' actual spending, or tax cuts, to boost demand. Economic policy makers hoped it would add 2.4 percentage points to growth the following year. Full year GDP growth rate 1%.

1993 **Stimulus** When the growth surge didn't materialize, out came two packages worth $118.7b. and $54b. in April and September respectively, with a total $78.2b. in real water. Full year GDP growth rate 0.3%.

1994 **Stimulus** Huge $148.7b. package in February with $100.8b. in real water, including a one-off income tax cut. Government economists thought this package could add 2 percentage points to growth. First-half GDP growth rate nearly 0.8% year on year.

Tightening Convinced that the economy had bottomed out, public investment drops sharply in the year's second half, with public fixed capital formation rising just 1.3% for the year instead of the initially estimated 12.5%. Full year GDP growth rate 0.6%.

1995 **Stimulus** April saw a $74.4b. package with $47.8b. in real water centered on public works following the Kobe earthquake. $151b. package with $95.7b. in spending centered on public works followed in September. Full year GDP growth rate 1.4%.

1996 No new package as the economy finally picks up steam. Full year GDP growth rate 3.5%.

1997 **Tightening** Convinced the economy is on a roll and eager to cut its deficit, the government in April raises the consumption tax to 5% from 3%, ends a temporary tax cut, and does not renew some 1996 public work spending.

Stimulus But the economy tanks. Facing recession, the government in December announces a $15.4b. temporary income tax cut. GDP growth rate 0.9% and headed down.

1998 **Stimulus** $123b. package with nearly $77b. in real water, including over $30b. in tax cuts spread over two years and $46b. in public works spending. More details to be announced shortly. With opinion divided on how effective the package will be, full year GDP growth rate forecasts range from -2% to 1%.

Freeing the Future

Big Bang is only the latest in a long series of reforms across many fields. But much more is needed, especially in areas such as the tax system and land use regulations.

1990 Foreign investment managers allowed to manage some corporate pensions.

1991 Toys 'R' Us opens first mega-store following revision of the Large-scale Retail Store Law.

1994 Four new entrants allowed into mobile phone sector. Customers allowed to own (instead of just rent) mobile phones.

1995 Foreign fund managers allowed to manage public pension funds. Investment trust companies allowed to distribute funds on their own.

1996 Domestic life and non-life insurers allowed into each other's markets, and given greater freedom in setting premiums.

1997 Barriers separating local, long-distance, and international service providers lifted. Companies outside the financial sector allowed to be holding companies.

1998 Wholly foreign-owned telecommunications carriers allowed into Japan. Self-service petrol stations introduced.

Big Bang

1998 Brokers' commissions on large-lot trades freed from control, and foreign exchange transactions liberalized. Pending: banks to be allowed to sell mutual funds, and new financial products to require only registration instead of pre-approval and licensing.

1999 Commissions on all securities transactions freed from control, and banks and brokerages allowed into each other's turfs.

2000 Accounting standards to meet international norms, using mark-to-market and consolidated accounting.

2001 Banks, brokerages, and insurers allowed into the others' markets.

INVESTOR TIPS

Don't be rigid in your pre-conceived notions about Japan, the Japanese, and being a foreigner in the country. Things are never exactly as they seem. Keep an open mind. One Hong Kong businessman says he was surprised to find that he was far more comfortable operating in Tokyo than he was in Singapore. The Japanese capital may be an expensive place to live, but it is both cosmopolitan and intimate, with its flashy commercial districts and quiet, leafy neighborhoods.

In the short term:

- Watch developments closely. Market liberalization is gradually taking place, with niches opening up for foreign players.

- Be realistic. Be patient. If you can't get your product to the Japanese, think of alternatives and ask how you can adapt to the local distribution and marketing system in order to succeed.

- Try to adapt. Learn the language or employ people who speak it. Pay attention to local customs and attitudes. It never hurts to be sensitive, particularly in Japan.

In the long term:

- Japan is going through the same sort of wrenching restructuring that the U.S. did in the 1980s amid the massive savings-and-loan crisis. It will probably take much longer, but Japan could emerge a more rational marketplace. Don't be paralyzed by fear of a pending collapse. Look now for ways to position yourself for the time when the economy will indeed be far more open than it is.

COMPANIES TO WATCH

- **Nintendo Co.**

Post-Super Mario Brothers, Nintendo's challenge is to stay on top of the video game and entertainment industry amid heightened competition. Run by billionaire Yamauchi Hiroshi.

- **Sony Corp.**

Stock pickers in these doldrum days tend to go with what are often called the 'Nifty Fifty,' a range of 50 or so companies that are mainly technology firms or household names, such as Toshiba and Mitsubishi. Leading the pack is Sony. In 1995, Idei Nobuyuki was picked to run the world-famous consumer-electronics giant. He has restructured and re-energized the global company which remains at the forefront of technological developments. The company has already racked up record profits for 1997. 'We cannot beat the competition unless consumers notice at a glance that our products are clearly new,' says Morimoto Masayoshi, Sony's senior managing director.

- **Toyota Motor Corp.**

Domestic sales may be flat, but Toyotas are all over the world. The auto company raked in $3 billion in profits for the year ending March 1997 on revenues of about $100 billion.

Malaysia: Do-it-Yourself Recovery

Of all the East Asian economies hit badly by the crisis, Malaysia has distinguished itself. Rather than seek aid from economic doctors of the International Monetary Fund (IMF), Kuala Lumpur went its own way, putting together a do-it-yourself economic recovery program. The IMF praised its efforts. Most analysts agreed that the fiercely independent country stood a good chance of achieving an economic 'soft landing' through tight monetary policies, avoiding any sudden deep decline – unlike its ailing neighbors.

But Malaysia's plunge has been steep. In January and February, manufacturing output dropped faster than it has ever done in the past decade. Domestic spending is quickly drying up, while business bankruptcies are sharply rising, resulting in mounting bad debt that is unsettling the already shaky financial system. Growth forecasts have been gradually revised downwards, with some private-sector economists predicting a mild recession for 1998. IMF projections released in April call for 2.5% growth this year, down from 7.8% in 1997. Inflation is expected to climb from 2.7% to 7.5%.

The negative signs are unfortunate, considering the start Malaysia made in containing damage from a 35% slide in the value of its currency, the ringgit. Thanks mainly to a relative lack of dollar-denominated debt, the country was on a firmer footing than Thailand and Indonesia when the region slipped into turmoil. An IMF bailout, and all the loss-of-face that may have involved, has not been needed. Malaysian officials independently mobilized a package of banking reforms and tight-money measures to stabilize the financial system. After a month-long review of the Malaysian economy, the IMF recently offered a vote of confidence. 'If fully and consistently implemented, this package would provide a strong basis for Malaysia to recover from its current difficulties and move to more rapid rates of growth over the medium term,' the IMF said.

Yet in the short term, the outlook is grim and getting more so. 'The risk of recession is growing,' says Daragh Maher, economist for ING Barings in Singapore. 'We are going to see some horrid numbers coming out of Malaysia.' The most troubling development is the unexpectedly disappointing performance of the country's export-oriented manufacturing sector. Output in the first two months of 1998 slid 1.1% compared to the same period a year ago. Analysts are predicting a 3.5% decline for the entire year. Partly to blame: more than 40% of Malaysia's exports go to Asia, including Japan, and regional demand has been crashing.

The toughest problem can be traced to the very nature of the economy's manufacturing base. Malaysia is Southeast Asia's largest electronics exporter, and prices for personal computers, peripherals, semiconductors, and electronic components are mired in a global slump. 'Even if they can keep up [export] volumes, the value of their exports is continuing to fall,' says Tim Condon, economist for Morgan Stanley Asia. Prices for important Malaysian commodities, including oil, gas, and palm oil, have also declined sharply in the last 12 months. 'It's a double whammy for them,' says Condon.

Make that a triple-whammy. Domestic demand 'is collapsing,' says Rajeev Malik, regional economist at Jardine Fleming in Singapore. Car sales fell 70% in the first quarter of 1998 compared to a year ago. Malaysia will not be able to stimulate consumers with government spending programs, and several ambitious infrastructure projects are already on indefinite hold. Nor would it be advisable for interest rates to be cut to bring out buyers. Doing so could force the ringgit into a free-fall and crack the thin veneer of confidence that has taken months to develop.

Table 7: Malaysia's Top Enterprises

Rank	Company	Main Business	Sales $ Millions	Profit $ Millions	Profit as % of sales	1000 Rank
1	PETROLIAM NASIONAL	Oil, gas, refining	11,480.0	2,892.0	25.2	96
2	SIME DARBY	Trading, commodities	5,260.9	332.2	6.3	233
3	TENAGA NASIONAL	Power generation	3,237.8	317.1	9.8	375
4	EON	Car dealership	2,769.8	180.6	6.5	461
5	MALAYSIAN AIRLINE SYSTEM	Air transport	2,577.6	132.3	5.1	498
6	TELEKOM MALAYSIA	Telecommunications	2,550.3	747.8	29.3	504
7	BERJAYA GROUP	Diversified	2,524.6	32.3	1.3	513
8	PROTON	Cars	2,473.2	297.9	12.1	530
9	PERLIS PLANTATIONS	Sugar, flour, property	2,336.5	71.2	3.1	560
10	AMSTEEL CORP.	Steel, retailing	2,295.7	50.9	2.2	572
11	MALAYSIA LNG	Gas	1,894.0	346.2	18.3	698
12	PETRONAS DAGANGAN	Oil marketing	1,549.3	62.7	4.1	851
13	FEDERAL FLOUR MILLS	Flour, animal feed	1,473.5	45.6	3.1	883
14	UMW HOLDINGS	Vehicle assembly	1,462.1	92.9	6.4	892
15	ORIENTAL HOLDINGS	Car assembly, dealership	1,250.4	156.8	12.5	—
16	TAN CHONG MOTOR	Car assembly	1,125.2	103.3	9.2	—
17	HICOM HOLDINGS	Cars	1,111.1	256.3	23.1	—
18	MAGNUM CORP.	Property, betting	1,110.4	112.8	10.2	—
19	GENTING	Gaming, investment	1,031.7	227.1	22.0	—
20	SHELL REFINING CO. (FOM)	Oil refining	980.0	44.5	4.5	—

Indeed, even after a measure of stability returned to the markets, foreign investors have remained skeptical that leaders have the will to carry out structural reforms. Since the crisis hit, several politically well-connected tycoons have received government-blessed bailouts when their business interests were imperiled. Among those rescued: a transportation company controlled by Prime Minister Mahathir Mohamad's son Mirzan, as well as companies owned by cronies Tajudin Ramli and Halim Saad. What is most important in attracting investors back is consistency and transparency, in both policies and financial matters. A classic example of what not to do is to send conflicting messages. Speaking recently after one of several such flip-flops at the top of Malaysia's leadership, James Travis, president of the American-Malaysian Chamber of Commerce, said: 'In the last 10 days, investor confidence in Malaysia's recovery has declined primarily due to inconsistencies.' Travis also cited 'some bailouts causing international fund managers to raise eyebrows.'

If Kuala Lumpur had called in the IMF and been forced to adhere to an imposed reform program, investor confidence might have been better grounded. But the wisdom of calling in the financial surgeons is now a moot point. 'Part of the problem is Malaysia is trying home-grown solutions without the discipline the IMF enforces,' says Malik. For all its efforts, unless lost-cause businesses are allowed to fail the country may be merely postponing a reckoning that will be made all the more painful by shortsighted, self-interested solutions.

Still, there are those who accentuate the positive. 'The worst is over' for Malaysia, said Hew See Tong, vice president of the All-Malaysia Chinese Mining Association in March. 'We will have recovered in one and a half to two years.' Many point out that Malaysia has not raised interest rates too much and is still seeing a strengthening currency and moderate inflation.

'People are not queuing up at foreign banks to deposit their money anymore,' says Malaysian education minister Najib Tun Razak. But Bank of America economist Andrew Freris says, 'The ringgit could take additional blows, which combined with a tight fiscal policy could result in a prolonged cycle that will see the country bottoming out eight to 12 months after the rest of the Asian economies.' And eventually, authorities will have to either arrange capital infusions for shaky lenders or shut them down to assure the public that no unsound bank will be allowed to accept deposits.

INVESTOR TIPS

The investor environment in Malaysia could become highly fluid. There are moves to open up sectors to foreign investment and to set aside the long-held *bumiputra* policy of ownership preferences for ethnic Malays. The question is whether any changes to the law will be temporary. Malaysian leaders have given mixed signals on their intentions. 'If it's temporary, no investor would go in,' says Chia Siow Yue, director of Singapore's Institute of Southeast Asian Studies. 'You cannot play hot and cold on foreign investment depending on how desperate you are.'

In the short term:

- Find out the true value of any assets you want to purchase. This goes without saying, but with the financial system very fluid, it pays to exercise due diligence.

- Just because a company is export-oriented doesn't mean it will ride an export-led recovery. Check where its main markets are and where its raw materials are sourced.

- Take in the air in Kuala Lumpur and try the water tap. Consider whether the haze and water shortage problems in Malaysia will pose any difficulties, personal or otherwise, for you.

In the long term:

- If Malaysia sticks to its own reform program, and once it pulls through its slump, the potential for strong growth will still be there. The more grandiose infrastructure projects may be on hold, but some key ones are going ahead — for example, the new international airport outside the capital. Investors should pay attention to policy decisions made in coming months that will have a long-term effect on the commercial environment. Of paramount interest: what, if anything, Kuala Lumpur does to revise the *bumiputra* policy.

COMPANIES TO WATCH

- **Berjaya Group**

The stable of tycoon Vincent Tan, a friend of Prime Minister Mahathir. Its gaming operation, Berjaya Sports Toto, is highly regarded because of low gearing and high liquidity, with limited foreign-exchange exposure. A prolonged tourism slump will hurt the group's hotel interests.

- **Petroliam Nasional**

Known as Petronas, the state petroleum company has consistently been a major profit generator. Its new twin-tower headquarters is the world's tallest building. Count on Petronas to remain a major profit-maker for the country.

- **Sime Darby**

A diversified blue-chip conglomerate that, among other things, exports palm oil. Subsidiary, Sime Bank, which is being sold to financial house Rashid Hussain Berhad, was hit hard by the economic crisis.

Philippines: Not Bad, But Could Do Better

1998 was supposed to be a year of celebration for the Philippines and Philippine democracy. In June, the country celebrated 100 years since revolutionaries declared independence from Spain. Just a month before the centenary, Joseph Estrada was elected president with a record breaking 10.5 million votes, marking the second time since the fall of dictator Ferdinand Marcos in 1986 that government authority has changed hands following democratic polls. Another key landmark was achieved at the end of March: Manila graduated from 35 years under the tutelage of the International Monetary Fund (IMF). Ironically, the conclusion of IMF supervision came at a time when three of the Philippines' neighbors are struggling to come to terms with IMF-imposed reforms, some of which the country had already been through.

The IMF strings have not been cut completely. Manila will maintain a two-year standby arrangement that will provide access to $1.6 billion in emergency funds if necessary. By doing so, says Ray Jovanovich, a Hong Kong-based director of fund managers Indocam Asia, the Philippines 'has re-enrolled in an executive MBA course, so to speak. This will help reassure investors.' Still, 'independence' from the IMF is no small achievement for a country once labeled Asia's 'sick man,' the one ASEAN economy to have missed out on the East Asian miracle.

The economic crisis that has seen the peso plunge dramatically along with most other East Asian currencies is fair warning that the Philippines must keep to the reform and liberalization path. 'Export growth [at an average 21% annually over the past five years] has been the strongest in Asia for the past two years,' says Tim Condon, Southeast Asia analyst for Morgan Stanley Dean Witter in Hong Kong. 'The source of this strong export growth lies in structural economic reforms that have increased the Philippines' attractiveness as a destination for foreign direct investment. Reforms undertaken in the early 1990s signaled a shift toward an outward-oriented approach [and] away from decades of inward-oriented, import-substitution policies.'

Fortunately for the Philippines, borrowing in its banking system was not as over-extended as in other economies, and investment in property had not run rampant as, say, in Thailand or Indonesia. The result: the economy has been spared the kind of whiplash suffered by some of its neighbors. The country has nevertheless taken a skid. GDP growth forecasts vary from flat to 2.5% in 1998, down from a peak of 5.7% in 1996. Property markets are soft but holding up better than those in neighboring countries. Interest rates, sometimes reaching 30%, are damaging businesses, but there is very little room to cut rates without putting pressure on the peso. A drought, particularly in the south, is causing agricultural shortages and accelerating price hikes. Inflation could reach 10% this year.

The May presidential elections have added some political uncertainty, as the economic discipline imposed during former president Fidel Ramos' six years in office was put to test when President Estrada immediately began favouring Marcos-era cronies: Eduardo Cojuanco took the helm of San Miguel; partial amnesty for tax evader Lucio Tan; Subic Bay boss Richard Gordon was sacked. The unease surrounding his first weeks in office, raised some doubt about the future of Ramos' economic reforms.

On the banking front, although bad loans are piling up at some banks, recapitalization needs are expected to be relatively small. Export growth is expected to stay strong, although a global falloff in demand for electronics could cut profits. Says Condon: 'Unlike Thailand and much more so Indonesia where debt problems, corporate bankruptcy, and a credit squeeze are slowing the export recovery, Philippine exporters are in a better position to take advantage of the more competitive exchange

Table 8: The Philippines' Top Enterprises

Rank	Company	Main Business	Sales $ Millions	Profit $ Millions	Profit as % of sales	1000 Rank
1	SAN MIGUEL CORP.	Beer, food, beverages	3,242.6	232.3	7.2	374
2	NATIONAL POWER CORP.	Power generation	2,427.3	211.4	8.7	538
3	MANILA ELECTRIC CO.	Electricity distribution	2,247.1	193.2	8.6	590
4	PETRON CORP.	Oil refining, distribution	2,037.4	161.7	7.9	645
5	PILIPINAS SHELL PETRO.	Oil refining, distribution	1,825.9	96.1	5.3	726
6	CALTEX (PHILIPPINES)	Oil refining, distribution	1,281.5	28.2	2.2	986
7	PHILIPPINE AIRLINES	Air transport	1,183.7	-95.4	-8.1	—
8	AYALA CORP.	Property, finance	1,130.1	237.6	21.0	—
9	PLDT	Telecommunications	1,093.1	245.7	22.5	—
10	TEXAS INSTRUMENTS (PHIL.)	Semiconductors	962.5	8.1	0.8	—
11	COCA-COLA BOTTLERS	Soft drinks	910.7	112.4	12.3	—
12	NESTLE PHILIPPINES	Food	840.2	83.0	9.9	—
13	JG SUMMIT HOLDINGS	Food	700.8	136.8	19.5	—
14	TOYOTA MOTOR PHIL.	Car assembly, sales	625.1	25.7	4.1	—
15	ZUELLIG PHARMA	Distribution	618.6	7.7	1.2	—
16	MERCURY DRUG	Pharmaceuticals retailing	599.2	9.4	1.6	—
17	RFM CORPORATION	Food, drinks	521.1	19.2	3.7	—
18	MITSUBISHI MOTORS PHIL.	Car assembly	519.3	49.8	9.6	—
19	NATIONAL STEEL	Steel	479.3	-96.5	-20.1	—
20	SHOE MART	Department stores	445.5	65.1	14.6	—

rate.' The Philippines has gone through several boom–bust cycles in the past 30 years, which means bureaucrats and businessmen are more experienced at handling adversity than some of their counterparts in the region.

Little surprise then that in February this year, the Soros Fund Management group of Hungarian-born tycoon George Soros allotted $45 million for the Philippines, with $10 million going into the London-listed Philippine Discovery Fund and the rest to strategic and long-term investments in local companies. For Patrick Go, managing director of Next Century Partners, the Manila-based conduit for Soros's funds and managers of the Discovery Fund, the American philanthropist's decision to put money into the Philippines is a welcome sign. 'Confidence is coming back,' Go said in March. 'The Philippines has done much better than its neighbors. It has been de-linked by investors from the problems of other countries like Indonesia.'

To be sure, the Philippines is not without its problems, all of which dogged the economy even before the economic crisis. Among the difficulties on the investors' litany of complaints: lack of infrastructure, a grinding legal system, cliquish business groups, and prevalent graft and corruption. But the Philippines, particularly in recent years, has managed to hold its own as an investment destination. The advantages investors rave about include the country's high literacy rate, the widespread use of the English language, the availability of highly skilled workers including computer-savvy technicians and programmers, and the quality of local managers, many of whom boast degrees from Western universities.

'When you ask the larger electronics companies where they prefer to establish facilities,' says Indocam's Jovanovich, 'the Philippines stacks up as No. 1 not only in wages but also in productivity, adaptability of the workforce, and ease of flow of products from factories to ports.' But as its neighbors implement their own deep reforms and improvements, Manila's new leadership will have to ensure that the Philippines stays the course and does not get left behind again.

INVESTOR TIPS

The Philippines is certainly no Singapore. Take a look at the list of the country's top enterprises. Only six of them rank among the top 1000 in the region. (In Thailand, 15 companies make it, while in Taiwan, 18 do.)

In the short term:

🌐 If you are worried about the post-election political situation, then hold off on making a move. Most other investors will be doing the same.

🌐 After elections, there are always changes in the business landscape as supporters of the winners and backers of the losers reposition themselves or get themselves repositioned. Another reason to tread carefully.

🌐 But don't miss out on an attractive opportunity by being faint of heart. Due diligence is the key. It may come as a surprise to some, but it is arguably more important in the Philippines than in other economies to link up with a credible local partner you can trust. The business community is still parochial, despite the fact that many top managers have been schooled abroad. Many local dealmakers think nothing of renegotiating contracts even after signing.

In the long term:

🌐 Think export growth. The Philippines has yet to harness its full potential to become an Asian export powerhouse. Post-crisis, this could be its chance. The country is rich in natural resources, and many areas of the country, particularly in the south, have hardly been developed. If the country can overcome infrastructure bottlenecks and the inefficient deployment of its skilled labor force, investors will have much less to complain about.

COMPANIES TO WATCH

- **Ayala Corp.**

A family conglomerate, Ayala is one of the best managed companies in the country. No wonder that picky Bill Gates recently chose to tie up with the group. Among its prized possessions: the listed Bank of the Philippine Islands, which has already reported a 14% profits rise for fiscal 1997.

- **Philippine Long Distance Telephone Co.**

The country's premier telecommunications operator, PLDT is a blue-chip giant on everybody's portfolio of Philippine holdings. It should prosper as the nation's economic prospects improve.

- **San Miguel**

Though burdened by debts, San Miguel remains the major food-and-beverage group in the Philippines. It also has operations around the region, including a growing presence in China. One of the first steps of President Estrada, was to allow Marcos-crony tycoon Eduardo Cojuanco back at the helm. He took immediate action to cut debt ($443 million) by selling its stake in Coca-Cola Beverages for $555 million.

Hong Kong-based conglomerate First Pacific, controlled by Indonesia's Salim Group, could try to translate its small shareholding into a larger stake.

Singapore: The Best of a Bad Lot

Recession is almost an alien concept to Singaporeans. The last time the Lion City weathered an economic contraction was in 1985. It is unlikely that growth will turn negative again this year. GDP forecasts range from zero to 5.5% growth. In February, the government slashed its 1998 economic growth forecast to 2.5-to-4.5% from 5-to-7%. GDP growth in 1997 was 7.8%, higher than the previously announced 7.6%.

Last year, the haze plaguing Southeast Asia from forest fires in Indonesia and the region's economic downturn hit Singapore's tourism and retailing sectors especially hard. The return of the haze threatens to do the same in 1998. Property prices are down by as much as 35% from their peak, but by limiting new supply, the Singapore government has steadied the market. Companies that expanded regionally, urged on by the government's regionalization drive, are suffering from the economic morass in Thailand, Malaysia, and Indonesia.

A quick glance at the list of the top 20 enterprises in the island republic reveals how important the energy and electronics sectors are to the economy. Seven of the companies are oil traders, while eight are producers of consumer appliances, computer equipment, or semiconductors. The economic crisis has driven down petroleum demand in East Asia, while electronics have been in a lingering slump. Singapore's electronics-based manufacturing sector depends heavily on U.S. demand. A regional glut in computer disk-drive manufacturing capacity is hurting profits, as is a slowdown in PC sales in Asia. Only a modest revival is expected in 1998. Singapore's dollar was hit by devaluation, though it held up better than the currencies of neighboring countries.

All indications are that Singapore, as expected, will rebound quickly. After all, in 1997, the economy turned in the sort of robust performance Lion City citizens are accustomed to. Inflation is likely to remain low; it rose to 2.3% from 2% in 1997. Singaporeans must be counting their blessings. The country has a huge current account surplus, equivalent to 16% of GDP, according to some estimates. Although most banks may have substantial exposure to the region, they are well-capitalized and could write off bad loans with barely a break in stride. A slight devaluation in currency and falling office rents have enhanced competitiveness over rival Hong Kong, which has stuck to a U.S. dollar peg for its currency.

There are more encouraging signs. Manufacturing growth in 1997 rose to 4.3% from 3% the year before. Transport and communications rose to 9.2% from 8.1%, while financial and business services growth rose to 11% from 7.8%.

Construction growth slowed to 13.3% from 19.5% in 1996 as the property market slump began, while commerce growth declined to 5.8% from 6.2% as retail cash registers were hit by a plunge in consumer confidence and tourist arrivals. Real estate prices are expected to continue to fall through 1998 and possibly into 1999.

But recovery will not be achieved easily. Troubles in Indonesia and Malaysia are headaches for Singapore. The regional turmoil is hitting the financial and business services and commerce badly. Entrepôt trade, tourism, and retail industries are also suffering. Expect more moderate growth in construction and manufacturing, as well as in the transport and communications sector. With the regional demand for oil likely to stay down, growth in the petroleum industry will continue to slow. Corporate balance sheets have yet to reflect the full effects of the crisis.

Financial results for the 187 listed companies reporting at the end of 1997 showed that combined earnings plummeted 26% over 1996, the first drop in a dozen years. Nearly 13% of the enterprises were in the red, with more than two-thirds turning in a loss after registering a

Table 9: Singapore's Top Enterprises

Rank	Company	Main Business	Sales $ Millions	Profit $ Millions	Profit as % of sales	1000 Rank
1	CALTEX TRADING	Oil trading	9,872.6	10.5	0.1	116
2	SEAGATE TECHNOLOGY INTL.	Disk drives	6,242.6	797.2	12.8	179
3	HEWLETT-PACKARD	Computers	5,839.1	1040.7	17.8	197
4	SINGAPORE AIRLINES	Air transport	5,121.6	731.6	14.3	239
5	ASIA MATSUSHITA ELECTRIC	Consumer electronics	4,336.2	44.7	1.0	286
6	YUKONG INTERNATIONAL (S)	Oil trading	3,875.8	13.0	0.3	325
7	NISSHO IWAI PETROLEUM	Oil trading	3,686.8	-0.8	—	342
8	HONG LEONG INVESTMENT	Investment	3,457.8	244.1	7.1	362
9	BP SINGAPORE	Oil trading, refining	3,182.4	59.3	1.9	384
10	HITACHI ASIA	Electronics	3,164.5	3.5	0.1	390
11	SINGAPORE TELECOM	Telecommunications	3,135.4	1,176.2	37.5	395
12	TEXAS INSTRUMENTS SING.	Semiconductors	2,887.7	48.0	1.7	437
13	MARUBENI INTL. PETROLEUM	Oil trading	2,782.1	13.2	0.5	459
14	MOBIL OIL SINGAPORE	Oil trading, refining	2,661.0	126.7	4.8	477
15	SGS-THOMSON MICROELECT. ASIA	Semiconductors	2,390.8	31.6	1.3	548
16	WESTERN DIGITAL (SING.)	Disk drives	2,296.5	111.3	4.8	569
17	KUOK OILS & GRAINS	Commodities trading	2,275.0	6.6	0.3	582
18	PHILIPS (SINGAPORE)	Consumer electronics	2,244.1	24.2	1.1	593
19	ITOCHU PETROLEUM	Oil trading	2,136.1	-0.4	—	617
20	CYCLE & CARRIAGE	Cars, property, food	2,135.4	141.9	6.6	618

profit the previous year. Of the profitable firms, more than half posted lower profits. The fashion among companies is to announce substantial provisions for potential red ink.

The Singapore government is banking heavily on the financial sector to secure the island's future as Southeast Asia's services hub. In this year's budget, Finance Minister Richard Hu offered tax incentives for fund management and venture capital firms. The aim, though not officially stated, is clear: to challenge Hong Kong. But Singapore has a long way to go. Its corporate income tax rate is 26%, compared to Hong Kong's 16%, and personal tax rates are much higher than its rival's. While Hong Kong is a much pricier place to live, it is beyond compare as a gateway to China. Singapore's niche is as a base for companies covering markets in Southeast Asia, particularly Indochina. The efficient infrastructure of the island, particularly its airport and high-tech port area, are still far ahead of what the neighbors have to offer.

But the neighbors are catching up. To stay ahead, Singapore has been seeking to re-invent itself. Manufacturing has been moving upscale. 'With weakening currencies, (other Asian nations) are going to be even more competitive relative to our lower-level exports, so it is even more important to upgrade as quickly as possible to reduce reliance on our lower-productivity labor and move to high value-added brainpower-type industries,' says Hu. The authorities have been pushing companies, including its large government-linked companies, to expand into the region's emerging markets, including China and India. The campaign has had mixed results. But for Singapore, an island of just 3.1 million people, there is probably no alternative.

INVESTOR TIPS

Many investors approach Singapore with a bagful of preconceptions. Sure, the place is clean and orderly, and the fines and penalties for breaking the rules can be severe. But it pays to discard the stereotypes and take a good sense of humor with you. Singapore is not as boring as casual visitors claim it is. The food is varied and tasty. And the city is a safe place to raise a family.

In the short term:

The finance sector is likely to see rapid liberalization in the near term. Keep an eye on developments even if you aren't a banker. Opening up of this industry will inevitably attract more investors to move into the Lion City and make it their Southeast Asian base.

🌐 Looking for a potentially lucrative property play? The Singapore real-estate market plunged further in the doldrums as a result of the crisis. But recovery is expected going into 1999. This could be one chance to buy low.

🌐 Even in Singapore, due diligence is important. Check company parentage. Who knows? Your potential partner could be some cash-strapped entity in Indonesia tottering on the brink of bankruptcy.

In the long term:

🌐 Singapore's future lies outside. Outward-looking companies with a smart global or regional strategy will prosper. If you are thinking of basing your operations on the island, be prepared. This is no free-wheeling Hong Kong yet. By-rote education has not fostered the kind of creative, enterprise culture you might find in Taiwan. As its economy has proven amid the crisis, what Singapore offers is stability.

COMPANIES TO WATCH

- **Keppel Corp.**

A major government-linked conglomerate with investments around the region. Its businesses include shipbuilding and shipyard operation, property development, and banking. It often takes the lead management position in government-sponsored flagship projects such as Singapore's industrial township in Suzhou, near Shanghai.

- **Singapore Airlines**

The economic crisis has thrown up the biggest challenge the air carrier has ever faced. But this profitable airline is certainly one of the best prepared to weather the turbulence. It will be rough, but the management knows what it takes.

- **Singapore Telecom**

The island's highly profitable telecommunications giant that is fighting to stay dominant despite the introduction of feisty competition. It is unlikely to lose.

South Korea: On the Bumpy Road to Recovery

Big is no longer beautiful in South Korea. *Chaebol*, or large industrial conglomerates, have been among the hardest hit by the economic crisis, most of them saddled with massive foreign debts. Some groups had already been feeling the pinch even before last year's financial meltdown hit. In 1997, about 10 *chaebol* went under, leaving banks holding more than $27 billion in bad debts. Hanbo Iron & Steel Co., the flagship enterprise of the country's 14th-largest business group, crumbled in January under $6.5 billion in debts. Kia Motors, the nation's third-biggest automaker, went into receivership in July.

Despite these high-profile corporate collapses, even as late as October 1997, nobody predicted that Korea — paragon of the East Asian economic miracle after Japan — would be brought to its knees the following month. Judging by fiscal 1996 corporate results, it is no wonder that pessimists were scarce. Take giants like Samsung, the country's top firm by sales, Daewoo, and LG International (once known as Lucky-Goldstar). For these three groups, 1996/97 was a healthy year, with each seeing about a 25% increase in total turnover. Senior executives attributed the glowing performance to their global presence in four key industries: consumer electronics and semiconductors, automobiles, ships and machinery, and petrochemicals. About 38% of Korea's global exports go to neighbors in Asia, excluding Japan. For Samsung, the figure is 45%.

But with the crisis, the picture has changed. In October 1997, the precipitous fall of the local currency, the won, over a matter of weeks led to a severe cash crunch, as Seoul's foreign reserves were rapidly depleted. By early November, the government of then-president Kim Young Sam had issued an SOS to the International Monetary Fund (IMF) — Korea was practically broke. And with many of Korea's major trading partners in the region similarly in trouble, reliance on Asian markets had turned into something of a liability. As company sales in East Asia have slowed going into 1998, corporate performance has suffered as a consequence. Look at Korean Air. While not one of Korea's top 20 enterprises, it is No. 298 on the *Asiaweek* 1000 list. In March 1998, the airline announced that, though sales rose 17% over 1996, it had posted its biggest ever loss of $248 million in 1997, due mainly to huge foreign exchange losses. It saw its debt-equity ratio rise from an already high 916% to a staggering 1128%. With passenger and cargo traffic in and out of Korea down because of the economic turmoil, the outlook for the nation's flag carrier is bleak. And the company is certainly not the only Korean enterprise bleeding because of the crisis.

Despite the grim prospects, Korea has managed to fight back from the brink. The election in December 1997 of opposition leader Kim Dae Jung to the presidency fueled the beginnings of a revival. Initially a skeptic, the new leader grudgingly accepted the IMF bailout package. When Seoul successfully negotiated a rollover of short-term debt in January, the tide of pessimism eased. The won rose 22% against the U.S. dollar and the Seoul stock market surged 48% in dollar terms in the first three months of 1998. Surging exports and sharply lower imports have produced large trade surpluses over the same period, a soothing balm to the country's deep economic wounds. The new president started calling the shots almost as soon as he was elected. By the time he had taken office in February, Kim had pushed through revisions in investment regulations and IMF-imposed financial and economic reforms that will see major shifts in Korea's corporate landscape. Among the key changes: wider opportunities for foreign investors to buy stakes in Korean companies.

Still, the economic picture is likely to remain gloomy through 1999. High interest rates of over 20% have strangled small and mid-sized companies. The corporate sector, dominated by the conglomerates, continues to struggle with its massive foreign debt burden. A stronger won coupled with a weaker yen could derail an export-led recovery as Japanese goods become more competitive. Dramatically weaker domestic demand has prompted the government to ease its austerity campaign. Forecasters are expecting an economic contraction of up to 5% this year, although some analysts still believe zero growth is achievable. Companies are restructuring by selling assets, narrowing their business lines, and shedding staff. Unemployment is soaring beyond the levels initially anticipated, and militant trade unions are likely to oppose additional layoffs. Social unrest could rise.

But if Seoul sticks to its reform program, real recovery should start sometime in 1999. Savvy investors are not waiting until then. There are definite signs. A strong inflow of foreign investment generated a $500 million capital account surplus in February, the country's first since November. Though Korea actively engaged the world in trade and commerce, back home, its own business sector remained largely closed to foreigners.

That is changing rapidly, as the government peels away layers of rules that once prevented or made it difficult for overseas interests to buy into the economy. Outsiders were prohibited from taking over a Korean company, appointing directors to corporate boards and, except in a few cases, buying property. Even when it joined the Organization of Economic Cooperation and Development (OECD) in 1997, Korea managed to win concessions allowing it to delay implementing such liberalization measures as opening up its bond market.

The losers will be the *chaebol*, which are mostly family-run behemoths that now look decidedly like dinosaurs heading toward extinction or at least major surgery to turn them into smaller, sleeker, and more accountable enterprises that will have to face greater competition and little, if any, government coddling. With the over-borrowing and over-investment of the conglomerates mainly to blame for Korea's economic turmoil, few are sad to see them cut down to size. President Kim has promised 'to give foreigners the same treatment that Koreans enjoy.' Foreigners will be able to buy up to a third of a company's outstanding common stock without the approval of its board of directors, up from the current 10% ceiling. They would also be able to buy as much as 55% of the outstanding stock directly from the market. Hostile takeovers by foreign companies should be easier, with the threshold stake coming down from 40% to 20%.

So where are the bargains in the new Korea? Automotive and electronic parts companies are considered good bets. These firms not only have a thick portfolio of supply contracts with Korea's leading producers but are also thinly capitalized. Retailers, particularly those burdened by poor management, might also prove attractive buys.

Table 10: South Korea's Top Enterprises

Rank	Company	Main Business	Sales $ Millions	Profit $ Millions	Profit as % of sales	1000 Rank
1	SAMSUNG CO.	Trading, investment	29,997.8	54.1	0.2	24
2	HYUNDAI CORP.	Trading, investment	25,548.9	15.3	0.1	30
3	DAEWOO CORP.	Trading, investment	23,633.9	90.7	0.4	33
4	SAMSUNG ELECTRONICS	Electronics, appliances	19,733.4	204.1	1.0	38
5	LG INTERNATIONAL CORP.	Trading, investment	17,454.3	26.9	0.2	49
6	KOREA ELECTRIC POWER	Power generation	14,393.4	742.8	5.2	65
7	HYUNDAI MOTOR	Cars	14,282.8	107.9	0.8	66
8	POHANG IRON & STEEL	Steel	11,989.7	735.1	6.1	86
9	YUKONG LTD.	Oil refining, exploration	10,345.1	84.8	0.8	112
10	LG ELECTRONICS	Consumer electronics	9,326.2	80.6	0.9	126
11	SSANGYONG CORP.	General trading	9,161.9	3.5	0.0	128
12	KOREA TELECOM	Telecommunications	8,904.3	224.3	2.5	131
13	KIA MOTORS	Cars, trucks	8,213.2	8.7	0.1	142
14	HYUNDAI MOTOR SERVICE	Car dealership	7,272.1	39.6	0.5	159
15	LG CALTEX OIL CORP.	Oil refining	6,920.3	15.2	0.2	165
16	DAEWOO HEAVY INDUSTRIES	Shipbuilding, machinery	6,400.0	92.0	1.5	176
17	HYUNDAI ENG. & CONST.	Construction	5,882.4	26.3	0.4	193
18	SUNKYONG LTD.	General trading, oil	5,826.8	10.6	0.2	198
19	HYUNDAI HEAVY INDS.	Shipbuilding, machinery	5,824.4	17.4	0.3	200
20	SSANGYONG OIL REFINING	Oil refining	5,545.7	154.6	2.8	219

INVESTOR TIPS

In the short term:

 Keep an eye out for developments in investment regulations. The reform process is moving quickly. What was prohibited one day could be allowed the next.

 Companies have been going bust every day. With the situation so fluid, it pays to exercise extra due diligence. Triple check any potential partners and their shareholders.

 Just because a business is associated with a *chaebol*, even one that went bankrupt, does not automatically mean that the enterprise is not worth a second look. It may be on sale precisely because its business is viable. Indeed, buying even a small piece of a *chaebol* could prove to be a smart play.

In the long term:

 The global strategy is still in play. Companies with strong sales in traditional markets such as the U.S. and Europe will pull through the crisis in better shape. Those with growing sales in emerging markets like Asia and Eastern Europe are likely to be the next generation of winners. And Korea, like other East Asian economies that have seen currencies plunge and asset values drop, is suddenly among the most competitive. When looking at an investment, think about how you can buy into that new competitiveness. Korean steelmakers, for example, were already among the most productive in the world before the crisis; now they could become unbeatable.

COMPANIES TO WATCH

A hard choice, given the dramatically changing corporate landscape. Still, the best-looking megacompanies are likely to be the familiar names.

• Daewoo

Saudi Prince al-Waleed bin Talal Abdel Aziz, the jet-setting royal tycoon, invested in a very grateful Daewoo. Big will not necessarily be beautiful in post-crisis Korea, but Daewoo remains a formidable *chaebol* with wide interests, competent management, and healthy profits. The group is likely to boost sales through growing operations in Eastern Europe.

• Hyundai Motor

Another company to receive money from Prince al-Waleed. The carmaker can take advantage of cheaper costs at home and the prospect of higher sales in key overseas markets such as the U.S. and Europe.

• Pohang Iron & Steel

Referred to as Posco, the steelmaker should benefit from the won devaluation, particularly if export markets in the West stay healthy and the regional market recovers. It was one of the most cost-effective steel producers before the crisis; post-devaluation, Posco could steamroller the competition.

Taiwan: Calm Island, Tense Island

Ironically, cash-rich Taiwan's decision to stop defending the local dollar and let it depreciate partly contributed to the currency meltdown that hit the region last year. Though the island government was sitting on top of about $80 billion in foreign exchange reserves, Taipei lost its nerve. The NT dollar slid, but it did not plunge in free-fall. The stock market was unsettled, but did not go into a prolonged slump. And even as the rest of East Asia was enveloped in the crisis, Taiwan stood out as a healthy exception. The reason: the island's competitiveness in key export sectors such as its bread-and-butter electronics. Simply put, Taiwan is plugged into the global market more than most of its neighbors. Says Joseph Stiglitz, the World Bank's chief economist: 'One thing that has served Taiwan well is its competitive market structure, so that the fortunes of one, two or three companies do not affect the fortunes of the country as a whole. It's a diversified economy.'

The diversification hailed by Stiglitz is evident in the list of top enterprises in Taiwan. In the ranking are companies representing a wide range of sectors from computers to cars, plastics to power generation. But Taiwan is distinctive for two other reasons. First, instead of depending largely on huge conglomerates similar to the Korean *chaebol*, the island has a well-developed enterprise culture. In many ways, its miracle was built on the growth of small and medium-sized companies. Second, Taiwan has for years developed its high-technology sector, benefiting immensely from the high standards of its local universities, as well as from the brain power it recruited from among its citizens who left the island to study in the best schools in the West and Japan. Diversification, entrepreneurship, and education. These are three areas in which Taiwan has had a head start. Its rivals should take notes.

There are, of course, other factors that have contributed to Taiwan's success. The island has been able to transform itself from a labor-intensive manufacturing center for low-end products into a maker of more sophisticated goods. The cheap stuff — the shoes, the toys, the garments — is now being made in Taiwan-funded factories in Southeast Asia and across the strait. Since Taipei permitted investment across the strait, the island has become one of the biggest investors in the mainland, with funding channeled through Hong Kong. The interest of Taiwan companies in China became so intense that the Taipei government became concerned that the island would become too dependent on the mainland. The authorities decided to slow down investments and call for its businessmen to 'go south' and spread the money around. With Southeast Asia in economic trouble, the strategy has been intensified as Taipei seeks to enhance its diplomatic influence by offering financial help. Taiwan leaders have been popping up in Southeast Asian capitals in recent months.

To be sure, Taiwan authorities know that their economic success may be built on sound foundations, but paradoxically it also hangs by a thread. The island of calm is also an island of extreme stress. The political limbo it inhabits is an obvious strain on the economy. Whatever its commercial aspirations, Taiwan will never fully achieve them until there is some satisfactory resolution to the cross-strait division. Limited direct shipping between the island and the mainland was introduced in 1997 and is set to expand. Air links could begin within the next few years. Improved U.S.–China relations have seen a parallel thaw in cross-strait ties.

But the fact is that a settlement of the China–Taiwan issue is a long way off, and not getting any easier to bring about. Taiwan has become a vibrant democracy, while in China, political reform is taking place at a very slow pace. As Taiwan's political system evolves, the gap between the two is widening. There are likely to be periods of cross-strait tension every so often. The Chinese missile testing that took place off Taiwan in March 1996 probably did more to undermine confidence in the island than the economic crisis. The reality is that the potential for conflict in the Taiwan Strait remains very high. China-watchers are already pondering what Beijing's response would be should a pro-Taiwan Independence candidate emerge as the island's leader in presidential elections scheduled for 2000. China has threatened to use military force before.

Investors looking at Taiwan have to live with this situation. But if they look beyond it, the island has much to offer. It has certainly proved its mettle through the crisis period. In the first quarter of 1998, fund managers from Hong Kong to London were overweighting Taiwan because it is one of the few Asian markets offering high economic and corporate earnings growth. 'Our market decoupled from the rest of Asia quite a long time ago,' says analyst Stephen Wang at HSBC James Capel Taiwan. 'We are being driven on the strength of our domestic economy and our competitive position in global electronics.' HSBC James Capel forecasts that listed Taiwan companies will post strong 19% growth in earnings per share in 1998, on top of the 45% recovery last year from a dismal 1996. The Asian Development Bank expects Taiwan's GDP to rise 5.8% in 1998 versus 6.8% in 1997.

There are clouds threatening. Taiwan's index of leading economic indicators slid 0.6% month-on-month in March, the third decline in a row. 'The trade numbers out of Taiwan recently have been disappointing,' says Eddie Wong of ABN Amro. 'The weaker yen is hurting Taiwan. Even the PC market in the U.S. and Europe isn't growing as fast as people had anticipated.' The quasi-official Chung-Hua Institution for Economic Research is warning that exports could drop 1.52% this year over 1997, the first annual decline in more than 10 years.

Exports of chemicals, plastics, and textiles are falling because of the Asian slump. But some analysts argue that, into the first few months of 1998, surging electronics exports with 13–14% growth expected this year, are more than compensating. While many investors worry that East Asia's slowdown will eventually hit Taiwan's personal computer and peripheral makers, Rick Hsu at Capital Securities in Taipei says such concerns are overblown. 'Our companies are world-class suppliers and they depend mainly on [sales to] North America and Europe, with Asia being a small portion of the market.'

Acer, the island's best-known personal computer maker, is a turnaround story cited by almost every Taiwan promoter. In 1997, the company's memory chip joint venture TI-Acer lost a bundle as prices fell. Now, as memory prices firm, the venture is bouncing back and Acer is benefiting. Losses from Acer America are also down sharply. Still, given the consolidation at the top end of the global PC industry as seen in the merger of U.S. giants Compaq and Digital, Acer faces stiffening competition. But Hsu says: 'Acer has shown before it can catch up fast. It has the products, it has cut costs, and it has a good marketing strategy in place.' And even if similarly small brands may find the going tougher, Acer is still a top contract manufacturer with big revenue streams from peripherals and components. Its own-brand PCs account for just 40% of total sales.

There are more Acers in the making in Taiwan. No surprise then that investors who before may have been spooked by the cross-strait problem are taking second and third looks at the island. Taipei approved foreign investment worth $640 million in the first quarter to March this year, up 51% from the same period in 1997, according to the Investment Commission.

Table II: Taiwan's Top Enterprises

Rank	Company	Main Business	Sales $ Millions	Profit $ Millions	Profit as % of sales	1000 Rank
1	CHINESE PETROLEUM CORP.	Oil exploration, refining	12,019.4	276.4	2.3	85
2	TAIWAN POWER	Power generation	8,510.3	1,247.9	14.7	136
3	CHUNGHWA TELECOM	Telecommunications	6,036.9	1,998.3	33.1	188
4	ACER	Computers	5,893.0	188.0	3.2	192
5	NAN YA PLASTICS	Petrochemicals	3,712.7	282.9	7.6	338
6	TAIWAN TOBACCO & WINE	Trading, distribution	3,585.5	NA	—	349
7	CHINA STEEL CORP.	Steel products	3,199.3	491.9	15.4	380
8	TATUNG	Consumer electronics	3,039.0	269.4	8.9	413
9	PRESIDENT ENTERPRISES	Drinks, food	2,480.2	116.6	4.7	526
10	HOTAI MOTOR	Car dealership	2,103.2	29.4	1.4	625
11	CHINA AIRLINES	Air transport	1,845.3	57.8	3.1	719
12	YULON MOTOR	Cars	1,771.7	57.2	3.2	747
13	EVERGREEN MARINE	Shipping	1,667.6	117.0	7.0	794
14	FORMOSA PLASTICS	Plastics	1,596.8	221.9	13.9	831
15	FORMOSA CHEM. & FIBRE	Textiles	1,517.4	125.6	8.3	862
16	FORD LIO HO MOTOR	Cars	1,479.0	NA	—	877
17	MITAC INTERNATIONAL CORP.	Computers	1,370.0	4.9	0.4	936
18	SAN YANG INDUSTRY	Cars, motorcycles	1,304.6	47.6	3.6	976
19	CHI MEI CORP.	Plastics	1,251.1	104.7	8.4	—
20	HUALON	Textiles	1,247.9	41.5	3.3	—

INVESTOR TIPS

Visitors to Taipei who have not been in the city for some time may be pleasantly surprised. The streets are cleaner and traffic moves faster. Drivers and motorcyclists are even behaving. The municipal authorities under Mayor Chen Shui-bian, Taiwan's leading opposition figure, have been widely applauded for their success. Chen's performance has made him the most popular politician and a serious contender for the presidency in 2000. The catch is that he belongs to the pro-Independence Democratic Progressive Party.

One other warning: English is not as widely spoken as in Hong Kong or Singapore. Mandarin and sometimes Japanese will get you around, but in some areas, particularly in the southern part of the island, even those languages won't help. These days, everybody speaks Taiwanese, which the Nationalist government once suppressed.

In the short term:

Think outward. Taiwan companies plugged into the region, into the mainland, and into the global grid are the ones to watch.

Think competitiveness. The island's electronics sector can compete with the best in the world. Often, they do so quietly. Take scanners: Taiwan has an enormous slice of this niche market. It's the same with golf clubs.

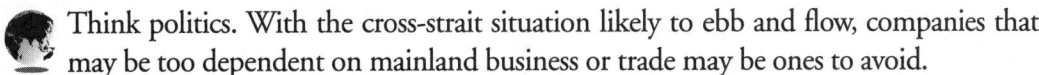

Think politics. With the cross-strait situation likely to ebb and flow, companies that may be too dependent on mainland business or trade may be ones to avoid.

In the long term:

Think politics, again. If you can't take the heat, stay out of the kitchen. Any investor will have to take the long-term political risk of a Taiwan presence into consideration. Consider how operating on the island may or may not affect investments in Hong Kong or the mainland. Many multinationals, such as petrochemical giant Du Pont, are now taking a Greater China approach. Taiwan can indeed become a useful source of expert personnel for investors in the management-starved mainland. But contingency plans should be in place, should cross-strait ties become unsettled.

COMPANIES TO WATCH

- **Acer**

Stan Shih and his team have built Acer into the most widely known Taiwan-born brand name in the world. The computer maker has reinvented itself with Shih's decentralized management system and his encouragement of entrepreneurship among his staff.

- **Formosa Plastics and Nan Ya Plastics**

The two flagships of dour multibillionaire Wang Yung-ching. They are expanding and moving into upstream and downstream products. Despite the regional overcapacity in petrochemicals and plastics and the slump in Asian demand, these are two globally competitive blue chips that should perform well in the medium-to-long term.

- **President Enterprises**

This diversified group's core business is food and beverages. It is one of Taiwan's biggest investors in the mainland.

Thailand: First in, First out ?

Recession arrived officially in Thailand in the fourth quarter of 1997. How long it stays depends upon the success of aggressive reform efforts. Some economists say the country is in for only a year of contraction; others say two. The baht has stabilized and interest rates are likely to ease. As 1998 progresses, however, the bad news will continue. There is worldwide overcapacity in petrochemicals, automobiles, and auto parts, which were targeted as Thailand's key growth sectors. Sluggish demand for its electronics is also slowing recovery efforts. Tourism, inspired by bargain hotel rates and airfares, was supposed to provide a kick, but visitor traffic has been discouraging. Inflation may hit nearly 10% this year, and unemployment is expected to continue rising until early next year. Social unrest could develop. 'The magnitude of this problem is unprecedented as more than one-and-a-half and possibly up to two million people may be unemployed by the end of the year,' admits Thai prime minister Chuan Leekpai.

The best news is that the government has moved resolutely to restructure the banking and financial system. Thailand's new leadership that took over in November last year amid the crisis has been lauded for monetary discipline, market-friendly policies, and its determination to adhere to the International Monetary Fund (IMF) program. Thai exports have picked up well in recent months; the country now has a trade surplus and trade financing is again available.

First in, first out. Amazingly, many investors, as well as eager-to-please Bangkok officials, are now betting that Thailand, the country that led Asia into its seven-month-old economic crisis, will also be the first to emerge from it. Improving macroeconomic numbers began enticing punters back into the market in mid-January. Two weeks later, the central bank abolished the two-tier exchange rate imposed at the height of the currency crisis. It was a red flag for the bulls, who sent the Bangkok bourse's SET index rocketing. 'You have to ask how long a crisis is a crisis,' says Ian McLennan, head of research at SBC Warburg in Bangkok. 'We're still facing very difficult conditions, but the baht is relatively stable and the government's performance has impressed somewhat.'

Still, while the big picture is improving, the nitty gritty hides dangers. 'The corporate outlook is still poor,' warns Suraphol Thipvilai, assistant research manager at Vickers Ballas in Bangkok. He warns that the baht, even if it has recovered somewhat from the depths it reached, is still a serious burden for companies with foreign debt. The Thai bourse may have scraped the bottom, but analysts caution that the market remains susceptible to bad news and could suddenly slump.

What have the experts been saying? First off, don't dive into blue chips. Their valuations have been stretched beyond all reason for now, as portfolio managers who wrote off Thailand last year pour back into the market. Find smaller and overlooked stocks — those with low foreign debt, good long-term demand for their products, and cheap valuations. Investors with a budget might be well advised to get some exposure now and take a further plunge later in the year. Advice from the fund masters should serve other direct investors just as well. Those without a presence in Thailand looking to make a strategic buy will want to make their first moves with caution. Like punters in equities, those wanting to get in for the long term should focus on companies with healthy revenue streams and strong earnings potential in deregulated environments such as telecommunications. As in the other bombed-out economies, double due diligence is key, even at the risk of missing out on a dirt-cheap asset.

Yet investors should not take too long. Economic recovery will take time, but the window of opportunity for bargain hunters may be open for only a limited period. Says Chalongphob Sussangkarn, president of the Thailand Development Research Institute: 'You have to make foreign

Table 12: Thailand's Top Enterprises

Rank	Company	Main Business	Sales $ Millions	Profit $ Millions	Profit as % of sales	1000 Rank
1	PETROLEUM AUTHORITY	Oil refining, distribution	6,538.8	327.5	5.0	171
2	ELEC. GENERATING AUTHORITY	Power generation	4,316.3	1,069.1	24.8	287
3	SIAM CEMENT	Cement	4,232.8	267.8	6.3	293
4	THAI AIRWAYS INTERNATIONAL	Air transport	3,078.6	133.5	4.3	406
5	TOYOTA MOTOR (THAILAND)	Car assembly, sales	2,785.5	34.2	1.2	456
6	THAI OIL	Oil refining	2,477.0	8.8	0.4	528
7	TRI PETCH ISUZU SALES	Car dealership	2,290.7	22.6	0.0	576
8	ESSO STANDARD THAILAND	Oil refining, distribution	2,049.9	-54.9	—	639
9	SHELL CO. OF THAILAND	Oil refining, distribution	1,872.6	52.7	2.8	713
10	TELEPHONE ORGANIZATION	Telecommunications	1,650.6	830.4	50.3	803
11	MMC SITTIPOL	Car assembly, sales	1,510.7	0.2	0.0	865
12	BOONRAWD TRADING	Beer & soft drink sales	1,364.5	2.4	0.2	939
13	SIAM MOTORS	Car assembly, distributor	1,346.2	38.9	2.9	955
14	BOONRAWD BREWERY	Beer, soft drinks	1,325.1	44.9	3.4	968
15	BANGCHAK PETROLEUM	Oil products	1,306.2	40.4	3.1	975
16	SIAM MAKRO	Cash and carry wholesale	1,249.1	30.1	2.4	—
17	SIAM NISSAN AUTOMOBILE	Car assembly, car parts	1,237.5	57.5	4.6	—
18	COMMUNICATIONS AUTH. OF THAI.	Telecommunications	1,090.2	294.5	27.0	—
19	HONDA CARS	Car distribution	1,028.0	6.5	0.6	—
20	CHAROEN POKPHAND FEEDMILL	Animal Feed	1,027.7	53.6	5.2	—

investors feel that the currency has hit bottom. In Thailand, once the currency begins to turn around, the longer you wait, the more expensive things become.'

Investors should also remember that stability is one thing, recovery another. Thailand's economy is far from out of the woods. Early in 1998, it was looking more like a bottomless pit. Even with the IMF bailout and a reform-minded government in place, analysts have now postponed much chance of a real rebound for at least three years. This crisis is the country's deepest downturn in 15 years. The IMF is forecasting a 3.1% contraction this year, after negative 0.4% growth in 1997. Inflation is expected to climb from 5.6% last year to 11.6% in 1998.

While the liquidity crisis that caused the closure of 56 finance companies has eased somewhat, surviving banks now must meet tough new reserve requirements set by the IMF. Attracting foreign investors to help recapitalize the banks will be difficult; there is competition for funds throughout the hard-hit region. Domestic demand has evaporated, depressing prospects for manufacturers of consumer durable goods and for real estate. The country's auto industry is facing drastic production cutbacks and massive layoffs as consumers in the region put off purchases. Total domestic car sales plunged 38.4% in 1997. Export-oriented companies will be helped by the greatly devalued baht, but only those that don't rely on imported inputs and have few U.S. dollar debts.

Still, wise investors are not standing still. In April, the local subsidiary of Swedish car manufacturer Volvo announced plans to export built-up cars from Thailand in reaction to the decline of the domestic market and weather the slump. 'Thailand was the first country in Asia hit by the economic crisis,' says Volvo Thailand managing director Pascal Bellemans. 'The country will be the first to come out of the crisis.' Volvo is investing $7.7 million to set up two assembly lines in their existing facilities to produce sedans and station wagons for the ASEAN, Japanese, and European markets.

INVESTOR TIPS

Thailand is one of the three East Asian economies in intensive care. Bangkok has moved quickly to tackle its economic problems, implementing the IMF-recommended reform program with determination. Still, investors should be mindful that a battle-scarred corporate landscape is a tricky minefield to navigate.

In the short term:

 Take the time to check out potential purchases and prospective partners.

🌐 With state enterprises on the block, it may be tempting to make a privatization play. But privatized state firms may need a lot of restructuring to whip them into shape. Consider the time and money you will need to do the needed repairs.

🌐 Be sensitive. With unemployment rising and foreign investors snapping up bargain assets, the chances of social unrest and nationalist sentiment growing are high.

In the long term:

🌐 Thailand will doubtless prove to be a tremendously satisfying buy for the long-term investor looking to make a strategic investment in Asia. The country is a good base for the emerging Indochina market, despite its infrastructure problems and current economic difficulties. The next few years will be tough ones, but the new post-reform Thailand will be more competitive and more attractive than before the crisis. Get in now, but proceed with extreme caution.

COMPANIES TO WATCH

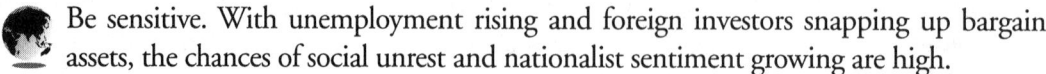

With Bangkok opening up markets, the corporate landscape is changing rapidly. Sectors to watch: telecommunications and autos.

• **Telephone Organization**

Profits will be slashed by the crisis and greater competition, and other companies may be more exciting. Watch developments in the fast-changing telecommunications sector.

• **Thai Airways International**

Set to be privatized (another prime privatization target is the Petroleum Authority). The airline is struggling amid the crisis, but new management could work wonders with a carrier that has a good international network and favorable reputation.

• **Toyota Motor (Thailand)**

Before the crisis, Thailand was looking to become Asia's Detroit. It could still move in that direction. One hitch for Toyota: troubles at home could spell trouble for its Thai unit.

Chapter Five

TOP ENTERPRISES BY INDUSTRY

Appliances and Consumer Electronics

If there is one potential bright spot, this could be it. The global electronics and computer market is forecast to grow 17% in 1998, maintaining the pace of the last two years despite the turmoil in Asia. The region is a key supplier to the world. Everyone from the giants in Japan, such as Toshiba and NEC, to the hustling memory chip, monitor, and disk drive makers of Korea, Taiwan, and Malaysia are being counted on to lead an export-driven recovery, especially since weak Asian currencies have boosted their price competitiveness. The trouble is, they all invested in capacity, expecting the over-20% growth rates of the early 1990s to return. So expect margin-busting price cuts.

Rank	Company	Country	Sales $ Millions	Profit $ Millions	Profit as % of Sales	Profit as % of Assets	1000 Rank
1	MATSUSHITA ELECTRIC INDL.	JAPAN	70,563.6	1,267.3	1.8	1.6	10
2	SONY CORP.	JAPAN	52,060.4	1,282.0	2.5	2.5	12
3	SAMSUNG ELECTRONICS	SOUTH KOREA	19,733.4	204.1	1.0	1.0	38
4	SANYO ELECTRIC CO.	JAPAN	16,972.1	162.5	0.0	0.7	52
5	SHARP	JAPAN	16,460.6	446.3	2.7	2.4	55
6	LG ELECTRONICS	SOUTH KOREA	9,326.2	80.6	0.9	0.9	126
7	VICTOR CO. OF JAPAN	JAPAN	8,185.1	42.2	0.5	0.8	143
8	MATSUSHITA-KOTOBUKI	JAPAN	5,713.6	193.5	3.4	5.4	209
9	PIONEER ELECTRONIC	JAPAN	5,079.8	23.1	0.5	0.5	241
10	DAEWOO ELECTRONICS	SOUTH KOREA	4,438.0	60.2	1.4	1.3	280
11	ASIA MATSUSHITA ELECTRIC	SINGAPORE	4,336.2	44.7	1.0	4.4	286
12	ALPS ELECTRIC	JAPAN	4,195.1	44.5	1.1	0.0	299
13	HYUNDAI ELECTRON. INDUSTRIES	SOUTH KOREA	3,937.2	88.4	2.2	1.1	322
14	NIKON	JAPAN	3,484.9	183.3	5.3	4.3	358
15	HITACHI ASIA	SINGAPORE	3,164.5	3.5	0.1	0.4	390
16	AIWA	JAPAN	3,127.9	58.5	1.9	3.4	397
17	SAMSUNG DISPLAY DEVICES	SOUTH KOREA	3,058.8	204.1	6.7	6.2	409
18	TATUNG	TAIWAN	3,039.0	269.4	8.9	6.4	413
19	SANYO LIFE ELECTRONICS	JAPAN	2,969.8	4.7	0.2	—	421
20	NIPPON ELECTRIC GLASS	JAPAN	2,897.0	120.0	4.2	2.7	434

The weaker yen has helped Japan's Toshiba boost exports. But the company is finding the competition in its prime market stiff. 'Price competition is fierce in the U.S. PC market now that $1000 models have made their debut,' says Wada Kozo, Toshiba's senior vice president. 'The Southeast Asian market is also expected to stagnate in the first quarter of 1998.' Another downside to intensifying exports is that it could re-ignite the old trade dispute between Japan and the U.S.

The picture is bleaker outside the computer arena. Not only are factories in China, Malaysia, and elsewhere making more TVs and VCRs that customers want to buy, but the consumer electronics segment hasn't had a big hit since CD players wiped out record turntables. Christmas 1997 was supposed to be the year for the DVD (digital video, or versatile, disc), the high-capacity disc format that could eventually replace video tapes, CDs, and CD-ROMs, but that did not happen largely due to the lack of software. Now analysts are saying it may not take place until 2000 to 2003, depending on the market. Toshiba, which launched its first DVD player in November 1996, is pushing from the other side of the market by investing in Japan's largest video/CD rental chain, which will start renting DVD software. Wada is optimistic about the future. 'Sales have been growing at a far faster pace than [for] existing media such as LD players or CD players,' he says. 'We expect an attractive multimedia market, steadily growing in tandem with the ongoing development of digital technology.' Not right away, though. The company expects consolidated sales growing a mere 1% and profits dropping 11% for the year ending March 1998.

Beverages, Food and Tobacco

Agricultural and food companies from Australia, the U.S. and Canada are taking the long-term view by increasing investment in rural infrastructure and food processing in countries like Thailand, China, Indochina and the Philippines which are moving along the deregulation path. In line with this, Taiwan and the World Bank have announced major investments in China's agriculture resources. Japanese imports from the region are expected to remain low, so a Japanese demand-driven boost is not expected in the short term. Brewers throughout the region have maintained sales growth, though profit margins continue to decline.

Rank	Company	Country	Sales $ Millions	Profit $ Millions	Profit as % of Sales	Profit as % of Assets	1000 Rank
1	JAPAN TOBACCO	JAPAN	34,622.4	794.7	2.3	4.0	20
2	KIRIN BREWERY	JAPAN	14,675.1	316.1	2.2	2.3	63
3	SNOW BRAND MILK PRODS.	JAPAN	11,165.4	48.7	0.4	0.0	101
4	ASAHI BREWERIES	JAPAN	11,142.2	75.7	0.7	0.5	102
5	SUNTORY	JAPAN	10,344.0	204.2	1.0	1.7	113
6	NIPPON MEAT PACKERS	JAPAN	7,653.5	26.8	0.4	0.5	151
7	AJINOMOTO	JAPAN	7,247.7	140.9	1.9	1.9	160
8	SAPPORO BREWERIES	JAPAN	6,117.9	35.0	0.6	0.4	184
9	YAMAZAKI BAKING	JAPAN	6,105.5	122.8	2.0	3.2	186
10	NICHIREI	JAPAN	5,434.7	18.2	0.3	0.5	225
11	MEIJI MILK PRODUCTS	JAPAN	5,309.5	22.5	0.4	0.9	232
12	MORINAGA MILK INDUSTRY	JAPAN	4,615.0	30.3	0.7	1.3	268
13	ITOHAM FOODS	JAPAN	4,279.6	8.9	0.2	0.4	291
14	NEW ZEALAND DAIRY BOARD	NEW ZEALAND	4,214.7	7.8	0.2	0.3	296
15	OTSUKA PHARMACEUTICAL	JAPAN	3,475.0	124.4	3.6	4.6	360
16	NISSHIN FLOUR MILLING	JAPAN	3,345.0	57.7	1.7	2.5	370
17	MEIJI SEIKA	JAPAN	3,318.8	41.0	1.2	1.4	371
18	SAN MIGUEL CORP.	PHILIPPINES	3,242.6	232.3	7.2	6.2	374
19	Q.P. CORP.	JAPAN	3,115.4	45.1	1.4	1.0	402
20	GOODMAN FIELDER	AUSTRALIA	2,943.3	89.8	3.1	5.2	424

Chemicals

The massive oil refinery or petrochemical plant used to be a symbol of economic development, and just about every Asian nation tried to become a regional leader in chemicals and petrochemicals. The result? A glut of plants and products. The huge facilities must be kept running as near capacity as possible to achieve economies of scale. Then mix in the soft price of the main raw material, oil, and weak regional demand. What do you get? Price cuts by producers desperate to keep operating.

Ethylene prices have halved in less than two years. Pure terephthalic acid, which goes into polyester fiber, has also dropped over the same period. Salomon Brothers initially forecast some

Rank	Company	Country	Sales $ Millions	Profit $ Millions	Profit as % of Sales	Profit as % of Assets	1000 Rank
1	CHINA PETROCHEMICAL CORP.	CHINA	26,874.5	662.6	2.5	1.8	29
2	MITSUBISHI CHEMICAL CORP.	JAPAN	15,924.7	-110.1	—	—	58
3	SUMITOMO CHEMICAL	JAPAN	9,299.5	197.4	2.1	1.6	127
4	DAINIPPON INK & CHEM.	JAPAN	8,696.2	79.0	0.9	0.8	133
5	UBE INDUSTRIES	JAPAN	5,821.7	93.3	1.6	1.1	202
6	SHIN-ETSU CHEMICAL	JAPAN	5,740.1	373.4	6.5	4.4	207
7	SHOWA DENKO	JAPAN	5,242.8	28.1	0.5	0.4	235
8	MITSUI CHEMICALS	JAPAN	4,599.6	24.1	0.5	0.3	269
9	LG CHEMICAL	SOUTH KOREA	4,306.4	4.1	0.1	0.1	288
10	MITSUI PETROCHEMICAL	JAPAN	3,672.0	106.3	2.9	2.3	344
11	TOSOH CORP.	JAPAN	3,560.8	55.8	1.6	1.2	351
12	IDEMITSU PETROCHEMICAL	JAPAN	3,189.6	10.1	0.3	—	382
13	NIPPON STEEL CHEMICAL	JAPAN	3,165.3	-392.9	—	—	389
14	MITSUBISHI GAS CHEMICAL	JAPAN	3,035.7	102.5	3.4	2.3	414
15	KANEKA CORP.	JAPAN	2,827.5	60.3	2.1	1.9	448
16	ICI AUSTRALIA	AUSTRALIA	2,746.1	154.3	5.6	6.9	466
17	NIPPON SANSO	JAPAN	2,456.3	19.0	0.8	0.7	533
18	DAICEL CHEMICAL INDS.	JAPAN	2,398.3	28.9	1.2	0.7	546
19	MATSUSHITA BATTERY INDL.	JAPAN	2,295.9	121.7	5.3	6.3	571
20	DENKI KAGAKU KOGYO	JAPAN	2,276.1	9.3	0.4	0.3	581

recovery in the global chemical industry by the end of 2000. Now, due to Asia's economic woes and continued price deflation, that has been pushed back to 2003. Hardest hit will be the countries with the greatest overcapacity — notably South Korea, Thailand, Singapore, and China, as well as Indonesia and Malaysia for some products.

As producers try to export their way out of trouble, they will push prices even lower. Meanwhile, their costs are going up because oil, even when weak, is denominated in strong U.S. dollars.

All of that means producers must do more than cut costs and sell harder; they have to match their products and markets like never before. Taiwan petrochemical giant Formosa Plastics expects 1998 to be a good year. Its edge is the shortage of petrochemical products within Taiwan, where it sells 90% of its output, says President C.T. Lee. If domestic demand falters, Lee sees imports suffering before local products. Formosa Plastics even has a new naphtha cracker facility coming on line this year, but its output will be absorbed by the company's downstream production of intermediates and end-products like PVC pipes and polyester. In contrast, Lee says, South Korean producers export half their output. Formosa Plastics is not entirely immune; its sales of acrylic fiber, which finds half its market offshore, are likely to be hit hard.

Clothing, Textiles and Accessories

Hong Kong, Taiwan and South Korean companies with textile and shoe production facilities in China and markets in Europe and the U.S. are weathering the Asian crisis. Japanese textile companies are also expanding in China looking to the domestic markets of China and home. While China itself is struggling with falling domestic and export prices as well as the closing of inefficient state factories. The Philippines and Indonesia are into double-digit falls in textile output, although foreign investment is still finding its way in. Taiwan, in an effort to boost domestic demand and to counter offshore (notably Indonesia) production losses, is setting up two high-tech textile zones, involving 25 textile companies.

Rank	Company	Country	Sales $ Millions	Profit $ Millions	Profit as % of Sales	Profit as % of Assets	1000 Rank
1	TORAY INDUSTRIES	JAPAN	9,623.4	213.0	2.2	1.7	120
2	TEIJIN LTD.	JAPAN	5,876.1	104.4	1.8	1.3	194
3	SEIKO EPSON	JAPAN	5,726.2	32.2	0.6	—	208
4	KANEBO	JAPAN	5,591.9	-3.6	—	—	215
5	TOYOBO	JAPAN	4,367.9	36.3	0.8	0.7	284
6	CITIZEN WATCH	JAPAN	3,612.1	89.8	2.5	2.5	346
7	MITSUBISHI RAYON	JAPAN	3,209.4	75.4	2.4	1.0	379
8	UNITIKA	JAPAN	3,193.6	-36.9	—	—	381
9	KURARAY	JAPAN	3,126.6	107.9	3.5	2.3	398
10	RELIANCE INDUSTRIES	INDIA	2,463.9	373.3	15.2	6.8	532
11	NISSHINBO INDUSTRIES	JAPAN	2,153.6	21.7	1.0	0.7	611
12	RENOWN	JAPAN	1,984.1	-36.0	—	—	662
13	ONWARD KASHIYAMA	JAPAN	1,970.6	99.9	5.1	4.1	668
14	KOWA	JAPAN	1,933.6	51.4	2.7	3.5	683
15	GUNZE	JAPAN	1,841.7	32.0	1.8	1.7	720
16	WORLD	JAPAN	1,834.1	33.1	1.8	1.4	722
17	WACOAL	JAPAN	1,547.4	67.4	4.4	3.7	852
18	FORMOSA CHEM. & FIBRE	TAIWAN	1,517.4	125.6	8.3	4.7	862
19	HYOSUNG T&C CO.	SOUTH KOREA	1,491.9	43.9	2.9	1.0	873
20	SEIKO INSTRUMENTS	JAPAN	1,465.1	NA	—	—	891

Construction

Investment in infrastructure by governments and foreign investors is the name of the game throughout the region. Major highway projects have been announced in Thailand, the Philippines, Indochina, China and even Japan in an effort to boost the construction sector. In Japan domestic construction is down 18% (housing starts are 56% down) and sliding, while overseas orders are down 18%. One of the bright lights in the region is China which has seen a 50% boost in commercial housing sales on a 10% rise in prices. Investment in real estate developments are expected to rise by 14% in the short-to medium-term.

Rank	Company	Country	Sales $ Millions	Profit $ Millions	Profit as % of Sales	Profit as % of Assets	1000 Rank
1	KAJIMA CORP.	JAPAN	19,311.5	67.5	0.3	0.3	39
2	TAISEI CORP.	JAPAN	18,221.8	53.2	0.3	0.2	43
3	SHIMIZU CORP.	JAPAN	15,793.7	48.8	0.3	0.2	60
4	TAKENAKA CORP.	JAPAN	14,215.1	176.4	1.2	1.2	68
5	OBAYASHI CORP.	JAPAN	14,170.7	125.2	0.9	0.6	69
6	SEKISUI HOUSE	JAPAN	13,147.7	391.7	2.0	2.4	75
7	DAIWA HOUSE INDUSTRY	JAPAN	10,923.8	390.3	3.6	3.7	106
8	SEKISUI CHEMICAL	JAPAN	10,869.4	285.3	2.6	3.2	108
9	KUMAGAI GUMI	JAPAN	9,732.9	-67.6	—	—	119
10	FUJITA CORP.	JAPAN	6,867.9	5.0	0.1	0.0	166
11	NISHIMATSU CONSTRUCTION	JAPAN	6,691.8	115.5	1.7	1.4	169
12	TODA CORP.	JAPAN	6,337.5	62.9	0.0	0.9	178
13	HYUNDAI ENG. & CONSTRUCTION	SOUTH KOREA	5,882.4	26.3	0.4	0.3	193
14	SATO KOGYO	JAPAN	5,825.7	-45.3	—	—	199
15	TOKYU CONSTRUCTION	JAPAN	5,629.3	-132.2	—	—	212
16	HAZAMA	JAPAN	5,545.1	-45.1	—	—	220
17	DAIKYO	JAPAN	5,083.4	-8.6	—	—	240
18	PENTA-OCEAN CONSTRUCTION	JAPAN	5,062.5	34.0	0.7	0.7	242
19	CHINA STATE CONST. ENG.	CHINA	4,951.8	55.1	1.1	0.9	249
20	MISAWA HOMES	JAPAN	4,704.6	26.5	0.6	0.5	262

Electric Power

Although there is a short-term decline in demand for electric power in Thailand and various development projects are on hold, the forecast demand is an annual rate of 7% up until 2000. A whole slew of nuclear power projects in China has attracted interest from U.S. and Japanese companies like Tokyo Electric Power. South Korea has opened state-owned power generation to foreign investors, while India has once again relaxed restrictions on investment in utilities. The leading Japanese power companies have begun shedding jobs on weak domestic demand.

Rank	Company	Country	Sales $ Millions	Profit $ Millions	Profit as % of Sales	Profit as % of Assets	1000 Rank
1	TOKYO ELECTRIC POWER	JAPAN	46,320.0	750.2	1.6	0.6	16
2	KANSAI ELECTRIC POWER	JAPAN	24,000.3	507.2	2.1	0.8	32
3	CHUBU ELECTRIC POWER	JAPAN	19,956.2	352.9	1.8	0.6	37
4	KOREA ELECTRIC POWER	SOUTH KOREA	14,393.4	742.8	5.2	1.7	65
5	TOHOKU ELECTRIC POWER	JAPAN	13,899.8	251.1	1.8	0.7	71
6	KYUSHU ELECTRIC POWER	JAPAN	12,998.6	364.2	2.8	0.0	77
7	CHUGOKU ELECTRIC POWER	JAPAN	9,569.4	250.3	2.6	0.9	121
8	TAIWAN POWER	TAIWAN	8,510.3	1,247.9	14.7	3.6	136
9	EAST CHINA ELECTRIC POWER	CHINA	5,817.1	221.3	3.8	1.9	204
10	SHIKOKU ELECTRIC POWER	JAPAN	5,545.0	197.3	3.6	1.5	221
11	HOKKAIDO ELECTRIC POWER	JAPAN	4,952.0	141.7	2.9	1.1	248
12	HOKURIKU ELECTRIC POWER	JAPAN	4,549.0	77.2	1.7	0.6	273
13	ELEC. GENERATING AUTHORITY	THAILAND	4,316.3	1,069.1	24.8	9.2	287
14	ELECTRIC POWER DEVT.	JAPAN	4,146.9	50.9	1.2	0.3	306
15	PER. LISTRIK NEGARA (PLN)	INDONESIA	4,020.9	498.1	12.4	2.2	316
16	TENAGA NASIONAL	MALAYSIA	3,237.8	317.1	9.8	2.5	375
17	CHINA HUANENG GROUP	CHINA	2,490.4	128.9	5.2	0.0	524
18	NATIONAL POWER CORP.	PHILIPPINES	2,427.3	211.4	8.7	1.2	538
19	NATIONAL THERMAL POWER	INDIA	2,395.0	381.7	15.9	5.0	547
20	CHINA LIGHT & POWER	HONG KONG	2,387.2	620.0	25.0	14.1	549

Heavy Industry and Engineering

Foreign investment in South Korea has been steadily increasing, mostly in the form of mergers and acquisitions. Most notably Volvo's takeover of Samsung Heavy Industry for $180 million. This is not the case for Japanese companies. However, in response to the collapse in consumer demand, Japan's heavy industry companies are cutting capital expenditure by up to 5% in the short term. China has been consistently recording 8% growth in heavy industrial output, which is expected to continue.

Rank	Company	Country	Sales $ Millions	Profit $ Millions	Profit as % of Sales	Profit as % of Assets	1000 Rank
1	MITSUBISHI HEAVY INDUSTRIES	JAPAN	28,888.3	1,136.3	3.9	2.8	26
2	KAWASAKI HEAVY INDUSTRIES	JAPAN	11,254.4	207.5	1.8	1.7	99
3	ISHIKAWAJIMA-HARIMA	JAPAN	9,853.4	126.1	1.3	1.0	117
4	HITACHI ZOSEN	JAPAN	5,839.6	107.8	1.8	1.6	196
5	HYUNDAI HEAVY INDUSTRIES	SOUTH KOREA	5,824.4	17.4	0.3	0.2	200
6	SUMITOMO HEAVY INDUSTRIES	JAPAN	5,575.8	54.4	0.0	0.8	216
7	KINDEN	JAPAN	5,203.7	165.6	3.2	2.9	236
8	KANDENKO	JAPAN	4,778.7	66.1	1.4	1.6	260
9	MITSUI ENG. & SHIPBUILDING	JAPAN	4,569.0	-41.2	—	—	271
10	CHIYODA CORP.	JAPAN	4,094.0	-490.2	—	—	310
11	SAMSUNG HEAVY INDUSTRIES	SOUTH KOREA	4,047.1	-366.2	—	—	314
12	KOREA HEAVY INDUSTRIES	SOUTH KOREA	3,483.4	187.3	5.4	5.3	359
13	HITACHI PLANT ENG. & CON.	JAPAN	2,518.3	44.4	1.8	2.2	515
14	JGC CORP.	JAPAN	2,514.2	-128.6	—	—	516
15	KYUDENKO CORP.	JAPAN	2,504.5	41.3	1.6	1.8	521
16	SANKI ENGINEERING	JAPAN	2,424.0	29.3	1.2	1.3	539
17	TOENEC	JAPAN	2,377.6	25.2	1.1	1.3	552
18	TAKASAGO THERMAL ENG.	JAPAN	2,361.5	36.4	1.5	1.4	554
19	NIIGATA ENGINEERING	JAPAN	2,261.5	-19.9	—	—	587
20	YURTEC	JAPAN	2,186.3	51.9	2.4	3.6	603

Industrial and Farm Equipment

Asia's woes have moved to the U.S., where wholesale prices of imported industrial equipment have weakened. Again for Japan, overseas orders for industrial machinery have dried up on top of sluggish domestic demand. China and Taiwan remain the best markets in Asia for machinery and farm equipment. Construction machinery sales have also followed the lead downwards of the construction industry, although sales to the U.S. and Europe and are up.

Rank	Company	Country	Sales $ Millions	Profit $ Millions	Profit as % of Sales	Profit as % of Assets	1000 Rank
1	KUBOTA	JAPAN	10,493.7	266.1	2.5	2.2	110
2	KOMATSU LTD.	JAPAN	10,102.2	166.9	1.7	1.2	114
3	FUJI ELECTRIC	JAPAN	8,690.8	75.3	0.9	0.9	134
4	DAEWOO HEAVY INDUSTRIES	SOUTH KOREA	6,400.0	92.0	1.5	0.8	176
5	OMRON	JAPAN	5,462.0	144.7	2.6	2.7	224
6	TOYODA AUTOMATIC LOOM	JAPAN	5,127.7	164.8	3.2	3.2	238
7	EBARA CORP.	JAPAN	4,974.1	90.5	1.8	1.8	246
8	NSK	JAPAN	4,424.9	80.0	1.8	1.3	282
9	DAIKIN INDUSTRIES	JAPAN	4,161.4	61.1	1.5	1.6	304
10	KOYO SEIKO	JAPAN	3,275.1	50.5	1.5	1.4	373
11	SHIN CATERPIL'R MITSUBISHI	JAPAN	3,223.1	48.5	1.5	1.8	377
12	HYUNDAI PRECISION & IND.	SOUTH KOREA	3,046.4	25.0	0.8	0.9	411
13	NTN CORP.	JAPAN	3,013.7	72.9	2.4	1.7	416
14	HITACHI CONST. MACHINERY	JAPAN	2,829.0	30.3	1.1	0.0	446
15	MINEBEA	JAPAN	2,784.4	81.5	2.9	1.6	457
16	YOKOGAWA ELECTRIC	JAPAN	2,577.9	35.4	1.4	0.9	497
17	YANMAR DIESEL ENGINE	JAPAN	2,317.0	16.2	0.7	0.7	564
18	YASKAWA ELECTRIC	JAPAN	2,275.3	11.1	0.5	0.5	583
19	YANMAR AGRI. EQUIPMENT	JAPAN	2,179.4	3.3	0.1	0.3	605
20	MEIDENSHA	JAPAN	2,161.3	12.4	0.6	0.6	610

Information Technology

Despite the slowdown in the computer market, the IT services market continues to grow, as many see it as "the cornerstone for survival". By mid-1998 Asia, outside Japan, accounted for 5% of the $302 billion worldwide IT services market. Compound growth of 24% to 2002 is expected, well above the world average of 15%. The largest IT market is Australia (32%), followed by India (14%), China and South Korea (11%), and Taiwan, Singapore and Hong (7%). By 2002 the world market will be worth $1.7 trillion, with Asia's share at $47 billion (now $15 billion).

Rank	Company	Country	Sales $ Millions	Profit $ Millions	Profit as % of Sales	Profit as % of Assets	1000 Rank
1	HITACHI LTD.	JAPAN	78,351.7	812.0	1.0	0.9	9
2	TOSHIBA CORP.	JAPAN	50,132.3	616.6	1.2	1.2	13
3	NEC CORP.	JAPAN	45,490.3	841.9	1.9	1.9	17
4	FUJITSU LTD.	JAPAN	41,399.8	424.2	1.0	0.0	18
5	MITSUBISHI ELECTRIC CORP.	JAPAN	34,245.2	78.4	0.2	0.2	21
6	CANON	JAPAN	23,517.4	865.8	3.7	3.6	34
7	IBM JAPAN	JAPAN	13,100.5	511.2	3.9	5.9	76
8	RICOH	JAPAN	12,098.5	265.9	2.2	1.8	81
9	FUJI XEROX	JAPAN	7,951.9	247.2	3.1	3.9	144
10	OKI ELECTRIC INDUSTRY	JAPAN	6,731.2	29.7	0.4	0.4	167
11	KYOCERA CORP.	JAPAN	6,570.7	419.7	6.4	4.6	170
12	SEAGATE TECHNOLOGY INTL.	SINGAPORE	6,242.6	797.2	12.8	43.2	179
13	ACER	TAIWAN	5,893.0	188.0	3.2	4.5	192
14	HEWLETT-PACKARD	SINGAPORE	5,839.1	1,040.7	17.8	23.9	197
15	MATSUSHITA ELECTRONICS	JAPAN	4,430.9	66.6	1.5	—	281
16	CASIO COMPUTER	JAPAN	4,220.5	34.0	0.8	0.7	295
17	MINOLTA	JAPAN	4,119.1	94.6	2.3	2.5	308
18	MATSUSHITA ELEC. COMP.	JAPAN	3,741.8	71.5	1.9	2.0	334
19	KYUSHU MATSUSHITA ELEC.	JAPAN	3,173.6	12.9	0.4	0.5	387
20	MURATA MFG.	JAPAN	3,039.3	299.6	9.9	5.1	412

Media and Communications

Telecom giants throughout the region have seen business slow, some have quickened the pace of privatisation, while others are repositioning themselves. Singapore, for one, is looking to China as the catalyst for growth. Malaysian and Thai telecoms have opened to foreign investment. Foreigners can now own 60% of Malaysia's telecoms. While in Australia, plans for Telstra to be fully privatised foundered and remains 60% government–owned. The printing industry, also in the doldrums, is expected to improve as the region's currencies stabilise.

Rank	Company	Country	Sales $ Millions	Profit $ Millions	Profit as % of Sales	Profit as % of Assets	1000 Rank
1	NIPPON TELEGRAPH & TEL.	JAPAN	81,097.5	2,311.6	2.9	1.5	8
2	DENTSU	JAPAN	13,612.8	124.8	0.9	1.7	73
3	TELSTRA	AUSTRALIA	12,084.9	1,265.0	10.5	6.3	82
4	DAI NIPPON PRINTING	JAPAN	12,043.6	516.3	4.3	3.0	83
5	NEWS CORP.	AUSTRALIA	11,716.9	563.7	4.8	1.7	90
6	TOPPAN PRINTING	JAPAN	11,714.8	198.8	1.7	1.9	91
7	DDI CORP.	JAPAN	9,343.6	-240.5	—	—	125
8	KOREA TELECOM	SOUTH KOREA	8,904.3	224.3	2.5	1.2	131
9	NIPPON SHUPPAN HANBAI	JAPAN	7,508.9	14.8	0.2	0.5	155
10	MATSUSHITA COMM. INDL.	JAPAN	7,486.3	263.7	3.5	5.9	156
11	TOHAN	JAPAN	7,328.7	30.4	0.4	—	158
12	CHUNGHWA TELECOM	TAIWAN	6,036.9	1,998.3	33.1	13.3	188
13	HAKUHODO	JAPAN	5,991.7	43.0	0.7	1.9	190
14	NTT DATA CORP.	JAPAN	5,622.4	130.9	2.3	1.7	213
15	HONGKONG TELECOM	HONG KONG	4,176.6	1,433.0	34.3	23.5	302
16	ASAHI SHIMBUN PUBLISHING	JAPAN	3,842.1	31.2	0.8	—	329
17	KDD	JAPAN	3,688.4	118.2	3.2	2.0	341
18	JAPAN TELECOM	JAPAN	3,455.2	233.9	6.8	5.4	363
19	RECRUIT	JAPAN	3,141.1	18.0	0.6	0.2	394
20	SINGAPORE TELECOM	SINGAPORE	3,135.4	1,176.2	37.5	15.3	395

Materials

Tyre sales are in short-term decline, but the diversified leading companies expect sales growth on weaker currencies. Cement and building products have followed the construction industry pattern: falling markets, with the expectation of benefiting from region-wide infrastructure plans. The chemical and plastics industries on the one hand are gaining from cheaper raw materials, while on the other are hit by a short-term drop in Asian markets.

Rank	Company	Country	Sales $ Millions	Profit $ Millions	Profit as % of Sales	Profit as % of Assets	1000 Rank
1	BRIDGESTONE CORP.	JAPAN	17,999.9	646.6	3.6	3.0	44
2	ASAHI GLASS	JAPAN	12,293.6	222.2	1.8	1.3	80
3	ASAHI CHEMICAL INDUSTRY	JAPAN	11,873.5	233.1	1.0	2.0	88
4	FUJI PHOTO FILM	JAPAN	11,510.5	784.6	6.8	4.3	95
5	MATSUSHITA ELEC. WORKS	JAPAN	10,960.6	286.5	2.6	2.4	105
6	MITSUBISHI MATERIALS	JAPAN	10,909.3	135.5	1.2	0.9	107
7	BTR NYLEX	AUSTRALIA	6,006.5	-169.7	—	—	189
8	TDK	JAPAN	5,705.0	554.3	9.7	9.2	210
9	SUMITOMO RUBBER INDS.	JAPAN	5,353.6	43.1	0.8	0.7	229
10	KONICA	JAPAN	5,314.2	41.7	0.8	0.8	231
11	CSR	AUSTRALIA	5,040.2	166.1	3.3	2.7	243
12	HITACHI CHEMICAL	JAPAN	4,920.4	71.4	1.5	1.8	252
13	CHICHIBU ONODA CEMENT	JAPAN	4,759.3	89.3	1.9	1.2	261
14	BORAL	AUSTRALIA	4,624.5	315.8	6.8	6.4	267
15	TOTO	JAPAN	4,341.5	109.1	2.5	2.3	285
16	SIAM CEMENT	THAILAND	4,232.8	267.8	6.3	3.8	293
17	YKK ARCH. PRODUCTS	JAPAN	3,986.5	29.2	0.7	1.3	319
18	NAN YA PLASTICS	TAIWAN	3,712.7	282.9	7.6	5.9	338
19	YOKOHAMA RUBBER	JAPAN	3,701.5	34.5	0.9	0.9	340
20	NIHON CEMENT	JAPAN	3,124.4	1.7	0.1	0.0	399

Metals

Major Japanese steel manufacturers, to make up for the shortfall in domestic demand and taking advantage of the weak yen, are increasing exports of steel products to the US. By the end of the third quarter 1998, steel exports will be doubled that for the same period in 1997 (to 1.5 million tonnes) primarily for gas-pipeline and rail projects. South Korean steel product producers are having a harder time, however, blast furnace operators have found ready US markets for pig iron and steel ingots. While the Thai steel industry has shut down 50% of operations, with few expectations of recovery.

Rank	Company	Country	Sales $ Millions	Profit $ Millions	Profit as % of Sales	Profit as % of Assets	1000 Rank
1	NIPPON STEEL CORP.	JAPAN	28,142.0	31.7	0.1	0.1	27
2	NKK CORP.	JAPAN	17,261.0	153.4	0.9	0.6	51
3	KOBE STEEL	JAPAN	14,096.9	160.9	1.1	0.7	70
4	SUMITOMO METAL INDUSTRIES	JAPAN	13,400.9	243.8	1.8	1.1	74
5	POHANG IRON & STEEL	SOUTH KOREA	11,989.7	735.1	6.1	3.8	86
6	SUMITOMO ELECTRIC INDS.	JAPAN	11,610.5	296.1	2.6	2.4	93
7	KAWASAKI STEEL	JAPAN	11,329.0	73.3	0.6	0.4	98
8	FURUKAWA ELECTRIC	JAPAN	6,933.9	116.6	1.7	1.4	164
9	TOYO SEIKAN	JAPAN	6,721.5	152.1	2.3	2.3	168
10	TOSTEM CORP.	JAPAN	6,225.3	173.5	2.8	2.6	182
11	SHANGHAI BAOSHAN IRON	CHINA	5,820.0	290.1	4.0	2.4	203
12	NIPPON LIGHT METAL	JAPAN	5,761.0	-13.9	—	—	206
13	HITACHI METALS	JAPAN	4,230.5	60.9	1.4	1.2	294
14	NISSHIN STEEL	JAPAN	4,211.4	47.5	1.1	0.8	297
15	DAIDO STEEL	JAPAN	3,764.2	23.6	0.6	0.6	331
16	HITACHI CABLE	JAPAN	3,713.4	86.2	2.3	2.3	336
17	MITSUI MINING & SMELTING	JAPAN	3,680.4	49.8	1.4	1.2	343
18	STEEL AUTHORITY OF INDIA	INDIA	3,604.2	145.4	4.0	—	347
19	FUJIKURA	JAPAN	3,460.1	65.8	1.9	1.6	361
20	CHINA STEEL CORP.	TAIWAN	3,199.3	491.9	15.4	6.7	380

Motor Vehicles

A year ago, Malaysian car-buyers lusting after a new Proton Saga had to wait up to four months for delivery due to short supplies. Today, you can choose from 40,000 cars that sit idle in showrooms or storage lots. Picking a model from Hyundai, Daewoo, or Kia? No waiting necessary. There are at least 100,000 brand-new Korean vehicles with odometers stuck around zero.

A car glut of unprecedented proportions is looming in Asia. Even before the tiger economies were declawed, car-makers were grappling with overcapacity thanks to huge investments in new plants this decade. Now, as demand withers in most countries across the region, the wheels are coming off. Analysts predict the Asian car market may shrink by as much as 4% this year. Auto-

Rank	Company	Country	Sales $ Millions	Profit $ Millions	Profit as % of Sales	Profit as % of Assets	1000 Rank
1	TOYOTA MOTOR CORP.	JAPAN	112,555.9	3,547.7	3.2	3.0	6
2	NISSAN MOTOR	JAPAN	61,214.1	714.7	1.2	1.0	11
3	HONDA MOTOR	JAPAN	48,660.6	2,033.2	4.2	5.3	14
4	MITSUBISHI MOTORS	JAPAN	33,756.0	106.6	0.3	0.4	22
5	ISUZU MOTORS	JAPAN	17,680.3	88.1	0.5	0.6	46
6	MAZDA MOTOR CORP.	JAPAN	17,413.1	-161.3	—	—	50
7	HYUNDAI MOTOR	SOUTH KOREA	14,282.8	107.9	0.8	1.1	66
8	SUZUKI MOTOR	JAPAN	13,811.6	308.8	2.2	3.3	72
9	FUJI HEAVY INDUSTRIES	JAPAN	11,243.0	364.0	3.2	5.2	100
10	DAIHATSU MOTOR	JAPAN	8,361.5	181.3	2.2	3.4	139
11	KIA MOTORS	SOUTH KOREA	8,213.2	8.7	0.1	0.1	142
12	SHANGHAI AUTOMOTIVE	CHINA	7,889.4	801.6	10.2	12.1	145
13	YAMAHA MOTOR	JAPAN	7,822.3	125.1	1.6	2.1	147
14	HINO MOTORS	JAPAN	5,816.5	66.5	1.1	1.8	205
15	DAEWOO MOTOR	SOUTH KOREA	5,426.7	64.5	1.2	0.0	226
16	TOYOTA AUTO BODY	JAPAN	4,922.0	33.8	0.7	1.8	251
17	ASTRA INTERNATIONAL	INDONESIA	4,688.0	200.4	4.3	2.8	264
18	NISSAN SHATAI	JAPAN	4,200.3	20.8	0.5	1.2	298
19	NISSAN DIESEL MOTOR	JAPAN	3,114.9	30.9	0.0	0.0	403
20	KANTO AUTO WORKS	JAPAN	3,062.2	10.7	0.4	0.6	408

makers are slashing production, staff, and investment in order to cope. A multi-billion-dollar new Proton plant in Malaysia has been shelved indefinitely, while the country's other local car-maker, Perodua, expects to slash 1998 output by one-third. In Thailand, General Motors, Honda, and Toyota are deferring planned investments.

Hyundai, the top car-maker in Korea and one of the largest in Asia outside Japan, cut its 1998 domestic sales target by 26% compared to 1997, the first year-over-year reduction in its history. To move inventory, the company has resorted to leasing schemes and no-interest financing, despite the burden on its own bottom line. Hyundai also suspended some model lines and plans to cut its workforce by 5000 over the next two years. One sector the company is counting on to be bright is exports. If the plunging won settles at 1200 to the dollar, it figures its price competitiveness will improve 10%-15%, and plans to export 720,000 units in 1998.

But is there salvation in exports? Probably not too much. Devalued currencies mean Asia-built cars will cost less in other markets, but within the region sales will be stifled by tariffs as well as the economic malaise. Competition will be fierce in the U.S. and Europe, the world's top two markets, and new plants are mushrooming in Latin America and Eastern Europe. By 2002, factories worldwide will be capable of churning out 20 million more cars a year than markets can absorb. Asia's ambitious auto-makers are set to suffer from reverse sticker shock for years to come.

Oil and Gas

Oil and oil product companies have been hit by overcapacity, which has led to a price war. Immediately affected were the state-owned oil companies, which saw significant falls in profits. However, as output stabilises demand should settle down. Despite the regional market weakness, China, Malaysia and Indonesia are looking to the future and have embarked on exploration and equipment programs backed by foreign investment. For Thailand this means foreign ownership of the country's two largest oil companies.

Rank	Company	Country	Sales $ Millions	Profit $ Millions	Profit as % of Sales	Profit as % of Assets	1000 Rank
1	NIPPON OIL	JAPAN	24,456.5	115.6	0.5	0.4	31
2	PERTAMINA	INDONESIA	19,276.5	578.1	2.0	4.1	40
3	IDEMITSU KOSAN	JAPAN	18,903.4	31.0	0.2	0.2	41
4	JAPAN ENERGY CORP.	JAPAN	18,520.3	-425.5	—	—	42
5	INDIAN OIL	INDIA	17,615.6	393.1	2.2	—	47
6	COSMO OIL	JAPAN	15,899.0	81.2	0.5	0.7	59
7	SHOWA SHELL SEKIYU	JAPAN	14,709.2	55.7	0.4	0.6	62
8	CHINESE PETROLEUM CORP.	TAIWAN	12,019.4	276.4	2.3	1.4	85
9	PETROLIAM NASIONAL	MALAYSIA	11,480.0	2,892.0	25.2	10.7	96
10	MITSUBISHI OIL	JAPAN	11,008.5	-95.7	—	—	104
11	YUKONG LTD.	SOUTH KOREA	10,345.1	84.8	0.8	0.7	112
12	TOKYO GAS	JAPAN	9,083.3	141.9	1.6	0.9	129
13	OSAKA GAS	JAPAN	7,702.4	155.3	2.0	1.4	150
14	LG CALTEX OIL CORP.	SOUTH KOREA	6,920.3	15.2	0.2	0.2	165
15	PETROLEUM AUTHORITY	THAILAND	6,538.8	327.5	5.0	7.1	171
16	NIPPON PETROLEUM REFINING	JAPAN	6,535.4	25.8	0.4	0.5	172
17	TONEN	JAPAN	6,116.2	92.3	1.5	1.5	185
18	ESSO SEKIYU	JAPAN	5,549.4	19.8	0.4	0.9	218
19	SSANGYONG OIL REFINING	SOUTH KOREA	5,545.7	154.6	2.8	3.2	219
20	GENERAL SEKIYU	JAPAN	5,334.5	44.2	0.8	1.2	230

Resources

International mining companies are on the hunt for bargains in Asia. Despite potential political risks, Indonesia has attracted their attention - notably tin giant Tambang Timah. Australian companies, dependent on Japan sales of iron ore, coal, aluminium, etc, are seeing sales and profit slumps. Falling prices and a short-term oversupply of paper, has sparked sharp competition - to the point where Australia has accused Japanese, South Korean and European companies of dumping paper products.

Rank	Company	Country	Sales $ Millions	Profit $ Millions	Profit as % of Sales	Profit as % of Assets	1000 Rank
1	BROKEN HILL PROPRIETARY	AUSTRALIA	17,474.4	320.0	1.8	1.1	48
2	OJI PAPER CO.	JAPAN	10,417.4	118.8	1.1	0.7	111
3	NIPPON PAPER INDUSTRIES	JAPAN	10,050.0	263.2	2.6	2.2	115
4	MARUHA CORP.	JAPAN	8,991.9	6.8	0.1	0.2	130
5	RIO TINTO	AUSTRALIA	8,452.0	1,098.4	12.0	6.4	137
6	SUMITOMO FORESTRY	JAPAN	7,519.3	120.0	1.6	3.1	154
7	FLETCHER CHALLENGE	NEW ZEALAND	5,861.9	114.1	1.9	1.2	195
8	AMCOR	AUSTRALIA	4,918.3	-85.8	—	—	253
9	SUMITOMO METAL MINING	JAPAN	4,826.0	118.4	2.5	2.2	256
10	JAPAN PULP & PAPER	JAPAN	4,377.0	18.5	0.4	0.8	283
11	NIPPON SUISAN	JAPAN	4,284.1	46.2	1.1	1.8	290
12	DAISHOWA PAPER MFG.	JAPAN	3,502.4	69.0	1.0	1.2	355
13	DAIO PAPER	JAPAN	2,891.5	46.6	1.6	1.2	435
14	RENGO	JAPAN	2,681.7	29.5	1.1	1.1	475
15	DOWA MINING	JAPAN	2,653.8	88.0	3.4	2.8	484
16	WMC	AUSTRALIA	2,376.6	232.7	9.8	3.9	553
17	NICHIRO CORP.	JAPAN	2,284.9	10.2	0.4	0.8	577
18	MITSUBISHI PAPER MILLS	JAPAN	2,093.7	40.0	1.9	1.3	627
19	CARTER HOLT HARVEY	NEW ZEALAND	2,022.0	172.6	8.5	3.3	650
20	M.I.M. HOLDINGS	AUSTRALIA	1,824.8	48.1	2.6	1.3	727

Retailing

Retailing is one of the worst hit by the Asian crisis. Consumer spending throughout the region had dropped drastically, with few signs of a turnaround. Shop closures, particularly for garments, are widespread. The contribution of the retailing sector to unemployment figures is disproportionately high. What retailers hope for is the return of tourists seeking cheaper prices, although they will have to do without intra-Asian tourists (one of the biggest sources in recent years) for the short- to medium-term.

Rank	Company	Country	Sales $ Millions	Profit $ Millions	Profit as % of Sales	Profit as % of Assets	1000 Rank
1	DAIEI	JAPAN	28,922.1	-109.5	—	—	25
2	ITO-YOKADO	JAPAN	27,752.0	683.3	2.5	4.1	28
3	JUSCO	JAPAN	20,576.2	279.0	1.4	2.0	36
4	MYCAL CORP.	JAPAN	16,552.5	139.7	0.8	0.9	53
5	COLES MYER	AUSTRALIA	14,229.2	219.5	1.5	3.0	67
6	WOOLWORTHS	AUSTRALIA	12,446.6	201.0	1.6	7.2	79
7	SEIYU	JAPAN	11,938.0	-27.5	—	—	87
8	TAKASHIMAYA	JAPAN	11,429.8	85.6	0.7	1.1	97
9	MITSUKOSHI	JAPAN	9,507.2	-7.2	—	—	122
10	UNY	JAPAN	8,541.9	90.6	1.1	1.6	135
11	DAIMARU	JAPAN	7,879.5	19.1	0.2	0.5	146
12	DAIRY FARM	HONG KONG	6,968.4	41.5	0.6	1.3	163
13	ISETAN	JAPAN	5,654.3	48.5	0.9	1.1	211
14	SEIBU DEPARTMENT STORES	JAPAN	5,602.3	28.4	0.5	0.7	214
15	MARUI	JAPAN	4,969.8	174.0	3.5	2.6	247
16	MATSUZAKAYA	JAPAN	4,855.6	12.9	0.3	0.5	255
17	TOKYU DEPARTMENT STORE	JAPAN	4,808.0	-10.4	—	—	258
18	HUTCHISON WHAMPOA	HONG KONG	4,700.3	1,015.4	21.6	6.0	263
19	HANKYU DEPT. STORES	JAPAN	4,055.8	26.6	0.7	0.8	313
20	IZUMIYA	JAPAN	3,849.7	61.8	1.6	2.3	327

Trading

The leading trading companies in Asia, are also the biggest companies (sales) in the region. Each of them is a diversified group, from telecommunications to construction, and each has a worldwide market base. Each is an excellent position not only to survive the Asian crisis, but also in a position to take up opportunities in other temporarily undervalued blue-chip companies. However, the majority of trading companies have been hit by weak demand and spiralling currencies.

Rank	Company	Country	Sales $ Millions	Profit $ Millions	Profit as % of Sales	Profit as % of Assets	1000 Rank
1	MITSUI & CO.	JAPAN	150,081.5	333.4	0.2	0.5	1
2	MITSUBISHI CORP.	JAPAN	145,174.5	408.0	0.3	0.5	2
3	ITOCHU CORP.	JAPAN	140,347.6	114.8	0.1	0.2	3
4	MARUBENI CORP.	JAPAN	128,424.1	184.9	0.1	0.3	4
5	SUMITOMO CORP.	JAPAN	123,510.3	-1,338.6	—	—	5
6	NISSHO IWAI CORP.	JAPAN	81,719.2	141.8	0.2	0.3	7
7	TOMEN CORP.	JAPAN	48,155.1	43.7	0.1	0.2	15
8	NICHIMEN CORP.	JAPAN	35,769.8	45.2	0.1	0.2	19
9	KANEMATSU CORP.	JAPAN	31,963.2	-253.1	—	—	23
10	SAMSUNG CO.	SOUTH KOREA	29,997.8	54.1	0.2	0.7	24
11	HYUNDAI CORP.	SOUTH KOREA	25,548.9	15.3	0.1	2.7	30
12	DAEWOO CORP.	SOUTH KOREA	23,633.9	90.7	0.4	0.8	33
13	SINOCHEM	CHINA	17,953.0	71.3	0.4	1.1	45
14	LG INTERNATIONAL CORP.	SOUTH KOREA	17,454.3	26.9	0.2	1.6	49
15	TOYOTA TSUSHO	JAPAN	16,497.4	56.0	0.3	0.8	54
16	KAWASHO CORP.	JAPAN	12,985.7	11.4	0.1	0.2	78
17	COFCO	CHINA	12,021.9	92.9	0.8	2.2	84
18	JARDINE MATHESON	HONG KONG	11,605.0	536.1	4.6	3.8	94
19	SUMIKIN BUSSAN	JAPAN	10,612.1	6.9	0.1	0.1	109
20	CALTEX TRADING	SINGAPORE	9,872.6	10.5	0.1	1.0	116

Transportation

Asian airlines' hopes used to fly one way up. Now, slowing economies and surging costs have brought them down to earth. It may be years before things look up. 'The worst is yet to come,' says Peter Harbinson, head of the Center for Asia-Pacific Aviation. 'We will see more over-capacity, lower yields, bigger losses, more price cutting and even fewer passengers.' Economic worries at home mean a cut in people traveling for pleasure, especially to countries where their money is now worth less. Korean, Japanese, and Taiwan tourists used to fill most of the seats. Now only the Taiwanese are still traveling. In the beginning of 1997, airlines expected the number of passengers to grow some 12% a year for the next five years.

Rank	Company	Country	Sales $ Millions	Profit $ Millions	Profit as % of Sales	Profit as % of Assets	1000 Rank
1	EAST JAPAN RAILWAY	JAPAN	23,108.9	649.6	2.8	0.0	35
2	NIPPON EXPRESS	JAPAN	16,413.7	252.8	1.5	2.5	56
3	JAPAN AIRLINES	JAPAN	14,406.4	-133.1	—	—	64
4	CENTRAL JAPAN RAILWAY	JAPAN	11,764.6	334.6	2.8	0.6	89
5	WEST JAPAN RAILWAY	JAPAN	11,116.6	327.6	2.9	1.3	103
6	NIPPON YUSEN	JAPAN	9,416.5	125.0	1.3	0.0	123
7	ALL NIPPON AIRWAYS	JAPAN	9,392.7	39.5	0.4	0.3	124
8	KINKI NIPPON RAILWAY	JAPAN	8,730.4	59.7	0.7	0.4	132
9	MITSUI O.S.K. LINES	JAPAN	7,151.1	55.8	0.8	0.5	161
10	YAMATO TRANSPORT	JAPAN	6,527.8	143.5	2.2	2.8	173
11	QANTAS	AUSTRALIA	6,504.0	197.8	3.0	2.5	174
12	ODAKYU ELECTRIC RAILWAY	JAPAN	5,371.0	34.2	0.6	0.3	228
13	SINGAPORE AIRLINES	SINGAPORE	5,121.6	731.6	14.3	7.1	239
14	SWIRE PACIFIC	HONG KONG	4,917.4	981.3	19.0	6.1	254
15	KOREAN AIR	SOUTH KOREA	4,555.4	-261.7	—	—	272
16	KAWASAKI KISEN	JAPAN	4,530.7	57.9	1.3	1.1	276
17	KEIO TEITO ELECTRIC RAILWAY	JAPAN	4,289.7	57.5	1.3	1.1	289
18	CATHAY PACIFIC AIRWAYS	HONG KONG	4,151.4	488.3	11.8	5.7	305
19	HANKYU CORP.	JAPAN	3,904.5	56.1	1.4	0.5	323
20	NAGOYA RAILROAD	JAPAN	3,543.3	48.3	1.4	0.5	353

Now they hope for 6% annually up to 2001. Airlines are particularly vulnerable to the currency devaluations in the region. Around half their revenue is in local currency, but they have to pay U.S. dollars for fuel and aircraft. Most airlines are already feeling the cash crunch. Korean Air said in December last year that it will sell five passenger aircraft to its creditors, and lease them back. In Hong Kong, Cathay Pacific has laid off staff and decided to hold off buying several Boeing 777s. Garuda Indonesia has been badly battered by the rupiah's plunge. If the currency does not recover to a sound level by next year, airline officials say the company could go bust. Other Indonesian carriers are also in serious trouble.

Weaker currencies in destination countries may eventually get tourists, particularly from long-haul markets, to travel, but some airlines are not waiting. After Cathay's revenues fell 17% below target in October, the Hong Kong carrier launched a 'Super Offer' including two-for-one fares to the territory plus hotel rooms. The deal was a hit in Taiwan, Australia, and the U.S. but failed to lure back many Japanese tourists, and its benefits are still being assessed. 'We did not expect immediate profit,' said spokesman Kwan Chuk-fai. 'But we expected it to bring long-term positive effects.' In January, Cathay brought the Takarazuka Revue, the Japanese all-female variety troupe, to Hong Kong. 'The troupe has a huge loyal following in Japan. Wherever the revue goes, a small army of fans is sure to follow,' Kwan says. More such efforts are on the way, but with Japan's economy having its own troubles and the yen on the slide, the return of the big-spending Japanese tourist is not about to happen anytime soon.

State Enterprises

Except for Japan and Taiwan, state enterprises throughout the region have been forced into deregulation and privatisation. The process has been going on for some years in China, the latest move being the carve-up the PLA's far-flung businesses. South Korea is the most active with all 12 government enterprises up for grabs. Thailand is to retain 50% ownership of its enterprises and Malaysia will keep 39%. Indonesia, on the verge of political and corporate reform, plan to privatise PT Telecom and Indostat, with other state assets likely to follow.

Rank	Company	Country	Sales $ Millions	Profit $ Millions	Profit as % of Sales	Profit as % of Assets	1000 Rank
1	NIPPON TELEGRAPH & TEL.	JAPAN	81,097.5	2,311.6	2.9	1.5	8
2	JAPAN TOBACCO	JAPAN	34,622.4	794.7	2.3	4.0	20
3	CHINA PETROCHEMICAL CORP.	CHINA	26,874.5	662.6	2.5	1.8	29
4	INDIAN OIL	INDIA	17,615.6	393.1	2.2	—	47
5	JIANGSU SUP. & MKTG. CO-OP.	CHINA	16,303.3	185.9	1.1	2.8	57
6	KOREA ELECTRIC POWER	SOUTH KOREA	14,393.4	742.8	5.2	1.7	65
7	TELSTRA	AUSTRALIA	12,084.9	1,265.0	10.5	6.3	82
8	CHINESE PETROLEUM CORP.	TAIWAN	12,019.4	276.4	2.3	1.4	85
9	PETROLIAM NASIONAL	MALAYSIA	11,480.0	2,892.0	25.2	10.7	96
10	KOREA TELECOM	SOUTH KOREA	8,904.3	224.3	2.5	1.2	131
11	TAIWAN POWER	TAIWAN	8,510.3	1,247.9	14.7	3.6	136
12	SHANGHAI AUTOMOTIVE	CHINA	7,889.4	801.6	10.2	12.1	145
13	PETROLEUM AUTHORITY	THAILAND	6,538.8	327.5	5.0	7.1	171
14	QANTAS	AUSTRALIA	6,504.0	197.8	3.0	2.5	174
15	CHUNGHWA TELECOM	TAIWAN	6,036.9	1,998.3	33.1	13.3	188
16	SHANGHAI BAOSHAN IRON	CHINA	5,820.0	290.1	4.0	2.4	203
17	EAST CHINA ELECTRIC POWER	CHINA	5,817.1	221.3	3.8	1.9	204
18	SINGAPORE AIRLINES	SINGAPORE	5,121.6	731.6	14.3	7.1	239
19	ELEC. GENERATING AUTHORITY	THAILAND	4,316.3	1,069.1	24.8	9.2	287
20	BHARAT PETROLEUM	INDIA	4,183.3	108.9	2.6	9.0	300

Chapter Six

TOP ENTERPRISES IN ASEAN

ASEAN: Friendship Has Its Costs

For the Association of Southeast Asian Nations, or ASEAN, the statement was almost revolutionary. On December 1 last year, finance ministers from the nine member nations meeting in Kuala Lumpur agreed that they should keep a much closer eye on each other's economies. Said their joint statement: 'Peer surveillance' will be used to evaluate 'potential economic and financial risks of member countries.' When it comes to such matters, the ministers seemed to say, 'constructive engagement'— the guiding buzzphrase of intra-ASEAN relations for the organization's three decades — may not be enough.

The months since July 1997, when the Thai baht's flotation triggered the regional currency meltdown, have made clear that ASEAN members cannot isolate themselves from each other's economic performance, policies, or problems. As the Asian flu spread from Thailand to Indonesia and on to Malaysia, the Philippines, and even Singapore and Brunei, the region's currency and stock markets fell ill. Later, South Korea and Japan, both already ailing from their own home-grown diseases, caught the bug. But that's old news. As demonstrated at the finance ministers' conference in Malaysia's capital (attended by Australia, China, Hong Kong, Japan, South Korea, and the U.S., as well as ASEAN), the focus has turned to figuring out how to get East Asia through the crisis and how to prevent similar contagion in the future.

It is well worth putting the current turmoil in context. Thirty years ago, the region was dominated by sleepy fishing villages and paddy fields. Back then, time passed in seasons, measured by the winds, rain, and the changing color of crops. But today, the pace of life is fast, the fishing villages are likely to be golf resorts, and the rice paddies have turned into housing developments. Among the five original ASEAN members, per capita GDP today averages more than 20 times what it was three decades ago. Exports have increased on average more than 70 times since ASEAN's founding.

But the economic miracle of year-upon-year of relentless growth for most of the economies (the Philippines is a glaring exception) hid mounting problems. Just as a frenetic stock trader might ignore a swelling drug addiction, so long as the good times and the money to pay for them kept flowing, Thailand (and, to a lesser extent, Indonesia and Malaysia) became dependent on easy credit. This opiate fed unproductive investment and property speculation. And when finance companies and other lenders could no longer maintain the habit, currencies and asset prices crashed.

Does the finance ministers' meeting in Kuala Lumpur and their pledge to liberalize financial services and to develop deep, liquid debt markets signal real reform? It depends on who you listen to. Malaysian prime minister Mahathir Mohamad has continued to blame hedge fund managers like George Soros for many of Asia's problems. Michel Camdessus, managing director of the International Monetary Fund (IMF), which is studying the effect of currency trading on markets, told the same finance ministers' meeting, 'It would be a mistake to blame hedge funds as the central agent of turmoil in Asia.' Instead, he faults poor economic fundamentals and governments' unwillingness to fix them. But, in the same speech, Camdessus praised as a positive development the so-called Manila Framework, the peer pressure mechanism drafted in the Philippine capital in November, applauded by participants at the Asia-Pacific Economic Cooperation forum meeting that same month, and endorsed in Kuala Lumpur.

Words about economic cooperation in Southeast Asia are nearly as old as ASEAN itself. But until now, they haven't amounted to very much. Twenty years ago, the group devoted months to assembling lists of tariff-free goods, only to realize that half the items were different sizes and types of nails.

Nevertheless, dreams of greater trade within the region persisted. One long-held goal, but dismissed by some, including committed auto executives, as a pipe dream: an ASEAN automobile, built from parts manufactured throughout the region. Malaysia's Proton uses Thai components as well as materials from Singapore. But in reality, the car is more representative of Mitsubishi Motors than ASEAN. The Japanese company is one of the few multinationals to employ an ASEAN-wide strategy to order and distribute parts made in Malaysia, Thailand, Indonesia, and the Philippines for its cars and trucks. The Mitsubishi experience demonstrates that private industry can often do more to promote intra-ASEAN trade than governments.

That's partly why Manu Bhaskaran, chief economist with SocGen Securities in Singapore, believes that regional recovery after this worst crisis to hit the region since the Second World War depends on deregulation: 'Root out inefficiencies, reduce protectionism, pull down all sorts of barriers, and do away with the licenses, monopolies and tendency to think they can pick winners instead of letting market forces decide.' Jardine Fleming economist Rajeev Malik in Singapore figures Malaysia, for instance, will be forced to accept significantly lower growth because of a fundamental imbalance in its economy: 'Its big problem is it doesn't have enough skilled workers to allow fresh foreign investment to move to the next level of high value-added exports.' Malik believes that because of this skills shortage, such ASEAN members as the Philippines, Indonesia, and Thailand will be forced to turn the clocks back and focus on natural resources. 'That's their comparative advantage,' he says. 'If ASEAN countries are to move forward, this misallocation of resources needs to be corrected.'

The obvious model for many of these changes may be Singapore. After all, the Lion City has retained and nurtured a manufacturing sector and has taken steps to cool property speculation and keep a lid on inflation. Pre-crisis, the monetary authorities were allowing the Singapore dollar to depreciate slowly, thus retaining the city-state's competitiveness along with its position as a safe haven. And Singapore has continued to invest in education, training and technology — in other words, the future.

But it may be futile to try applying Singapore solutions to anywhere more than one island in Indonesia. The city state, whose population is a quarter the size of Metro Manila, is unique. For example, Singapore has not had to concern itself with raising the quality of life in vast rural areas while maintaining city services. Similarly, Brunei can offer practical insights only to economies

Table 13: Asean's Top Enterprises   **1 to 25**

Rank	Company	Country	Sales $ Millions	Profit $ Millions	Profit as % of Sales	Assets $ Millions	Work Force	1000 Rank
1	PERTAMINA	INDONESIA	19,276.5	578.1	2.0	14,205.5	33,333	40
2	PETROLIAM NASIONAL	MALAYSIA	11,480.0	2,892.0	25.2	27,090.1	14,094	96
3	CALTEX TRADING	SINGAPORE	9,872.6	10.5	0.1	1,037.4	84	116
4	PETROLEUM AUTHORITY	THAILAND	6,538.8	327.5	5.0	4,583.4	3,430	171
5	SEAGATE TECHNOLOGY INTL.	SINGAPORE	6,242.6	797.2	12.8	1,843.0	19,528	179
6	HEWLETT-PACKARD	SINGAPORE	5,839.1	1,040.7	17.8	4,356.1	9,000	197
7	SIME DARBY	MALAYSIA	5,260.9	332.2	6.3	15,242.5	37,000	233
8	SINGAPORE AIRLINES	SINGAPORE	5,121.6	731.6	14.3	10,298.7	27,241	239
9	ASTRA INTERNATIONAL	INDONESIA	4,688.0	200.4	4.3	7,143.8	123,000	264
10	ASIA MATSUSHITA ELECTRIC	SINGAPORE	4,336.2	44.7	1.0	1,009.2	636	286
11	ELEC. GENERATING AUTHORITY	THAILAND	4,316.3	1,069.1	24.8	11,678.8	32,867	287
12	SIAM CEMENT	THAILAND	4,232.8	267.8	6.3	7,094.1	5,500	293
13	PER. LISTRIK NEGARA (PLN)	INDONESIA	4,020.9	498.1	12.4	22,449.6	56,476	316
14	YUKONG INTERNATIONAL (S)	SINGAPORE	3,875.8	13.0	0.3	622.0	12	325
15	NISSHO IWAI PETROLEUM	SINGAPORE	3,686.8	-0.8	—	95.6	7	342
16	HONG LEONG INVESTMENT	SINGAPORE	3,457.8	244.1	7.1	12,887.9	30,000	362
17	SAN MIGUEL CORP.	PHILIPPINES	3,242.6	232.3	7.2	3,772.7	28,544	374
18	TENAGA NASIONAL	MALAYSIA	3,237.8	317.1	9.8	12,913.1	23,565	375
19	BP SINGAPORE	SINGAPORE	3,182.4	59.3	1.9	1,191.4	450	384
20	HITACHI ASIA	SINGAPORE	3,164.5	3.5	0.1	890.1	792	390
21	SINGAPORE TELECOM	SINGAPORE	3,135.4	1,176.2	37.5	7,701.4	10,388	395
22	THAI AIRWAYS INTERNATIONAL	THAILAND	3,078.6	133.5	4.3	5,197.3	22,136	406
23	TEXAS INSTRUMENTS SING.	SINGAPORE	2,887.7	48.0	1.7	883.0	2,184	437
24	GUDANG GARAM	INDONESIA	2,799.9	279.7	9.0	1,841.9	45,000	453
25	TOYOTA MOTOR (THAILAND)	THAILAND	2,785.5	34.2	1.2	1,285.8	6,075	456

that rely almost exclusively on oil. Might the Philippines be a better model? In the years since ASEAN was formed, the Philippines has lagged badly, growing between one-half and one-tenth as much as its fellow members. Until the end of March 1998, the country had been under IMF tutelage for about the same time that ASEAN has existed. But that means it has, to some extent and with mixed success, confronted the crony capitalism and asset bubbles now facing its neighbors. Certainly, the newest ASEAN members — Laos, Myanmar, and Vietnam — have a

26 to 50

Rank	Company	Country	Sales $ Millions	Profit $ Millions	Profit as % of Sales	Assets $ Millions	Work Force	1000 Rank
26	MARUBENI INTL. PETROLEUM	SINGAPORE	2,782.1	13.2	0.5	271.6	27	459
27	EON	MALAYSIA	2,769.8	180.6	6.5	3,483.0	3,435	461
28	MOBIL OIL SINGAPORE	SINGAPORE	2,661.0	126.7	4.8	2,360.7	610	477
29	MALAYSIAN AIRLINE SYSTEM	MALAYSIA	2,577.6	132.3	5.1	5,822.0	22,545	498
30	TELEKOM MALAYSIA	MALAYSIA	2,550.3	747.8	29.3	7,946.7	27,516	504
31	BERJAYA GROUP	MALAYSIA	2,524.6	32.3	1.3	4,954.7	22,500	513
32	THAI OIL	THAILAND	2,477.0	8.8	0.4	2,819.9	980	528
33	PROTON	MALAYSIA	2,473.2	297.9	12.1	1,849.6	5,400	530
34	NATIONAL POWER CORP.	PHILIPPINES	2,427.3	211.4	8.7	17,458.1	14,686	538
35	SGS-THOMSON MICROELEC. ASIA	SINGAPORE	2,390.8	31.6	1.3	407.1	550	548
36	PERLIS PLANTATIONS	MALAYSIA	2,336.5	71.2	3.1	1,518.7	9,600	560
37	WESTERN DIGITAL (SING.)	SINGAPORE	2,296.5	111.3	4.8	662.4	4,731	569
38	AMSTEEL CORP.	MALAYSIA	2,295.7	50.9	2.2	3,783.3	NA	572
39	TRI PETCH ISUZU SALES	THAILAND	2,290.7	22.6	0.0	1,392.9	900	576
40	KUOK OILS & GRAINS	SINGAPORE	2,275.0	6.6	0.3	254.3	137	582
41	MANILA ELECTRIC CO.	PHILIPPINES	2,247.1	193.2	8.6	2,587.0	7,793	590
42	PHILIPS (SINGAPORE)	SINGAPORE	2,244.1	24.2	1.1	801.3	8,000	593
43	TELKOM	INDONESIA	2,167.0	641.8	29.6	7,592.2	37,644	609
44	ITOCHU PETROLEUM	SINGAPORE	2,136.1	-0.4	—	274.2	22	617
45	CYCLE & CARRIAGE	SINGAPORE	2,135.4	141.9	6.6	1,629.4	5,141	618
46	SINGAPORE POWER	SINGAPORE	2,056.7	546.8	26.6	7,787.2	4,500	636
47	ESSO STANDARD THAILAND	THAILAND	2,049.9	-54.9	—	1,530.5	1,600	639
48	KEPPEL CORP.	SINGAPORE	2,046.6	144.8	7.1	13,382.9	14,320	641
49	PETRON CORP.	PHILIPPINES	2,037.4	161.7	7.9	1,827.5	1,267	645
50	FRASER & NEAVE	SINGAPORE	1,993.9	154.9	7.8	4,499.8	10,064	659

rich set of economic experiences from which to choose. (Cambodia, whose membership has been put on hold because of internal political turmoil, could complete the ASEAN 10 by the end of this year.)

ASEAN comprises a wide mix of nations bound by geographic proximity, cultural similarities and, now, economic troubles. But the recent crises, including the recurring problem of the suffocating haze, may force ASEAN to finally come to grips with its interconnectedness. It has reached a defining moment. The watchful eyes of neighbors can be as comforting to a community of friends as they are intrusive to strangers. Yet enhancing cooperation and moving toward what Europeans called 'an ever-closer union' spooks many. With possibly 10 members by the turn of the millennium, the family may be too large, too diverse, and too physically spread out to stay together. Geopolitics gurus say the threat of Chinese expansionism and lingering distrust of Japan will keep the body together. That may prove true, but ASEAN may be doomed to be no more than a regional trade group whose members, behind the smiles and linked arms, harbor deep-seated resentment of each other. Dysfunctional families have been known to self-destruct. To enhance cohesion requires frank and open talk about the issues that divide. So far, that has not been an integral part of the ASEAN way.

The list of the top 50 enterprises in ASEAN is clearly dominated by Singapore, the region's financial and commercial hub. Some Indonesian tycoons may be wealthier, but the Lion City's companies rule. Besides, a lot of Southeast Asia's money is parked in the city state. Post-crisis, expect the rankings to be fluid. Most of the companies have been hard hit by the turmoil. Singapore firms may increase their representation at the expense of enterprises in Thailand, Malaysia, and Indonesia. A few more Philippine companies could make it on the list in coming years. Figure on strong export-earners to stay on top as the region begins to recover. Airlines are likely to fall because of flagging tourism. So too will petroleum-sector players. Electronics manufacturers may hold their ground or sink, depending on where their markets are and what they produce. Those relying on sales in Asia will certainly hurt. After the turmoil, the mantra for recovery has to be: go global.

Another Important Title from Asiaweek:
Asia's Financial 500:
A Guide to the Region's Banking and Finance Industry

0-471-82901-3   220pp   Paper   December 1998   US$19.95*

In 1998 Japan will implement its Big Bang policy and open up its previously protected financial markets to the outside world. At the same time a World Trade Organization directive will encourage other Asian countries to follow suit. This book provides an important snapshot of Asia's top 500 financial institutions prior to these changes and offers analysis of the changes to come and their implications for world banking. This book will be beneficial to Banking and Financial Professionals, Business People, Asian Analysts, Corporate Strategists, Investors, Economists, Students and Academics.

Features:

- Key information and analysis of Asia's banking industry from Asiaweek's top regional reporters
- Comprehensive coverage of key Asian countries
- Directory section on all listed banks
- Sections such as Biggest Profits/Largest Gain in Profits/Highest Return on Equity/ Highest Growth in Assets/Biggest Loans etc. will prove invaluable to investors and those in corporate finance
- Provides a benchmark for the US and European Banking Community

Look out for this invaluable release in December in your local bookshop. Should you encounter difficulties, please contact the publisher at:

John Wiley & Sons (Asia) Pte Ltd
2 Clementi Loop #02-01 Singapore 129809
Tel: 463 2400   Fax: 463 4604 / 463 4605 / 463 4606
Email: enquiry@wiley.com.sg
Visit our Wiley Homepage at : http://www.wiley.com

DIRECTORY

A

Acer Group, The
Stan Shih
Chairman
6/F, 156 Ming-Shen E. Road
Section 3, Taipei
Taiwan
Tel: 88-6-2-545-5288
Fax: 88-6-2-545-5308

Aichi Machine Industry Co., Ltd.
Yoshiyuki Miyakawa
President
1-12 Kawanami-Cho, Atsuta-Ku
Nagoya 456
Japan
Tel: 81-52-681-1111
Fax: 81-52-681-6871

Aichi Steel Works, Ltd.
Masaaki Ohashi
President
1 Wanowari, Arao-Cho
Tokai-Shi
Aichi-Ken 476
Japan
Tel: 81-52-604-1111
Fax: 81-52-601-0301

Aichi Toyota Motor Co., Ltd.
Naoki Yamaguchi
President
6-8 Takatsuji-Cho, Showa-Ku
Nagoya-Shi 466
Japan
Tel: 81-52-871-4511
Fax: 81-52-871-5800

Air China
Chen Guangyi
Bureau Chief
A2 Jing Xin Mansion
Dong San Huan
North Road, Beijing
China
Tel: 86-10-6401-2233
Fax: 86-10-6455-3201

Air New Zealand Limited
James McCrea
Managing Director
Quay Tower, 29 Customs Street
West, Auckland
New Zealand
Tel: 64-9-366-2400
Fax: 64-9-366-2764

Aisin Aw Co., Ltd.
Haruo Mori
President
10 Takane, Fujii-Cho, Anjo City
Aichi Pref. 444-11
Japan
Tel: 81-566-73-1111
Fax: 81-566-73-1380

Aisin Seiki Co., Ltd.
Kanshiro Toyoda
President
2-1 Asahi-Machi, Kariya City
Aichi Pref. 448
Japan
Tel: 81-566-24-8231
Fax: 81-566-24-8848

Aiwa Co., Ltd.
Yoshio Ishigaki
President
1-2-11 Ikenohata, Taito-Ku
Tokyo 110
Japan
Tel: 81-3-3827-3111
Fax: 81-3-3827-2578

Ajinomoto Co., Ltd.
Shunsuke Inamori
President
1-15-1 Kyobashi, Chuo-Ku
Tokyo 104, Japan
Tel: 81-3-5250-8159/8111
Fax: 81-3-5250-8378

Alcoa of Australia Limited
Roger A. G. Vines
Chairman & Managing Director
Cnr Davy & Marmion Streets
Booragoon, Western Australia 6154
Australia
Tel: 61-8-9316-5111
Fax: 61-8-9316-5228

All Nippon Airways Co., Ltd.
Seiji Fukatsu
President
Kasumigaseki Bldg.
3-2-5 Kasumigaseki
Chiyoda-Ku, Tokyo 100
Japan
Tel: 81-3-3592-3065/3049
Fax: 81-3-3592-3039

Alps Electric Co., Ltd.
Masataka Kataoka
President
1-7 Yukigaya, Otsuka-Cho
Ota-Ku, Tokyo 145
Japan
Tel: 81-3-3726-1211
Fax: 81-3-3728-1741

Amada Co., Ltd.
Nobuyuki Ueda
President
200 Ishida, Isehara City
Kanagawa Pref. 259-11
Japan
Tel: 81-463-96-1111
Fax: 81-463-93-1323

Amcor Limited
Donald B. Macfarlane
Managing Director
Level 23, Southgate Tower East
40 City Road
South Melbourne
Victoria 3205
Australia
Tel: 61-3-9694-9000
Fax: 61-3-9686-2924

Amsteel Corporation
Y. Bhg. Tan Sri William H.J.Cheng
Managing Director
Level 46, Menara Lion
165 Jalan Ampang
Kuala Lumpur 50450
Malaysia
Tel: 60-3-262-2155
Fax: 60-3-262-6497

Amway Japan Limited
Richard S. Johnson
President
Arco Tower
1-8-1 Shimomeguro
Meguro-Ku
Tokyo 153
Japan
Tel: 81-3-5434-8484
Fax: 81-3-5434-4899

Ando Corporation
Kosaku Okita
President
3-12-8 Shibaura-Cho
Minato-Ku
Tokyo 108
Japan
Tel: 81-3-3457-0111
Fax: 81-3-3451-1606

Ansett Australia Holdings Limited
Rod Eddington
Chairman
501 Swanston Street
Melbourne, Victoria 3000
Australia
Tel: 61-3-9623-3333
Fax: 61-3-9623-2400

Aoki Corporation
Yoichiro Yano
President
2-17-3 Shibuya
Shibuya-Ku, Tokyo
Japan
Tel: 81-3-3407-8511
Fax: 81-3-3407-4428

Aoyama Trading Co., Ltd.
Shohzo Miyamae
President
1-3-5 Ohji-Cho, Fukuyama-Shi
Hiroshima-Ken 721
Japan
Tel: 81-849-20-0050
Fax: 81-849-21-8111

Arabian Oil Company, Ltd.
Keiichi Konaga
President
Seiroka Tower 8-1
Akashi-Cho, Chuo-Ku, Tokyo 104
Japan
Tel: 81-3-3547-0226
Fax: 81-3-547-0246

Araco Corporation
Masanao Shiomi
President
25 Kamifjiike, Yoshiwara-Cho
Toyota City, Aichi Pref. 473
Japan
Tel: 81-565-52-4141
Fax: 81-565-51-2295

Arai-Gumi, Ltd.
Shojiro Hanafusa
President
12-20 Ikeda-Cho
Nishinomiya City, Hyogo Pref 662
Japan
Tel: 81-798-26-3111
Fax: 81-798-33-6111

Asahi Breweries, Ltd.
Yuzo Seto
President
1-23-1 Azumabashi, Sumida-Ku
Tokyo 130
Japan
Tel: 81-3-5608-5112
Fax: 81-3-5608-7111

Asahi Chemical Industry Co., Ltd.
Kazumoto Yamamoto
President
1-1-2 Yuraku-Cho
Chiyoda-Ku, Tokyo 100
Japan
Tel: 81-3-3507-2060
Fax: 81-3-3507-2495

Asahi Food Co., Ltd.
Takeuchi Katsuyuki
President
2-15-5 Minamiharimaya-Cho
Kochi-City, Kochi Pref. 780
Japan
Tel: 81-888-82-7111
Fax: 81-888-82-7119

Asahi Glass Co., Ltd.
Hiromichi Seya
President
2-1-2 Marunouchi
Chiyoda-Ku, Tokyo 100
Japan
Tel: 81-3-3218-5741/5555
Fax: 81-3-3201-5390

Asahi Kasei Homes
Yuji Tsuchiya
President
24/F., Shinjuku Monoris
2-3-1 Nishi-Shinjuku
Shinjuku-Ku
Tokyo 160-09
Japan
Tel: 81-3-3344-7171
Fax: 81-3-3344-7050

Asahi National Broadcasting Co., Ltd.
Kunio Ito
President
1-1-1 Roppongi, Minato-Ku
Tokyo 106
Japan
Tel: 81-3-3587-5111
Fax: 81-3-3505-3539

Asahi Shimbun Publishing Co.
Muneyuki Matsushita
President
3-2-4 Nakanoshima, Kita-Ku
Osaka
Japan
Tel: 81-6-231-0131
Fax: 81-6-201-8599

Asanuma Corporation
Kenichi Asanuma
President
12-6 Higashikozu-Cho
Tennoji-Ku
Osaka 543-91
Japan
Tel: 81-6-768-5222
Fax: 81-6-763-6336

Asatsu Inc.
Tsutomu Takeda
President
7-16-12 Ginza, Chuo-Ku
Tokyo 104
Japan
Tel: 81-3-3547-2111
Fax: 81-3-3547-2091

Asia Matsushita Electric (Singapore) Pte. Ltd.
K. Yuasa
Managing Director
300 Beach Road
#16-01, The Concourse
Singapore 199555
Tel: 65-299-8400
Fax: 65-299-7600

Asia Motors
Cho Rae-Sung
President
15 Youido-Dong
Yongdungpo-Gu
Seoul
South Korea
Tel: 82-2-788-8497
Fax: 82-2-780-1037

Asia Pulp & Paper Co., Ltd.
Suresh Kilam
Managing Director
1 Maritime Square
10-01 World Trade Centre
Singapore 099253
Tel: 65-272-9288
Fax: 65-272-9133

Asiana Airlines, Inc.
Park Sam-Koo
President
Asiana Bldg., 10-1
2-Ka, Hoehyun-Dong
Chung-Ku
Seoul 100-052
South Korea
Tel: 82-2-758-8114
Fax: 82-2-758-8008

Asmo Co., Ltd.
Yoshimichi Shirai
President
390 Umeda, Kosai-Shi
Shizuoka 431-04
Japan
Tel: 81-53-572-3311
Fax: 81-53-572-3575

Astra International
Theodore Permadi Rachmat
President Director
22, Jalan Ir. H. Juanda
Jakarta 10120
Indonesia
Tel: 62-21-231-2555
Fax: 62-21-345-3358

Australia Post
Graeme T. John
Managing Director
321 Exhibition Street
Melbourne
Victoria 3000
Australia
Tel: 61-3-9204-7171
Fax: 61-3-9663-1160

Australian National Industries Limited
P.W. Stancliffe
Managing Director
Level 5, Merlin Centre
235 Pyrmont Street
Pyrmont
NSW 2009
Australia
Tel: 61-2-9577-6700
Fax: 61-2-9577-6888

Australian Petroleum Pty. Ltd. (Ampol)
Ian Blackburne
Managing Director
Level 12, MLC Centre
19-29 Martin Place
Sydney, NSW 2000
Australia
Tel: 61-2-9250-5000
Fax: 61-2-9250-5742

Australian Wheat Board
John Lawrenson
Managing Director
Ceres House, 528 Lonsdale Street
Melbourne
Victoria 3000
Australia
Tel: 61-3-9209-2000
Fax: 61-3-9670-2782

Autobacs Seven Co., Ltd.
Koichi Sumino
President
Senri Asahi Hankyu Bldg.
5-3 Shinsenri-Higashimachi
1-Chome, Toyonaka
Osaka 565
Japan
Tel: 81-3-3454-0433
Fax: 81-3-3454-0166

B

Bandai Co., Ltd.
Takashi Mogi
President
5-4 Komagata, 2-Chome
Taito-Ku
Tokyo 111-81
Japan
Tel: 81-3-3847-5005
Fax: 81-3-3847-5067

Bangchak Petroleum Public Company Ltd.
Sophon Supapong
President
38 Srinakarin Road, Prawet
Bangkok 10260
Thailand
Tel: 662-301-2700
Fax: 662-399-1051

Banyu Pharmaceutical Co., Ltd.
Kenjiro Nagasaka
President
2-2-3 Nihonbashi-Honcho
Chuo-Ku
Tokyo 103
Japan
Tel: 81-3-5203-8111
Fax: 81-3-3246-2130

Beijing Yanshan Petrochemical Corp.
Liu Haiyan
President
Fangshan District
Beijing 102500
China
Tel: 86-10-6934-2281
Fax: 86-10-6934-2736

Benesse Corporation
Soichiro Fukutake
President
3-7-17 Minamigata
Okayama City
Okayama 700-88
Japan
Tel: 81-86-225-1100
Fax: 81-86-227-6112

Berjaya Group Berhad
Tan Sri Vincent Tan Chee Yioun
Chairman
Level 18
Shahzan Prudential Tower
30 Jalan Sultan Ismail
Kuala Lumpur 50250
Malaysia
Tel: 60-3-242-2622 /244-4333
Fax: 60-3-248-4866

Best Denki Co., Ltd.
Yasumitsu Kitada
President
2-1-12 Nanotsu
Chuo-Ku, Fukuoka-Shi
Fukuchi
Japan
Tel: 81-92-781-7161
Fax: 81-92-752-1956

Bharat Heavy Electricals Ltd.
R.K.D. Shah
Chairman & Managing Director
Bhel House, Siri Fort
New Delhi 110 049
India
Tel: 91-11-649-3031/3008
Fax: 91-11-649-3021/3153

Bharat Petroleum Corporation Ltd.
U. Sundararajan
Chairman & Managing Director
Bharat Bhavan, 4&6 Currimbhoy
Road, Ballard Estate
Mumbai 400 001
India
Tel: 91-22-261-8281/8061
Fax: 91-22-261-6793

BMW Japan Corporation
Yoshikazu Nakashima
President
1-10-2 Nakase, Mihama-Ku
Chiba City, Chiba 261
Japan
Tel: 81-43-297-7070
Fax: 81-43-297-7077

Boonrawd Brewery Co., Ltd.
Piya Bhirombhakdi
President & Chairman
999 Samsen Road, Dusit
Bangkok 10300, Thailand
Tel: 66-2-241-1361-9/243-4731
Fax: 66-2-243-1740

Boonrawd Trading
Piya Bhirombhakdi
Chairman
1003 Samsen Road
Bangkrabue, Bangkok 10300
Thailand
Tel: 662-243-4731
Fax: 662-243-1740

Boral Limited
Tony Berg
Managing Director
Level 39, AMP Centre, 50 Bridge
Street, Sydney, NSW 2000
Australia
Tel: 61-2-9220-6300
Fax: 61-2-9233-6605

BP Australia Holdings Limited
Ronald A. McGimpsey
Managing Director
Level 21-34, The Tower
Melbourne Central
360 Elizabeth Street
Melbourne
Victoria 3000
Australia
Tel: 61-3-9268-4111
Fax: 61-3-9268-3321

BP Singapore Pte. Ltd.
D.D.Straun Robertson
Chief Executive Officer
24/F., BP Tower
396 Alexandra Road
Singapore
Tel: 65-371-8888
Fax: 65-371-8801

Brambles Industries Limited
John Fletcher
Chief Executive
Level 40, 'Gateway'
1 Macquarie Place
Sydney
NSW 2000
Australia
Tel: 61-2-9256-5222
Fax: 61-2-9256-5299

Bridgestone Corporation
Yoichiro Kaizaki
President
1-10 Kyobashi, 1-Chome
Chuo-Ku
Tokyo 104
Japan
Tel: 81-3-3563-6811
Fax: 81-3-3567-4615

Brierley Investments Limited
Paul Collins
Chief Executive
Level 6, Colonial Bldg.
22-24 Victoria Street
Wellington
New Zealand
Tel: 64-4-470-8800
Fax: 64-4-470-8831

Broken Hill Proprietary Co., Ltd.
John B. Prescott
Managing Director
48/F., BHP Tower
Bourke Place
600 Bourke Street
Melbourne
Victoria 3000
Australia
Tel: 61-3-9609-3333
Fax: 61-3-9609-3624

Brother Industries, Ltd.
Yoshihiro Yasui
President
15-1 Naeshiro-Cho
Mizuho-Ku, Nagoya-Shi 467
Japan
Tel: 81-52-824-2511
Fax: 81-52-821-7628

BTR Nylex Limited
Elwvn Elledge
Chairman
15/F., 390 St Kilda Road
Melbourne
Victoria 3004
Australia
Tel: 61-3-9222-5700
Fax: 61-3-9867-4103

Burns, Philp & Co. Ltd.
Thomas Degnan
Managing Director
7 Bridge Street
Sydney
NSW 2000
Australia
Tel: 61-2-9259-1111
Fax: 61-2-9251-3254

C

C.P. Pokphand Co., Ltd.
Dhanin Chearavanont
Chairman
22/F., Far East Finance Centre
16 Harcourt Road
Central
Hong Kong
Tel: 852-2520-1601
Fax: 852-2861-2514

Calsonic Corporation
Haruo Ohno
President
5-24-15 Minamidai, Nakano-Ku
Tokyo 164
Japan
Tel: 81-3-5385-0111
Fax: 81-3-3380-7331

Caltex (Philippines) Inc.
Clilcon G. Hon
President
6/F., 6750 Bldg.
Ayala Avenue
Makati City, Metro-Manila
Philippines
Tel: 63-2-813-6001
Fax: 63-2-813-6078

Caltex Trading Pte. Ltd.
L.G. Lonergan
Chairman
30 Raffles Place #25-00
Caltex House
Singapore 048622
Tel: 65-439-1101
Fax: 65-439-1700

Canon Inc.
Fujio Mitarai
President
3-30-2 Shimomaruko, Ohta-Ku
Tokyo 146
Japan
Tel: 81-3-3758-2111
Fax: 81-3-5482-5135

Canon Sales Co., Inc.
Hideharu Takemoto
President
3-11-28 Mita, Minato-Ku
Tokyo 108
Japan
Tel: 81-3-3455-9111
Fax: 81-3-5476-7924

Carter Holt Harvey Limited
John V. Faraci
Managing Director
640 Great South Road
Manukau City, Auckland
New Zealand
Tel: 64-9-262-6000
Fax: 64-9-262-0956

Casio Computer Co., Ltd.
Kazuo Kashio
President
6-1 Nishi-Shinjuku, 2-Chome
Shinjuku-Ku, Tokyo 163
Japan
Tel: 81-3-3347-4852
Fax: 81-3-3347-4850

Cathay Pacific Airways Limited
Peter Sutch
Chairman
4/F., Swire House
9 Connaught Road, Central
Hong Kong
Tel: 852-2747-5000
Fax: 852-2868-0176

Cecile Co., Ltd.
Michikazu Masaoka
President
2-10-20 Taga-Cho
Takamatsu-Shi 760
Japan
Tel: 81-120-70-8888
Fax: 81-878-35-4432

Central Glass Co., Ltd.
Hirotaro Okazaki
President
3-7-1 Kanda-Nishikicho,
Chiyoda-Ku Tokyo 101
Japan
Tel: 81-3-3259-7111
Fax: 81-3-3259-7394

Central Japan Railway Company
Yoshiyuki Kasai
President
15/F., Sumitomo Seimei Bldg.
2-14-19 Meieki Minami
Nakamura-Ku, Nagoya City 450
Japan
Tel: 81-52-564-2317
Fax: 81-52-587-1300

Chain Store Okuwa Co., Ltd.
Ikuji Okuwa
President
185-3 Nakajima, Wakayama-Shi 641
Japan
Tel: 81-734-25-2481
Fax: 81-734-26-1049

Cheil Jedang Corp.
Sohn Kyong-Sik
President
500 Namdaemunno 5-Ga
Chung-Gu, Seoul
South Korea
Tel: 82-2-726-8114
Fax: 82-2-751-8529

Cheung Kong (Holdings) Limited
Li Ka-shing
Chairman & Managing Director
18-22/F., China Building
29 Queen's Road Central
Hong Kong
Tel: 852-2526-6911
Fax: 852-2845-2940

Chichibu Onoda Cement Corporation
Kazutsugu Hiraga
President
2-14-1 Nishi-Shinbashi, Minato-Ku
Tokyo 105
Japan
Tel: 81-3-5512-5222
Fax: 81-3-5512-5231

China Airlines
Fu Chun-Fan
President
131, Sec. 3, Nanking E. Road
Taipei, Taiwan
Tel: 886-2-715-2233
Fax: 886-2-514-5754

China Huaneng Enterprise Group
Li Xiaopeng
General Manager
23 Fuxing Road, Haidian District
Beijing
China
Tel: 86-10-6829-7749
Fax: 86-10-6822-3349

China Light & Power Co., Ltd.
Ross Edward Sayers
Managing Director
147 Argyle Street
Kowloon
Hong Kong
Tel: 852-2760-6111
Fax: 852-2760-6379

China National Agri. Means of Production Group Corp.
Wang Xiao-Min
President
25 Chegong Zhuang Lu
Haidian District
Beijing
China
Tel: 86-10-6841-3322/8353
Fax: 86-10-6841-5090

China National Offshore Oil Corp.
Wang Yan
President
Jia 2, North Dongsanhuan Lu
Chao Yang Qu
Beijing 100027
China
Tel: 86-10-6466-9001
Fax: 86-10-6466-2994

China Petrochemical Corporation
Sheng Huaren
President
A6 Huixindong Street
Chaoyang District
Beijing 100029
China
Tel: 86-10-6499-9249
Fax: 86-10-6421-2429

China State Construction Engineering Corp.
Ma Ting-Gui
General Manager
Bai-Wan-Zhuang
Beijing 100835
China
Tel: 86-10-6834-7766
Fax: 86-10-6831-4326

China Steel Corporation
J.Y. Chen
President
1 Chung Kang Road
Hsiao Kang
Lin Hai Industrial District
Kaohsiung 81233
Taiwan
Tel: 886-7-802-1111
Fax: 886-7-802-2511/801-9427

Chinese Petroleum Corporation
S.J. Lee
Chairman
83 Chung-Hwa Road
Section 1
Taipei 10031
Taiwan
Tel: 886-2-361-0221
Fax: 886-2-331-9645

Chiyoda Co., Ltd.
Masao Funahashi
President
4-39-8 Narita-Higashi
Suginami-Ku
Tokyo 166
Japan
Tel: 81-3-3316-4131
Fax: 81-3-3317-2852

Chiyoda Corporation
Masato Kitagawa
President
12-1 Tsurumichuo, 2-Chome
Tsurumi-Ku, Yokohama 230
Japan
Tel: 81-45-521-1231
Fax: 81-45-503-0200

Chizaki Kogyo Co., Ltd.
Akiie Chizaki
President
2-23-1 Nishi-Shinbashi
Minato-Ku, Tokyo 105
Japan
Tel: 81-3-3436-3175
Fax: 81-3-5472-5266

Chori Co., Ltd.
Hisao Nakamura
President
2-4-7 Kawara-Machi
Chuo-Ku, Osaka 541
Japan
Tel: 81-6-228-5086
Fax: 81-6-228-5083

Chubu Electric Power Co., Inc.
Hiroji Ota
President
1 Higashi-Shincho, Higashi-Ku
Nagoya 461-8680
Japan
Tel: 81-52-951-8211
Fax: 81-52-962-4624

Chudenko Corporation
Kouichi Ikeuchi
President
6-12 Koami-Cho, Naka-Ku
Hiroshima-Shi 733
Japan
Tel: 81-82-291-7411
Fax: 81-82-293-6903

Chugai Boyeki Co., Ltd.
Utaro Doi
President
2-15-13 Tsukishima, Chuo-Ku
Tokyo 104
Japan
Tel: 81-3-3536-4600
Fax: 81-3-3536-4701

Chugai Pharmaceutical Co., Ltd.
Osamu Nagayama
President
2-1-9 Kyobashi, Chuo-Ku
Tokyo 104
Japan
Tel: 81-3-3281-6611
Fax: 81-3-3281-2828

Chugoku Electric Power Co., Inc.
Shitomi Takasu
President & Director
4-33 Komachi, Naka-Ku
Hiroshima 730-91
Japan
Tel: 81-82-241-0211
Fax: 81-82-242-8437

Chunghwa Telecom Co., Ltd.
Shyue-Ching Lu
President
31 Ai-Kuo E. Road
Taipei 106
Taiwan
Tel: 886-2-344-3691
Fax: 886-2-394-7324

Chunichi Shimbun
Bungo Shirai
President
1-6-1 Sannomaru, Naka-Ku
Nagoya 460-11
Japan
Tel: 81-52-201-8811
Fax: 81-52-201-4331

Chuo Gyorui Co., Ltd.
Hiroyasu Ito
President
5-2-1 Tsukiji, Chuo-Ku
Tokyo 104
Japan
Tel: 81-3-3541-2500
Fax: 81-3-3545-9747

CITIC
Wang Jun
Chairman
8/F., Capital Mansions
6 Xinyuannan Road
Chaoyang District
Beijing 100004
China
Tel: 86-10-6466-0088
Fax: 86-10-6466-1186

CITIC Pacific Limited
Larry Yung Chi-kin
Chairman
Level 35, Two Pacific Place
88 Queensway
Hong Kong
Tel: 852-2820-2111
Fax: 852-2877-2771

Citizen Watch Co., Ltd.
Hiroshi Haruta
President
20/F., Shinjuku Mitsui Bldg.
2-1-1 Nishi-Shinjuku
Shinjuku-Ku
Tokyo 163-04
Japan
Tel: 81-3-3342-1231
Fax: 81-3-3342-1280

City Developments Limited
Kwek Leng Beng
Executive Chairman
36 Robinson Road
#20-01 City House
Singapore 068877
Tel: 65-221-2266
Fax: 65-223-2746

Clarion Co., Ltd.
Ichizo Ishitsubo
President
2-22-3 Shibuya, Shibuya-Ku
Tokyo 150
Japan
Tel: 81-3-3400-1121
Fax: 81-3-3400-8505

Coca-Cola Amatil Limited
N.P. Cole
Managing Director
71 Macquarie Street
Sydney, NSW 2000
Australia
Tel: 61-2-9259-6666
Fax: 61-2-9259-6626

COFCO
Ming Chen Zhou
General Manager
8 Jiangnomen,
Nei Dajie, Beijing 100005
China
Tel: 86-10-6526-8888
Fax: 86-10-6527-8612

Coles Myer Limited
Peter T. Bartels
Managing Director
800 Toorak Road, Tooronga
Victoria 3146
Australia
Tel: 61-3-9829-3111
Fax: 61-3-9829-6787

Comalco Limited
W.T.Palmer
Chief Executive Officer
Level 33, 55 Collins Street
Melbourne
Victoria 3000
Australia
Tel: 61-3-9283-3000
Fax: 61-3-9283-3707

Conagra Holdings (Australia) Pty. Ltd.
Leon Baronet
Managing Director
109 Doherty's Road
Altona
North Victoria 3025
Australia
Tel: 61-3-9360-3200
Fax: 61-3-9360-9632

Consumers Co-Operative Kobe
Shigenori Takemoto
President
1-4 Aoyama, 7-Chome
Shijimi-Cho, Miki City
Hyogo Pref. 673-05
Japan
Tel: 81-794-87-3248
Fax: 81-794-87-3935

Cosmo Oil Co., Ltd.
Keiichiro Okabe
President
1-1-1 Shibaura, Minato-Ku
Tokyo 105
Japan
Tel: 81-3-3798-3211
Fax: 81-3-3798-3411

Cosmo Oil International Pte. Ltd.
Keizo Morikawa
Managing Director
6 Shenton Way
#24-08, DBS Bldg Tower Two
Singapore 068809
Tel: 65-324-3722
Fax: 65-324-1022

CSR Limited
Geoffrey Kells
Managing Director
Level 24, 1 O'Connell Street
Sydney
NSW 2000
Australia
Tel: 61-2-9235-8000
Fax: 61-2-9235-8044

Cycle & Carriage Ltd.
Philip Eng Heng Nee
Group Managing Director
239 Alexandra Road
Singapore 159930
Tel: 65-473-3122
Fax: 65-475-7088

Daelim Industrial Co., Ltd.
Lee Jong-Guk
Chairman
23-9 Yoido-Dong
Youngdungpo-Ku
Seoul
South Korea
Tel: 82-2-368-7114
Fax: 82-2-368-7700

Daewoo Corporation
Kang Byong-Ho
Chairman
541 Namdaemunno 5-Ga
Chung-Gu
Seoul
South Korea
Tel: 82-2-759-2114
Fax: 82-2-753-9489

Daewoo Electronics
Bae Sun-Hun
President
541 Namdaemunno 5-Ga
Chung-Gu
Seoul
South Korea
Tel: 82-2-360-7114
Fax: 82-2-360-7861

Daewoo Heavy Industries Limited
Yune Won-Seok
Chairman
541 Namdaemunno 5-Ga
Chung-Gu
Seoul
South Korea
Tel: 82-2-726-3114/1500
Fax: 82-2-756-2679/4390

Daewoo Motor Company Limited
Kim Tae-Goo
President
199 Chungchun-Dong, Book-Gu
Inchon
South Korea
Tel: 82-32-520-2277
Fax: 82-32-528-7973

Daewoo Motor Sales Corp.
Chung Hae-Young
President
426-1 Chung Chun-Dong
Bupyung-Gu, Inchon
South Korea
Tel: 82-32-510-4321
Fax: 82-42-627-5951

Dai Nippon Construction
Tetsuji Motai
President
1-6-8 Usa Minami, Gifu 500
Japan
Tel: 81-3-3267-7086
Fax: 81-3-3267-7668

Dai Nippon Printing Co., Ltd.
Yoshitoshi Kitajima
President
1-1-1 Ichigaya-Kagacho, Shinjuku-Ku
Tokyo 162-01
Japan
Tel: 81-3-3266-2111
Fax: 81-3-3266-2129

Dai-Dan Co., Ltd.
Setu Sugaya
President
1-9-25 Edobori, Nishi-Ku
Osaka 550
Japan
Tel: 81-6-441-8231
Fax: 81-6-448-5628

Daicel Chemical Industries, Ltd.
Akiro Kojima
President
1 Teppo-Cho
Sakai City, Osaka Pref. 590
Japan
Tel: 81-722-27-3111
Fax: 81-722-27-3000

Daido Kogyo Co., Ltd.
Nobuo Ohba
President
Kogin Bldg
1-11-18, Naka-Ku, Nishiki
Nagoya City 460
Japan
Tel: 81-52-201-4905
Fax: 81-52-201-6120

Daido Steel Co., Ltd.
Kanji Tomita
President
1-11-18 Nishiki, Naka-Ku
Nagoya-Shi 460
Japan
Tel: 81-52-201-5116
Fax: 81-52-201-5754

Daiei, Inc.
Isao Nakauchi
President
4-1-1 Minatojima Nakamachi
Chuo-Ku, Kobe 650
Japan
Tel: 81-78-302-5001
Fax: 81-78-302-5572

Daiei Papers Ltd.
Tatsuyuki Imai
President
6-26 Akashi-Cho
Chuo-Ku
Tokyo 104
Japan
Tel: 81-3-3542-2891
Fax: 81-3-3545-9450

Daifuku Co., Ltd.
Susumu Ito
President
3-2-11 Mitejima
Nishi-Yodogawaku, Osaka 555
Japan
Tel: 81-6-476-2531
Fax: 81-6-476-2567

Daihatsu Motor Co., Ltd.
Iichi Shingu
President
1-1 Daihatsu-Cho, Ikeda City
Osaka 563
Japan
Tel: 81-727-54-3047
Fax: 81-727-53-6880

Daiho Corporation
Kotaro Uchida
President
1-24-4 Shinkawa, Chuo-Ku
Tokyo 104
Japan
Tel: 81-3-3553-4311
Fax: 81-3-3553-4176

Daiichi Pharmaceutical Co., Ltd.
Tadashi Suzuki
President
3-14-10 Nihonbashi, Chuo-Ku
Tokyo 103
Japan
Tel: 81-3-3272-0611
Fax: 81-3-3272-7348

Daiken Corporation
Joji Muguruma
President
2-3-18 Nakanoshima, Kita-Ku
Osaka-Shi 530
Japan
Tel: 81-6-228-3350
Fax: 81-6-228-3535

Daikin Industries, Ltd.
Noriyuki Inoue
President
Umeda Center Bldg.
2-4-12 Nakazaki-Nishi, Kita-Ku
Osaka 530
Japan
Tel: 81-6-373-4351
Fax: 81-6-373-4388

Daiko Advertising Inc.
Takeshi Adachi
President
3-39, 4-Chome, Miyahara
Yodogawa-Ku
Osaka 532
Japan
Tel: 81-6-392-8111
Fax: 81-6-392-8004

Daikuma Co., Ltd.
Shigenori Morita
President
62-1 Yuhigaoka
Hiratsuka-Shi
Kanagawa-Ken 254
Japan
Tel: 81-463-23-6111
Fax: 81-463-23-6129

Daikyo Inc.
Hasegawa Masaharu
President
Sendagaya No. 21 Daikyo Bldg.
4-24-13 Sendagaya
Shibuya-Ku
Tokyo 151
Japan
Tel: 81-3-3475-1111
Fax: 81-3-3479-3727

Daimaru, Inc.
Tsutomu Okuda
President
4-10, 4-Chome, Minamisemba
Chuo-Ku
Osaka
Japan
Tel: 81-6-281-9002
Fax: 81-6-245-1343

Dainichiseika Color & Chemicals Mfg. Co., Ltd.
Osamu Takahashi
President
1-7-6 Bakuro-Cho, Nihonbashi
Chuo-Ku
Tokyo 103
Japan
Tel: 81-3-3662-7111
Fax: 81-3-3669-3936

Dainippon Ink & Chemicals, Incorporated
Takemitsu Takahashi
President
35-38, Sakashita, 3-Chome
Itabashi-Ku
Tokyo 174
Japan
Tel: 81-3-3272-4511
Fax: 81-3-3278-8558

Dainippon Pharmaceutical Co., Ltd.
Takeshi Tomotake
President
2-6-8 Dosho-Machi, Chuo-Ku
Osaka 541
Japan
Tel: 81-6-203-5307
Fax: 81-6-203-6581

Dainippon Screen Mfg. Co., Ltd.
Akira Ishida
President
Tenjinkita-Cho 1-1
Teranouchi-Agaru, 4-Chome
Horikawa-Dori, Kamigyo-Ku
Kyoto 602
Japan
Tel: 81-75-414-7111
Fax: 81-75-451-9603

Daio Paper Corporation
Tamotsu Ohsawa
President
2-7-2 Yaesu, Chuo-Ku
Tokyo 104
Japan
Tel: 81-3-3271-1961
Fax: 81-896-24-3860

Dairy Farm International Holdings Ltd.
Graeme Seabrook
Managing Director
33/F., Windsor House
311 Gloucester Road
Causeway Bay
Hong Kong
Tel: 852-2837-6483
Fax: 852-2576-9734

Daishowa Paper Mfg. Co., Ltd.
Shogo Nakano
President
4-1-1 Imai, Fuji-Shi
Shizuoka-Ken 417
Japan
Tel: 81-545-30-3000
Fax: 81-545-30-3111

Daisue Construction Co., Ltd.
Hiroshi Tsujimori
President
6-8-10 Fukushima, Fukushima-Ku
Osaka 553
Japan
Tel: 81-6-456-3737
Fax: 81-6-456-3802

Daito Gyorui Co., Ltd.
Keiichi Suzuki
President
5-2-1 Tsukiji, Chuo-Ku, Tokyo 104
Japan
Tel: 81-3-5565-8169
Fax: 81-3-3248-2546

Daito Trust Construction Co., Ltd.
Katsumi Tada
President
2-4-1 Shiba-Koen, Minato-Ku
Tokyo 105
Japan
Tel: 81-3-3473-9111
Fax: 81-3-5488-3349

Daiwa Can Company
Hisakazu Yamaguchi
President
2-1-10 Nihonbashi, Chuo-Ku
Tokyo 103
Japan
Tel: 81-3-3272-0561
Fax: 81-3-3281-8167

Daiwa House Industry Co., Ltd.
Nobuyasu Ishibashi
President
1-5-16 Awaza, Nishi-Ku
Osaka 550
Japan
Tel: 81-6-538-5111
Fax: 81-6-532-5806

Davids Limited
Don Bourke
Chairman
46-48 Pyrmont Bridge Road
Pyrmont
NSW 2009
Australia
Tel: 61-2-9298-3222
Fax: 61-2-9298-3200

DDI Corporation
Yusai Okuyama
President
8 Ichibanchou, Chiyoda-Ku
Tokyo 102
Japan
Tel: 81-3-3221-9512
Fax: 81-3-3221-9696

Denki Kagaku Kogyo K.K. (Denka)
Tsuneo Yano
President
Sanshin Bldg., 1-4-1
Yurakucho, Chiyoda-Ku
Tokyo 100
Japan
Tel: 81-3-3507-5071/5055
Fax: 81-3-3507-5059/3508-9479

Denso Corporation
Hiromu Okabe
President
1-1 Showa-Cho
Kariya City, Aichi Pref. 448
Japan
Tel: 81-566-25-5846
Fax: 81-566-25-4537

Dentsu Inc.
Yutaka Narita
President
1 Tsukiji, 1-Chome, Chuo-Ku
Tokyo 104
Japan
Tel: 81-3-5551-5111
Fax: 81-3-5551-2013

Deodeo Corporation
Masataka Kubo
President
2-1-18 Kamiya-Cho, Naka-Ku
Hiroshima-Shi 730
Japan
Tel: 81-82-247-5111
Fax: 81-82-240-1556

Dia Kensetsu Co., Ltd.
Hironori Shimotsu
President
6-28-7 Shinjuku, Shinjuku-Ku
Tokyo 160
Japan
Tel: 81-3-3205-5555
Fax: 81-3-3205-8106

Dong Kuk Steel Mill
Chang Sang-Tae
President
50 Suha-Dong
Chung-Gu, Seoul
South Korea
Tel: 82-2-317-1114
Fax: 82-2-317-1391

Dong-Ah Construction Industrial
Ryu Sung-Yong
President
120-33 Sosomun-Dong
Chung-Gu, Seoul
South Korea
Tel: 82-2-3709-2114
Fax: 82-2-3709-3821

Dongfeng Motors Corporation
Ma Yue
President
Shiyan City, Hubei 442001
China
Tel: 86-719-822-1114
Fax: 86-719-822-1198

Dowa Mining Co., Ltd.
Kenzo Harada
President
1-8-2 Marunouchi
Chiyoda-Ku
Tokyo 100
Japan
Tel: 81-3-3201-1062
Fax: 81-3-3201-1297

Duskin Co., Ltd.
Koji Chiba
President
1-33 Toyotsu-Cho, Suita-Shi
Osaka 564
Japan
Tel: 81-6-821-5006
Fax: 81-6-821-5357

E

East China Electric Power Group Corp.
Qian Zhongwei
General Manager
201 Nanjing East Road
Shanghai 200002
China
Tel: 86-21-6329-0000
Fax: 86-21-6329-0727

East Japan Kiosk Co., Ltd.
Yoshiyuki Yamamoto
President
5-1 Kojimachi, Chiyoda-Ku
Tokyo 102
Japan
Tel: 81-3-5275-6712
Fax: 81-3-5275-6750

East Japan Railway Company
Masatake Matsuda
President
2-2 Yoyogi, 2-Chome, Shibuya-Ku
Tokyo 151
Japan
Tel: 81-3-5334-1309
Fax: 81-3-5334-1297

Ebara Corporation
Shigeru Maeda
President
11-1 Haneda Asahi-cho
Ohta-Ku
Tokyo 144
Japan
Tel: 81-3-3743-6111
Fax: 81-3-3745-3356

Edaran Otomobil Nasional Berhad (EON)
Y. Bhg Dato Seri Yahaya Bin Ahmad
Chairman
Eon Head Office Complex
Jalan Kerjaya
Seksyen Utara Satu
40000 Shah Alam
Selangor Darul Ehsan
Malaysia
Tel: 60-3-703-1111
Fax: 60-3-703-0009

Eisai Co., Ltd.
Haruo Naito
President
4-6-10 Koishikawa
Bunkyo-Ku
Tokyo 112-88
Japan
Tel: 81-3-3817-3700
Fax: 81-3-3811-3305

Electric Power Development Co., Ltd.
Hirosi Sugiyama
President
6-15-1 Ginza Chuo-Ku
Tokyo 104
Japan
Tel: 81-3-3546-2211
Fax: 81-3-3546-9532

Electricity Generating Authority of Thailand
Preecha Chungwatana
Governor
53 Charan Sanit Wong Road
Bang Kruai
Nonthaburi 11130
Thailand
Tel: 662-436-4800
Fax: 662-436-4879

Email Limited
John M. Hanna
Managing Director
Joynton Avenue
Waterloo
NSW 2017
Australia
Tel: 61-2-9690-7333
Fax: 61-2-9699-3190

EnergyAustralia
Ted Woodley
Managing Director
570 George Street
Sydney
NSW 2000
Australia
Tel: 61-2-9269-2172
Fax: 61-2-9269-2830

Epson Hanbai Co., Ltd.
Toshio Kimura
President
11/F., N.S. Bldg.,
2-4-1 Nishi-Shinjuku, Shinjuku-Ku
Tokyo 163-08
Japan
Tel: 81-3-5321-4111
Fax: 81-3-5321-4123

Esso Australia Limited
Charles E. Fields
Chairman & Managing Director
12 Riverside Quay
Southbank
Victoria 3006
Australia
Tel: 61-3-9270-3333
Fax: 61-3-9270-3995

Esso Sekiyu K.K.
W.R.K. Innes
President
5-3-3 Akasaka, Minato-Ku
Tokyo 107
Japan
Tel: 81-3-5561-1000
Fax: 81-3-3584-0388

Esso Standard Thailand Ltd.
David Henry Ledlie
Managing Director
3195/17-29 Rama IV Road
Klongtoey
Bangkok 10110
Thailand
Tel: 662-262-4000
Fax: 662-661-3148

Evergreen Marine Corporation (Taiwan) Ltd.
George Hsu
President
Evergreen Bldg
No.166, Sec. 2
Minsheng East Road
Taipei
Taiwan
Tel: 88-6-2-505-7766
Fax: 88-6-2-505-5256

Ezaki Glico Co., Ltd.
Katsuhisa Ezaki
President
4-6-5 Utajima, Nishiyodogawa-Ku
Osaka 555
Japan
Tel: 81-6-477-8351
Fax: 81-6-477-8250

F.H. Faulding & Co., Ltd.
Edward Twedell
Group Managing Director
115 Sherrif Street
Underdale
South Australia 5032
Australia
Tel: 61-8-8205-6500
Fax: 61-8-8234-5648

Fanuc Limited
Dr. Eng. Seiuemon Inaba
Chairman
3580 Shibokusa, Aza-Komanba
Oshino-Mura, Minamitsuru-Gun
Yamanashi Pref. 401-05
Japan
Tel: 81-555-84-5555
Fax: 81-555-84-5512

Federal Flour Mills Berhad
Oh Siew Nam
Managing Director
16/F., Wisma Jerneh
38 Jalan Sultan Ismail
Kuala Lumpur 50250
Malaysia
Tel: 60-3-242-4077
Fax: 60-3-241-4059

First Pacific Co., Ltd.
Manuel V. Pangilinan
Managing Director
24/F., Two Exchange Square
8 Connaught Place
Central
Hong Kong
Tel: 852-2842-4388
Fax: 852-2845-2943

Fletcher Challenge Limited
Hugh A. Fletcher
Managing Director
Fletcher Challenge House
810 Great South Road
Penrose
Auckland
New Zealand
Tel: 64-9-525-9000
Fax: 64-9-525-9023

Food Corporation of India
Shri K.A. Nambiar
Chairman
16-20 Khadya Sadan
Barakhamba Lane
New Delhi 110001
India
Tel: 91-11-331-6160
Fax: 91-11-331-6873

Foodland Associated Limited
Barry Alty
Managing Director
218 Bannister Road
Canning Vale
Western Australia 6155
Australia
Tel: 61-8-9311-6000
Fax: 61-8-9311-6013

Ford Lio Ho Motor Company
Michael R. McKelvie
President
705 Chunghwa Road
Section 1, Chungli Taoyuan 320
Taiwan
Tel: 88-6-3-455-3131
Fax: 88-6-3-455-1474

Ford Motor Company of Australia Ltd.
David Morgan
President
1735 Sydney Road
Campbellfield
Victoria 3061
Australia
Tel: 61-3-9359-8211
Fax: 61-3-9359-8266

Formosa Chemicals & Fibre Corporation
Yeong Ching-Wang
Chairman
201 Tung Hwa North Road
Taipei 10591
Taiwan
Tel: 88-6-2-712-2211
Fax: 88-6-2-713-3229

Formosa Plastics Corporation
Wang Yung-Ching
Chairman
201 Tung Hwa North Road
Taipei 10591
Taiwan
Tel: 88-6-2-712-2211
Fax: 88-6-2-717-5287

Foster's Brewing Group Limited
E.T. Kunkel
President
77 Southbank Boulevard
Southbank
Melbourne
Victoria 3006
Australia
Tel: 61-3-9633-2000
Fax: 61-3-9633-2002

Franklins Holdings Limited
Don Fraser
Managing Director
62 Hume Highway
Chullora
NSW 2190
Australia
Tel: 61-2-9722-1400
Fax: 61-2-9722-1733

Fraser and Neave Limited
Michael Fam
Executive Chairman
438 Alexandra Road
21/F., Alexandra Point
Singapore 119958
Tel: 65-272-9488
Fax: 65-271-0811

Fudo Construction Co., Ltd.
Masanobu Ichiyoshi
President
2-1 Taito, 1-Chome, Taito-Ku
Tokyo
Japan
Tel: 81-3-3837-6038
Fax: 81-3-3831-9455

Fuji Co., Ltd.
Norikuni Tokito
President
1-2-1 Miyanishi
Matsuyama City 790,
Japan
Tel: 81-89-926-7111
Fax: 81-89-925-6981

Fuji Denki Reiki Co., Ltd.
Tatsuo Komine
President
6-15-12 Soto-Kanda
Chiyoda-Ku, Tokyo 101
Japan
Tel: 81-3-3832-1251
Fax: 81-3-3832-7380

Fuji Electric Co., Ltd.
Yoshihiko Nakazato
President
Shin Yurakucho Bldg.
1-12-1 Yuraku-Cho
Chiyoda-Ku, Tokyo 100
Japan
Tel: 81-3-3211-7111
Fax: 81-3-3215-8321

Fuji Heavy Industries, Ltd.
Takeshi Tanaka
President
1-7-2 Nishi-Shinjuku
Shinjuku-Ku, Tokyo 160
Japan
Tel: 81-3-3347-2111
Fax: 81-3-3347-2338

Fuji Oil Co., Ltd.
Nobutaka Kengaku
President
8-1 Akashi-Cho
Chuo-Ku, Tokyo 104
Japan
Tel: 81-3-3547-0011
Fax: 81-3-3547-0051

Fuji Photo Film Co., Ltd.
Masayuki Muneyuki
President
2-26-30 Nishiazabu
Minato-Ku, Tokyo 106
Japan
Tel: 81-3-3406-2111
Fax: 81-3-3406-2193

Fuji Television Network, Inc.
Hisashi Hieda
President
2-4-8 Daiba, Minato-Ku
Tokyo 137-88
Japan
Tel: 81-3-5500-8888
Fax: 81-3-5500-8027

Fuji Xerox Co., Ltd.
Akira Miyahara
President
2-17-22 Akasaka, Minato-Ku
Tokyo 107
Japan
Tel: 81-3-3585-3211
Fax: 81-3-3505-1609

Fujikura Limited
Shigenobu Tanaka
President
1-5-1 Kiba, Koto-Ku
Tokyo 135
Japan
Tel: 81-3-5606-1111
Fax: 81-3-5606-1532

Fujisash Co., Ltd.
Shigeru Morita
President
135 Nakamaruko, Nakahara-Ku
Kawasaki-Shi 211
Japan
Tel: 81-44-435-3977
Fax: 81-44-422-1183

Fujisawa Pharmaceutical Co., Ltd.
Akira Fujiyawa
President
4-7 Doshomachi, 3-Chome
Chuo-Ku, Osaka 541
Japan
Tel: 81-6-206-7857
Fax: 81-6-206-5016

Fujita Corporation
Kazunori Fujita
President
4-6-15 Sendagaya, Shibuya-Ku
Tokyo 151
Japan
Tel: 81-3-3402-1911
Fax: 81-3-3796-2346

Fujitsu Business Systems Ltd.
Mikio Ohtsuki
President
1-7-27 Kouraku, Bunkyo-Ku
Tokyo
Japan
Tel: 81-3-5804-8111
Fax: 81-3-5804-8136

Fujitsu General Ltd.
Tuguo Yagi
President
1116 Suenaga, Takatsu-Ku
Kawasaki 213,
Japan
Tel: 81-44-866-1716
Fax: 81-44-861-7875

Fujitsu Ltd.
Tadashi Sekizawa
President
6-1 Marunouchi, 1-Chome
Chiyoda-Ku, Tokyo 100
Japan
Tel: 81-3-3216-3211
Fax: 81-3-3213-7174

Fukuda Corporation
Minoru Fukuda
President
3-10 Ichibanbori-Dori-Machi
Niigata City, Niigata Pref. 951
Japan
Tel: 81-25-266-9121
Fax: 81-25-266-5591

Fukujin Co., Ltd.
Kunio Fukujin
President
1-12-1 Uchi-Kanda
Chiyoda-Ku, Tokyo 101
Japan
Tel: 81-3-3292-3331
Fax: 81-3-3292-3339

Fukuyama Transporting Co., Ltd.
Shigehiro Komaru
President
4-20-1 Higashi, Fukazu-Cho
Fukuyama City
Hiroshima Pref. 721
Japan
Tel: 81-849-24-2000
Fax: 81-849-31-4865

Furukawa Co., Ltd.
Akitaka Nakai
President
2-6-1 Marunouchi
Chiyoda-Ku
Tokyo 100
Japan
Tel: 81-3-3212-6561
Fax: 81-3-3287-0696

Furukawa Electric Co., Ltd.
Junnosuke Furukawa
President
2-6-1 Marunouchi
Chiyoda-Ku
Tokyo 100
Japan
Tel: 81-3-3286-3001
Fax: 81-3-3286-3694

Fushun Petrochemical Company
Zhong-Cheng Sun
Chief Executive
3 East 2nd Street
Fushun
Liaoning
China
Tel: 86-413-225-777
Fax: 86-413-221-115

Futuris Corporation Ltd.
Alan Newman
Chief Executive Officer
Level 1, 66 Kings Park Road
West Perth
Western Australia 6005
Australia
Tel: 61-8-9481-1433
Fax: 61-8-9324-1294

G

Gakken Co., Ltd.
Toshiro Komatsu
President
4-40-5 Kami-Ikedai, Ohta-Ku
Tokyo 145
Japan
Tel: 81-3-3726-8120
Fax: 81-3-3726-8859

Garuda Indonesia
Soe Pandi
President
15/F., Garuda Indonesia Bldg.
13, Jalan Merdeka Selatan
Jakarta 10110
Indonesia
Tel: 62-21-231-1801
Fax: 62-21-365-986

Gas Authority of India Ltd.
C.R. Prasad
Managing Director
16 Bikaji Cama Place
New Delhi 110066
India
Tel: 91-11-610-2077
Fax: 91-11-610-3055

General Sekiyu K.K.
Masayoshi Okai
President
2-8-6 Nishi-Shinbashi
Minato-Ku
Tokyo 105
Japan
Tel: 81-3-3595-8300
Fax: 81-3-3595-8316

GMH Automotive Limited
James R. Wiemels
Chairman & Managing Director
241 Salmon Street
Port Melbourne
Victoria 3207
Australia
Tel: 61-3-9647-1111
Fax: 61-3-9647-2550

Goodman Fielder Limited
David L.G. Hearn
Chief Executive Officer
Level 42, Grosvenor Place
225 George Street
Sydney
NSW 2000
Australia
Tel: 61-2-9258-4000
Fax: 61-2-9247-3145

Gunze Limited
Masashi Nagaoka
President
Osakadaiichi Bldg
1-8-17 Umeda, Kita-Ku
Osaka 530
Japan
Tel: 81-6-348-1313
Fax: 81-6-348-4813

Gunze Sangyo, Inc.
Yoshiaki Shikata
President
3-1 Kudanminani, 2-Chome
Chiyoda-Ku
Tokyo 102
Japan
Tel: 81-3-5211-1800
Fax: 81-3-5211-1900

H

Hakuhodo Incorporated
Takashi Shoji
President
4-1 Shibaura, 3-Chome
Minato-Ku
Tokyo 108
Japan
Tel: 81-3-5446-6161
Fax: 81-3-5446-6166

Hanjin Shipping Company
Sooho Cho
President
25-11 Yoido-Dong
Youngdeungpo-Ku 150-010
Seoul
South Korea
Tel: 82-2-3770-6114
Fax: 82-2-3770-6759

Hankook Tire Mfg. Co., Ltd.
Hong Geun-Hi
President
647-15 Yoksam-Dong
Kangnam-Gu
Seoul
South Korea
Tel: 82-2-222-1000
Fax: 82-2-222-1100

Hankyu Corporation
Motohiro Sugai
President
1-16-1 Shibata Kita-Ku
Osaka 530
Japan
Tel: 81-6-373-5085
Fax: 81-6-373-5670

Hankyu Department Stores, Inc.
Hidesaburo Matsuda
President
8-7 Kakuda-Cho, Kita-Ku
Osaka 530
Japan
Tel: 81-6-361-1381
Fax: 81-6-367-8145

Hanshin Construction
Song Chol-Ho
President
65-32 Jamwon-Dong, Socho-Gu
Seoul
South Korea
Tel: 82-2-590-7114
Fax: 82-2-593-9007

Hanwa Co., Ltd.
Shuji Kita
President
1-13-10 Tsukiji, Chuo-Ku
Tokyo 104
Japan
Tel: 81-3-3544-2171
Fax: 81-3-3544-2351

Hanwha Chemical Corporation
Lee Chong-Hak
President
1 Changgyo-Dong, Chung-Gu
Seoul
South Korea
Tel: 82-2-729-2700
Fax: 82-2-729-3000

Hanwha Energy
U. Wan-Sik
President
1 Changgyo-Dong
Chung-Gu, Seoul
South Korea
Tel: 82-2-729-2019
Fax: 82-2-729-2020

Haseko Corporation
Kohei Goda
President
2-32-1 Shiba
Minato-Ku
Tokyo 105
Japan
Tel: 81-3-3456-3900
Fax: 81-3-3456-6399

Hazama Corporation
Fumiya Yamato
President
5-8 Kita-Aoyama, 2-Chome
Minato-Ku
Tokyo 107
Japan
Tel: 81-3-3405-1111
Fax: 81-3-3405-1878

Heiwado Co., Ltd.
Hirakazu Natsuhara
President
31 Koizumi-Cho
Hikone-Shi
Shiga-Ken 522
Japan
Tel: 81-749-23-3111
Fax: 81-749-24-3005

Henderson Land Development Co. Ltd.
Lee Shau-kee
Chairman & Managing Director
6/F., World-Wide House
19 Des Voeux Road Central
Hong Kong
Tel: 852-2826-5222
Fax: 852-2810-6292

Hewlett-Packard Japan, Ltd.
Katsuto Kohtani
President
3-29-21 Takaido-Higashi
Suginami-Ku
Tokyo 168
Japan
Tel: 81-3-3331-6111
Fax: 81-3-3335-1478

Hewlett-Packard, Singapore (Private) Limited
Chaeh Kean Huat
Managing Director
450 Alexandra Road
Singapore 119960
Tel: 65-275-3888
Fax: 65-275-6839

Hikawa Shoji Kaisha, Ltd.
Michio Shiota
President
1-26-2 Shinkawa-NS Bldg.
Shinkawa, Chuo-Ku
Tokyo
Japan
Tel: 81-3-5541-3300
Fax: 81-3-5541-3271

Hindustan Lever Limited
S.M. Datta
Chairman
Hindustan Lever House
165/166 Backbay Reclamation
Mumbai 400 020
India
Tel: 91-22-287-0622/285-5898
Fax: 91-22-285-0552

Hindustan Petroleum Corporation Ltd.
H.L. Zutshi
Chairman & Managing Director
17 Jamshedji Tata Road
Mumbai 400 020
India
Tel: 91-22-202-6151
Fax: 91-22-287-2992

Hino Motor Sales, Ltd.
Akira Takeda
President
4-11-3 Shiba
Minato-Ku
Tokyo 108
Japan
Tel: 81-3-3456-8840
Fax: 81-3-3453-1909

Hino Motors, Ltd.
Hiroshi Yuasa
President
3-1-1 Hinodai, Hino-Shi
Tokyo 191
Japan
Tel: 81-425-86-5011
Fax: 81-425-86-5038

Hitachi Asia (Pte.) Limited
Akira Yukawa
Managing Director
16 Collyer Quay
21/F., Hitachi Tower
Singapore 049318
Tel: 65-535-0533
Fax: 65-535-1533

Hitachi Building Systems E & S Co., Ltd.
Toshihiko Fukayama
President
1-6 Kanda-Nishikicho
Chiyoda-Ku
Tokyo 101
Japan
Tel: 81-3-3295-1211
Fax: 81-3-3219-9191

Hitachi Cable, Ltd.
Seiji Hara
President
2-1-2 Chiyoda Bldg.
Marunouchi
Chiyoda-Ku
Tokyo 100
Japan
Tel: 81-3-5252-3261
Fax: 81-3-3214-5779

Hitachi Chemical Co., Ltd.
Takeshi Tanno
President
2-1-1 Nishi-Shinjuku, Shinjuku-Ku
Tokyo 163-04
Japan
Tel: 81-3-3346-3111
Fax: 81-3-3346-2977

Hitachi Construction Machinery Co., Ltd.
Ryuichi Seguchi
President
6-2 Nippon Bldg., 2-Chome
Otemachi, Chiyoda-Ku
Tokyo 100
Japan
Tel: 81-3-3245-6390
Fax: 81-3-3246-2609

Hitachi Electronics Services Co., Ltd.
Yasuhiko Tani
President
504-2 Shinano-Cho
Totsuka-Ku
Yokohama City 244
Japan
Tel: 81-45-822-1111
Fax: 81-45-824-0796

Hitachi Koki Co., Ltd.
Tadashi Onose
President
6-2 Nippon Bldg., 2-Chome
Otemachi, Chiyoda-Ku
Tokyo 100
Japan
Tel: 81-3-3270-6130
Fax: 81-3-3270-2847

Hitachi Ltd.
Tsutomu Kanai
President
6 Kanda-Surugadai, 4-Chome
Chiyoda-Ku
Tokyo 101
Japan
Tel: 81-3-3258-1111
Fax: 81-3-3258-5480

Hitachi Maxell, Ltd.
Toori Sato
President
1-1-88 Ushitora
Ibaraki City
Osaka Pref. 567
Japan
Tel: 81-726-23-8101
Fax: 81-726-26-0325

Hitachi Metals, Ltd.
Tetsuya Eda
President
1-2 Chiyoda Bldg.
2-Chome, Marunouchi
Chiyoda-Ku
Tokyo 100
Japan
Tel: 81-3-3284-4511
Fax: 81-3-3287-1956

Hitachi Plant Engineering & Construction Co., Ltd.
Masataka Nishi
President & Representative Director
1-14 Uchikanda, 1-Chome
Chiyoda-Ku
Tokyo 101
Japan
Tel: 81-3-3292-8111
Fax: 81-3-3292-8401

Hitachi Transport System, Ltd.
Hisanobu Naka
President
7-2-18, Toyo Koto-Ku
Tokyo 135
Japan
Tel: 81-3-5634-0333
Fax: 81-3-5634-0299

Hitachi Zosen Corporation
Iso Minami
President
3-28 Nishikujo, 5-Chome
Konohana-Ku
Osaka 554
Japan
Tel: 81-6-466-7500
Fax: 81-6-466-7576/7572

Hokkaido Electric Power Co., Inc.
Seiji Izumi
President
2 Higashi, 1-Chome, Ohdori
Chuo-Ku
Sapporo 060-91
Japan
Tel: 81-11-251-1111
Fax: 81-11-251-0329

Hokuriku Electric Power Co., Inc.
Keizo Yamada
President
15-1 Ushijima-Cho
Toyama-Shi 930
Japan
Tel: 81-764-41-2511
Fax: 81-764-33-9985

Honda Motor Co., Ltd.
Nobuhiko Kawamoto
President & Representative Director
2-1-1-Chome
Minami-Aoyama
Minato-Ku
Tokyo 107
Japan
Tel: 81-3-3423-1111
Fax: 81-3-3423-2442

Hong Leong Investment Holdings Pte. Ltd.
Kwek Leng Peck
Executive Director
16 Raffles Quay
26/F., Hong Leong Bldg.
Singapore 048581
Tel: 65-220-8411
Fax: 65-224-6771

Hongkong Telecom
Linus W.L. Cheung
Chief Executive
39/F., Hongkong Telecom Tower
Taikoo Place, 979 Kings Road
Quarry Bay
Hong Kong
Tel: 852-2888-2888
Fax: 852-2877-8877

Hotai Motor Co. Ltd.
Y.H. Su
Chairman
8-13/F., 121 Sung Chiang Road
Taipei
Taiwan
Tel: 88-6-2-506-2121
Fax: 88-6-2-509-5521

House Foods Corporation
Kunihiko Otsuka
President
1-5-7 Mikuriya-Sakaemachi
Higashi, Osaka City
Osaka Pref. 577
Japan
Tel: 81-6-788-1231
Fax: 81-6-788-1271

Howard Smith Limited
Dr. Ken Moss
Managing Director
Level 22, 1 York Street
Sydney
NSW 2000
Australia
Tel: 61-2-9230-1777
Fax: 61-2-9251-1190

Hoya Corporation
Mamoru Yamanaka
President
7-5 Naka-Ochiai, 2-Chome
Shinjuku-Ku
Tokyo 161
Japan
Tel: 81-3-3952-1151
Fax: 81-3-3952-1314

Hung Kuk Sang Sa Company Limited
Suh Jung-Bo
President
948-1 Daichi-3 Dong
Kangnam-Ku
Seoul
South Korea
Tel: 82-2-222-0114
Fax: 82-2-222-0115

Hutchison Whampoa Limited
Li Ka-shing
Chairman
22/F., Hutchison House
10 Harcourt Road
Central
Hong Kong
Tel: 852-2523-0161
Fax: 852-2810-0705

Hyosung Corporation
Won Mu-Hyon
President
21-1 Sosomun-Dong, Chung-Gu
Seoul
South Korea
Tel: 82-2-3707-1114
Fax: 82-2-754-9983

Hyosung T.& C. Co.
Kim In-Hwan
President
450 Kongdok-Dong, Mapo
Mapo-Gu
Seoul
South Korea
Tel: 82-2-707-7000
Fax: 82-2-707-3155

Hyundai Corporation
Park Se-Yong
President
140-2 Hyundai Bldg., Kye-Dong
Chongro-Ku
Seoul 110-793
South Korea
Tel: 82-2-746-1172
Fax: 82-2-746-1092

Hyundai Electronics Industries Co.
Kim Ju-Yong
President
San 136-1, Ami-Ri, Boobal-Up
Ichon-Gun, Kyunggi
South Korea
Tel: 82-336-30-4114
Fax: 82-2-741-0737

Hyundai Engineering & Construction Co., Ltd.
Chung Mong-Hun
Representative Director & Chairman
140-2 Kye-Dong, Chongro-Ku
Seoul
South Korea
Tel: 82-2-746-1114
Fax: 82-2-743-8963

Hyundai Heavy Industries Co.
Kim Jung-Kook
President
1 Jonha-Dong
Dong-Gu
Ulsan-Shi, Kyungnam
South Korea
Tel: 82-522-30-2114
Fax: 82-522-34-3470

Hyundai Ind. Devel. & Const. Co.
Ryu In-Gyun
President
27-8 Chamwon-Dong
Socho-Gu
Seoul
South Korea
Tel: 82-2-519-9114
Fax: 82-2-540-0740

Hyundai Merchant Marine Co., Ltd.
Park Se-Yong
President
96 Mugyo Hyundai Bldg.
Mugyo-Dong, Chung-Gu
Seoul
South Korea
Tel: 82-2-3706-5114
Fax: 82-2-775-8788

Hyundai Motor Company
Park Byong-Jae
President
140-2 Kye-Dong
Chongro-Gu
Seoul
South Korea
Tel: 82-2-746-1114
Fax: 82-2-741-0470

Hyundai Motor Service Company
Yang Rai-Cho
President
113-25, 4-Ka, Wonhyo-Ro
Yongsan-Ku
Seoul 140-711
South Korea
Tel: 82-2-717-6111
Fax: 82-2-715-8265

Hyundai Oil Refinery Co. Ltd.
Chung Mong-Hyuck
President
Choong-Nam, Suh-San Shi
Dae-San Ub, Dae-Joong-Ri 640-6
South Korea
Tel: 82-455-60-5114
Fax: 82-455-60-5111

Hyundai Precision & Industry
Yu Chol-Gin
President
140-2 Kye-Dong, Chongno-Gu
Seoul
South Korea
Tel: 82-2-746-1114
Fax: 82-2-741-4244

IBM Australia Limited
Bob Savage
Chairman
2 Coonara Avenue
West Pennant Hills
NSW 2125
Australia
Tel: 61-2-9354-4000
Fax: 61-2-9354-7766

IBM Japan Ltd.
Kakutaro Kitashiro
President
3-2-12 Roppongi, Minato-Ku
Tokyo 106, Japan
Tel: 81-3-3586-1111
Fax: 81-3-3589-4645

ICI Australia Limited
Phil Weickhardt
Managing Director
1 Nicholson Street, Melbourne
Victoria 3000
Australia
Tel: 61-3-9665-7111
Fax: 61-3-9665-7937

Idemitsu International (Asia) Pte. Ltd.
Mr. Zenichi Suda
Managing Director
16 Raffles Quay #31-01
Hong Leong Bldg.
Singapore 048581
Tel: 65-222-6477
Fax: 65-224-0508

Idemitsu Kosan Co., Ltd.
Yuji Idemitsu
President
3-1-1 Marunouchi
Chiyoda-Ku, Tokyo 100
Japan
Tel: 81-3-3213-3115
Fax: 81-3-3213-9354

Idemitsu Petrochemical Co., Ltd.
Eijiro Kono
President
Idemitsu Mita Bldg.
5-6-1 Shiba, Minato-Ku, Tokyo 108
Japan
Tel: 81-3-3457-8610
Fax: 81-3-3457-8657

IKKO
Keiko Yano
President
Ikkoh Park Sakae Bldg.
1-9-26 Higashisakura
Higashi-Ku
Nagoya-Shi 461
Japan
Tel: 81-52-962-3071
Fax: 81-52-951-4619

Inaba Denkisangyo Co., Ltd.
Yasuo Inaba
President
1-6-4 Kyomachibori, Nishi-Ku
Osaka 550
Japan
Tel: 81-6-444-1781
Fax: 81-6-449-0880

Inabata & Co., Ltd.
Katsuo Inabata
President
1-15-14 Minami-Senba, Chuo-Ku
Osaka-Shi 542
Japan
Tel: 81-6-267-6051
Fax: 81-6-267-6043

Inageya Co., Ltd.
Seiji Sawatari
President
6-1-1 Sakae-Cho
Tachikawa City
Tokyo 190
Japan
Tel: 81-425-37-5111
Fax: 81-425-37-5355

Inax Corporation
Chikahisa Mizutani
President
5-1 Honmachi, Koie
Tokoname City
Aichi Pref. 479
Japan
Tel: 81-569-35-2700
Fax: 81-569-35-5813/34-2045

Inchon Iron & Steel
Paek Chang-Gi
President
1 Songhyun-Dong
Tong-Gu, Inchon
South Korea
Tel: 82-32-760-2114
Fax: 82-32-763-5046

Indian Oil Corporation Limited
R.K. Narang
Chairman
Scope Complex, Core-2
7 Institutional Area, Lodhi Rd
New Delhi 110 003
India
Tel: 91-11-436-0243
Fax: 91-11-436-0822

Inoac Corporation
Soichi Inoue
President
2-13-4 Meieki-Minami
Nakamura-Ku
Nagoya-Shi 450
Japan
Tel: 81-52-581-1086
Fax: 81-52-581-4726

Iseki & Co., Ltd.
Yukiji Horie
President
5-3-14 Nishinippori
Arakawa-Ku
Tokyo 116
Japan
Tel: 81-3-5604-7602
Fax: 81-3-5604-7701/7707

Isetan Co., Ltd.
Kazumasa Koshit
President
14-1 Shinjuku, 3-Chome
Shinjuku-Ku
Tokyo 160
Japan
Tel: 81-3-3352-1111
Fax: 81-3-5273-5321

Ishikawajima-Harima Heavy Industries Co., Ltd.
Toshifumi Takei
President
Shin Otemachi Bldg.
2-2-1 Otemachi
Chiyoda-Ku
Tokyo 100
Japan
Tel: 81-3-3244-5111
Fax: 81-3-3244-5131

Isuzu Motors Limited
Kazuhira Seki
President
6-26-1 Minami-Oi
Shinagawa-Ku
Tokyo 140
Japan
Tel: 81-3-5471-1111
Fax: 81-3-5471-1043

ITC Limited
Yogesh Chander Deveshwar
Chairman
Virginia House
37 Chowringhee
Calcutta 700 071
India
Tel: 91-33-246-9373/226-5337
Fax: 91-33-245-2257

Ito-Yokado Co., Ltd.
Toshifumi Suzuki
President
1-4 Shibakoen, 4-Chome
Minato-Ku
Tokyo 105
Japan
Tel: 81-3-3459-2111
Fax: 81-3-3434-8378

Itochu Australia Limited
Hidekazu Suzaki
Managing Director
Level 29, Grosvenor Place
225 George Street
Sydney
NSW 2000
Australia
Tel: 61-2-9239-1500
Fax: 61-2-9241-3955

Itochu Corporation
Minoru Murofushi
President
2-5-1 Kita-Aoyama
Minato-Ku
Tokyo 107-77
Japan
Tel: 81-3-3497-2121
Fax: 81-3-3497-7296

Itochu Fuel Corporation
Hideo Matsumura
President
1-24-1 Meguro
Meguro-Ku
Tokyo
Japan
Tel: 81-3-5436-8200
Fax: 81-3-5436-8227

Itochu Kenzai Corporation
Yasuhiro Miya
President
6-2, 3-Chome, Honmachi
Nihonbashi
Chuo-Ku
Tokyo 103
Japan
Tel: 81-3-3661-3281
Fax: 81-3-5644-7847

Itochu Petroleum Co. (S) Pte. Ltd.
Junji Taniuchi
Managing Director
9 Raffles Place
48-01 Republic Plaza
Singapore 048619
Tel: 65-230-0695
Fax: 65-532-3809

Itochu Shokuhin Co., Ltd.
Ozaki Hiromu
President
2-1-6 Kouraibashi
Chuo-Ku
Osaka-Shi 541
Japan
Tel: 81-6-204-5901/ 204-5900
Fax: 81-6-204-5970

Itoham Foods Inc.
Kenichi Ito
President
4-27 Takahata-Cho
Nishinomiya City, Hyogo Pref. 663
Japan
Tel: 81-798-66-1231
Fax: 81-798-64-1140

Itokin Co., Ltd.
Koichi Tsujimura
President
2-4-25 Kyutaro-Machi
Chuo-Ku, Osaka 541
Japan
Tel: 81-6-262-2345
Fax: 81-3-3746-0484

Iwatani International Corporation
Koji Saito
President
3-4-8 Honmachi
Chuo-Ku, Osaka 541
Japan
Tel: 81-6-267-3131
Fax: 81-3-3555-5876

Izumi Co., Ltd.
Yasuaki Yamanishi
President
2-22 Kyobashi-Cho, Minami-Ku
Hiroshima-Shi 732
Japan
Tel: 81-82-264-3211
Fax: 81-82-261-5895

Izumiya Co., Ltd.
Akio Wada
President
1-4-4 Hanazono-Minami
Nishinari-Ku, Osaka 557
Japan
Tel: 81-6-657-3355
Fax: 81-6-657-3398

J

James Hardie Industries Limited
R. Keith Barton
Managing Director
9/F., James Hardie House
65 York Street
Sydney, NSW 2000
Australia
Tel: 61-2-9290-5333
Fax: 61-2-9262-4394

Japan Air System Co., Ltd.
Hiromi Funabiki
President
37 Mori Bldg.
3-5-1 Toranomon
Minato-Ku
Tokyo 105
Japan
Tel: 81-3-5473-4012
Fax: 81-3-5472-7760

Japan Airlines Co., Ltd.
Akira Kondo
President
4-11 Higashi-Shinagawa, 2-Chome
Shinagawa-Ku
Tokyo 140
Japan
Tel: 81-3-5460-3191
Fax: 81-3-5460-5929

Japan Atomic Power Company
Takeshi Abiru
President
Otemachi Bldg.
1-6-1 Otemachi
Chiyoda-Ku
Tokyo 100
Japan
Tel: 81-3-3201-6631
Fax: 81-3-3215-2067

Japan Energy Corporation
Akihiko Nomiyama
President
2-10-1 Toranomon
Minato-Ku
Tokyo 105
Japan
Tel: 81-3-5573-6100
Fax: 81-3-5573-6784

Japan Freight Railway Company
Yoshio Kaneda
President
3-19 Koura Ku, 2-Chome
Bunkyou-Ku
Tokyo 112
Japan
Tel: 81-3-3816-9700
Fax: 81-3-3816-9720

Japan Oil Development Co., Ltd.
Haruyo Matsubara
President
Yamato Life Insurance Bldg.
1-1-7 Uchisaiwai-Cho
Chiyoda-Ku
Tokyo 100
Japan
Tel: 81-3-3508-5521
Fax: 81-3-3508-5619

Japan Pulp & Paper Co., Ltd.
Kyoichi Hirato
President
6-11 Nihonbashi
Hongoku-Cho, 4-Chome
Chuo-Ku
Tokyo 103
Japan
Tel: 81-3-3270-1311
Fax: 81-3-5201-6352

Japan Radio Co., Ltd.
Hiroshi Yokomizo
President
2-17-22 Akasaka, Minato-Ku
Tokyo 107
Japan
Tel: 81-3-3584-8836
Fax: 81-3-3584-8878

Japan Steel Works, Ltd.
Keizo Ohnishi
President
1-1-2 Yuraku-Cho
Chiyoda-Ku, Tokyo 100
Japan
Tel: 81-3-3501-6111
Fax: 81-3-3595-4629

Japan Synthetic Rubber Co., Ltd.
Eiichi Matsumoto
President
2-11-24 Tsukiji, Chuo-Ku
Tokyo 104
Japan
Tel: 81-3-5565-6500
Fax: 81-3-5565-6630

Japan Telecom Co., Ltd.
Koichi Sakata
President
4-7-1 Hatcho-Bori
Chuo-Ku, Tokyo 104
Japan
Tel: 81-3-5540-8016
Fax: 81-3-5543-1968

Japan Tobacco Inc.
Masaru Mizuno
President
2-1 Toranomon, 2-Chome
Minato-Ku
Tokyo 105
Japan
Tel: 81-3-3582-3111
Fax: 81-3-5572-1441

Japan Travel Bureau, Inc.
Ryuji Funayama
President
1-6-4 Marunouchi
Chiyoda-Ku, Tokyo 100
Japan
Tel: 81-3-3284-7046/7502
Fax: 81-3-3284-7504

Jardine International Motors Holdings Limited
Peter T. Ward
Chief Executive
1/F., Bonaventure House
91 Leighton Road
Causeway Bay
Hong Kong
Tel: 852-2895-7288
Fax: 852-2890-7017

Jardine Matheson Holdings Limited
Henry Keswick
Chairman
48/F., Jardine House
Connaught Place
Central
Hong Kong
Tel: 852-2843-8388
Fax: 852-2845-9005

Jardine Pacific Limited
Blair Pickerell
Managing Director
25/F., Devon House
Taikoo Place
Quarry Bay, 979 Kings Road
Hong Kong
Tel: 852-2579-2888
Fax: 852-2856-9868

Jatco Corporation
Kenichi Sasaki
President
700-1 Aza-Kamoda Imaizumi
Fuji-Shi
Shizuoka 417
Japan
Tel: 81-545-51-0047
Fax: 81-545-52-6944

JDC Corporation
Akihiro Tsujioka
President
4-9-9 Akasaka, Minato-Ku
Tokyo 107
Japan
Tel: 81-3-5410-5850
Fax: 81-3-3405-0185

JGC Corporation
Yoshihiro Shigehisa
President
2-2-1 Ohtemachi
Chiyoda-Ku
Tokyo 100
Japan
Tel: 81-3-3279-5441
Fax: 81-3-3273-8047

Jiangsu Supply & Marketing Co-Op. (Group) Gen. Corp.
Zhou Xu-De
General Manager
101 Zhong-Shan-Bei Lu
Nanjing
Jiangsu
China
Tel: 86-25-330-0580
Fax: 86-25-330-5259

Joshin Denki Co., Ltd.
Yoshiaki Ueda
President
1-6-5 Nipponbashi-Nishi
Naniwa-Ku
Osaka 556
Japan
Tel: 81-6-631-1161
Fax: 81-6-649-7557

JS Corporation
Shigefumi Ito
President
1-9 Kanda, Nishiki-Cho
Chiyoda-Ku
Tokyo 101
Japan
Tel: 81-3-3294-3381
Fax: 81-3-3294-7880

Jusco Co., Ltd.
Motoya Okada
President
1-5-1 Nakase, Mihama-Ku
Chiba 261
Japan
Tel: 81-43-212-6000
Fax: 81-43-212-6809

Kajima Corporation
Umeda Sadao
President
1-2-7 Moto-Akasaka, Minato-Ku
Tokyo 107
Japan
Tel: 81-3-3404-3311
Fax: 81-3-3470-1444/5

Kajima Road Co., Ltd.
Atsushi Seki
President
Koraku Kajima Bldg.
1-7-27 Koraku, Bunkyo-Ku
Tokyo 102, Japan
Tel: 81-3-5802-8000
Fax: 81-3-5802-8017

Kamei Corporation
Shogo Kamei
President
3-1-18 Kokubun-Cho, Aoba-Ku
Sendai-Shi 980
Japan
Tel: 81-22-264-6111
Fax: 81-22-264-6020

Kamigumi Co., Ltd.
Mutsumi Ozaki
President
4-1-11 Hamabe-Dori, Chuo-Ku
Kobe 651
Japan
Tel: 81-78-271-5110
Fax: 81-78-271-5210

Kanden Kogyo, Incorporated
Mikio Kitada
President
2-9-18 Honjo Higashi, Kita-Ku
Osaka-Shi 531
Japan
Tel: 81-6-372-1151
Fax: 81-6-354-7622

Kandenko Co., Ltd.
Satoshi Hoshino
President
4-8-33 Shibaura, Minato-Ku
Tokyo 108
Japan
Tel: 81-3-5476-2111
Fax: 81-3-5476-3454

Kanebo, Ltd.
Soichi Ishihara
President
1-5-90 Tomobuchi-Cho
Miyakojima-Ku
Osaka 534
Japan
Tel: 81-6-922-8151
Fax: 81-6-922-8093

Kaneka Corporation
Takeshi Furuta
President
3-2-4 Nakanoshima, Kita-Ku
Osaka 530
Japan
Tel: 81-6-226-5050
Fax: 81-6-226-5037

Kanematsu Corporation
Masao Yosomiya
President
Seavans North, 2-1, Shibaura
1-Chome
Minato-Ku
Tokyo 105-05
Japan
Tel: 81-3-5440-8111
Fax: 81-3-5440-6500

Kansai Electric Power Co., Inc.
Yoshihisa Akiyama
President
3-3-22 Nakanoshima, Kita-Ku
Osaka 530-70
Japan
Tel: 81-6-441-8821
Fax: 81-6-441-0569

Kansai Paint Co., Ltd.
Yoshio Sasaki
President
3-6 Fushimi-Machi, 4-Chome
Chuo-Ku
Osaka 541
Japan
Tel: 81-6-203-6530
Fax: 81-6-232-0714

Kanto Auto Works, Ltd.
Fumio Agetsuma
President
Mubanchi, Taura-Minatocho
Yokosuka City
Kanagawa Pref. 237
Japan
Tel: 81-468-61-5111
Fax: 81-468-61-2329

Kao Corporation
Fumikatsu Tokiwa
President
1-14-10 Nihonbashi-Kayabacho
Chuo-Ku
Tokyo 103
Japan
Tel: 81-3-3660-7111
Fax: 81-3-3660-7092

Kashima Oil Co., Ltd.
Takeji Fukuda
President
Kioicho Park Bldg.
3-6 Kioi-Cho
Chiyoda-Ku
Tokyo 102
Japan
Tel: 81-3-5276-9540
Fax: 81-3-3265-0430

Kasho Co., Ltd.
Seishichi Ito
President
14-9 Nihonbashi, 2-Chome
Chuo-Ku, Tokyo 103
Japan
Tel: 81-3-3276-7726
Fax: 81-3-3276-7585

Kasumi Co., Ltd.
Akio Kambayashi
President
1-3 Higashi-Nakanukimachi
Tsuchiura-Shi, Ibaraki-Ken 300
Japan
Tel: 81-298-50-1850
Fax: 81-298-50-1823

Kato Sangyo Co., Ltd.
Kato Takeo
President
9-20 Matsubara-Cho
Nishinomiya-Shi, Hyogo-Ken 662
Japan
Tel: 81-798-33-7650
Fax: 81-798-22-5637

Katokichi Co., Ltd.
Yoshikazu Kato
President
1490-1 Ko, Kanonji-Cho
Kanonji-Shi, Kagawa Pref. 768
Japan
Tel: 81-875-56-1100
Fax: 81-875-56-1109

Kawasaki Heavy Industries, Ltd.
Hiroshi Ohba
Chairman
4-1 Hamamatsu-Cho, 2-Chome
Minato-Ku, Tokyo 105
Japan
Tel: 81-3-3435-2111
Fax: 81-3-3436-3037

Kawasaki Kisen Kaisha, Ltd.
Isao Shintani
President
Hibiya Central Bldg.
2-9 Nishi-Shinbashi, 1-Chome
Minato-Ku
Tokyo 105
Japan
Tel: 81-3-3595-5082
Fax: 81-3-3595-6126

Kawasaki Steel Corporation
Kanji Emoto
President
Hibiya Kokusai Bldg.
2-2-3 Uchisaiwaicho, Chiyoda-Ku
Tokyo 100
Japan
Tel: 81-3-3597-3111
Fax: 81-3-3597-4860

Kawasho Corporation
Mitsuru Shiokawa
President
World Trade Center Bldg.
2-4-1 Hamamatsu-Cho
Minato-Ku
Tokyo 105-62
Japan
Tel: 81-3-3578-5111
Fax: 81-3-3578-5924

Kayaba Industry Co., Ltd.
Kiyoshi Hosomi
President
World Trade Centre Bldg.
2-4-1 Hamamatsu-Cho
Minato-Ku
Tokyo 105
Japan
Tel: 81-3-3435-3511
Fax: 81-3-3436-6759

Keihan Electric Railway
Akio Kinba
President
2-27 Shiromi, 1-Chome
Chuo-Ku
Osaka City 540
Japan
Tel: 81-6-944-2549
Fax: 81-6-944-2501

Keihin Electric Express Railway Co., Ltd.
Masaru Kotani
President & Representative Director
2-20-20 Takanawa
Minato-Ku
Tokyo 108
Japan
Tel: 81-3-3280-9120
Fax: 81-3-3280-9193

Keio Teito Electric Railway Co., Ltd.
Hiroichi Nishiyama
President
1-9-1 Sekido, Tama City
Tokyo 206
Japan
Tel: 81-423-37-3112
Fax: 81-423-74-9810

Keiyo Co., Ltd.
Ken Nagai
President
1-28-1 Mitsuwadai
Wakaba-Ku
Chiba 264
Japan
Tel: 81-43-255-1111
Fax: 81-43-253-5951

Kenwood Corporation
Makoto Oka
President
14-6 Dogenzaka, 1-Chome
Shibuya-Ku
Tokyo 150
Japan
Tel: 81-3-5457-7120
Fax: 81-3-5457-7110

Keppel Corporation Limited
Sim Kee Boon
Executive Chairman
325 Telok Blangah Road
Singapore 098831
Tel: 65-270-6666
Fax: 65-274-0645

Kia Motors Corporation
Kim Young-Kwi
Chairman
15-21 Yoido-Dong
Youngdeungpo-Ku
Seoul
South Korea
Tel: 82-2-788-1114
Fax: 82-2-788-1162

Kikkoman Corporation
Yuzaburo Mogi
President
339 Noda
Noda-Shi
Chiba-Ken 278
Japan
Tel: 81-471-23-5111
Fax: 81-471-23-5200

Kinden Corporation
Taizo Oka
President
2-3-41 Honjo-Higashi
Kita-Ku
Osaka-Shi 531
Japan
Tel: 81-6-375-6000
Fax: 81-6-375-6370

Kinki Coca-Cola Bottling Co., Ltd.
Akihiko Ikeda
President
7-9-31 Senrioka
Settsu-Shi
Osaka 566
Japan
Tel: 81-6-330-2222
Fax: 81-6-387-2116

Kinki Nippon Railway Co., Ltd.
Wa Tashiro
President
6-1-55 Uehommachi
Tennoji-Ku
Osaka 543
Japan
Tel: 81-6-775-3444
Fax: 81-6-775-3468

Kinsho-Mataichi Corporation
Toshio Kawachi
President
1-24-1 Shinkawa
Chuo-Ku
Tokyo 104
Japan
Tel: 81-3-3297-7300
Fax: 81-3-3297-7392

Kintetsu Department Store Co., Ltd.
Taro Tanaka
President
1-1-43 Abenotsuji
Abeno-Ku
Osaka-Shi 545
Japan
Tel: 81-6-624-1111
Fax: 81-6-662-2101

Kintetsu Real Estate Co., Ltd.
Michihiko Sekine
President
2-2-3 Nanba
Chuo-Ku
Osaka-Shi 542
Japan
Tel: 81-6-212-8236
Fax: 81-6-212-8299

Kintetsu World Express Inc.
Toshio Kumokawa
President
5/F., Otemachi Bldg. 1-6-1
Otemachi
Chiyoda-Ku
Tokyo 100
Japan
Tel: 81-3-3201-2580
Fax: 81-3-3201-2666

Kirin Beverage Corporation
Hiroki Abe
President
1 Kanda-Izumicho
Chiyoda-Ku
Tokyo 101
Japan
Tel: 81-3-5821-4001
Fax: 81-3-5821-4131

Kirin Brewery Co., Ltd.
Yasuhiro Satoh
President
10-1 Shinkawa, 2-Chome
Chuo-Ku
Tokyo 104
Japan
Tel: 81-3-5540-3411
Fax: 81-3-5540-3547

Koa Oil Co., Ltd.
Masao Segawa
President
3-4-1 Shibaura
Minato-Ku
Tokyo 108
Japan
Tel: 81-3-3241-8611
Fax: 81-3-3270-6928

Kobayashi Pharmaceutical Co., Ltd.
Kobayashi Kazumasa
President
4-3-6 Doshomachi
Chuo-Ku
Osaka 541
Japan
Tel: 81-6-222-0210
Fax: 81-6-222-4261

Kobe Steel, Ltd.
Masahiro Kumamoto
President
8-2 Marunouchi, 1-Chome
Chiyoda-Ku
Tokyo 100
Japan
Tel: 81-3-3218-7111
Fax: 81-3-3218-6330

Kodansha Ltd., Publishers
Sawako Noma
President
2-12-21 Otowa, Bunkyo-Ku
Tokyo 112-01
Japan
Tel: 81-3-3945-1111
Fax: 81-3-3944-9915

Koito Manufacturing Co., Ltd.
Yoshiro Nagamura
President
4-8-3 Takanawa
Minato-Ku
Tokyo 108
Japan
Tel: 81-3-3443-7111
Fax: 81-3-3447-1520

Kokubu & Co., Ltd.
Kanbei Kokubu
President
1-1-1 Nihonbashi
Chuo-Ku
Tokyo 103
Japan
Tel: 81-3-3276-4121
Fax: 81-3-3273-7305

Kokusai Denshin Denwa Co., Ltd. (KDD)
Tadashi Nishimoto
President
2-3-2 Nishi-Shinjuku
Shinjuku-Ku
Tokyo 163-03
Japan
Tel: 81-3-3347-7111
Fax: 81-3-3347-7000

Kokusai Electric Co., Ltd.
Endo Makoto
President
3-14-20 Higashi Nakano
Nakano-Ku
Tokyo 164
Japan
Tel: 81-3-3368-6111
Fax: 81-3-3365-9119

Kokuyo Co., Ltd.
Akihiro Kuroda
President
6-1-1 Ohimazato-Minami
Higashinari-Ku
Osaka 537
Japan
Tel: 81-6-976-1221
Fax: 81-6-972-9589

Kolon International Corporation
Kwon O-Sang
President
45 Mugyo-Dong
Chung-Gu
Seoul
South Korea
Tel: 82-2-311-8001
Fax: 82-2-754-5314

Komatsu Ltd.
Satoru Anzaki
President
2-3-6 Akasaka
Minato-Ku
Tokyo 107
Japan
Tel: 81-3-5561-2616
Fax: 81-3-3505-9662

Konica Corporation
Tomiji Uematsu
President
26-2 Nishishinjuku, 1-Chome
Shinjuku-Ku
Tokyo 163-05
Japan
Tel: 81-3-3349-5251
Fax: 81-3-3349-8998

Konoike Construction Co., Ltd.
Kazusue Konoike
President
3-6-1 Kita-Kyuhoji-Machi
Chuo-Ku
Osaka 541
Japan
Tel: 81-6-244-3553
Fax: 81-6-244-3690

Korea Electric Power Corporation
Chong-Hun Rieh
President
167 Samsong-Dong
Kangnam-Gu
Seoul 135-791
South Korea
Tel: 82-2-3456-3114
Fax: 82-2-3456-5981

Korea Heavy Industries & Construction Co., Ltd. (Hanjung)
Un-Sun Park
Chairman & President
555 Guygok-Dong
Changwon-City
Kyongsangnam-Do 641-792
Seoul
South Korea
Tel: 82-551-78-6114
Fax: 82-551-64-5551/5552

Korea Telecom
Lee Jun
President
100 Sejongno, Chongno-Gu
Seoul
South Korea
Tel: 82-2-750-3114/3210
Fax: 82-2-750-3543

Korean Air
Cho Choong-Hoon
Chairman
41-3 Sosomun-Dong, Chung-Ku
Seoul
South Korea
Tel: 82-2-756-2000
Fax: 82-2-755-5220

Kotobukiya Co., Ltd.
Hirokazu Ishii
President
3-3-3 Honjo, Kumamoto City
Kumamoto Pref. 860
Japan
Tel: 81-96-366-3111
Fax: 81-96-362-3036

Kowa Co., Ltd.
Yoshihiro Miwa
President
3-6-29 Nishiki, Naka-Ku
Nagoya 460
Japan
Tel: 81-52-963-3040
Fax: 81-52-963-3045

Koyo Seiko Co., Ltd.
Hiroshi Inoue
President
3-5-8 Minami-Funaba, Chuo-Ku
Osaka-Shi 542
Japan
Tel: 81-6-271-8451
Fax: 81-6-245-7892

Kubota Corporation
Kohei Mitsui
President
1-2-47 Shikitsu-Higashi
Naniwa-Ku
Osaka 556
Japan
Tel: 81-6-648-2111
Fax: 81-6-648-3862

Kumagai Gumi Co., Ltd.
Taichiro Kumagai
President
2-1 Tukudo-Cho
Shinjuku-Ku
Tokyo 162
Japan
Tel: 81-3-3260-2111
Fax: 81-3-3235-3308

Kumho Tire Company
Nam Il
President
Asiana B/D
10-1 Hoehyon-Dong, 2-Ga
Chung-Gu
Seoul
South Korea
Tel: 82-2-758-1114
Fax: 82-2-758-1515

Kuok Oils & Grains Pte. Ltd.
Kwok Kian Hai
Managing Director
1 Kim Seng Promenade
05-01 Great World City
Singapore 237994
Tel: 65-738-8622
Fax: 65-735-6366

Kurabo Industries, Ltd.
Kozo Shindo
President
2-4-31 Kyutaro-Machi
Chuo-Ku
Osaka 541
Japan
Tel: 81-6-266-5111
Fax: 81-6-266-5555

Kuraray Co., Ltd.
Hiroto Matsuo
President
1-12-39 Shin-Hankyu Bldg.
Umeda, Kita-Ku
Osaka 530
Japan
Tel: 81-6-348-2111
Fax: 81-6-348-2165

Kuraya Corporation
Sadatake Kumakura
President
3-12 Kioi-Cho
Chiyoda-Ku
Tokyo 102
Japan
Tel: 81-3-3238-2700
Fax: 81-3-3238-2672

Kurimoto, Ltd.
Tsutomu Igarashi
Chairman
1-12-19 Kita-Horie
Nishi-Ku
Osaka-Shi 550
Japan
Tel: 81-6-538-7731
Fax: 81-6-538-7756

Kurita Water Industries Limited
Kazuo Taketoshi
President
3-4-7 Nishi-Shinjuku
Shinjuku-Ku
Tokyo 160
Japan
Tel: 81-3-3347-3111
Fax: 81-3-3347-3904

Kygnus Sekiyu K.K.
Takao Hashimoto
President
Nittohbo Bldg.
2-8-1 Yaesu Chuo-Ku
Tokyo 104
Japan
Tel: 81-3-3276-5211
Fax: 81-3-3276-5390

Kyocera Corporation
Kensuke Itoh
President
5-22 Kitainoue-Cho, Higashino
Yamashina-Ku
Kyoto 607
Japan
Tel: 81-75-592-3851
Fax: 81-75-501-6536

Kyokuto Boeki Kaisha, Ltd.
Motoo Imakita
President
7/F., New Otemachi Bldg.
2-2-1 Otemachi
Chiyoda-Ku
Tokyo 100-91
Japan
Tel: 81-3-3244-3511
Fax: 81-3-3246-2148

Kyokuto Petroleum Industries, Ltd.
Takeshi Okada
President
8-7 Kyobashi Nisshoku Bldg.
Kyobashi 1-Chome
Chuo-Ku
Tokyo 100
Japan
Tel: 81-3-5250-2681
Fax: 81-3-5250-2692

Kyokuyo Co., Ltd.
Mikio Inoue
President
3-1-15 Kawara-Machi
Chuo-Ku
Osaka 541
Japan
Tel: 81-6-229-7600
Fax: 81-6-229-7640

Kyokuyo Company Limited
Kazumasa Ishise
President
Chiyoda Bldg.
2-1-2 Marunouchi
Chiyoda-Ku
Tokyo 100
Japan
Tel: 81-3-3211-0134
Fax: 81-3-3211-6921

Kyowa Exeo Corporation
Tadasu Murakami
President
4-13-13 Akasaka
Minato-Ku
Tokyo 107
Japan
Tel: 81-3-5570-8001
Fax: 81-3-5570-8181

Kyowa Hakko Kogyo Co., Ltd.
Kannosuke Nakamura
Chairman of the Board of Directors
1-6-1 Ohtemachi
Chiyoda-Ku
Tokyo 100
Japan
Tel: 81-3-3282-0007
Fax: 81-3-3284-1839

Kyudenko Corporation
Tsukasa Shiraishi
President
1-23-35 Nanokawa
Minami-Ku
Fukuoka 815
Japan
Tel: 81-92-523-1231
Fax: 81-92-524-3269

Kyushu Electric Power Co., Inc.
Shigeru Ohno
President
2-1-82 Watanabe-Dori
Chuo-Ku
Fukuoka 810-91
Japan
Tel: 81-92-761-3031
Fax: 81-92-713-9192

Kyushu Matsushita Electric Co., Ltd.
Sakai Hajima
President
4-1-62 Minoshima
Hakata-Ku
Fukuoka-Shi 812
Japan
Tel: 81-92-431-2111
Fax: 81-92-477-1222

Kyushu Oil Co., Ltd.
Takao Katsumata
President
2-1-1 Iino Bldg.
Uchisaiwai-Cho
Chiyoda-Ku
Tokyo 100
Japan
Tel: 81-3-3502-3651
Fax: 81-3-3502-9840

Kyushu Railway Company
Koji Tanaka
President
1-1 Hakataeki-Chuogai
Hakata-Ku
Fukuoka 812
Japan
Tel: 81-92-474-2501
Fax: 81-92-474-9745

L

Larsen & Toubro Limited
S.D. Kulkarni
Managing Director
L & T House, Ballard Estate
Mumbai 400 001
India
Tel: 91-22-261-8181
Fax: 91-22-262-0223

Leighton Holdings Limited
Wal King
Chief Executive Officer
472 Pacific Highway
St.Leonards
NSW 2065
Australia
Tel: 61-2-9925-6666
Fax: 61-2-9925-6005

Lend Lease Corporation Limited
David Higgins
Managing Director
Level 45, Australia Square Tower
Sydney
NSW 2000
Australia
Tel: 61-2-9236-6111
Fax: 61-2-9237-5346

LG Cable
Kwon Mun-Ku
President
20 Youido-Dong
Yongdungpo-Gu
Seoul
South Korea
Tel: 82-2-787-1114
Fax: 82-2-785-1905

LG Chemical
Song Jae-Gap
President
20 Youido-Dong
Youngdungpo-Gu
Seoul
South Korea
Tel: 82-2-787-1114
Fax: 82-2-787-7039

LG Construction Co., Ltd.
Ku Ja-Song
President
537 Namdaemunno, 5-Ga
Chung-Gu
Seoul
South Korea
Tel: 82-2-787-1114
Fax: 82-2-774-6610

LG Electronics Inc.
Ku Ja-Hong
President
20 Youido-Dong
Yongdungpo-Gu
Seoul
South Korea
Tel: 82-2-787-5114
Fax: 82-2-787-3400

LG Industries
20 Youido-Dong
Yongdungpo-Gu
Seoul
South Korea
Tel: 82-2-3777-1114
Fax: 82-2-3777-5330

LG International Corporation
Soo-Ho Lee
President
20 Youido-Dong
Yongdungpo-Gu
Seoul
South Korea
Tel: 82-2-3773-1114
Fax: 82-2-785-7762/7763

LG Metals
Lee Jong-Song
President
20 Youido-Dong
Yongdungpo-Gu
Seoul
South Korea
Tel: 82-2-787-1114
Fax: 82-2-761-3188

LG Oil Products Sales Co., Ltd.
Koo Jin-Hoe
President
Namkyung Bldg.
8-2 Samsung-Dong
Kangnam-Gu
Seoul
South Korea
Tel: 82-2-546-5151
Fax: 82-2-545-4437

LG Semicon Co., Ltd.
Chung-Hwan Mun
President
891 LG Bldg.
Daechi-Dong, Kangnam-Gu
Seoul 135-280
South Korea
Tel: 82-2-3777-1114
Fax: 82-2-3459-3535/3434

LG-Caltex Oil Corporation
Huh Dong-Soo
President
LG Twin Towers (West Tower)
20 Yoido-Dong
Youngdungpo-Ku
Seoul
South Korea
Tel: 82-2-3777-1114
Fax: 82-2-787-6051

Li & Fung Limited
Dr. Victor Fung Kwok-king
Group Chairman
Level 13, Lifung Tower
China Hong Kong City
33 Canton Road
Kowloon
Hong Kong
Tel: 852-2736-1111
Fax: 852-2736-1167

Life Corporation
Nobutsugu Shimizu
President
1-19-4 Higashi-Nakajima
Higashi-Yodogawa-Ku
Osaka 533
Japan
Tel: 81-6-815-2600
Fax: 81-6-815-2688

Lion Corporation
Michinao Takahashi
President
1-3-7 Honjo
Sumida-Ku
Tokyo 130
Japan
Tel: 81-3-3621-6211
Fax: 81-3-3621-6029

Lotte Co., Ltd.
Takeo Shigemitsu
President
3-20-1 Nishishinjuku
Shinjuku-Ku
Tokyo 160
Japan
Tel: 81-3-3375-1211
Fax: 81-3-3374-7254

Lotte Shopping Company
Kang Jin-Woo
President
1 Sokong-Dong
Choong-Gu
Seoul
South Korea
Tel: 82-2-771-2500
Fax: 82-2-752-6471/319-6522

M

Maeda Corporation
Yasuji Maeda
President
2-10-26 Fujimi, Chiyoda-Ku
Tokyo 102
Japan
Tel: 81-3-5276-5154/5155
Fax: 81-3-3262-3339

Maeda Road Construction Co., Ltd.
Masatsugu Okabe
President
3-14-12 Kami-Ohsaki
Shinagawa-Ku
Tokyo 141
Japan
Tel: 81-3-3447-0781
Fax: 81-3-3473-3529

Mainichi Newspapers Co., Ltd.
Koike Tadao
President
1-1-1 Hitotsubashi
Chiyoda-Ku
Tokyo 100-51
Japan
Tel: 81-3-3212-0321
Fax: 81-3-3210-3449

Makita Corporation
Masahiko Goto
President
3-11-8 Sumiyoshi-Cho
Anjo City
Aichi Pref. 446
Japan
Tel: 81-566-98-1711
Fax: 81-566-98-5580

Malaysia LNG Sdn. Bhd.
Abdul Hamid Ibrahim
Managing Director
Tanjung Kidurong
Bintulu 97007
Sarawak
Malaysia
Tel: 60-86-251-301/320
Fax: 60-86-252-626

Malaysian Airline System Berhad
Tan Sri Datoō Tajudin Ramli
Chairman
34/F., Bangunan Mas
Jalan Sultan Ismail
Kuala Lumpur 50250
Malaysia
Tel: 60-3-261-0555
Fax: 60-3-261-3472

Mando Machinery
Chong Mong-Won
President
730 Tang-Dong
Kunpo-Shi
Kyonggi
South Korea
Tel: 82-343-50-6114
Fax: 82-343-59-6380

Manila Electric Company (Meralco)
Manuel M. Lopez
President
Ortigas Avenue
Pasig City
Philippines 0300
Tel: 63-2-16220
Fax: 63-2-1622-8501

Marubeni Australia Limited
Yoshiki Watanabe
Chairman & Managing Director
Level 31, Chifley Tower
2 Chifley Square
Sydney
NSW 2000
Australia
Tel: 61-2-9931-2222
Fax: 61-2-9931-2299

Marubeni Corporation
Iwao Toriumi
President
1-4-2 Otemachi
Chiyoda-Ku
Tokyo 100-88
Japan
Tel: 81-3-3282-2111
Fax: 81-3-3282-7456

Marubeni Energy Corporation
Yasushi Otsuka
President
2-2 Surugadai, Kanda
Chiyoda-Ku
Tokyo 101
Japan
Tel: 81-3-3293-4401
Fax: 81-3-3293-4079

Marubeni International Petroleum (Singapore) Pte. Ltd.
Kazuyuki Ishida
Managing Director
16 Raffles Quay
#39-02, Hong Leong Bldg.
Singapore 048581
Tel: 65-224-0446
Fax: 65-221-5458

Marudai Food Co., Ltd.
Yoshiyuki Komori
President
21-3 Midori-Cho
Takatsuki-Shi
Osaka 569
Japan
Tel: 81-726-61-2518
Fax: 81-726-61-5006

Maruetsu, Inc.
Kazuo Kawa
President
5-51-12 Higashi-Ikebukro
Tosima-Ku
Tokyo 170
Japan
Tel: 81-3-3590-1110
Fax: 81-3-3590-4642

Maruha Corporation
Keijiro Nakabe
President
1-1-2 Otemachi
Chiyoda-Ku
Tokyo 100
Japan
Tel: 81-3-3216-0821
Fax: 81-3-3216-0342

Marui Co., Ltd.
Tadao Aoi
President
4-3-2 Nakano
Nakano-Ku
Tokyo 164-01
Japan
Tel: 81-3-3384-0101
Fax: 81-3-3380-0107

Maruichi Co., Ltd.
Hirotoshi Nishina
President
3-48 Ichiba
Nagano City
Nagano Pref. 381-22
Japan
Tel: 81-26-285-4101
Fax: 81-26-285-3401

Maruti Udyog Limited
R.C. Bhargava
Managing Director
11/F., Jeevan Prakash Bldg.
25 Kasturba Gandhi Road
New Delhi 110 001
India
Tel: 91-11-331-6831/332-8668
Fax: 91-11-331-8754/371-3575

Marutomi Group Co., Ltd.
Shuji Yamada
President
2-7-28 Kakeage
Minami-Ku
Nagoya-Shi, Aichi 457
Japan
Tel: 81-52-821-9631
Fax: 81-52-822-6888

Maruzen Co., Ltd.
Nobuo Suzuki
President
2-3-10 Nihombashi
Chuo-Ku
Tokyo 103
Japan
Tel: 81-3-3272-7211
Fax: 81-3-3274-4695

Maruzen Petrochemical Co., Ltd.
Iwao Umehara
President
2-25-10 Hacchobori
Chuo-Ku
Tokyo 104
Japan
Tel: 81-3-3552-9361
Fax: 81-3-5566-8391

Matsumura-Gumi Corporation
Kosaku Fukuda
President
1-10-20 Higashi-Tenma
Kita-Ku
Osaka 530
Japan
Tel: 81-6-353-1131
Fax: 81-6-353-7282

Matsushita Battery Industrial Co., Ltd.
Yukinobu Yasuda
President
1-1 Matsushita-Cho
Moriguchi-Shi
Osaka 570
Japan
Tel: 81-6-991-1141
Fax: 81-6-998-8873

Matsushita Communication Industrial Co., Ltd.
Takashi Kawada
President
4-3-1 Tsunashima-Higashi
Kohoku-Ku
Yokohama 223
Japan
Tel: 81-45-531-1231
Fax: 81-45-542-5105

Matsushita Electric Industrial Co., Ltd.
Yoichi Morishita
President
1006 Kadoma
Kadoma City
Osaka 571
Japan
Tel: 81-6-908-1121
Fax: 81-6-908-2351

Matsushita Electric Works, Ltd.
Kiyosuke Imai
President
1048 Kadoma
Kadoma City
Osaka 571
Japan
Tel: 81-6-908-1131
Fax: 81-6-909-4694

Matsushita Electronic Components Co., Ltd.
Kazumasa Yoshida
President
1006 Kadoma
Kadoma City
Osaka 571
Japan
Tel: 81-6-908-1101
Fax: 81-6-906-3612

Matsushita Electronics Industry Corporation
Kazuhiro Mori
President
1-1 Saiwai-Cho
Takatsuki-Shi
Osaka 569
Japan
Tel: 81-726-82-5521
Fax: 81-726-83-2416

Matsushita Refrigeration Co.
Tadashi Kubota
President
4-2-5 Takaida Hondori
Higashi, Osaka City
Osaka Pref. 577
Japan
Tel: 81-6-784-7004
Fax: 81-6-784-7015

Matsushita-Kotobuki Electronics Industries, Ltd.
Takashi Honjo
President
8-1 Furujin-Machi
Takamatsu
Kagawa 760
Japan
Tel: 81-878-51-7228
Fax: 81-878-51-1047

Matsuzakaya Co., Ltd.
Akira Ito
President
3-16-1 Sakae
Naka-Ku
Nagoya 460
Japan
Tel: 81-52-251-1111
Fax: 81-52-264-7040

Mayne Nickless Limited
Robert R. Dalziel
Managing Director
21/F., 390 St. Kilda Road
Melbourne
Victoria 3004
Australia
Tel: 61-3-9868-0700
Fax: 61-3-9868-0751

Mazda Motor Corporation
Henry D.G. Wallace
President
3-1 Shinchi, Fuchu-Cho
Aki-Gun
Hiroshima Pref. 730-91
Japan
Tel: 81-82-282-1111
Fax: 81-82-287-5190

McDonald's Co. (Japan), Ltd.
Den Fujita
President
39/F., Shinjuku I-Land Tower
6-5-1 Nishi Shinjuku
Shinjuku-Ku
Tokyo 163-13
Japan
Tel: 81-3-3344-6251
Fax: 81-3-3344-6769

Meidensha Corporation
Keiji Kojima
President
36-2 Riverside Bldg.
Nihonbashi Hakozakicho
Chuo-Ku
Tokyo 103
Japan
Tel: 81-3-5641-7000
Fax: 81-3-5641-7001

Meidi-Ya Co., Ltd.
Keiichi Isono
President
2-8 Kyobashi, 2-Chome
Chuo-Ku
Tokyo 104
Japan
Tel: 81-3-3271-1111
Fax: 81-3-3278-1422

Meiji Milk Products Co., Ltd.
Hisashi Nakayama
President
2-3-6 Kyobashi
Chuo-Ku
Tokyo 104
Japan
Tel: 81-3-3281-6118
Fax: 81-3-3281-4717

Meiji Seika Kaisha, Ltd.
Ichiro Kitasato
President
4-16 Kyobashi, 2-Chome
Chuo-Ku
Tokyo 104
Japan
Tel: 81-3-3272-6511
Fax: 81-3-3271-3528

Meiwa Trading Co., Ltd.
Zenshiro Nagasaka
President
3-3-1 Marunouchi
Chiyoda-Ku
Tokyo 100
Japan
Tel: 81-3-3240-9534
Fax: 81-3-3240-9561

Milx Corporation
Kazuyoshi Tsuda
President
Meikai Kyobashi Bldg.
2-18-2 Kyobashi
Chuo-Ku
Tokyo 104
Japan
Tel: 81-3-3567-7700
Fax: 81-3-3567-7701

MIM Holdings Limited
Nick W. Stump
Director
Level 1, MIM Plaza
410 Ann Street
Brisbane
Queensland 4000
Australia
Tel: 61-7-3833-8000
Fax: 61-7-3832-2426

Minebea Co., Ltd.
Goro Ogino
President
4106-73, Oaza Miyota
Miyota-Machi, Kitasaku-Gun
Nagano 389-02
Japan
Tel: 81-267-32-2200
Fax: 81-267-31-1330

Minerals & Metals Trading Corporation of India Ltd.
S.N. Malik
Chairman & Managing Director
Scope Complex, Core 1
7 Lodi Road, Institutional Area
New Delhi 110 003
India
Tel: 91-11-436-2200/1603
Fax: 91-11-436-2072/0724/2224

Minolta Co., Ltd.
Osamu Kanaya
President
3-13 Azuchi-Machi, 2-Chome
Chuo-Ku
Osaka 541
Japan
Tel: 81-6-271-2251
Fax: 81-6-266-1010

Misawa Homes Co., Ltd.
Chiyoji Misawa
President
2-4-5 Takaido-Higashi
Suginami-Ku
Tokyo 168
Japan
Tel: 81-3-3331-1111
Fax: 81-3-3349-8074

Mitac International Corporation
Matthew F.C. Miau
Chairman
40 Wen Hwa 2nd Road
Kwei Shan Hsiang
Taoyuan
Taiwan
Tel: 886-3-3289-000
Fax: 886-3-3277-591

Mitani Corporation
Yoshinori Suzuki
President
1-3-1 Toyoshima
Fukui City 910
Japan
Tel: 81-776-20-3111
Fax: 81-776-21-0993

Mitsubishi Australia Limited
Noriyuki Nagagawa
Managing Director
Level 43, Gateway Bldg.
1 Macquarie Place
Sydney
NSW 2000
Australia
Tel: 61-2-9951-4807
Fax: 61-2-9951-4928

Mitsubishi Cable Industries, Ltd.
Harunosuke Fuji
President
New Kokusai Bldg.
3-4-1 Marunouchi
Chiyoda-Ku
Tokyo 100
Japan
Tel: 81-3-3216-1551
Fax: 81-3-3201-2239/3948

Mitsubishi Chemical Corporation
Akira Miura
President
5-2 Marunouchi, 2-Chome
Chiyoda-Ku
Tokyo 100
Japan
Tel: 81-3-3283-6274
Fax: 81-3-3283-6287

Mitsubishi Construction Co., Ltd.
Yoshihiko Ota
President
3-6 Wakamatsu Bldg.
Nihonbashi-Honcho, 3-Chome
Chuo-Ku
Tokyo 103
Japan
Tel: 81-3-3270-0932
Fax: 81-3-3270-0118

Mitsubishi Corporation
Minoru Makihara
President
6-3 Marunouchi, 2-Chome
Chiyoda-Ku
Tokyo 100-86
Japan
Tel: 81-3-3210-2121
Fax: 81-3-3210-8051/8841

Mitsubishi Electric Building Techno-Service Co., Ltd.
Gai Kobayashi
President
2-6-2 Otemachi
Chiyoda-Ku
Tokyo 100
Japan
Tel: 81-3-3279-8000
Fax: 81-3-3245-0242

Mitsubishi Electric Corporation
Takashi Kitaoka
President
2-3 Marunouchi, 2-Chome
Chiyoda-Ku
Tokyo 100
Japan
Tel: 81-3-3218-2111
Fax: 81-3-3218-2431

Mitsubishi Estate Co., Ltd.
Takeshi Fukuzawa
President
Marunouchi Bldg.
2-7-3 Marunouchi
Chiyoda-Ku
Tokyo 100
Japan
Tel: 81-3-3287-5100
Fax: 81-3-3214-7036

Mitsubishi Gas Chemical Co., Inc.
Akira Ohira
President
2-5-2 Marunouchi
Chiyoda-Ku
Tokyo 100
Japan
Tel: 81-3-3283-5000
Fax: 81-3-3287-0833

Mitsubishi Heavy Industries, Ltd.
Nobuyuki Masuda
President
2-5-1 Marunouchi
Chiyoda-Ku
Tokyo 100
Japan
Tel: 81-3-3212-3111
Fax: 81-3-3212-9860

Mitsubishi Logistics Corp.
Tsuyoshi Miyazaki
President
1-19-1 Nihonbashi
Chuo-Ku
Tokyo 103
Japan
Tel: 81-3-3278-6511
Fax: 81-3-3278-6594

Mitsubishi Materials Corporation
Yumi Akimoto
President
1-5-1 Otemachi
Chiyoda-Ku
Tokyo 100
Japan
Tel: 81-3-5252-5201
Fax: 81-3-5252-5270

Mitsubishi Motors Australia Limited
Michael Quinn
Managing Director
1284 South Road
Clovelly Park
Adelaide
South Australia 5042
Australia
Tel: 61-8-8275-7111
Fax: 61-8-8275-6841

Mitsubishi Motors Corporation
Takemune Kimura
President
5-33-8 Shiba
Minato-Ku
Tokyo 108
Japan
Tel: 81-3-3456-1111
Fax: 81-3-5232-7731

Mitsubishi Oil Co., Ltd.
Yoshihiko Izumitani
President
1-6-41 Konan Minato-Ku
Tokyo 108
Japan
Tel: 81-3-3595-7663
Fax: 81-3-3508-2521

Mitsubishi Paper Mills, Ltd.
Yoshihiro Onda
President
2-4 Marunouchi, 3-Chome
Chiyoda-Ku
Tokyo 100
Japan
Tel: 81-3-3213-3732
Fax: 81-3-3215-8157

Mitsubishi Paper Sales Co., Ltd.
Noboru Kurushima
President
2-6-4 Kyobashi
Chuo-Ku
Tokyo 101
Japan
Tel: 81-3-3566-2300
Fax: 81-3-3272-0192

Mitsubishi Plastics, Inc.
Yoshikazu Miyabe
President
2-5-2 Marunouchi
Chiyoda-Ku
Tokyo 100
Japan
Tel: 81-3-3283-4049
Fax: 81-3-3213-4089

Mitsubishi Rayon Co., Ltd.
Eiichi Taguchi
President
3-19 Kyobashi, 2-Chome
Chuo-Ku
Tokyo 104
Japan
Tel: 81-3-3245-8734
Fax: 81-3-3245-8789

Mitsui Chemicals, Inc.
Akio Sato
President
2-5 Kasumigaseki
3-Chome, Chiyoda-Ku
Tokyo 100
Japan
Tel: 81-3-3592-4111
Fax: 81-3-3592-4267

Mitsui & Co. (Australia) Limited
Mr. Fuyuki Kitahara
Chairman & Managing Director
Level 46, Gateway Bldg.
1 Macquarie Place
Sydney
NSW 2000
Australia
Tel: 61-2-9256-9500
Fax: 61-2-9251-1788

Mitsui & Co., Ltd.
Shigeji Ueshima
President
1-2-1 Otemachi
Chiyoda-Ku
Tokyo 100
Japan
Tel: 81-3-3285-1111
Fax: 81-3-3285-9800

Mitsui Construction Co., Ltd.
Kazuhiro Inamura
President
3-10-1 Iwamoto-Cho
Chiyoda-Ku
Tokyo 101
Japan
Tel: 81-3-5821-7051
Fax: 81-3-5821-7605

Mitsui Engineering & Shipbuilding Co., Ltd.
Jiro Hoshino
President
5-6-4 Tsukiji
Chuo-Ku
Tokyo 104
Japan
Tel: 81-3-3544-3147
Fax: 81-3-3544-3050

Mitsui Fudosan Co., Ltd.
Jun-Ichiro Tanaka
President
2-1-1 Nihonbashi-Muromachi
Chuo-Ku
Tokyo 103
Japan
Tel: 81-3-3246-3055
Fax: 81-3-3241-2870

Mitsui Home Co., Ltd.
Shiro Akai
President
2-1-1 Nishi-Shinjuku
Shinjuku-Ku
Tokyo 163-04
Japan
Tel: 81-3-3346-4411
Fax: 81-3-3346-4400

Mitsui Mining Co., Ltd.
Tadashi Harada
President
2-1-1 Nihonbashi-Muromachi
Chuo-Ku
Tokyo 103
Japan
Tel: 81-3-3241-1334
Fax: 81-3-3241-8684

Mitsui Mining & Smelting Co., Ltd.
Shinpei Miyamura
President
2-1-1 Nihonbashi-Muromachi
Chuo-Ku
Tokyo 103
Japan
Tel: 81-3-3246-8000
Fax: 81-3-3246-8050

Mitsui O.S.K. Lines, Ltd.
Masaharu Ikuta
President
2-1-1 Toranomon
Minato-Ku
Tokyo 105-91
Japan
Tel: 81-3-3587-7111
Fax: 81-3-3587-7702

Mitsui Oil & Gas Co., Ltd.
Teiichi Kinoshita
President
1-32-2 Honmachi
Nakano-Ku
Tokyo 164
Japan
Tel: 81-3-5334-0700
Fax: 81-3-5512-3642

Mitsui Petrochemical Industries, Ltd.
Shigenori Koda
President
2-5 Kasumigaseki Bldg.
Kasumigaseki, 3-Chome
Chiyoda-Ku
Tokyo 100
Japan
Tel: 81-3-3580-2012
Fax: 81-3-3593-0027

Mitsukoshi, Ltd.
Shoji Tsuda
President
1-4-1 Nihonbashi-Muromachi
Chuo-Ku
Tokyo 103-01
Japan
Tel: 81-3-3241-3311
Fax: 81-3-3241-5298

Mitsumi Electric Co., Ltd.
Itsuo Moribe
President
8-8-2 Kokuryo-Cho
Chofu-Shi
Tokyo 182
Japan
Tel: 81-3-3489-5333
Fax: 81-3-3488-3031

Mizuno Corporation
Masato Mizuno
President
12-35 Nanko-Kita, 1-Chome
Suminoe-Ku
Osaka 559
Japan
Tel: 81-6-614-8315
Fax: 81-6-614-8389

MMC Sittipol Co., Ltd.
Takashi Muiasawa
President
1990 Ramkhamhaeng Road
Huamarkbantkiti
Bangkok 10240
Thailand
Tel: 662-908-8000
Fax: 662-318-3060

Mobil Oil Australia Limited
Richard V. Pisarczyk
Chairman & Managing Director
417 St. Kilda Road
Melbourne
Victoria 3000
Australia
Tel: 61-3-9252-3341/3923
Fax: 61-3-9252-3728

Mobil Oil Singapore Pte. Ltd.
(Renamed Mobil Asia Pacific Pte. Ltd.)
Lucille J. Cavanaugh
Chairman
18 Pioneer Road
Singapore 628498
Tel: 65-660-6000
Fax: 65-739-5600

Mobil Sekiyu K.K.
I.F. Scoble
President
1-7-2 Otemachi
Chiyoda-Ku
Tokyo 100
Japan
Tel: 81-3-3244-4691
Fax: 81-3-3244-4528

Morinaga & Co., Ltd.
Akio Matsuzaki
President
33-1 Shiba, 5-Chome
Minato-Ku
Tokyo 108
Japan
Tel: 81-3-3456-0150
Fax: 81-3-3452-7438

Morinaga Milk Industry Co., Ltd.
Akira Ohno
President
5-33-1 Shiba
Minato-Ku
Tokyo 108
Japan
Tel: 81-3-3798-0111
Fax: 81-3-3798-0101

Moritani & Co., Ltd.
Shohei Moritani
President
1-4-22 Yaesu
Chuo-Ku
Tokyo 103
Japan
Tel: 81-3-3278-6000
Fax: 81-3-3278-6255

Motorola Electronic (China) Ltd.
A39 Zizuyuanlu
Haidian District
Beijing 100081
China
Tel: 86-10-6843-7222

Motorola Electronics Pte. Ltd.
Y.F. Tan
Vice President
12 Ang Mo Kio Street 64
Singapore 569088
Tel: 65-481-2000
Fax: 65-482-3879

Murata Manufacturing Co., Ltd.
Yasutaka Murata
President
26-10 Tenjin, 2-Chome
Nagaokakyo-Shi
Kyoto 617
Japan
Tel: 81-75-955-6786
Fax: 81-75-958-2219

Mycal Corporation
Kohtaro Utsunomiya
President
2-9 Awajimachi, 2-Chome
Chuo-Ku
Osaka 541
Japan
Tel: 81-6-203-7817
Fax: 81-6-203-6387

N

Nachi-Fujikoshi Corporation
Masamichi Honda
President
1-1-1 Fujikoshihoumachi
Toyama-Shi
Toyama 930
Japan
Tel: 81-764-23-5111
Fax: 81-764-93-5211

Nagasakiya Co., Ltd.
Tamio Inoue
President
3-7-14 Higashi-Nihonbashi
Chuo-Ku
Tokyo 103
Japan
Tel: 81-3-3661-3810
Fax: 81-3-3663-7792

Nagase & Co., Ltd.
Hideo Nagase
President
1-1-17 Shin-Machi
Nishi-Ku
Osaka 550
Japan
Tel: 81-6-535-2114
Fax: 81-6-535-2160

Nagoya Mitsukoshi Limited
Keiichiro Iwase
President
3-5-1 Sakai
Naka-Ku
Nagoya-Shi 460
Japan
Tel: 81-52-252-1111
Fax: 81-52-252-1549

Nagoya Railroad Co., Ltd.
Soukichi Minoura
President
1-2-4 Meieki
Nakamura-Ku
Nagoya-Shi 450
Aichi
Japan
Tel: 81-52-571-2111
Fax: 81-52-581-6060

Nakaizumi
Yoshio Hosoya
Representative Director
1-3-4 Tsukishima
Chuo-Ku
Tokyo 104
Japan
Tel: 81-3-5560-1361
Fax: 81-3-5560-1371

Nakano Vinegar Co., Ltd.
Matazaemon Nakano
President
2-6 Nakamura-Cho
Handa City
Aichi Pref. 475
Japan
Tel: 81-569-21-3331
Fax: 81-569-24-5019

Nan Ya Plastics Corporation
Yeong Ching Wang
Chairman & President
201 Tung Hwa North Road
Taipei
Taiwan
Tel: 88-6-2-712-2211
Fax: 88-6-2-717-8533

Nankai Electric Railway
Taiji Kawakatsu
President
5-1-60 Nanba, Chuo-Ku
Osaka 542
Japan
Tel: 81-6-644-7121
Fax: 81-6-644-7123

Narasaki Sangyo Co., Ltd.
Yasuaki Mabuchi
President
2-7-1 Nihonbashi-Honcho
Chuo-Ku
Tokyo 103
Japan
Tel: 81-3-3666-2341
Fax: 81-3-3249-0756

National House Industrial Co., Ltd.
Akihiko Nishioka
President
1-1-4 Nishi-Machi, Shinsenri
Toyonaka-Shi
Osaka 565
Japan
Tel: 81-6-834-5111
Fax: 81-6-834-1586

National Power Corporation
Guido Alfredo A. Delgado
President
Agham Road Cor. Quezon Ave.
Diliman
Quezon City
Philippines
Tel: 63-2-921-2998
Fax: 63-2-922-4339

National Thermal Power Corporation Ltd.
Rajendra Singh
Chairman & Managing Director
Ntpc Bhawan, Core 7
Scope Complex
Lodi Road
New Delhi 110 003
India
Tel: 91-11-436-0044/0608
Fax: 91-11-436-3050

Natsteel Ltd.
Ang Kong Hua
President
22 Tanjong Kling Road
Jurong Town
Singapore 628048
Tel: 65-265-1233
Fax: 65-265-8317

Navix Line, Ltd.
Noriaki Hori
President
1-1 Hitotsubashi, 1-Chome
Chiyoda-Ku
Tokyo 100
Japan
Tel: 81-3-3282-7500
Fax: 81-3-3282-7600

NEC Corporation
Hisashi Kaneko
President
5-7-1 Shiba
Minato-Ku
Tokyo 108-01
Japan
Tel: 81-3-3454-1111
Fax: 81-3-3457-7249

NEC Home Electronics, Ltd.
Tomoo Miyawaki
President
5-37-8 Shiba
Minato-Ku
Tokyo 108
Japan
Tel: 81-3-3454-5111
Fax: 81-3-3798-6966

NEC System Integration & Construction, Ltd.
Koh Fukuda
President
1-39-9 Higashishinagawa
Shinagawa-Ku
Tokyo 140
Japan
Tel: 81-3-5463-1111
Fax: 81-3-5463-7781

Neptune Orient Lines Ltd.
Lua Cheng Eng
Chief Executive Officer
456 Alexandra Road
6/F., NOL Building
Singapore 119962
Tel: 65-278-9000
Fax: 65-278-4900

Nestlé Australia Ltd.
Ernest Pope
Managing Director
60 Bathurst Street
Sydney
NSW 2000
Australia
Tel: 61-2-9931-2345
Fax: 61-2-9931-2610/2602

Nestlé Japan Limited
F.M W. Van Dijk
President
Rokko Island Bldg.
2-10 Naka, Koyo-Cho
Higashinada-Ku, Kobe-Shi
Hyogo
Japan
Tel: 81-78-857-4300
Fax: 81-3-3432-8263

New World Development Co., Ltd.
Cheng Yu-tung
Chairman
30/F., New World Tower
16-18 Queen's Road Central
Hong Kong
Tel: 852-2523-1056
Fax: 852-2810-4673

New Zealand Dairy Board
Warren A. Larsen
Chief Executive Officer
Pastoral House
25 The Terrace
Wellington
New Zealand
Tel: 64-4-471-8300
Fax: 64-4-471-8600

New Zealand Dairy Group
Pryme Footner
Chief Executive
Anchor House
80 London Street
Hamilton
New Zealand
Tel: 64-7-839-8398
Fax: 64-7-839-8123

News Corporation
Rupert Murdoch
Chairman
2 Holt Street
Surry Hills
NSW 2010
Australia
Tel: 61-2-9288-3000
Fax: 61-2-9288-3292

NGK Insulators, Ltd.
Masaharu Shibata
President
2-56 Suda-Cho
Mizuho-Ku
Nagoya 467
Japan
Tel: 81-52-872-7230
Fax: 81-52-872-7160

NGK Spark Plug Co., Ltd.
Kaneo Okamura
President
14-18 Takatsuji-Cho
Mizuho-Ku
Nagoya 467
Japan
Tel: 81-52-872-5915
Fax: 81-52-872-5999

NHK Spring Co., Ltd.
Tsuguhiro Maeda
President
3-10 Fukuura, Kanazawa-Ku
Yokohama 236
Japan
Tel: 81-45-786-7511
Fax: 81-45-786-7598/7599

Nichiei Co., Ltd.
Koichiro Hirata
President
4-33-1 Tsurumi-Cho
Tsurumi-Ku
Yokohama 230
Japan
Tel: 81-45-521-6161
Fax: 81-45-501-9484

Nichimen Corporation
Akira Watari
President
1-23 Shiba, 4-Chome
Minato-Ku
Tokyo 108
Japan
Tel: 81-3-5446-1111
Fax: 81-3-5446-1010

Nichirei Corporation
Tadashi Teshima
President
6-19-20 Tsukiji, Chuo-Ku
Tokyo 104
Japan
Tel: 81-3-3248-2101
Fax: 81-3-3248-2119

Nichiro Corporation
Keinosuke Hisai
President
1-12-1 Yuraku-Cho
Chiyoda-Ku
Tokyo 100
Japan
Tel: 81-3-3240-6211
Fax: 81-3-5252-7966

Nihon Cement Co., Ltd.
Michio Kimura
President
6/F., Otemachi Bldg
Chiyoda-Ku, Otemachi
Tokyo 100
Japan
Tel: 81-3-3201-1731
Fax: 81-3-3284-1722

Nihon Keizai Shimbun, Inc.
Takuhiko Tsuruta
President
1-9-5 Otemachi
Chiyoda-Ku
Tokyo 100-66
Japan
Tel: 81-3-3270-0251
Fax: 81-3-5255-2661

Nihon Shurui Hanbai Co., Ltd.
Nobuyoshi Shinoda
President
2-2-1 Yaesu
Chuo-Ku
Tokyo 104
Japan
Tel: 81-3-3273-1751
Fax: 81-3-3242-0457

Nihon Unisys, Ltd.
Junichi Amano
President
1-1-1 Toyosu
Koto-Ku
Tokyo 135
Japan
Tel: 81-3-5546-4111
Fax: 81-3-5546-7800

Niigata Engineering Co., Ltd.
Yoshihiro Muramatsu
President
10-1 Kamatahomcho, 1-Chome
Ohta-Ku
Tokyo 144
Japan
Tel: 81-3-5710-7700
Fax: 81-3-5710-4750

Nikon Corporation
Shoichiro Yoshida
President
2-3 Fuji Bldg., Marunouchi
3-Chiyome, Chiyodaku
Tokyo 100
Japan
Tel: 81-3-3214-5311
Fax: 81-3-3201-5856

Nintendo Co., Ltd.
Hiroshi Yamauchi
President
60 Kamitakamatsu-Cho
Hukuiue
Higashiyama-Ku
Kyoto City
Japan
Tel: 81-75-541-6111
Fax: 81-75-531-7996

Nippon Comsys Corporation
Shozo Iwasaki
President
3-23-14 Takanawa
Minato-Ku
Tokyo 108
Japan
Tel: 81-3-3448-7031
Fax: 81-3-3447-3993

Nippon Densetsu Kogyo Co., Ltd.
Tatsuyuki Enomoto
President
1-2-23 Ikenohata
Taito-Ku
Tokyo 110
Japan
Tel: 81-3-3822-8811
Fax: 81-3-3822-8960

Nippon Electric Glass Co., Ltd.
Tetsuji Mori
President
2-7-1 Seiran
Otsu
Shiga 520
Japan
Tel: 81-775-37-1700
Fax: 81-775-34-4967

Nippon Express Co., Ltd.
Shoichiro Hamanaka
President
3-12-9 Soto-Kanda
Chiyoda-Ku
Tokyo 101
Japan
Tel: 81-3-5294-5031
Fax: 81-3-5294-5039

Nippon Flour Mills Co., Ltd.
Hiroshi Sawada
President
5-27-5 Sendagaya
Shibuya-Ku
Tokyo 151
Japan
Tel: 81-3-3350-2311
Fax: 81-3-3352-3048

Nippon Hodo Co., Ltd.
Yoshio Nibe
President
1-19-11 Kyobashi
Chuo-Ku
Tokyo 104
Japan
Tel: 81-3-3563-6751
Fax: 81-3-3567-4086

Nippon Hoechst Marion Roussel Ltd.
Marc Dunoyer
President
2-17-51 Akasaka
Minato-Ku
Tokyo 107
Japan
Tel: 81-3-5571-6331
Fax: 81-3-5571-6215

Nippon Light Metal Co., Ltd.
Yukoh Masuda
President
2-2-20 Higasishinagawa
Shinagawa-Ku
Tokyo 140
Japan
Tel: 81-3-5461-9281
Fax: 81-3-5461-9200

Nippon Meat Packers, Inc.
Hiroji Okoso
President
6-14 Minami-Honmachi
3-Chome, Chuo-Ku
Osaka 541
Japan
Tel: 81-6-282-3130
Fax: 81-6-282-1056

Nippon Oil Co., Ltd.
Hidejiro Ohsawa
President
1-3-12 Nishi-Shinbashi
Minato-Ku
Tokyo 105
Japan
Tel: 81-3-3502-1135
Fax: 81-3-3502-9352

Nippon Paint Co., Ltd.
Hiroshi Fujii
President
2-1-2 Oyodo-Kita
Kita-Ku
Osaka 531
Japan
Tel: 81-6-458-1111
Fax: 81-6-455-9261/9278

Nippon Paper Industries Co., Ltd.
Masao Kobayashi
President
1-12-1 Yurakucho Bldg.
Yurakucho, Chiyoda-Ku
Tokyo 100
Japan
Tel: 81-3-3218-8000
Fax: 81-3-3214-5226

Nippon Petrochemicals Co., Ltd.
Kenzo Saikawa
President
1-3-1 Saiwai Bldg., Uchisaiwai-Cho
Chiyoda-Ku
Tokyo 100
Japan
Tel: 81-3-3501-7313
Fax: 81-3-3501-7630

Nippon Petroleum Gas Co., Ltd.
Usio Fukuda
President
6/F., Shin-Nisseki Bldg.
3-4-2 Marunouchi
Chiyoda-Ku
Tokyo 100
Japan
Tel: 81-3-3286-4811
Fax: 81-3-3286-4837

Nippon Petroleum Refining Co., Ltd.
Jiro Yamamoto
President
1-3-12 Nishi-Shinbashi
Minato-Ku
Tokyo 105
Japan
Tel: 81-3-3502-1111
Fax: 81-3-3502-9351

Nippon Road Co., Ltd.
Sato Hiromichi
President
6-5 Shimbashi, 1-Chome
Minato-Ku
Tokyo 105
Japan
Tel: 81-3-3571-3890
Fax: 81-3-3289-4489

Nippon Sanso Corporation
Hiroo Tsutiya
President
1-16-7 Nishi-Shinbashi
Minato-Ku
Tokyo 105
Japan
Tel: 81-3-3581-8200
Fax: 81-3-3580-9425

Nippon Sheet Glass Co., Ltd.
Minoru Matsumura
President
2-1-7 Kaigan
Minato-Ku
Tokyo 105
Japan
Tel: 81-3-5443-9522
Fax: 81-3-5443-9440

Nippon Shokubai Co., Ltd.
Kenji Aida
President
4-1-1 Koraibashi
Chuo-Ku
Osaka 541
Japan
Tel: 81-6-223-9111
Fax: 81-6-201-3716

Nippon Shuppan Hanbai, Inc.
Kazuhiro Igarashi
President
4-3 Kanda-Surugadai
Chiyoda-Ku
Tokyo 101
Japan
Tel: 81-3-3233-1111
Fax: 81-3-3233-8521

Nippon Steel Chemical Co., Ltd.
Yamatoya Takaki
President
1-13 Sinkawa, 2-Chome
Chuo-Ku
Tokyo 104
Japan
Tel: 81-3-5541-3622
Fax: 81-3-5541-3562

Nippon Steel Corporation
Takashi Imai
President
6-3 Otemachi, 2-Chome
Chiyoda-Ku
Tokyo 100-71
Japan
Tel: 81-3-3242-4111
Fax: 81-3-3275-5607

Nippon Suisan Kaisha, Ltd.
Yasuo Kunii
President
2-6-2 Otemachi
Chiyoda-Ku
Tokyo 100
Japan
Tel: 81-3-3244-7000
Fax: 81-3-3244-7085

Nippon Telegraph and Telephone Corp.
Jun-Ichiro Miyazu
President
3-19-2 Nishi-Shinjuku
Shinjuku-Ku
Tokyo 163-19
Japan
Tel: 81-3-5359-2111
Fax: 81-3-3509-4290

Nippon Television Network Corp.
Seiichiro Ujiie
President
14 Niban-Cho
Chiyoda-Ku
Tokyo 102-40
Japan
Tel: 81-3-5275-1111
Fax: 81-3-5275-4008

Nippon Travel Agency Co., Ltd.
Teruo Shoji
President
2-20-15 Shimbashi
Minato-Ku
Tokyo 105
Japan
Tel: 81-3-3572-8718
Fax: 81-3-3574-9610

Nippon Yusen Kabushiki Kaisha
Kentaro Kawamura
President
2-3-2 Marunouchi
Chiyoda-Ku
Tokyo 100
Japan
Tel: 81-3-3284-5151
Fax: 81-3-3284-6361/6081

Nippon Zeon Co., Ltd
Katsuhiko Nakano
President
2-6-1 Marunouchi
Chiyoda-Ku
Tokyo 100
Japan
Tel: 81-3-3216-1772
Fax: 81-3-3216-0501

Nishi-Nippon Railroad Co., Ltd.
Hisayuki Hashimoto
President
1-11-17 Tenjin, Chuo-Ku
Fukuoka 810
Japan
Tel: 81-92-734-1217
Fax: 81-92-781-2583

Nishimatsu Construction Co., Ltd.
Yoshiharu Kanayama
President
1-20-10 Toranomon
Minato-Ku
Tokyo 105
Japan
Tel: 81-3-3502-0232
Fax: 81-3-3580-2745

Nissan Construction Co., Ltd.
Takeshi Fujita
President
1-2-6 Minamiaoyama
Minato-Ku
Tokyo 107
Japan
Tel: 81-3-3402-8161
Fax: 81-3-3478-3232

Nissan Diesel Motor Co., Ltd.
Masayuki Saito
President
1, 1-Chome, Ohaza, Ageo-Shi
Saitama-Ken 362
Japan
Tel: 81-48-781-2301
Fax: 81-48-781-7505

Nissan Motor Co., Ltd.
Yoshikazu Hanawa
President
6-17-1 Ginza
Chuo-Ku
Tokyo 104-23
Japan
Tel: 81-3-5565-2147
Fax: 81-3-3546-2669

Nissan Shatai Co., Ltd.
Shigenori Asano
President
10-1 Amanuma
Hiratsuka City
Kanagawa Pref. 254
Japan
Tel: 81-463-21-8001
Fax: 81-463-21-8155

Nissei Sangyo Co., Ltd.
Noriaki Higuchi
President
1-24-14 Nishishimbashi
Minato-Ku
Tokyo 105
Japan
Tel: 81-3-3504-7111
Fax: 81-3-3504-7123

Nisshin Flour Milling Co., Ltd.
Osamu Shoda
President
19-12 Nihonbashi-Koamicho
Chuo-Ku
Tokyo 103
Japan
Tel: 81-3-3660-3111
Fax: 81-3-3660-3841

Nisshin Oil Mills, Ltd.
Jokei Akitani
President
1-23-1 Shinkawa
Chuo-Ku
Tokyo 104
Japan
Tel: 81-3-3206-5025
Fax: 81-3-3206-6452

Nisshin Steel Co., Ltd.
Yasuyuki Hamada
President
Shin-Kokisai Bldg.
3-4-1 Marunouchi
Chiyoda-Ku
Tokyo 100
Japan
Tel: 81-3-3216-5511
Fax: 81-3-3214-1895

Nisshinbo Industries, Inc.
Akihiro Mochizuki
President
2-31-11 Ningyo-Cho
Nihonbashi, Chuo-Ku
Tokyo 103
Japan
Tel: 81-3-5695-8833
Fax: 81-3-5695-8970

Nissho Iwai Australia Ltd.
Kageyama Koichiro
Managing Director
Level 17, Gateway Bldg
1 Macquarie Place
Sydney
NSW 2000
Australia
Tel: 61-2-9234-0811
Fax: 61-2-9235-1080

Nissho Iwai Corporation
Masatake Kusamichi
President
4-5 Akasaka, 2-Chome
Minato-Ku
Tokyo 107
Japan
Tel: 81-3-3588-2111
Fax: 81-3-3588-4136

Nissho Iwai Petroleum Co. (Singapore) Pte. Ltd.
H. Soiri
Managing Director
#34-00 Hong Leong Bldg.
16 Raffles Quay
Singapore 048581
Singapore
Tel: 65-229-6147
Fax: 65-227-6281

Nissin Corporation
Hiroshi Tsutsui
President
5 Banchi, Sanban-Cho
Chiyoda-Ku
Tokyo 102
Japan
Tel: 81-3-3238-6666
Fax: 81-3-3238-6638

Nissin Food Products Co., Ltd.
Koki Ando
President
4-1-1 Nishi-Nakajima
Yodogawa-Ku
Osaka 532
Japan
Tel: 81-6-305-7711
Fax: 81-6-304-1288

Nittetsu Shoji Co., Ltd.
Minoru Sato
President
Nittetsu N.D. Tower 1-5-7
Kameido Koto-Ku
Tokyo 136
Japan
Tel: 81-3-5627-2905
Fax: 81-3-5627-2196

Nitto Boseki Co., Ltd
Atsuhiko Sagara
President
1-2-1 Nihonbashi-Hamacho
Chuo-Ku
Tokyo 103
Japan
Tel: 81-3-3865-6632
Fax: 81-3-3865-6725

Nitto Denko Corporation
Hideki Yamamoto
President
1-1-2 Shimohozumi
Ibaraki City
Osaka Pref. 567
Japan
Tel: 81-726-22-2981
Fax: 81-726-26-1505

Nittsu Shoji Co., Ltd.
Hisashi Ashikari
President
3-12-9 Soto-Kanda
Chiyoda-Ku
Tokyo 101
Japan
Tel: 81-3-5256-2111
Fax: 81-3-3251-5225

NKK Corporation
Yoichi Shimogaichi
President
1-1-2 Marunouchi
Chiyoda-Ku
Tokyo 100
Japan
Tel: 81-3-3212-7111
Fax: 81-3-3214-8400/8436

NKK Trading Inc.
Kazuo Takemura
President
Itoshige Bldg.
4-4 Hisamatsu-Cho
Nihonbashi, Chuo-Ku
Tokyo 103
Japan
Tel: 81-3-3660-0853
Fax: 81-3-3660-1572

NOF Corporation
Masayasu Uno
President
Yebisu Garden Place Tower
20-3 Ebisu, 4-Chome
Shibuya-Ku
Tokyo 150
Japan
Tel: 81-3-5424-6658
Fax: 81-3-5424-6802

NOK Corporation
Masato Tsuru
President
1-12-15 Shiba-Daimon
Minato-Ku
Tokyo 105
Japan
Tel: 81-3-3432-4211
Fax: 81-3-3432-5904

Nokyo Tourist Corporation
Kazuomi Sagara
President
1-8-3 Otemachi
Chiyoda-Ku
Tokyo 100
Japan
Tel: 81-3-3270-0081
Fax: 81-3-3270-2952

Nomura Real Estate Development Co., Ltd.
Junichi Nakano
President
Shimjuku Nomura Bldg.
1-26-2 Nishishinjuku
Shinjuku-Ku
Tokyo 163-05
Japan
Tel: 81-3-3348-8811
Fax: 81-3-3345-0381

Nomura Trading Co., Ltd.
Hiroshi Ikeda
President
1-4-5 Bingo-Machi
Chuo-Ku
Osaka-Shi 541
Japan
Tel: 81-6-268-8111
Fax: 81-6-268-8037

Noritz Corporation
Ryota Matsumoto
President
93 Edo-Machi
Chuo-Ku
Kobe 650
Japan
Tel: 81-78-361-1929
Fax: 81-78-332-3046

Novartis Japan K.K.
Paul A. Dudler
President
37/F., World Trade Center Bldg.
2-4-1 Hamamatsu-Cho
Minato-Ku
Tokyo 105
Japan
Tel: 81-3-5403-1485
Fax: 81-3-5403-1477

Nozaki & Co., Ltd.
Hiroshi Kohzu
President
2-2-6 Nihonbashi-Bakurocho
Chuo-Ku
Tokyo 103-91
Japan
Tel: 81-3-5641-4304
Fax: 81-3-5641-4382

NSK Limited
Tetsuo Sekiya
President
1-6-3 Nissei Bldg., Osaki
Shinagawa-Ku
Tokyo 141
Japan
Tel: 81-3-3779-7111
Fax: 81-3-3779-7431

NTN Corporation
Toyoaki Itoh
President
1-3-17 Kyomachibori
Nishi-Ku
Osaka-Shi 550
Japan
Tel: 81-6-443-5001
Fax: 81-6-443-6966

NTP Nagoya Toyopet Corporation
Nanao Oguri
President
2-22 Oto-Cho, Atsuta-Ku
Nagoya 456
Aichi
Japan
Tel: 81-52-683-2111
Fax: 81-52-681-1765

NTT Data Corporation
Tomeo Kambayashi
President
Toyosu Center Bldg.
3-3 Toyosu, 3-Chome
Koto-Ku, Tokyo 135
Japan
Tel: 81-3-5546-8202
Fax: 81-3-5546-2405

O

Obayashi Corporation
Shinji Mukasa
President
2-3 Kanda-Tsukasacho
Chiyoda-Ku
Tokyo
Japan
Tel: 81-3-3292-1111
Fax: 81-3-5247-8934

Obayashi Road Corporation
Akio Konishi
President
1-24-1 Minami-Aoyama
Minato-Ku
Tokyo 107
Japan
Tel: 81-3-3796-6500
Fax: 81-3-3796-6516

Odakyu Department Store Co., Ltd.
Kunio Toshimitsu
President
1-1-3 Nishi-Shinjuku
Shinjuku-Ku
Tokyo 160
Japan
Tel: 81-3-3342-1111
Fax: 81-3-5325-3605

Odakyu Electric Railway Co., Ltd.
Takashi Takigami
President
1-8-3 Nishi-Shinjuku
Shinjuku-Ku
Tokyo 160
Japan
Tel: 81-3-3349-2054
Fax: 81-3-3346-1899

Ohmoto Gumi Co., Ltd.
Eiichi Omoto
President
1-1-13 Uchisange
Okayama City 700
Japan
Tel: 81-86-225-5131
Fax: 81-86-226-3258

Oil & Natural Gas Commission
B.C. Bora
Chairman & Managing Director
Jeevan Bharati Bldg
Connaught Circus,
New Delhi 110001
India
Tel: 91-22-642-9983
Fax: 91-22-640-0282

OJI Paper Co., Ltd.
Masahiko Ohkuni
President
7-5 Ginza, 4-Chome
Chuo-Ku
Tokyo 104
Japan
Tel: 81-3-3563-1111
Fax: 81-3-3563-1135

Okamoto Co., Ltd.
Masao Okamoto
President
1-7-4 Nihonbashi-Honcho
Chuo-Ku
Tokyo 103
Japan
Tel: 81-3-3241-4141
Fax: 81-3-3241-4398

Okamura Corporation
Kikuo Nakamura
President
2-7-18 Kitasaiwai
Nishi-Ku
Yokohama 220
Japan
Tel: 81-45-319-3401
Fax: 81-45-319-3515

Okaya & Co., Ltd.
Tokuichi Okaya
President
2-4-18 Sakae
Naka-Ku
Nagoya 460-91
Japan
Tel: 81-52-204-8122
Fax: 81-52-204-8384

OKI Electric Industry Co., Ltd.
Shiko Sawamura
President
7-12 Toranomon, 1-Chome
Minato-Ku
Tokyo 105
Japan
Tel: 81-3-3501-3111
Fax: 81-3-3581-5522

Okumura Corporation
Shotaro Okumura
President
2-2-2 Matsuzaki-Cho
Abeno-Ku
Osaka 545
Japan
Tel: 81-6-621-1101
Fax: 81-6-623-7692

Okura & Co., Ltd.
Hiroshi Toyokawa
President
2-3-6 Ginza
Chuo-Ku
Tokyo 104
Japan
Tel: 81-3-3566-6000
Fax: 81-3-3566-2866

Okura Pulp and Paper Co., Ltd.
Akira Mutaguchi
President
8 Kanda-Nishiki-Cho
1-Chome, Chiyoda-Ku
Tokyo 101
Japan
Tel: 81-3-3259-5080
Fax: 81-3-3233-0991

Olympus Optical Co., Ltd.
Masatoshi Kishimoto
President
2-3-1 Nishi-Shinjuku
Shinjuku-Ku
Tokyo 163-09
Japan
Tel: 81-3-3340-2111/2121
Fax: 81-3-3340-2130/2098

Omron Corporation
Yoshio Tateisi
President
Karasuma Nanajo
Shimogyo-Ku
Kyoto 600
Japan
Tel: 81-75-344-7170
Fax: 81-75-344-7171

Onward Kashiyama Co., Ltd.
Akira Baba
President
3-10-5 Nihonbashi
Chuo-Ku
Tokyo 103
Japan
Tel: 81-3-3272-2317
Fax: 81-3-3272-2333

Optus Communications
Peter Howell-Davies
Chief Executive Officer
101 Miller Street
North Sydney
NSW 2060
Australia
Tel: 61-2-9243-7000
Fax: 61-2-9242-7895

Orient Overseas (International) Limited
C.C. Tung
Chairman & President
33/F., Harbour Centre
25 Harbour Road
Wanchai
Hong Kong
Tel: 852-2833-3838
Fax: 852-2531-8122

Oriental Land Co., Ltd.
Toshio Kagami
President
1-1 Maihama, Urayasu-Shi
Chiba-Ken 279
Japan
Tel: 81-47-381-3053
Fax: 81-47-355-9621

Osaka Gas Co., Ltd.
Shin-Ichiro Ryoki
President
4-1-2 Hirano-Cho
Chuo-Ku
Osaka 541
Japan
Tel: 81-6-202-2221
Fax: 81-6-226-1681

Osaka Uoichiba Co., Ltd.
Kunio Tetsumoto
President
1-1-86 Noda
Fukushima-Ku
Osaka 553
Japan
Tel: 81-6-469-2003
Fax: 81-6-469-2154

Otsuka Pharmaceutical Co., Ltd.
Akihiko Otsuka
President
2-9 Kanda Tsukasa-Cho
Chiyoda-Ku
Tokyo 101
Japan
Tel: 81-3-3292-0021
Fax: 81-3-3295-2058

Otsuka Shokai Co., Ltd.
Minoru Otsuka
President
2-12-1 Misaki-Cho
Chiyoda-Ku
Tokyo 101
Japan
Tel: 81-3-3264-7111
Fax: 81-3-3239-9614

P

Pacific Dunlop Limited
Rodney L. Chadwick
Managing Director
Level 41, 101 Collins Street
Melbourne, Victoria 3000
Australia
Tel: 61-3-9270-7270
Fax: 61-3-9270-7300

Pacific Petroleum & Trading Co., Ltd.
Yasuichi Arao
President
11/F., East Tower
Akasaka Twin Tower
17-22 Akasaka, 2-Chome
Minato-Ku, Tokyo
Japan
Tel: 81-3-5562-6501
Fax: 81-3-5562-6504

Pakistan State Oil Co., Ltd.
Jahangir N.W. Ansari
Managing Director
9/F., PSO House
Kheyaban-E-Iqbal, Clifton
Karachi
Pakistan
Tel: 92-21-920-3770
Fax: 92-21-920-3717

Paltac Corporation
Tadao Murakami
President
1-5-9 Minami-Kyuhojimachi
Chuo-Ku
Osaka 541
Japan
Tel: 81-6-262-1286
Fax: 81-6-264-6343

Parco Co., Ltd.
Masayoshi Yamada
Chairman
15-1 Udagawa-Cho
Shibuya-Ku
Tokyo 150
Japan
Tel: 81-3-3477-5737
Fax: 81-3-3464-1370

Penta-Ocean Construction Co., Ltd.
Rempei Mizuno
President
2-2-8 Koraku, Bunkyo-Ku
Tokyo 112
Japan
Tel: 81-3-3816-7111
Fax: 81-3-3816-7158

Perlis Plantations Berhad
Kuok Khoon Ean
Chairman
17/F., Wisma Jerneh
38 Jalan Sultan Ismail
Kuala Lumpur 50250
Malaysia
Tel: 60-3-241-2077
Fax: 60-3-241-8242

Pertamina
Falsal Abda Oe
President & Director
1a Jalan Merdeka Timur
Jakarta 10110
Indonesia
Tel: 62-21-381-5111
Fax: 62-21-384-6917

Perusahaan Listrik Negara (PLN)
Djiteng Marsudi.Ir.
President Director
Jalan Trunojoyo, Blok M I/135
Kebayoran Baru
Jakarta Selatan
Indonesia
Tel: 62-21-739-7765/726-2234
Fax: 62-21-722-1330

Perusahaan Otomobil Nasional Berhad (Proton)
Tan Sri Yahaya Ahmad
Chairman
Kawasan Perindustrian Hicom
Batu Tiga, 40000 Shah Alam
Selangor Darul Ehsan
Malaysia
Tel: 60-3-511-1055
Fax: 60-3-511-1252

Petroleum Authority of Thailand
Pala Sookawesh
Governor
555 Vibhavadi Rangsit Road
Chatuchak
Bangkok 10900
Thailand
Tel: 662-537-2000
Fax: 662-537-3498

Petroliam Nasional Berhad
Tan Sri Dato Mohd Hassan Bin Marican
President
Menara Dayabumi
Jalan Sultan Hishamuddin
Peti Surat 12444
Kuala Lumpur 50778
Malaysia
Tel: 60-3-274-8011/3833
Fax: 60-3-274-0217/2895

Petron Corporation
Ali A. Al-Ajmi
President
Petron Bldg.
7901 Makati Avenue
Makati City
Philippines
Tel: 63-2-892-9061
Fax: 63-2-817-6220

Petronas Dagangan Berhad
Anwarrudin Bin Ahamad Osman
Managing Director
Menara 1, Menara Faber
Jalan Desa Bahagia, Taman Desa
Off Jalan Kelang Lama
Kuala Lumpur 58100
Malaysia
Tel: 60-3-782-3700
Fax: 60-3-782-2520

PFU Limited
Eigo Kato
President
Nu 98-2, Unoke, Unokemachi
Kahoku-Gun
Ishikawa-Ken 929-11
Japan
Tel: 81-76-283-1212
Fax: 81-76-283-4689

Philips (Singapore) Pte. Limited
Victor K.H. Loh
Chairman & President
620A Lorong 1 Toa Payoh
Singapore 319762
Tel: 65-350-2000
Fax: 65-253-3395

Pilipinas Shell Petroleum Corporation
Reinier Willems
President
Shell House, 156 Valero Street
Salcedo Village
Makati City 1227
Philippines
Tel: 63-2-816-6501/6565/6089
Fax: 63-2-816-6565

Pioneer Electronic Corporation
Kaneo Ito
President
1-4-1 Meguro, Meguro-Ku
Tokyo 153
Japan
Tel: 81-3-3494-1111
Fax: 81-3-3495-4428

Pioneer International Limited
John Schubert
Managing Director
Level 46, Governor Phillip Tower
1 Farrer Place
Sydney
NSW 2000
Australia
Tel: 61-2-9323-4000
Fax: 61-2-9323-4009

Pohang Iron & Steel Company Limited
Mahn-Je Kim
Chairman
1 Koedong-Dong, Nam-Ku
Pohang City
Kyongsangbuk-Do 790-600
South Korea
Tel: 82-562-220-0114
Fax: 82-562-220-3399

Pola Chemical Industry, Inc.
Satoshi Suzuki
President
2-2-3 Nishi-Gotanda
Shinagawa-Ku
Tokyo 141
Japan
Tel: 81-3-3494-7111
Fax: 81-3-3494-8541

Pola Cosmetics Inc.
Nobuya Arai
President
2-2-3 Nishi-Gotanda
Shinagawa-Ku
Tokyo 141
Japan
Tel: 81-3-3494-7111
Fax: 81-3-3494-8141

President Enterprises Corp.
Lin Chang Sheng
President
301 Chung Chen Road
Yan Harng, Yeong Kang City
Tainan Hsien
Taiwan
Tel: 88-6-6-253-2121
Fax: 88-6-6-254-1770

Prima Meat Packers, Ltd.
Shinji Tateishi
President
3-2-5 Kasumigaseki
Chiyoda-Ku
Tokyo 100
Japan
Tel: 81-3-3593-6710
Fax: 81-3-3592-1591

Progressive Enterprises Limited
Graeme John Kelly
Managing Director
80 Favona Road
Mangere
Auckland
New Zealand
Tel: 64-9-275-2699
Fax: 64-9-275-0508

PT Gudang Garam
Rachman Halim
President Director
Jalan Semampir II/1
Kediri 64121
Indonesia
Tel: 62-354-82091
Fax: 62-354-81555

PT Indocement Tunggal Prakarsa
Sudwikatmono
President Director
8/F., Wisma Indosemen
Jalan Jend. Sudirman, Kav. 70-71
Jakarta 12910
Indonesia
Tel: 62-21-251-2121
Fax: 62-21-251-0066

Q

Qantas Airways Limited
James Strong
Managing Director
Level 9, Qantas Centre
Building A
203 Coward Street
Mascot
NSW 2020
Australia
Tel: 61-2-9691-3636
Fax: 61-2-9691-3339

Qilu Petrochemical Corp.
Guo Yankang
General Manager
Linzi District, Zibo
Shandong, 255436
China
Tel: 86-533-7180-777
Fax: 86-533-7180-406

Q.P. Corporation
Shiro Tarui
President
1-4-13 Shibuya
Shibuya-Ku
Tokyo 150
Japan
Tel: 81-3-3486-3331
Fax: 81-3-3498-1806

Queensland Sugar Corporation
Dr. David J.S. Rutledge
Chairman
20/F., 240 Queen Street
Brisbane
Queensland 4000
Australia
Tel: 61-7-3231-0199
Fax: 61-7-3221-2906

R

Recruit Co., Ltd.
Eiko Kono
President
Recruit Ginza 8 Bldg.
8-4-17 Ginza, Chuo-Ku
Tokyo 104
Japan
Tel: 81-3-3575-1111
Fax: 81-3-3575-5887

Recruit Cosmos Co., Ltd.
Satoshi Shigeta
President
3-9-15 Kaigan, Minato-Ku
Tokyo 108
Japan
Tel: 81-3-3571-1111
Fax: 81-3-5440-4004

Reliance Industries Limited
Dhirubhai H. Ambani
Chairman
3/F., Maker Chambers IV
222 Nariman Point
Mumbai 400 021
India
Tel: 91-22-283-1633/16-282-6070
Fax: 91-22-204-2268

Rengo Co., Ltd.
Kaoru Hasegawa
President
5-25 Umeda, 2-Chome
Kita-Ku
Osaka 530
Japan
Tel: 81-6-342-0266
Fax: 81-6-342-0379

Renown Inc.
Keiji Toyoda
President
2-34-18 Jingumae
Shibuya-Ku
Tokyo 150-07
Japan
Tel: 81-3-3478-9580
Fax: 81-3-3403-5366

Ricoh Co., Ltd.
Masamitsu Sakurai
President
1-15-5 Minami-Aoyama
Minato-Ku
Tokyo 107
Japan
Tel: 81-3-3479-3111
Fax: 81-3-3403-1578

Rinnai Corporation
Susumu Naito
President
2-26 Fukuzumi-Cho
Nakagawa-Ku
Nagoya 454
Japan
Tel: 81-52-361-8211
Fax: 81-52-353-9565

Rio Tinto Limited
Leon Davis
Chief Executive
55 Collins Street
Melbourne
Victoria 3000
Australia
Tel: 61-3-9283-3333
Fax: 61-3-9283-3257

Rohm Co., Ltd.
Ken Sato
President
21 Saiin Mizosaki-Cho
Ukyo-Ku
Kyoto 615
Japan
Tel: 81-75-311-2121
Fax: 81-75-315-0172

Rothmans Holdings Limited
Gary L. Krelle
Chief Executive Officer
Level 42, Northpoint
100 Miller Street
North Sydney
NSW 2060
Australia
Tel: 61-2-9956-0666
Fax: 61-2-9956-7860

Ryobi Limited
Hiroshi Urakami
President
3-15-1 Soto-Kanda
Chiyoda-Ku
Tokyo 101
Japan
Tel: 81-3-3257-1500
Fax: 81-3-3257-1513

Ryoden Trading Company, Ltd.
Hirohiko Sazuki
President
3-15-15 Higashi-Ikebukuro
Toshima-Ku
Tokyo 170
Japan
Tel: 81-3-5396-6119
Fax: 81-3-5396-6448

Ryosan Co., Ltd.
Tatsuo Ui
President
2-5-15 Higashi-Kanda
Chiyoda-Ku
Tokyo 101
Japan
Tel: 81-3-3862-2591
Fax: 81-3-3862-4385

Ryoshoku Limited
Tadashi Hirota
President
1-1 Heiwajima, 6-Chome
Ohta-Ku
Tokyo 143
Japan
Tel: 81-3-3767-5033
Fax: 81-3-3767-0450

S

S x L Corporation
Shogo Nakajima
President
2-12-1 Sonezaki
Kita-Ku
Osaka 530
Japan
Tel: 81-6-315-1131
Fax: 81-6-361-6072

Sagami Railway Co., Ltd.
Masahiro Hoshino
President
2-9-14 Kita-Saiwai
Nishi-Ku
Yokohama 220-91
Japan
Tel: 81-45-319-2057
Fax: 81-45-319-8989

Sam Yang Company
Kim Sang-Ung
President
263 Yeonji-Dong
Chongno-Gu
Seoul
South Korea
Tel: 86-2-740-7114
Fax: 86-2-740-7640

Samsung Company
Shin Se-Gil
President
250 Taepyongno, 2-Ga
Chung-Gu
Seoul
South Korea
Tel: 82-2-751-2114
Fax: 82-2-752-7926

Samsung Display Devices
Yun Jong-Yong
President
120 Taepyongno, 2-Ga
Chung-Gu
Seoul
South Korea
Tel: 82-2-727-3232
Tel: 82-2-727-3219

Samsung Electro-Mechanics Co., Ltd.
Lee Hyung-Do
President
314 Maetan 3 Dong, Paldal-Ku
Suwon, Kyungki-Do
South Korea
Tel: 82-331-210-5114
Fax: 82-331-210-6363

Samsung Electronics Co., Ltd.
Jong-Yong Yun
President
Samsung Main Bldg.
250, 2-Ka, Taepyung-Ro
Chung-Ku
Seoul 100-742
South Korea
Tel: 82-2-727-7114
Fax: 82-2-727-7985

Samsung Heavy Industries Co., Ltd.
Kyong Ju-Hyon
President
25 Pongrae-Dong, 1-Ga
Chung-Gu
Seoul
South Korea
Tel: 82-2-728-6200
Fax: 82-2-728-6161

San Miguel Corporation
Andres Soriano III
Chairman
40 San Miguel Avenue
Mandaluyong City 1550
Metro-Manila
Philippines
Tel: 63-2-632-3000
Fax: 63-2-632-3099

San Yang Industry Co. Ltd.
I-Hsiung Liu
President
124 Hsin Ming Road
Nei-Hu
Taipei
Taiwan
Tel: 88-6-2-791-2161
Fax: 88-6-2-791-2160

San-Ai Oil Co., Ltd.
Yoshiaki Ito
President
5-22-5 Higashiooi
Shinagawa-Ku
Tokyo 140
Japan
Tel: 81-3-5479-3180
Fax: 81-3-5479-3370

San-Mic Chiyoda Trading Co., Ltd.
Yoshiaki Himi
President
Kamakura Kashi Bldg.
2-2-1 Uchikanda
Chiyoda-Ku
Tokyo 101
Japan
Tel: 81-3-3252-1654
Fax: 81-3-3256-1063

Sanden Corporation
Masayoshi Ushikubo
President
20 Kotobuki-Cho
Isesaki-Shi
Gunma 372
Japan
Tel: 81-270-24-1211
Fax: 81-270-24-5338

Sankei Shimbun Co., Ltd.
Kiyohara Takehiko
President
1-7-2 Otemachi
Chiyoda-Ku
Tokyo 100
Japan
Tel: 81-3-3231-7111
Fax: 81-3-3275-8955

Sanken Electric Co., Ltd.
Koichi Kotani
President
3-6-3 Kitano
Niiza City
Saitama Pref. 352
Japan
Tel: 81-48-472-1111
Fax: 81-48-476-1778

Sanki Engineering Co., Ltd.
Takeshi Ohshima
President
Sanshin Bldg.
1-4-1 Yuraku-Cho
Chiyoda-Ku
Tokyo 100
Japan
Tel: 81-3-3502-6111
Fax: 81-3-3508-9658

Sankyo Aluminum Industry Co., Ltd.
Hisao Arai
President
70 Hayakawa
Takaoka-Shi
Toyama-Ken 933
Japan
Tel: 81-766-20-2101
Fax: 81-766-20-2082

Sankyo Co., Ltd.
Yoshibumi Kawamura
President
5-1 Nihonbashi-Honcho, 3-Chome
Chuo-Ku
Tokyo 103
Japan
Tel: 81-3-5255-7111
Fax: 81-3-5255-7035

Sankyu Inc.
Kimikazu Nakamura
President
1-4-28 Mita
Minato-Ku
Tokyo 108
Japan
Tel: 81-3-5484-3939
Fax: 81-3-3453-1858

Sanseido Co., Ltd.
Takashi Yamada
President
2-14-1 Yamamoto-Dori
Chuo-Ku
Kobe 650
Japan
Tel: 81-78-231-4341
Fax:81-78-222-0359/261-2221

Sanshin Electronics Co., Ltd.
Mitsumasa Matsunaga
President
4-4-12 Shiba
Minato-Ku
Tokyo 108
Japan
Tel: 81-3-3453-5111
Fax: 81-3-3451-2414

Sanwa Shutter Corporation
Toshitaka Takayama
President
2-1-1 Nishi-Shinjuku
Shinjuku-Ku
Tokyo 163-04
Japan
Tel: 81-3-3346-3019
Fax: 81-3-3346-3317

Sanyo Electric Co., Ltd.
Yasuaki Takano
President
2-5-5 Keihan-Hondori
Moriguchi City
Osaka Pref. 570
Japan
Tel: 81-6-991-1181
Fax: 81-6-991-6566

Sanyo Life Electronics Co., Ltd.
Hideaki Sasagawa
President
1-1 Dainichi-Higashi-Machi
Moriguchi-Shi
Osaka 570
Japan
Tel: 81-6-901-1111
Fax: 81-6-901-3400

Sanyo Shokai Ltd.
Masamichi Nakase
President
14 Honshio-Cho
Shinjuku-Ku
Tokyo 160
Japan
Tel: 81-3-3357-4111
Fax: 81-3-3226-8530

Sapporo Breweries Limited
Kenzo Edamoto
President
4-20-1 Ebisu
Shibuya-Ku
Tokyo 150
Japan
Tel: 81-3-5423-2111
Fax: 81-3-5423-2078

Sato Kogyo Co., Ltd.
Yoshitake Sato
President
12-20 Nihonbashi-Honcho
4-Chome, Chuo-Ku
Tokyo 103
Japan
Tel: 81-3-3661-1231
Fax: 81-3-3661-5473

Seagate Technology International
Steve Luczo
President & Chief Operating Officer
7000 Ang Mo Kio Avenue 5
Singapore 569877
Tel: 65-483-3888
Fax: 65-484-0110

Secom Co., Ltd.
Makoto Iida
Chairman
1-26-2 Nishi-Shinjuku
Shinjuku-Ku
Tokyo 163-05
Japan
Tel: 81-3-3348-7511
Fax: 81-3-3348-1799

Sega Enterprises, Ltd.
Hayao Nakayama
President
1-2-12 Haneda
Ohta-Ku
Tokyo 144
Japan
Tel: 81-3-5736-7034/7111
Fax: 81-3-5736-7078

Seibu Construction Co., Ltd.
Minoru Kashiwagi
President
1-11-2 Kusunokidai
Tokorozawa-Shi
Saitama-Ken 359
Japan
Tel: 81-429-26-3311
Fax: 81-429-26-3315

Seibu Department Stores, Ltd.
Hiroshi Kometani
President
1-28-1 Minami-Ikebukuro
Toshima-Ku
Tokyo 171
Japan
Tel: 81-3-3981-0111
Fax: 81-3-5992-8765

Seibu Oil Company Limited
Yasuto Kikuchi
President
Kowa Nishi-Shinbashi Bldg.
1-1 Nishi-Shinbashi, 2-Chome
Minato-Ku
Tokyo
Japan
Tel: 81-3-5512-3411
Fax: 81-3-5512-3444

Seibu Railway Co., Ltd.
Hiroyuki Toda
President
1-16-15 Minamiikebukuro
Toshima-Ku
Tokyo
Japan
Tel: 81-429-26-2044
Fax: 81-429-26-2237

Seika Corporation
Kousei Matsuo
President
3-3-1 Marunouchi
Chiyoda-Ku, Tokyo 100
Japan
Tel: 81-3-5221-7102
Fax: 81-3-5221-7125

Seiko Corporation
Chushichi Inoue
President
6-21 Kyobashi, 2-Chome
Chuo-Ku, Tokyo 104
Japan
Tel: 81-3-3563-2111
Fax: 81-3-3563-8496

Seiko Epson Corporation
Hideaki Yasukawa
President
3-5 Owa, 3-Chome
Suwa-Shi, Nagano-Ken 392
Japan
Tel: 81-266-52-3131
Fax: 81-266-53-4844

Seiko Instruments Inc.
Kiyoshi Ito
President
1-8 Nakase, Mihama-Ku
Chiba-City 261
Japan
Tel: 81-43-211-1111
Fax: 81-43-211-8029/8038

Seikodo Co., Ltd.
Iihara Shigeru
President
2-65-8 Itabashi
Itabashi-Ku, Tokyo
Japan 173
Tel: 81-3-3579-4511
Fax: 81-3-3579-5881

Seino Transportation Co., Ltd.
Yoshikazu Taguchi
President
1 Taguchi-Cho
Ohgaki City
Gifu Pref. 503
Japan
Tel: 81-584-81-1111
Fax: 81-584-82-5040

Seiyu Foods Co., Ltd.
Kunihiro Hashimoto
President
45/F., Sunshine 60 Bldg.
3-1-1 Higashi-Ikebukuro
Toshima-Ku
Tokyo 170
Japan
Tel: 81-3-3989-5734
Fax: 81-3-5396-6075

Seiyu Ltd., The
Katsuhiro Fujiseki
President
Sunshine 60 Bldg.
3-1-1 Higashi-Ikebukuro
Toshima-Ku
Tokyo 170
Japan
Tel: 81-3-3989-5069
Fax: 81-3-3982-3221

Sekisui Chemical Co., Ltd.
Susumu Nishizawa
President
4-4 Nishi-Tenma, 2-Chome
Kita-Ku
Osaka 530
Japan
Tel: 81-6-365-4122
Fax: 81-6-365-4370

Sekisui House Co., Ltd.
Isao Okui
President
Towereast, Umeda-Sky Bldg.
1-88 Naka, 1-Chome
Kita-Ku
Osaka 531
Japan
Tel: 81-6-440-3111
Fax: 81-6-440-3331

Semi-Tech (Global) Company Limited
James Henry Ting
Chairman & Chief Executive
Suite 3001-3004
Two Exchange Square
8 Connaught Place
Central
Hong Kong
Tel: 852-2524-1043
Fax: 852-2845-3558

Senko Co., Ltd.
Yasushi Shimamura
President
2-7-18 Shibata
Kita-Ku
Osaka 530
Japan
Tel: 81-6-372-1611
Fax: 81-6-372-1626

Senshukai Co., Ltd.
Takashi Miyaji
President & Representative Director
1-4-31 Doshin
Kita-Ku
Osaka 530
Japan
Tel: 81-6-881-3100
Fax: 81-6-881-3050

Seven-Eleven Japan Co., Ltd.
Ken Kudo
President
4-1-4 Shiba-Koen, Minato-Ku
Tokyo 105
Japan
Tel: 81-3-3459-3711
Fax: 81-3-3438-3724

SGS-Thomson Microelectronics Asia Pacific (Pte) Ltd.
Jean-Claude Marquet
Corporate Vice President
28 Ang Mo Kio Industrial Park II
Singapore 569508
Tel: 65-482-1411
Fax: 65-482-0240

Shanghai Automotive Industry (Group) Corp.
Chen Xiang Lin
President
390 Wu Kang Road
Shanghai 200031
China
Tel: 86-21-6433-6892
Fax: 86-21-6433-0518

Shanghai Baoshan Iron & Steel Corporation
Li Ming
Manager
Baoshan District, Shanghai 201900
China
Tel: 86-21-5664-8648
Fax: 86-21-5664-8046

Shanghai Petrochemical Co. Ltd.
Wang Jiming
Chairman
2 Wei Er Rd.
Jinshanwei Shanghai
China
Tel: 86-21-5794-3143
Fax: 86-21-5794-0050

Shanghai Volkswagen Automotive Co., Ltd.
Hong Jiming
Managing Director
Luo Pu Road
Anting
Shanghai 201805
China
Tel: 86-21-5957-7780/8888
Fax: 86-21-5957-2815

Sharp Corporation
Haruo Tsuji
President
22-22 Nagaike-Cho, Abeno Ku
Osaka-Shi 545
Japan
Tel: 81-6-625-3007
Fax: 81-6-628-1667

Shell Australia Limited
J.R. Williams
Chairman
1 Spring Street
Melbourne
Victoria 3000
Australia
Tel: 61-3-9666-5444
Fax: 61-3-9666-5008

Shell Company of Thailand Limited, The
M.S. Warwick
Chairman
Shell Bldg.
10 Soonthornkosa Road
Klongtoey
Bangkok 10110
Thailand
Tel: 66-2-249-0491
Fax: 66-2-249-3700

Shikoku Electric Power Co., Inc.
Kozo Kondo
President & Director
2-5 Marunouchi
Takamatsu City 760-91
Japan
Tel: 81-878-21-5061
Fax: 81-878-26-1250

Shimadzu Corporation
Kikuo Fujiwara
President
1 Nishinokyo-Kuwabaracho
Nakagyo-Ku
Kyoto 604
Japan
Tel: 81-75-823-1111
Fax: 81-75-811-3188

Shimizu Corporation
Harusuke Imamura
President
Seavans South
1-2-3 Shibaura
Minato-Ku
Tokyo 150-07
Japan
Tel: 81-3-5441-1111
Fax: 81-3-5441-0349

Shin Caterpillar Mitsubishi Limited
Kiyokazu Kawai
President
4-10-1 Yoga
Setagaya-Ku
Tokyo 158
Japan
Tel: 81-3-5717-1121
Fax: 81-3-5717-1129

Shin Nikkei Co., Ltd.
Ryozaburo Ogura
President
Dai Ichi Bldg.
2-7-23 Kiba
Koto-Ku
Tokyo 135
Japan
Tel: 81-3-3820-2100
Fax: 81-3-3820-2429

Shin-Etsu Chemical Co., Ltd.
Chihiro Kanagawa
President
2-6-1 Otemachi
Chiyoda-Ku
Tokyo 100
Japan
Tel: 81-3-3246-5111
Fax: 81-3-3246-5350

Shin-Idemitsu Co., Ltd.
Yoshihide Idemitsu
President
1-10 Kamigofuku-Machi
Hakata-Ku, Fukuoka City
Fukuoka
Japan
Tel: 81-92-291-4131
Fax: 81-92-271-0958

Shinmaywa Industries, Ltd.
Shiko Saikawa
President
1-5-25 Kosome-Cho
Nishinomiya City
Hyogo Pref. 663
Japan
Tel: 81-798-47-0331
Fax: 81-798-45-5743

Shinryo Corporation
Go Kagami
President
2-4 Yotsuya
Shinjuku-Ku
Tokyo 160
Japan
Tel: 81-3-3357-2151
Fax: 81-3-3353-3191

Shinsho Corporation
Miyaji Yoshiki
President
2-6-17 Kitahama
Chuo-Ku
Osaka 541
Japan
Tel: 81-6-206-7009
Fax: 81-6-206-7399

Shintoa Corporation
Sumio Arai
President
5/F., New Tokyo Bldg.
3-3-1 Marunouchi
Chiyoda-Ku
Tokyo 100
Japan
Tel: 81-3-3286-0211
Fax: 81-3-3213-2420

Shionogi & Co., Ltd.
Yoshihiko Shiono
President
3-1-8 Dosho-Machi
Chuo-Ku
Osaka 541
Japan
Tel: 81-6-202-2161
Fax: 81-6-229-9596

Shiseido Co., Ltd.
Akira Gemma
President
7-5-5 Ginza
Chuo-Ku
Tokyo 104-10
Japan
Tel: 81-3-3572-5111
Fax: 81-3-3574-8380

Shogakukan, Inc.
Masahiro Ooga
President
2-3-1 Hitotsubashi
Chiyoda-Ku
Tokyo 101-01
Japan
Tel: 81-3-3230-5296
Fax: 81-3-3230-5875

Shokusan Jutaku Sogo Co., Ltd.
Haruo Murozumi
President
2-11-17 Yoyogi
Shibuya-Ku
Tokyo 151
Japan
Tel: 81-3-3370-1214
Fax: 81-3-3370-1886

Shougang Corporation
Luo Bing-Sheng
President
Shi Jing Shan District
Beijing 100041
China
Tel: 86-10-6829-3520
Fax: 86-10-6829-3518

Showa Aluminum Corporation
Ichiro Anzai
President
3-6-5 Iidabashi
Chiyoda-Ku
Tokyo 102
Japan
Tel: 81-3-3239-5311
Fax: 81-3-3239-5306

Showa Denko K.K.
Mitsuo Ohashi
President
1-13-9 Daimon
Minato-Ku
Tokyo 105
Japan
Tel: 81-3-5470-3111
Fax: 81-3-3431-6442

Showa Electric Wire & Cable Co., Ltd.
Kaoru Murata
President
1-1-18 Toranomon
Minato-Ku
Tokyo 105
Japan
Tel: 81-3-3597-7011
Fax: 81-3-3503-4506

Showa Pharmaceutical Co., Ltd.
Futoshi Yokoi
President
2-173-2 Hongo Meito-Ku
Nagoya-Shi 465
Japan
Tel: 81-52-775-1111
Fax: 81-52-773-7962

Showa Sangyo Co., Ltd.
Mutsuo Kanehara
President
2-2-1 Kamakuragashi Bldg.
Uchi-Kanda
Chiyoda-Ku
Tokyo 101
Japan
Tel: 81-3-3257-2011
Fax: 81-3-3257-2180

Showa Shell Sekiyu K.K.
Tamotsu Yamazaki
President
Kasumigaseki Bldg.
3-2-5 Kasumigaseki
Chiyoda-Ku
Tokyo 100
Japan
Tel: 81-3-3580-0123
Fax: 81-3-3581-9347

Shueisha Inc.
Tamio Kojima
President
2-5-10 Hitotsubashi
Chiyoda-Ku
Tokyo 101-50
Japan
Tel: 81-3-3230-6111
Fax: 81-3-3238-9239

Siam Cement Public Company Ltd.
Sanya Dharmasakti
Chairman
1 Siam Cement Road
Bangsue
Bangkok 10800
Thailand
Tel: 66-2-586-3333/4444
Fax: 66-2-587-2199/2201

Siam Motors Co., Ltd.
Phornthep Phornprapha
President
891/1 Siam Motors Bldg.
Rama I Road
Pathumwan
Bangkok 10330
Thailand
Tel: 662-215-0830
Fax: 662-216-2114

Sichuan Changhong Elect. Co., Ltd.
Ni Run Feng
Chairman
4 Yue Road
Mian Yang, Sichuan
China
Tel: 86-816-2411-486
Fax: 86-816-2411-518

Sime Darby Berhad
Datuk Nik Mohamed Bin Nik Yaacob
Group Chief Executive
21/F., Wisma Sime Darby
Jalan Raja Laut
Kuala Lumpur 50350
Malaysia
Tel: 60-3-291-4122
Fax: 60-3-298-7398

Singapore Airlines Limited
Cheong Choong Kong
Deputy Chairman
Airline House
25 Airline Road
Singapore 819829
Tel: 65-542-3333
Fax: 65-545-5034

Singapore Petroleum Co., Ltd.
Jacobus Johannes Rinck
President
6 Shenton Way
#33-08 DBS Bldg.
Tower Two
Singapore 068809
Tel: 65-221-3166
Fax: 65-221-3691

Singapore Pools (Private) Ltd.
Goh Yong Hong
Chairman
10 Anson Road
#03-09 International Plaza
Singapore 079903
Tel: 65-222-9088
Fax: 65-323-6240

Singapore Power Limited
B.G. Boey Tak Hap
Chief Executive
111 Somerset Road #16-01
Singapore 238164
Tel: 65-733-1668
Fax: 65-831-8188

Singapore Telecommunications Ltd.
B. G. Lee Hsien Yang
Director
31 Exeter Road
Comcentre
Singapore 239732
Tel: 65-838-3388
Fax: 65-732-8428

Sinochem
Zheng Dunxun
President
Sinochem Tower
A2 Fuxingmenwai Dajie
Beijing 100045
China
Tel: 86-10-6856-8900/8888
Fax: 86-10-6856-8890

Sinopec Daqing Petrochemical Complex
Mr. Wang
Chairman
Wo Li Tuan
Long Feng District
Daqing City
China
Tel: 86-459-6763-028
Fax: 86-459-625-2024

Skylark Co., Ltd.
Tasuku Chino
President
6-14-1 Nishi-Shinjuku
Shinjuku-Ku
Tokyo 160
Japan
Tel: 81-3-3349-7595
Fax: 81-3-3346-0615

Snow Brand Milk Products Co., Ltd.
Sumio Katayama
President
13 Honshio-Cho
Shinjuku-Ku
Tokyo 160
Japan
Tel: 81-3-3226-2158
Fax: 81-3-3226-2150/2109

Sogo Co., Ltd.
Eiichi Iwamura
President
1-8-3 Shinsaibashi-Suji
Chuo-Ku
Osaka 542
Japan
Tel: 81-6-281-3111
Fax: 81-6-243-1867

Sogo Keibi Hosho Co., Ltd.
Eiji Uruma
President
1-6-6 Motoakasaka
Minato-Ku
Tokyo 107
Japan
Tel: 81-3-3470-6811
Fax: 81-3-3470-2626

Sony Corporation
Nobuyuki Idel
President
6-7-35 Kita-Shinagawa
Shinagawa-Ku
Tokyo 141
Japan
Tel: 81-3-5448-2111
Fax: 81-3-5448-2244/2183

Sony Music Entertainment (Japan) Inc.
Shugo Matsuo
President
1-4 Ichigaya-Tamachi
Shinjuku-Ku
Tokyo 162
Japan
Tel: 81-3-3266-5995
Fax: 81-3-3266-5936/0914

Southcorp Holdings Limited
Graham Kraehe
Managing Director
Level 23, 91 King William Street
Adelaide
South Australia 5000
Australia
Tel: 61-8-8239-7777
Fax: 61-8-8231-0886

Ssangyong Cement Industrial Co., Ltd.
Ki-Ho Kim
President
24-1 Cho-Dong, 2-Ga
Chung-Gu
Seoul
South Korea
Tel: 82-2-270-5114
Fax: 82-2-275-7040

Ssangyong Corporation
Ahn Chong-Won
President
24-1 Cho-Dong, 2-Ga
Chung-Gu
Seoul
South Korea
Tel: 82-2-270-8114
Fax: 82-2-273-0981

Ssangyong Engineering & Construction Co., Ltd.
Chang Ji Hwan
President
87 Samsung-Dong
Kangnam-Ku
Seoul 135-090
South Korea
Tel: 82-2-513-7509
Fax: 82-2-545-6111

Ssangyong Oil Refining
Kim Son-Dong
President
24-1 Cho-Dong, 2-Ga
Chung-Gu
Seoul
South Korea
Tel: 82-2-270-6114
Fax: 82-2-273-2170

Stanley Electric Co., Ltd.
Masahiro Shinoda
President
2-9-13 Nakameguro
Meguro-Ku
Tokyo 153
Japan
Tel: 81-3-3710-2222
Fax: 81-3-3792-0007

State Rail Authority of New South Wales
David Hill
Chief Executive Officer
Level 11, 31 York Street
Sydney
NSW 2000
Australia
Tel: 61-2-9379-3000
Fax: 61-2-9379-5310

Steel Authority of India Limited
M.R.R. Nair
Chairman
Ispat Bhavan
Lodi Road
New Delhi 110 003
India
Tel: 91-11-469-0481/0233
Fax: 91-11-461-6069/469-4015

Sumikin Bussan Ltd.
Yoshihide Yamamoto
President & Chairman
3-6-2 Hommachi
Chuo-Ku
Osaka 541
Japan
Tel: 81-6-244-8011
Fax: 81-6-244-8009

Sumisho Machinery Trade Corporation
Kaichi Takimoto
President
Kobun-Kosan Bldg.
2-4-3 Hitotsubashi, Chiyoda-Ku
Tokyo 101
Japan
Tel: 81-3-3230-7400
Fax: 81-3-3237-5252

Sumitomo 3M Limited
Ryoji Tamura
President
2-33-1 Tamagawadai
Setagaya-Ku
Tokyo 158
Japan
Tel: 81-3-3709-8111
Fax: 81-3-3709-9588

Sumitomo Australia Limited
Junichi Ishii
Chairman & Managing Director
Level 41, Governor Phillip Tower
1 Farrer Place
Sydney
NSW 2000
Australia
Tel: 61-2-9335-3700
Fax: 61-2-9335-3777

Sumitomo Bakelite Co., Ltd.
Naoto Enda
President
2-5-8 Higashishinagawa
Shinagawa-Ku
Tokyo 140
Japan
Tel: 81-3-5462-3434
Fax: 81-3-5462-4873

Sumitomo Chemical Co., Ltd.
Akio Kosai
President
4-5-33 Kitahama
Chuo-Ku
Osaka 541
Japan
Tel: 81-6-220-3287
Fax: 81-6-220-3497

Sumitomo Coal Mining Co., Ltd.
Yuji Momose
President
3-20-4 Nishi-Shinbashi
Minato-Ku
Tokyo 105
Japan
Tel: 81-3-5404-0401
Fax: 81-3-5404-0446

Sumitomo Construction Co., Ltd.
Shinsaku Sammoto
President
13-4 Araki-Cho
Shinjuku-Ku
Tokyo 160
Japan
Tel: 81-3-3225-5127
Fax: 81-3-3353-5559

Sumitomo Corporation
Kenji Miyahara
President
2-2 Hitotsubashi, 1-Chome
Chiyoda-Ku
Tokyo 100
Japan
Tel: 81-3-3217-5082
Fax: 81-3-3217-5128

Sumitomo Densetsu Co., Ltd.
Kozotanaka
President
2-1-4 Awaza, Nishi-Ku
Osaka 550
Japan
Tel: 81-6-537-3440
Fax: 81-6-537-3499

Sumitomo Electric Industries, Ltd.
Noritaka Kurauchi
President
4-5-33 Kitahama
Chuo-Ku
Osaka 541
Japan
Tel: 81-6-220-4141
Fax: 81-6-222-3380

Sumitomo Forestry Co., Ltd.
Hiroto Yamaguchi
President & Representative Director
7-28 Kitahama, 4-Chome
Chuo-Ku
Osaka
Japan
Tel: 81-6-220-8607
Fax: 81-6-220-8612

Sumitomo Heavy Industries, Ltd.
Mitoshi Ozawa
President
5-9-11 Kita-Shinagawa
Shinagawa-Ku
Tokyo 141
Japan
Tel: 81-3-5488-8219
Fax: 81-3-5488-8056

Sumitomo Light Metal Industries, Ltd.
Shiro Sato
President
Shimbashi Sumitomo Bldg.
5-11-3 Shimbashi
Minato-Ku
Tokyo 105
Japan
Tel: 81-3-3436-9700
Fax: 81-3-3434-6464

Sumitomo Metal Industries, Ltd.
Matao Kojima
President
4-5-33 Kitahama
Chuo-Ku
Osaka 541
Japan
Tel: 81-6-220-5111
Fax: 81-6-223-0563

Sumitomo Metal Mining Co., Ltd.
Moriki Aoyagi
President
5-11-3 Shimbashi
Minato-Ku
Tokyo 105
Japan
Tel: 81-3-3436-7701
Fax: 81-3-3434-2215

Sumitomo Osaka Cement Co., Ltd.
Shoichi Tatemoto
President
1 Kanda Mitoshiro-Cho
Chiyoda-Ku
Tokyo 101
Japan
Tel: 81-3-3296-9600
Fax: 81-3-3295-5156

Sumitomo Pharmaceuticals Co., Ltd.
Masayasu Takeuchi
President
2-2-8 Doshomachi
Chuo-Ku
Osaka 541
Japan
Tel: 81-6-229-5711
Fax:81-6-233-2288/222-2050

Sumitomo Realty & Development Co., Ltd.
Junji Takashima
President
2-4-1 Nishi-Shinjuku
Shinjuku-Ku
Tokyo 163-08
Japan
Tel: 81-3-3346-1011
Fax: 81-3-3344-6090

Sumitomo Rubber Industries, Ltd.
Naoto Saito
President
3-6-9 Wakinohama-Cho
Chuo-Ku
Kobe
Japan
Tel: 81-78-265-3000/ 3004
Fax: 81-78-265-3111/ 3113

Sumitomo Wiring Systems, Ltd.
Michio Moriya
President
1-14 Nishisuehiro-Cho
Yokkaichi City
Mie Pref. 510
Japan
Tel: 81-593-54-6200
Fax: 81-593-54-6318

Sun Hung Kai Properties Limited
Kwok Ping-sheung, Walter
Chairman
45/F., Sun Hung Kai Centre
30 Harbour Road
Wanchai
Hong Kong
Tel: 852-2827-8111
Fax: 852-2827-2862

Sun-S Inc.
Ken Suzuki
President
1-1 Otemachi
Aoba-Ku
Sendai 980
Japan
Tel: 81-22-266-4511
Fax: 81-22-266-3942

Sunkyong Limited
Kim Sung-Jong
President
36-1 Ulchiro, 2-Ga
Chung-Gu
Seoul
South Korea
Tel: 82-2-758-2114
Fax: 82-2-754-9414

Suntory Foods Limited
Nishishige Susumu
President
South Gate Shinjuku Bldg.
5-33-8 Sendagaya, Shibuya-Ku
Tokyo 151
Japan
Tel: 81-3-5360-1311
Fax: 81-3-5360-4601/4602

Suntory Limited
Shinichiro Torii
President
2-1-40 Dohjima-Hama
Kita-Ku
Osaka 530
Japan
Tel: 81-6-346-1150
Fax: 81-6-345-1169

Suzuken Co., Ltd.
Yoshiki Bessho
President
8 Higashi-Katahamachi
Higashi-Ku
Nagoya 461
Japan
Tel: 81-52-961-2331
Fax: 81-52-951-6696

Suzuki Motor Corporation
Osamu Suzuki
President
300 Takatsuka-Cho
Hamamatsu-Shi
Shizuoka-Ken 432-91
Japan
Tel: 81-53-440-2061
Fax: 81-53-445-0040

Suzuyo Shoji Co., Ltd.
Yoshihiro Masuda
President
Nisseki-Suzuyo Bldg.
1-3 Sakae-Cho, Shizuoka City
Shizuoka 420
Japan
Tel: 81-54-273-7759
Fax: 81-54-273-7763

Swire Pacific Limited
Peter D.A. Sutch
Chairman
4/F., Swire House
9 Connaught Road
Central
Hong Kong
Tel: 852-2840-8686
Fax: 852-2845-4876

TAB of New South Wales
Allen Windross
Chief Executive Officer
495 Harris Street
Ultimo
Sydney
NSW 2007
Australia
Tel: 61-2-9211-0188
Fax: 61-2-9211-5010

Tadano Limited
Sakae Tadano
President
Ko-34. Shinden-Cho
Takamatsu City 761-01
Japan
Tel: 81-878-39-5555
Fax: 81-878-39-5743

Tae Kwang Industrial Co., Ltd.
Lee Ki Hwa
Chairman
162-1 Changchung-Dong, 2-Ga
Chung-Ku
Seoul
South Korea
Tel: 82-2-273-3191
Fax: 82-2-277-2058

Taihei Kogyo Co., Ltd.
Koremasa Anami
President
1-23-4 Shinkawa
Chuo-Ku
Tokyo 104
Japan
Tel: 81-3-5543-6000
Fax: 81-3-5543-6007

Taikisha Limited
Teiichi Abe
President
2-6-1 Nishi-Shinjuku
Shinjuku-Ku
Tokyo 163-02
Japan
Tel: 81-3-3344-1851
Fax: 81-3-3342-5590

Taiko Trading Co., Ltd.
Yoshiyuki Nogawa
President
Anzen Bldg.
1-6-4 Moto Akasaka
Minato-Ku
Tokyo 107
Japan
Tel: 81-3-3423-2511
Fax: 81-3-5474-6076

Taisei Corporation
Osam Hirashima
President
1-25-1 Nishi-Shinjuku
Shinjuku-Ku
Tokyo 163-06
Japan
Tel: 81-3-3348-1111
Fax: 81-3-3345-0481

Taisei Rotec Corporation
Mishima Mareyuki
President
3-13-1 Kyobashi
Chuo-Ku
Tokyo 104
Japan
Tel: 81-3-3567-9431
Fax: 81-3-3567-8521

Taisho Pharmaceutical Co., Ltd.
Akira Uehara
President
3-24-1 Takada Toshima-Ku
Tokyo 171
Japan
Tel: 81-3-3985-1111
Fax: 81-3-3985-6485

Taiwan Power Company
Shih-Chi Hsi
President
242 Roosevelt Road
Section 3
Taipei 100
Taiwan
Tel: 88-6-2-365-1234
Fax: 88-6-2-367-8593

Taiwan Tobacco & Wine Monopoly Bureau
Shihu Yen-Shiang
Director-General
4 Nan Chang Road, Section 1
Taipei
Taiwan
Tel: 88-6-2-321-4567
Fax: 88-6-2-341-5200/397-2086

Taiyo Oil Co., Ltd.
Shigeyoshi Aoki
President
Hibiya Kokusai Bldg.
2-2-3 Uchisaiwai-Cho
Chiyoda-Ku
Tokyo 100
Japan
Tel: 81-3-3502-1601
Fax: 81-3-3508-0183

Takara Shuzo Co., Ltd.
Hisashi Omiya
President
Higashinotohinn Higashiiru
Shijoh Dori, Shimogyo-Ku
Kyoto Shi 600
Japan
Tel: 81-75-241-5110
Fax: 81-75-211-6385

Takara Standard Co., Ltd.
Rokuro Watanabe
President
1-2-1 Shigino-Higashi
Jyoto-Ku, Osaka-Shi
Osaka 536
Japan
Tel: 81-6-962-1531
Fax: 81-6-969-0404

Takasago Thermal Engineering Co., Ltd.
Masaru Ishii
President
4-2-8 Kanda-Surugadai
Chiyoda-Ku
Tokyo 101
Japan
Tel: 81-3-3255-8212
Fax: 81-3-3251-0914

Takashimaya Co., Ltd.
Tatsuro Tanaka
President
5-1-5 Namba
Chuo-Ku
Osaka 542
Japan
Tel: 81-6-631-1101
Fax: 81-6-631-9850

Takeda Chemical Industries, Ltd.
Kunio Takeda
President
1-1 Doshomachi, 4-Chome
Chuo-Ku
Osaka 541
Japan
Tel: 81-6-204-2111
Fax: 81-6-204-2880

Takenaka Civil Engineering & Construction Co., Ltd.
Fujio Nagasawa
President
8-21-1 Ginza
Chuo-Ku
Tokyo 104
Japan
Tel: 81-3-3542-6321
Fax: 81-3-3541-8825

Takenaka Corporation
Toichi Takenaka
President
4-1-13 Hommachi
Chuo-Ku
Osaka-Shi 541
Japan
Tel: 81-6-252-1201
Fax: 81-6-271-0398

Takisada & Co., Ltd.
Kinichiro Taki
President
2-13-19 Nishiki, Naka-Ku
Nagoya-Shi 460
Japan
Tel: 81-52-201-0779
Fax: 81-52-201-7367

Tanabe Seiyaku Co., Ltd.
Toshio Tanaka
President
3-2-10 Dosho-Machi
Chuo-Ku
Osaka 541
Japan
Tel: 81-6-205-5555
Fax: 81-6-205-5262

Tanaka Kikinzoku Kogyo K.K.
Tadahiko Fukami
President
2-6-6 Kayaba-Cho
Nihonbashi, Chuo-Ku
Tokyo 103
Japan
Tel: 81-3-3668-0111
Fax: 81-3-3668-4138

Tata Engineering & Locomotive Co., Ltd.
Ratan N. Tata
Executive Chairman
Bombay House
24 Homi Mody Street
Hutatma Chowk
Mumbai 400 001
India
Tel: 91-22-204-9131
Fax: 91-22-204-5474

Tata Iron & Steel Co. Ltd.
Ratan N. Tata
Chairman
Bombay House
24 Homi Mody Street
Mumbai 400 001
India
Tel: 91-22-204-9131
Fax: 91-22-204-9522

Tateyama Aluminum Industry Co., Ltd.
Eitaro Takehira
President
550 Hayakawa
Takaoka-Shi
Toyama-Ken 933
Japan
Tel: 81-766-20-3121
Fax: 81-766-20-3543

Tattersalls Sweep
David Jones
Managing Trustee
787 Dandenong Road
East Malvern
Victoria 3145
Australia
Tel: 61-3-9277-4000
Fax: 61-3-9277-4365/9572-2412

Tatung Company
Lin Ting-Sheng
President
22 Chungshan N. Road
Section 3
Taipei
Taiwan
Tel: 88-6-2-592-5252
Fax: 88-6-2-591-5185

TDK Corporation
Hiroshi Sato
President
13-1 Nihonbashi, 1-Chome
Chuo-Ku
Tokyo 103
Japan
Tel: 81-3-3278-5111
Fax: 81-3-5201-7110

TEAC Corporation
Norio Tamura
President
3-7-3 Naka-Machi
Musashino City
Tokyo 180
Japan
Tel: 81-422-52-5000
Fax: 81-422-55-8959

TEC Corporation
Mitsuo Kubo
President
Tokyo Tatemono Bldg.
1-14-10 Uchi-Kanda
Chiyoda-Ku
Tokyo 101
Japan
Tel: 81-3-3292-6223
Fax: 81-3-3292-6440

Teijin Limited
Hiroshi Itagaki
President
6-7 Minami-Honmachi, 1-Chome
Chuo-Ku
Osaka 541
Japan
Tel: 81-6-268-2132
Fax: 81-6-268-2133

Teijin Shoji Co., Ltd.
Yoshimasa Okamoto
President
6-21, 1-Chome
Minami-Honmachi
Chuo-Ku
Osaka 541
Japan
Tel: 81-6-266-8209
Fax: 81-6-244-1130

Tekken Corporation
Katsuyoshi Nagao
President
2-5-3 Misaki-Cho
Chiyoda-Ku
Tokyo 101
Japan
Tel: 81-3-3221-2193
Fax: 81-3-3234-8570

Telecom Corporation of New Zealand Limited
Roderick Deane
Managing Director
Level 3, North Tower
Telecom Networks House
68 Jervois Quay
Wellington
New Zealand
Tel: 64-4-801-9000
Fax: 64-4-473-6961

Telekom Malaysia Berhad
Dato Mohamed Said Bin Mohamed Ali
Chief Executive
1/F., Wisma Telekom
Jalan Pantai Baharu
Kuala Lumpur 50672
Malaysia
Tel: 60-3-208-9494
Fax: 60-3-757-4747

Telephone Organization of Thailand
Mr. Jumpone Herabat
President
89/2 Moo 3 Chaeng Wattana Road
Laksi, Don Muang
Bangkok 10210
Thailand
Tel: 662-505-1111
Fax: 662-574-9545

Telkom
Asman Akhir Nasution
President Director
1 Jalan Japati
Bandung 40133
Indonesia
Tel: 62-22-452-7110
Fax: 62-22-440-313

Telstra Corporation Limited
W. Frank Blount
Chief Executive Officer
33/242 Exhibition Street
Melbourne
Victoria 3000
Australia
Tel: 61-3-9634-2905
Fax: 61-3-9634-8826

Tenaga Nasional
Ani Bin Arope
Executive Chairman
129 Jalan Bangsar
Kuala Lumpur 59200
Malaysia
Tel: 60-3-282-5566/2121
Fax: 60-3-282-6754

Texas Instruments Japan Ltd.
Toshiaki Ikoma
President
Aoyama Fuji Bldg.
6-12, 3-Chome, Kita-Aoyama
Minato-Ku
Tokyo 107
Japan
Tel: 81-3-3498-2111
Fax: 81-3-3498-1089

Texas Instruments Singapore (Pte) Limited
Goh Geok Ling
Managing Director
990 Bendemeer Road
Singapore 339942
Tel: 65-290-2000
Fax: 65-296-5239

Thai Airways International Public Co., Ltd.
Thamnoon Wanglee
President
89 Vibhavadi Rangsit Road
Bangkok 10900
Thailand
Tel: 662-513-0121
Fax: 662-513-0203

Thai Oil Co., Ltd.
Kasame Chatikavanij
Chairman & Managing Director
15/F., Harindhorn Tower
54 North Sathorn Road
Silom
Bangrak
Bangkok 10500
Thailand
Tel: 66-2-231-7000
Fax: 66-2-231-7111/7222

Thomson Multimedia Asia Pte. Ltd.
Margery Chong Swee Meng
Chief Executive Officer
1000 Toa Payoh North
Singapore 318994
Tel: 65-253-8111
Fax: 65-250-7804

TNT Limited
David A. Mortimer
Chairman
TNT Plaza, Tower One
Lawson Square
Redfern
NSW 2016
Australia
Tel: 61-2-9699-2222
Fax: 61-2-9699-9238

Toa Corporation
Hiroshi Kitamura
President
5 Yonban-Cho
Chiyoda-Ku
Tokyo 102
Japan
Tel: 81-3-3262-5102
Fax: 81-3-3262-9536

Toa Steel Co., Ltd.
Satoru Nomura
President
6-2 Goban-Cho
Chiyoda-Ku
Tokyo 102
Japan
Tel: 81-3-3221-7121
Fax: 81-3-3221-9320

Toagosei Co., Ltd.
Akira Senda
President
1-14-1 Nishi-Shimbashi
Minato-Ku
Tokyo 105
Japan
Tel: 81-3-3597-7215
Fax: 81-3-3597-7217

Tobishima Corporation
Shoichiro Ishihara
President
2 Sanban-Cho
Chiyoda-Ku
Tokyo 102
Japan
Tel: 81-3-5214-7742
Fax: 81-3-3262-3255

Tobu Department Stores Co., Ltd.
Kan Yamanaka
President
1-1-25 Nishi-Ikebukuro
Toshima-Ku
Tokyo 171
Japan
Tel: 81-3-3981-2211/3989-8211
Fax: 81-3-3986-7508/0829

Tobu Railway Co., Ltd.
Takashige Uchida
President
1-1-2 Oshiage, Sumida-Ku
Tokyo 131
Japan
Tel: 81-3-3621-5055
Fax: 81-3-3621-5058

Toda Corporation
Moriji Toda
President
1-7-1 Kyobashi
Chuo-Ku
Tokyo 104
Japan
Tel: 81-3-3562-6111
Fax: 81-3-3561-5747

Toenec Corporation
Kinichiro Tsukada
Chairman
1-20-31 Sakae Naka-Ku
Nagoya 460
Japan
Tel: 81-52-221-1111
Fax: 81-52-219-1950

Tohan Corporation
Hirotada Kotaki
President
6-24 Higashi, Goken-Cho
Shinjuku-Ku
Tokyo 162
Japan
Tel: 81-3-3269-6111
Fax: 81-3-3235-1337

Toho Gas Co., Ltd.
Sadahiko Shimizu
President
19-18 Sakurada-Cho, Atsuta-Ku
Nagoya 456
Japan
Tel: 81-52-871-3511
Fax: 81-52-882-1307

Toho Pharmaceutical Co., Ltd.
Makoto Matsutani
President
5-2-1 Daisawa, Setagaya-Ku
Tokyo 155
Japan
Tel: 81-3-3419-7811
Fax: 81-3-3414-6042

Tohoku Electric Power Co., Inc.
Toshiaki Yashima
President
3-7-1 Ichiban-Cho
Aoba-Ku, Sendai
Miyagi 980
Japan
Tel: 81-22-225-2111
Fax: 81-22-222-2881

Tohoku Oil Co., Ltd.
Shozo Hosomura
President
1-1 Minato, 5-Chome
Miyagino-Ku, Sendai-Shi
Miyagi Pref. 985
Japan
Tel: 81-22-363-1111
Fax: 81-22-363-1125

Tohto Suisan Co., Ltd.
Yukiya Sekimoto
President
Tokyo Central Fish Market
5-2-1 Tsukiji, Chuo-Ku
Tokyo 104
Japan
Tel: 81-3-3542-1111
Fax: 81-3-3541-5225

Tokai Denpun Co., Ltd.
Kazunari Jinno
President
24-15 Tenma-Cho
Shizuoka City
Shizuoka Pref. 420
Japan
Tel: 81-54-253-1181
Fax: 81-54-205-0186

Tokai Kogyo Co., Ltd.
Kunihide Kobayashi
President
1-6 Yaesu, 1-Chome
Chuo-Ku
Tokyo 103
Japan
Tel: 81-3-5200-5141
Fax: 81-3-5200-5200

Tokai Rika Co., Ltd.
Akira Kisaki
President
1 Noda, Toyoda, Ohguchi-Cho
Niwa-Gun
Aichi Pref. 480-01
Japan
Tel: 81-587-95-5211
Fax: 81-587-95-6641

Tokai Rubber Industries, Ltd.
Akira Miyata
President
3600 Utazu
Kitatoyama
Komaki City
Aichi Pref. 485
Japan
Tel: 81-568-77-2121
Fax: 81-568-72-4537

Tokuyama Corporation
Yuichi Miura
President
Shibuya Konno Bldg.
3-1 Shibuya, 3-Chome
Shibuya-Ku
Tokyo 150
Japan
Tel: 81-3-3499-8023
Fax: 81-3-3499-8966

Tokyo Broadcasting System, Inc.
Yukio Sunahara
President
5-3-6 Akasaka
Minato-Ku
Tokyo 107-06
Japan
Tel: 81-3-3746-1111
Fax: 81-3-3224-2012

Tokyo Electric Power Co., Inc.
Hiroshi Araki
President
1-1-3 Uchisaiwai-Cho
Chiyoda-Ku
Tokyo 100
Japan
Tel: 81-3-3501-8111
Fax: 81-3-3592-1795

Tokyo Electron Limited
Terry Higashi
President
5-3-6 Akasaka
Minato-Ku
Tokyo 107
Japan
Tel: 81-3-5561-7000
Fax: 81-3-5561-7400

Tokyo Gas Co., Ltd.
Kunio Anzai
President
1-5-20 Kaigan
Minato-Ku
Tokyo 105
Japan
Tel: 81-3-3433-2111
Fax: 81-3-3432-4574

Tokyo Sangyo Co., Ltd.
Akira Monden
President
3-3-1 Marunouchi
Chiyoda-Ku
Tokyo 100
Japan
Tel: 81-3-3212-7611
Fax: 81-3-3287-0611

Tokyo Seika Co., Ltd.
Ichiro Sekiya
President
3-2-1 Tokai
Ota-Ku
Tokyo 143
Japan
Tel: 81-3-5492-2001
Fax: 81-3-5492-2400

Tokyo Steel Manufacturing Co., Ltd.
Masanari Iketani
President
22/F., Fukokuseimei Bldg.
2-2-2 Uchisaiwai-Cho
Chiyoda-Ku
Tokyo 100
Japan
Tel: 81-3-3580-8521
Fax: 81-3-3580-8837

Tokyo Tobacco Service Co., Ltd.
Keiji Takemoto
President
2/F., Alliance Bldg.
5-2-1 Minami Aoyama
Minato-Ku
Tokyo 107
Japan
Tel: 81-3-3400-2161
Fax: 81-3-3400-2453

Tokyo Toyopet Motor Sales Co., Ltd.
Kenichi Kato
President
3-23-10 Takanawa
Minato-Ku
Tokyo 108
Japan
Tel: 81-3-3443-1111
Fax: 81-3-3445-5701

Tokyu Agency Inc.
Kimio Arai
President
4-8-18 Akasaka
Minato-Ku
Tokyo 107
Japan
Tel: 81-3-3475-3641/3404-5321
Fax: 81-3-3405-5504/3423-2958

Tokyu Construction Co., Ltd.
Tetsu Gotoh
President
1-16-14 Shibuya
Shibuya-Ku
Tokyo 150
Japan
Tel: 81-3-5466-5111
Fax: 81-3-3400-4580

Tokyu Corporation
Shinobu Shimizu
President
5-6 Nanpeidai-Cho
Shibuya-Ku
Tokyo 150
Japan
Tel: 81-3-3477-6393
Fax: 81-3-3770-5545

Tokyu Department Store Co., Ltd.
Toru Uchiyama
President
2-24-1 Dogenzaka
Shibuya-Ku
Tokyo 150
Japan
Tel: 81-3-3477-3111
Fax: 81-3-3496-7200

Tokyu Land Corporation
Tetsuro Aki
President
1-21-2 Dogenzaka
Shibuya-Ku
Tokyo 150
Japan
Tel: 81-3-5458-0620
Fax: 81-3-5489-0876

Tokyu Store Chain Co., Ltd.
Hideo Harasawa
President
1-21-12 Kamimeguro
Meguro-Ku
Tokyo 153
Japan
Tel: 81-3-3714-2317
Fax: 81-3-3791-6521

Tomen Corporation
Akihiro Tsuji
President
Kokusai Shin Akasaka Bldg.
East Wing 2-14-27 Akasaka
Minato-Ku
Tokyo
Japan
Tel: 81-3-3588-7111
Fax: 81-3-3588-6627

Tonen Chemical Corporation
Tadashi Yokokura
President
Ebisu Prime Square Tower
1-39 Hiroo 1-Chome
Shibuya-Ku
Tokyo 150
Japan
Tel: 81-3-5778-5300
Fax: 81-3-5778-5309

Tonen Corporation
Tamehiko Tamahori
President
Ebisu Prime Square Tower
1-39 Hiroo, 1-Chome
Shibuya-Ku
Tokyo 150
Japan
Tel: 81-3-5778-5111
Fax: 81-3-5778-5120

Toppan Forms Co., Ltd.
Yasuhiro Fukuda
President
1-6, Suruga-Dai
Kanda, Chiyoda-Ku
Tokyo 101
Japan
Tel: 81-3-3259-2417
Fax: 81-3-3293-2729

Toppan Printing Co., Ltd.
Hiromichi Fujita
President
1 Kanda-Izumicho
Chiyoda-Ku
Tokyo 101
Japan
Tel: 81-3-3835-5741
Fax: 81-3-3835-0674

Topy Industries, Limited
Tomokatsu Kohtani
President
5-9 Yonban-Cho
Chiyoda-Ku
Tokyo 102
Japan
Tel: 81-3-3265-0111
Fax: 81-3-3234-7675

Toray Industries, Inc.
Katsuhiko Hirai
President
2-2-1 Nihonbashi-Muromachi
Chuo-Ku
Tokyo 103
Japan
Tel: 81-3-3245-5111
Fax: 81-3-3245-5555

Toshiba Corporation
Taizo Nishimuro
President
1-1-1 Shibaura
Minato-Ku
Tokyo 105-01
Japan
Tel: 81-3-3457-4511
Fax: 81-3-3456-4776

Toshiba Electronics Asia (S) Pte. Ltd.
T. Ogi
Managing Director
460 Alexandra Road
21/F. PSA Bldg.
Singapore 119963
Tel: 65-278-5252
Fax: 65-271-5155

Toshiba Lighting & Technology Corp.
Tadao Kanoh
President
2-13 Minamishinagawa
2-Chome
Shinagawa-Ku
Tokyo 140
Japan
Tel: 81-3-5463-8800
Fax: 81-3-5463-8830

Toshiba Machine
Sadao Okano
President
4-2-11 Ginza
Chuo-Ku
Tokyo 104
Japan
Tel: 81-3-3567-0520
Fax: 81-3-3562-5220

Toshoku Limited
Tetsuya Sato
President
2-4-3 Nihonbashi-Muromachi
Chuo-Ku
Tokyo 103
Japan
Tel: 81-3-3245-2211
Fax: 81-3-3245-2201

Tosoh Corporation
Madoka Tashiro
President
1-7-7 Akasaka
Minato-Ku
Tokyo 107
Japan
Tel: 81-3-3585-6707/3311
Fax: 81-3-3582-7846/0972

Tostem Corporation
Kenjiro Ushioda
President
2-1-1 Ojima
Koto-Ku
Tokyo 136
Japan
Tel: 81-3-3638-8115
Fax: 81-3-3638-8343

Toto Limited
Shigeru Ezoye
President
2-1-1 Nakashima
Kokurakita-Ku
Kitakyushu
Fukuoka 802
Japan
Tel: 81-93-951-2707
Fax: 81-93-922-6789

Tottori Sanyo Electric Co., Ltd.
Kotaro Yoneyama
President
7-101 Tachikawa-Cho
Tottori-Shi
Tottori-Ken 680
Japan
Tel: 81-857-21-2001
Fax: 81-857-21-2034

Towa Real Estate Development Co., Ltd.
Kimiyasu Fujita
President
2-3-13 Yaesu
Chuo-Ku
Tokyo 104
Japan
Tel: 81-3-3272-6331
Fax: 81-3-3272-1901

Toyo Construction Co., Ltd.
Akira Ohnishi
President
3-7-1 Kanda-Nishikicho
Chiyoda-Ku
Tokyo 101
Japan
Tel: 81-3-3296-4611
Fax: 81-3-3296-4692

Toyo Engineering Corporation
Morio Sonoda
President
3-2-5 Kasumigaseki Kasumigaseki
Chiyoda-Ku
Tokyo 100
Japan
Tel: 81-3-3592-7411/7421
Fax: 81-3-3593-0749

Toyo Ink Manufacturing Co., Ltd.
Mutsuo Nagashima
President
2-3-13 Kyobashi
Chuo-Ku
Tokyo 104
Japan
Tel: 81-3-3272-5731
Fax: 81-3-3278-8688

Toyo Seikan Kaisha, Ltd.
Hirofumi Miki
President
1-3-1 Uchi-Saiwaicho
Chiyoda-Ku
Tokyo 100
Japan
Tel: 81-3-3508-2112
Fax: 81-3-3592-9471

Toyo Suisan Kaisha, Ltd.
Teruaki Hashimoto
President
2-13-40 Konan
Minato-Ku
Tokyo 108
Japan
Tel: 81-3-3458-5111
Fax: 81-3-3471-1734

Toyo Tire & Rubber Co., Ltd.
Shozo Katayama
President
1-17-18 Edobori
Nishi-Ku
Osaka 550
Japan
Tel: 81-6-441-8801
Fax: 81-6-445-2225

Toyobo Co., Ltd.
Minoru Shibata
President
2-8 Dojima Hama, 2-Chome
Kita-Ku
Osaka-Shi 530
Japan
Tel: 81-6-348-3395
Fax: 81-6-348-3117

Toyoda Automatic Loom Works, Ltd.
Chisei Isogai
President
2-1 Toyoda-Cho
Kariya-Shi
Aichi-Ken 448
Japan
Tel: 81-566-22-2511
Fax: 81-566-27-5650

Toyoda Gosei Co., Ltd.
Tokio Horigome
President
1 Nagahata Ochiai Aza, Oaza
Kasuga-Cho
Nishi-Kasugai-Gun
Aichi-Ken 452
Japan
Tel: 81-52-400-1055
Fax: 81-52-409-7491

Toyoda Machine Works, Ltd.
Toyo Kato
President
1-1 Asahi-Machi, Kariya-Shi
Aichi-Ken 448
Japan
Tel: 81-566-25-5111
Fax: 81-566-25-5470

Toyoshima & Co., Ltd.
Tokuzo Toyoshima
President
2-14-27 Nishiki
Naka-Ku
Nagoya-Shi 460
Japan
Tel: 81-52-204-7711
Fax: 81-52-204-7442

Toyota Auto Body Co., Ltd.
Akira Iijima
President
100 Kanayama, Ichiriyama-Cho
Kariya-Shi, Aichi-Ken 448
Japan
Tel: 81-566-36-2121
Fax: 81-566-36-2195

Toyota Motor Corporation
Hiroshi Okuda
President
1 Toyota-Cho
Toyota City
Aichi Pref. 471-71
Japan
Tel: 81-565-28-2121
Fax: 81-565-23-5800

Toyota Motor Corporation Australia Limited
Osamu Komori
President
155 Bertie Street
Port Melbourne
Victoria 3207
Australia
Tel: 61-3-9647-4444
Fax: 61-3-9645-1311

Toyota Motor Sales Australia Limited
O. Komori
President
155 Bertie Street
Port Melbourne
Victoria 3207
Australia
Tel: 61-3-9647-4444
Fax: 61-3-9645-1311

Toyota Motor (Thailand) Co. Ltd.
Yoshiaki Muramatsu
President
186/1 Moo 1, Old Railway Road
Tambol Samrong Tai
Pra-Pradang District
Samutprakarn Province 10130
Thailand
Tel: 66-2-386-1000
Fax: 66-2-386-1891

Toyota Tsusho Corporation
Eizo Takeyama
President
7-23 Meieki, 4-Chome
Nakamura-Ku, Nagoya 450
Japan
Tel: 81-52-584-5000
Fax: 81-52-584-5636

Tri Petch Isuzu Sales Co., Ltd.
Hisashi Kunifusa
President
1088 Vibhavadi Rangsit Road
Ladyao, Chatuchak
Bangkok 10900
Thailand
Tel: 66-2-966-2111/2222
Fax: 66-2-966-2191

U

Ube Industries, Ltd.
Maomi Nagahiro
President
2-3-11 Higashi-Shinagawa
Shinagawa-Ku
Tokyo 140
Japan
Tel: 81-3-5460-3311
Fax: 81-3-5460-3388

UCC Ueshima Coffee Co., Ltd.
Tatsushi Ueshima
President
Kobe Main Office
7-7-7 Nakamachi, Minatojima
Chuo-Ku, Kobe-Shi
Hyogo 650
Japan
Tel: 81-78-304-8888
Fax: 81-78-304-8878

Uchida Yoko Co., Ltd.
Hitoshi Hisada
President
2-4-7 Shinkawa
Chuo-Ku, Tokyo 104
Japan
Tel: 81-3-5634-6043
Fax: 81-3-5634-6832

UMW Holdings Berhad
Wan Salleh Bin Mohd
Group Managing Director
3/F., The Corporate
Jalan Utas (15/7)
Batu Tiga Industrial Estate
40200 Shah Alam
Selangor Darul Ehsan
Malaysia
Tel: 60-3-559-1911
Fax: 60-3-550-2282

Uni-Charm Corporation
Keiichiro Takahara
President
3-25-23 Takanawa
Minato-Ku
Tokyo 108
Japan
Tel: 81-3-3447-5111
Fax: 81-3-3449-5927

Unisia Jecs Corporation
Kouichiro Tohda
President
1370 Onna, Atsugi City
Kanagawa Pref. 243
Japan
Tel: 81-462-25-8025
Fax: 81-462-23-1177

Unitika, Ltd.
Keita Taguchi
President
4-1-3 Kyutaro-Machi
Chuo-Ku
Osaka 541
Japan
Tel: 81-6-281-5695
Fax: 81-6-281-5697

UNY Co., Ltd.
Koji Sasaki
President
1 Amaikegotanda-Cho
Inazawa City
Aichi Pref. 492
Japan
Tel: 81-587-24-8111
Fax: 81-587-24-8042

V

Victor Company of Japan, Limited
Takeo Shuzui
President
3-12 Moriya-Cho
Kanagawa-Ku
Yokohama 221
Japan
Tel: 81-45-450-2837
Fax: 81-45-450-1574

Videsh Sanchar Nigam Limited
B.K. Syngal
Chairman & Managing Director
Videsh Sanchar Bhavan
Mahatma Gandhi Road
Mumbai 400 001
India
Tel: 91-22-262-4020/4300
Fax: 91-22-262-4027/4466

W

Wacoal Corporation
Yoshikata Tsukamoto
President
29 Nakajima-Cho
Kisshoin Minami-Ku
Kyoto 601
Japan
Tel: 81-75-682-5111
Fax: 81-75-682-5603

Wakachiku Construction Co., Ltd.
Kihei Ikebe
President
2-23-18 Shimo-Meguro
Meguro-Ku
Tokyo 153
Japan
Tel: 81-3-3492-0271
Fax: 81-3-3490-1019

Watanabe Pipe Co., Ltd.
Hajime Watanabe
President
1-4-7 Kamezawa
Sumida-Ku
Tokyo 130
Japan
Tel: 81-3-3626-3132
Fax: 81-3-3623-2481

Wesfarmers Limited
Michael Chanen
Managing Director
11/F., 40 The Esplanade
Perth
Western Australia 6000
Australia
Tel: 61-8-9327-4211
Fax: 61-8-9327-4216

West Japan Railway Company
Shojiro Nan-Ya
President
4-24 Shibata, 2-Chome
Kita-Ku
Osaka 530
Japan
Tel: 81-6-375-8939
Fax: 81-6-375-8862

Western Digital (Singapore) Pte. Ltd.
Arif Shakeel
Vice President — Asian Operations
Personal Storage Group
Chai Chee Industrial Park
750B Chai Chee Road
Singapore 469002
Tel: 65-240-0118
Fax: 65-449-4166

WMC Limited
Hugh M. Morgan
Managing Director
16/F., 60 City Road
Southbank
Melbourne
Victoria 3006
Australia
Tel: 61-3-9685-6000
Fax: 61-3-9686-3569

Woolworths Limited
Reg Clairs
Group Managing Director
Level 5, 534-540 George Street
Sydney
NSW 2000
Australia
Tel: 61-2-9323-1555
Fax: 61-2-9323-1599

World Co., Ltd.
Hirotoshi Hatasaki
President
6-8-1 Minatojima-Nakamachi
Chuo-Ku, Kobe-Shi
Hyogo 650
Japan
Tel: 81-78-302-3111
Fax: 81-78-302-2148

Y

Yachiyo Industry Co., Ltd.
Kazuhira Kato
President
27-12, 3-Chome, Nishiikebukuro
Toshima-Ku
Tokyo 171
Japan
Tel: 81-3-3986-0721
Fax: 81-3-3986-0796

Yagi & Co., Ltd.
Shigeo Yagi
President
2-2-8 Kyutaro-Machi
Chuo-Ku
Osaka 541
Japan
Tel: 81-6-266-7300
Fax: 81-6-266-7373

Yakult Honsha Co., Ltd.
Sumiya Hori
President
1-1-19 Higashi-Shinbashi
Minato-Ku
Tokyo 105
Japan
Tel: 81-3-3574-8960
Fax: 81-3-3574-7253

Yamae Hisano Co., Ltd.
Masato Hamamoto
President
2-13-34 Higashi
Hakataeki, Hakata-Ku
Fukuoka-Shi 812
Japan
Tel: 81-92-474-0661
Fax: 81-92-415-3353

Yamaha Corporation
Ishimura Kazukiyo
President
10-1 Nakazawa-Cho, Hamamatsu
Shizuoka Pref. 430
Japan
Tel: 81-53-460-2071
Fax: 81-53-464-8554

Yamaha Motor Co., Ltd.
Takehiko Hasegawa
President
2500 Shingai
Iwata-Shi
Shizuoka Ken 438
Japan
Tel: 81-538-32-1145
Fax: 81-538-37-4250

Yamanouchi Pharmaceutical Co., Ltd.
Masayoshi Onoda
President
2-3-11 Nihonbashi-Honcho
Chuo-Ku
Tokyo 103
Japan
Tel: 81-3-3244-3000
Fax: 81-3-5201-7473

Yamatake-Honeywell Co., Ltd.
Ichiro Ido
President
Totate International Bldg.
2-12-19 Shibuya
Shibuya-Ku
Tokyo 150
Japan
Tel: 81-3-3486-2111
Fax: 81-3-3400-5475/3409-7388

Yamato Transport Co., Ltd.
Keiji Aritomi
President
2-16-10 Ginza
Chuo-Ku
Tokyo 104
Japan
Tel: 81-3-3541-3411
Fax: 81-3-5565-3427

Yamazaki Baking Co., Ltd.
Nobuhiro Iijima
President
3-2-4 Iwamoto-Cho
Chiyoda-Ku
Tokyo 101
Japan
Tel: 81-3-3864-3111
Fax: 81-3-3864-3109

Yamazen Corporation
Shinzo Nakamichi
President
2-3-16 Itachibori
Nishi-Ku
Osaka 550
Japan
Tel: 81-6-534-3021
Fax: 81-6-534-3037

Yanase & Co., Ltd.
Takahide Inayama
President
1-6-38 Shibaura
Minato-Ku
Tokyo 105
Japan
Tel: 81-3-3452-4311
Fax: 81-3-3451-9931

Yanmar Agricultural Equipment Co., Ltd.
Yamaoka Tadao
President
1-32 Chaya-Machi
Kita-Ku
Osaka 530
Japan
Tel: 81-6-376-6299
Fax: 81-6-372-2455

Yanmar Diesel Engine Co., Ltd.
Tadao Yamaoka
President
1-32 Chaya Machi
Kita-Ku
Osaka-Shi 530
Japan
Tel: 81-6-376-6299
Fax: 81-6-372-2455

Yaohan Japan Corporation
Mitsumasa Wada
President
1256-1 Okanomiya
Numazu City
Shizuoka Pref. 410
Japan
Tel: 81-559-23-3234
Fax: 81-559-22-2812

Yaskawa Electric Corporation
Ko Kikuchi
President
2-1 Kurosakishiroishi
Yahata-Nishi-Ku
Kita-Kyushu 806
Japan
Tel: 81-93-645-8800
Fax: 81-93-631-8837

Yazaki Corporation
Yasuhiko Yazaki
President & Chairman
17/F., Mita-Kokusai Bldg.
1-4-28 Mita
Minato-Ku
Tokyo 108
Japan
Tel: 81-3-3455-8812
Fax: 81-3-3455-8802

YKK Architectural Products Inc.
Tadahiro Yoshida
President
1 Kanda Izumi-Cho
Chiyoda-Ku
Tokyo 101
Japan
Tel: 81-3-3864-2200
Fax: 81-3-3864-2280

YKK Corporation
Tadahiro Yoshida
President
1 Izumi-Cho
Kanda, Chiyoda-Ku
Tokyo
Japan
Tel: 81-3-3864-2000
Fax: 81-3-3866-5500

Yodogawa Steel Works, Ltd.
Tousuke Shibata
President
4-1-1 Minami-Honmachi
Chuo-Ku
Osaka 541
Japan
Tel: 81-6-245-1113
Fax: 81-6-282-0541

Yokogawa Electric Corporation
Eiji Mikawa
President
2-9-32 Naka-Machi
Musashino-Shi, Tokyo 180
Japan
Tel: 81-422-52-5526
Fax: 81-422-52-9803

Yokohama Rubber Co., Ltd.
Seiji Hagiwara
President
5-36-11 Shinbashi
Minato-Ku, Tokyo 105
Japan
Tel: 81-3-5400-4531
Fax: 81-3-3432-5616

York-Benimaru Co., Ltd.
Zenjiro Ohtaka
President
18-2 Asahi, 2-Chome
Koriyama City, Fukushima 963
Japan
Tel: 81-249-24-3211
Fax: 81-249-25-3439

Yoshino Kogyosho Co., Ltd.
Yataro Yoshino
President
3-2-6 Ojima, Koto-Ku
Tokyo 136
Japan
Tel: 81-3-3682-1141
Fax: 81-3-5609-7333

Yuasa Trading Co., Ltd.
Teruhisa Yuasa
President
13-10 Nihonbashi-Odenmacho
Chuo-Ku, Tokyo 103
Japan
Tel: 81-3-3665-6511
Fax: 81-3-3665-6837

Yukijirushi Access Inc.
Yuasa Sinitirou
President
1-1, 3-Chome, Nozawa
Seiagaya-Ku
Tokyo 154
Japan
Tel: 81-3-3410-1141
Fax: 81-3-3410-9240

Yukong International (S) Pte. Ltd.
C.K. Lee
Deputy Managing Director
5 Shenton Way
34-04 UIC Bldg.
Singapore 068808
Tel: 65-220-1266
Fax: 65-221-1225

Yukong Limited
Kyu Hyang Cho
President
26-4 Yukong Bldg.
Yoido-Dong
Yongdung Po-Gu
Seoul
South Korea
Tel: 82-2-788-5114
Fax: 82-2-788-7001/7002

Yulon Motor Co., Ltd.
Chen-Hwa Lee
President
39-1 Po Kung Keng
Shi-Hu-Tsuen San Yi
Miao Li Hsien
Taiwan
Tel: 88-6-37-871-801
Fax: 88-6-37-874-983

Yurtec Corporation
Hiroji Nakazawa
President
4-1-1 Tsutsujigaoka
Miyagino-Ku, Sendai
Miyagi Pref. 983
Japan
Tel: 81-22-296-2111
Fax: 81-22-296-2118

Z

Zenchiku Co., Ltd.
Seiichi Uzurahashi
President
2-5-7 Kounan
Minato-Ku
Tokyo 108
Japan
Tel: 81-3-3471-5521
Fax: 81-3-3471-5946

Zenitaka Corporation
Kazuyoshi Zenitaka
President
2-2-11 Nishi-Honmachi
Nishi-Ku
Osaka 550
Japan
Tel: 81-6-531-6431
Fax: 81-6-538-7900

Zexel Corporation
Yutaka Ota
President
3-6-7 Shibuya
Shibuya-Ku
Tokyo 150
Japan
Tel: 81-3-3400-1551
Fax: 81-3-3797-4774

ASIAWEEK

    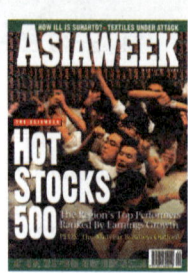

ASIAWEEK, the award-winning publisher of the original ASIAWEEK 1000 and ASIAWEEK FINANCIAL 500 Special Reports, is Asia's leading newsmagazine. ASIAWEEK puts you in the picture about key happenings in Asia better than any other printed source. Every week, your eye spans the Asian continent — in business, economics, investment, politics, social and cultural trends. ASIAWEEK is trusted by Asia's most influential business people as the one weekly publication they can count on to give them an unbiased and accurate view of events across the region.

To attract your readership we are prepared to make you an enticing proposition.

Subscribe to ASIAWEEK now and we'll add **Four Bonus Issues** to your subscription — that's One Month FREE. Plus you enjoy a substantial saving off the newsstand price.

UNCONDITIONAL MONEY-BACK GUARANTEE
If at any time you are not completely satisfied with ASIAWEEK, you may cancel your subscription and get a full refund on all undelivered issues.

COMPLETE THIS FORM TO RECEIVE FOUR BONUS ISSUES

YES, I accept your offer. Send me **4 BONUS ISSUES** of ASIAWEEK on top of my 1 year subscription.

Name : _____
Company : _____
Address : _____
_____
Telephone: _____ Fax: _____

• Cheque enclosed for _____ payable to Asiaweek Ltd.
• Debit my credit card: ❑Amex ❑Diners ❑Visa ❑Mastercard
Card No. : _____
Expiry date : _____
Debit Account for: _____

Signature : _____

Country	Subscription Rate* (52 weeks)	You Save
AUSTRALIA	A$206.50	33%
CANADA	C$202.00	35%
EUROPE	US$167.00	41%
NEW ZEALAND	NZ$237.5	42%
U.K.	GBP104.00	32%
USA	US$167.00	41%
ASIA		
Hong Kong	HK$478.00	73%
India	Rs. 1,560.00	50%
Indonesia	Rp. 130,000.00	58%
Japan	Yen 20,020.00	48%
Korea	Won 124,800.00	36%
Malaysia	RM$154.00	57%
Pakistan	Rs. 1,196.00	58%
Philippines	Peso 1,456.00	56%
Singapore	S$118.00	63%
Sri Lanka	Rs. 2,808.00	36%
Taiwan	NT$2,704.00	60%
Thailand	Baht1,404.00	73%

Mail or fax to Asiaweek Ltd., P.O. Box 60280, Tsat Tze Mui Post Office, Hong Kong.
Tel : (852) 2512-5688, Fax : (852) 2512-9790, E-mail: customer_service@asiaweek.com

ASIAWEEK is published weekly except for two issues combined into one at year end.
*Rates valid until Dec 31, 1998. Please contact our Customer Service Center after this date.